BRISTOL
BLENHEIM

BRISTOL BLENHEIM

THEO BOITEN

The Crowood Press

First published in 1998 by
The Crowood Press Ltd
Ramsbury, Marlborough
Wiltshire SN8 2HR

British Library Cataloguing in Publication Data

A catalogue record for this book
is available from the British Library.

ISBN 1 86126 115 2

Frontispiece: **Blenheim Mark IV L4843 TE-J of 53 Squadron
'A' Flight, showing its graceful lines in its natural element,
May 1939. A few months later, 53 Squadron was re-coded
PZ and sent to France, where it was badly mauled, with
thirteen aircraft destroyed during May 1940. L4843 went
missing on 16 May 1940, with P/O McPherson and his
crew taken prisoner.** Col. Dick Maydwell

Typeset by JP3 Ltd

Printed and bound in Great Britain by Butler & Tanner, Frome

Contents

Foreword by Wing Commander Hugh George, DFC, Chairman of the Blenheim Society   6

Preface   7

1   THE 'WONDER BOMBER': DEVELOPMENT
AND THE ROAD TO WAR, 1933–40   8

2   BLENHEIM OPERATIONAL TRAINING UNITS, 1940–44   20

3   NORDIC WARRIORS: THE FINNISH BLENHEIMS, 1936–58   32

4   CARNAGE AND RAW COURAGE: THE BATTLES
OF THE LOW COUNTRIES AND FRANCE, MAY–JUNE 1940   42

5   ON THE OFFENSIVE AND THE DEFENSIVE:
THE BATTLE OF BRITAIN, JULY–OCTOBER 1940   56

6   SHIPHUNTERS, CIRCUSES AND FRINGE RAIDERS, MARCH–JUNE 1941   70

7   THE CHARGE OF THE LIGHT BRIGADE: THE CRUEL SUMMER OF 1941   86

8   MALTA CRUSADE: HUNTING ROMMEL'S SUPPLIES, 1941–42   100

9   BLENHEIM WIRELESS OPERATOR/AIR GUNNER AT WAR   110

10   INTRUDERS, COMMANDOS, BATTLESHIPS
AND THE 'THOUSAND PLAN', DECEMBER 1941–43   120

11   FROM DEFEAT IN GREECE TO VICTORY IN *TORCH*, 1940–43   130

12   FIGHTING THE JAPANESE ASSAULT, DECEMBER 1941–43   146

13   THE SPIRIT OF THE BLENHEIM   160

Appendix I   Experiences   168

Appendix II   RAF and Commonwealth Squadrons Operating the Blenheim and the Bolingbroke   183

Appendix III   Royal Air Force Units, Other than Squadrons, Operating the Blenheim   184

Glossary   185

Bibliography   186

Acknowledgements   187

Index   188

Foreword

Theo Boiten has painstakingly researched the history of the Blenheim and has collected very many first-hand accounts of the experiences of aircrew who operated the aircraft. These he has recorded verbatim, without any embroidery or additional comment by any third party, and they form the basis of this book. Personally, having myself flown the Blenheim in anger through the dark days of 1940 and shared in the experiences and traumas of his contributors, I find *Bristol Blenheim* moving in the extreme, and it is I think a fitting tribute to the memory of those very many brave 'Blenheim Boys' who made the ultimate sacrifice.

The origin and evolution of the Blenheim is in itself a fascinating story and Theo traces this in his opening chapter, showing how at its concept in 1933 as a projected high speed six-seater transport, its military potential was realized by that great patriot, Lord Rothermere, who, with characteristic determination, lost no time in kindling the interest of the Air Ministry, as a result of which a revised, military, specification was evolved, and the Blenheim, the fastest bomber aircraft in the world at that time, was born.

WING COMMANDER HUGH GEORGE, DFC, Chairman of the Blenheim Society

Preface

The Bristol Blenheim's service, in the 1930s and in the desperate early war years, was as important and versatile as one of its famous successors, the De Havilland Mosquito. The big difference in the histories of these multirole combat aircraft is that the tale of the Blenheim is often the story of tragedy and defeat, whereas the Mosquito was a real 'war-winner'. Yet the aircraft deserves a place of honour in the annals of the Royal Air Force. The Blenheim was the first of a new generation of mass-produced, all-metal, stressed skin, twin-engined monoplanes with retractable undercarriage for the RAF, with no fewer than 6,260 being produced between 1935 and 1944. At the time of its introduction into service in 1937 it was the fastest bomber aircraft in the world, even outpacing any contemporary RAF fighter. Yet the frantic rate of progress in military aviation design was such that only two and a half years later the Blenheim was already obsolete and therefore vulnerable in combat.

On the eve of war the RAF had over a thousand Blenheims on strength, more than of any other type. Its gallant crews helped by holding the line in the dark days of 1940–42 when the Axis forces threatened to overpower the free world, suffering appallingly high casualties. The daylight raids carried out by the Blenheim in the first two years of the war proved to be the most hazardous type of operation, exacting the highest percentage of casualties in all three British fighting services during the whole course of the war. The Blenheim was thrown into the breach in just about every conceivable role, finding out operational tactics the hard way. Despite its puny capabilities as a bomber, strike aircraft and long-range fighter, its crews pioneered tactical daylight raids, the strategic night bombing offensive against Germany, in radar-controlled night fighting, low-level anti-shipping strike operations (both by day and by night), in close support operations, and in photo-reconnaissance and night intrusion, until the Blenheim could be replaced by more potent aircraft such as the Boston, Beaufighter, Mitchell and Mosquito. Moreover, the aircraft served with distinction in many foreign air forces such as the Canadian, the Finnish and the Free French, both on operations and in training.

In this book I have endeavoured to highlight the many roles and campaigns in which the Blenheim and its crews carried out sterling work. As a tool of war, any aircraft reaps fame only through the deeds of the young men who work with it, and through the men who fly, fight and die in it. I have therefore laid emphasis on the personal experiences of the crews who flew and serviced the aircraft and on the photographs from their wartime albums.

THEO E.W. BOITEN
Almere, The Netherlands
September 1997

CHAPTER ONE

The 'Wonder Bomber':

Development and the Road to War, 1933–40

The genesis of the large family of the successful twin-engined Bristol Blenheim, Beaufort and Beaufighter (fighter) bombers can be traced back to July 1933. During that month Bristol Aeroplane Company's Chief Designer, Capt Frank Barnwell, and Leslie Frise designed a

The Bristol Aeroplane Company

After being bitten by the aviation bug at the age of fifty-five in 1909, Sir George White, one of Britain's major figures in the transport world, established British and Colonial Aircraft one year later. Based at Filton on the outskirts of Bristol, this firm became the Bristol Aeroplane Company, or Bristol for short. One of Britain's visionary aviation pioneers, it was White's firm intention to develop reliable civil and military aeroplanes. Famous and successful designs in the early years were the Boxkite and, after the designer Frank Barnwell joined the company, the successful, single-engined, fighter the Bristol Scout and F2B Fighter established the firm's place as one of the leaders in the nation's aviation industry during World War I. Bristol's next step was to get involved in aero-engine design, employing Roy Fedden as chief engine designer in 1920. This led to a range of highly successful, air-cooled radial engines: the Jupiter, Mercury, Pegasus, Hercules and Centaurus were in world-wide use for well over forty years. Successful Bristol aircraft designs in the 1920s and the 1930s were the Bristol Bulldog fighter and the Bombay troop transport. After struggling in the mid 1930s with an unsuccessful series of single-engined aircraft, Bristol re-established itself in 1938–39 as the world's largest aircraft manufacturer once Blenheim production got into full stride.

small, twin-engined, low-wing, cabin monoplane, intended as a six-seater, high-speed transport with a crew of two. The project, christened Type 135, was brought to the attention of Lord Rothermere, owner of the *Daily Mail*, early in the next year. Rothermere, keen on encouraging British aviation, had recently boasted that he intended to buy the fastest commercial aeroplane in Europe for his private use. Barnwell estimated the top speed of Type 135, fitted with the latest 650hp Mercury VIS 2 engines, at 250mph at 6,500ft, whereupon Rothermere placed an immediate order for the aircraft, now designated Type 142. It was the most advanced aeroplane design in Europe, its semi-monocoque, all-metal stressed skin construction being highly innovative. This new building method was made possible by the recent introduction into the American aviation industry of the light yet strong Alclad composite-alloy skins. These skins were held in place by light alloy frames and stringers as a semi-monocoque, resulting in far lighter and stronger structures than were possible previously. Type 142 was the first European design using this revolutionary production method. With the aviation industry at this time still struggling to build wings strong enough to withstand loads without any external bracing struts and wires, the 142's clean monoplane design was innovative, as were

The Bristol Mercury Engine

In late 1916 the Admiralty issued a specification for the ideal engine for the Royal Naval Air Service: a static, air-cooled radial producing 300hp of no more than 3ft 6in in diameter. In response, Roy Fedden had designed and built the Mercury within six months; it was an immediate success. Fedden (at that time Chief Engineer at Straker Squire, car and aero-engine builders in Bristol) was one of the famous pioneers in British aircraft engine design, together with the likes of Montague Napier, John Siddeley and Henry Royce. In early 1918, with his experience in building the Mercury, Fedden finished a superb 400hp, single-row, nine-cylinder radial of 28 litres which he called the Jupiter. The Jupiter was further developed during the 1920s, as a reliable 550hp engine used around the world in the period between the two World Wars. From the Jupiter design, Fedden developed a 420hp (supercharged), single-row, nine-cylinder, air-cooled radial in 1928, which he again named Mercury. This engine was further developed over the next thirteen years into a 1,050hp (supercharged) radial. It had a 5.75in (146mm) bore and a 6.5in (165mm) stroke, giving 169cu in (2,765cc) per cylinder, and a capacity of 1,520cu in (24,983 litres). It was a most reliable engine, equipping an impressive number of British aircraft such as the 'Britain First', Blenheim, Lysander, Gladiator, Gauntlet, Skua, Master, Martinet, Hamilcar X, and the Sea Otter seaplane. Foreign aircraft designs powered by the Mercury during the 1930s were the Dutch Fokker G1 twin-engined fighter and the Polish PZL P11 single-engined fighter.

its enclosed cockpit, retractable undercarriage and safety flaps.

Type 142 was first flown at Filton on 12 April 1935. Rothermere gave it much publicity in his newspaper, and its dazzling performance swiftly attracted the Air Ministry's attention, which Rothermere had always had in the back of his mind. After fitting two-position, three-bladed metal propellors instead of the original fixed-pitch, four-bladed wooden ones, the sleek all-metal aircraft reached a top speed of 307mph. It was some 70mph faster than the contemporary first-line RAF biplane Gloster Gauntlet fighter, and 50mph faster than the Gloster Gladiator, which at that

Captain Frank Sowter Barnwell, OBE, AFC, BSc, Chief Designer of the Bristol Blenheim

Born in 1880 in Lewisham in south-east London, Frank Barnwell was educated at Glasgow University. He started building gliders as a teenager and in 1905 designed and built his first aeroplane fitted with a motor-cycle engine. It was not a success, nor was a monoplane he built together with his brother in 1908. In 1911 he joined Bristol as chief draughtsman, where two years later he was responsible for the design of the famous Bristol Scout. After the outbreak of World War I, Barnwell joined the RFC but was returned to Bristol, where he went on to build the Bristol F2B Fighter and the Bulldog. In all, he designed the amazing total of over 150 types of aircraft for Bristol between 1911 and 1938. Sadly he died at the controls of a privately-designed monoplane in a crash on 2 August 1938. Barnwell had three sons; all joined the Royal Air Force in the late 1930s. Plt Off John Barnwell, flying a fighter Blenheim in 29 Squadron, was probably killed by return fire on 18/19 June 1940 after shooting down a He 111 bomber. Barnwell's two other sons were also destined to be killed on active service in the early years of the war.

Bristol Type 143 with two of the new 500hp Bristol Aquila I sleeve-valve, radial engines, the intended commercial successor to Type 135. By the time Type 143 had been completed, Bristols was too deeply involved in the Blenheim programme to be able to develop the 143, and the project was abandoned in 1938. Peter G. Cooksley

K7033, the first production Blenheim is seen here at Filton in June 1936 where it made its first flight on the 25th before going on to Martlesham Heath for official acceptance trials. Peter G. Cooksley

time had just been ordered as the new frontline fighter for the RAF. When the Air Ministry asked to retain the aircraft for full evaluation as a potential high-speed, medium bomber, Lord Rothermere, a great patriot, decided to donate his aircraft to the Air Council, dubbing it 'Britain First'. The Air Ministry wasted no time in evaluating Type 142, now with the serial number K7557, issuing a retroactive specification B28/35, which Bristols met with the Type 142M (for Military), and which was officially named Blenheim Mk I in May 1936. The original design was altered to a mid-wing aircraft, to make room for a bomb bay below the wing spars. More powerful 840hp Mercury VIII nine-cylinder, air-cooled radials were fitted, a bomb aimer's position was provided in the nose, a dorsal semi-retractable gun turret was added, and the whole structure was strengthened: the 'Wonder Bomber' was

born. Converting the civilian type 142 into the military Blenheim I led to an increase in weight from 9,800 to 12,250lb, plus extra drag, which inevitably had an adverse effect on its performance. Even though the Mercury engines were uprated

from 650 to 840hp, the aircraft's maximum speed fell by some 28mph to 279mph. Still, it remained far faster than the RAF's contemporary fighters.

The Air Ministry had great plans for the Blenheim I in the RAF's Expansion

Programme, which was gathering pace during 1935 and 1936. As one facet of Scheme C, the first in this programme, a batch of 150 aircraft (K7033 to K7182) were ordered straight off the drawing

Specification of the Bristol Type 142	
ENGINES	two 650hp Bristol Mercury VI.S.2
WINGSPAN	56ft (17.08m)
WING AREA	469sq ft (43.57sq m)
LENGTH	39ft 4in (11.98m)
WEIGHT EMPTY	6,830lb (3,105kg)
WEIGHT LOADED	9,630lb (4,377kg)
RANGE	1,000miles (1,610km)
MAX. SPEED (WITH MAX. LOAD)	285mph (459kmh)
MAX. SPEED (WITH LIGHT LOAD)	307mph (490kmh)

board in September 1935.

The frantic pace of rearmament during these years is clearly illustrated by the government's orders for the aviation industry in 1936. The new Scheme F proposed to expand production from 3,800

Specification of the Blenheim Mk I	
ENGINES	two 840hp Bristol Mercury VIII nine-cylinder, air-cooled, supercharged radials
WINGSPAN	56ft 4in (17.16m)
WING AREA	469sq ft (43.64sq m)
LENGTH	39ft 9in (12.12m)
HEIGHT	9ft 10in (3.00m)
WEIGHT EMPTY	7,409lb (3,368kg)
FULL LOAD	4,400lb (2,000kg)
MAX. BOMB LOAD	1,150lb (523kg)
MAX. ALL-UP WEIGHT	12,030lb (5,468kg)
PERFORMANCE (WITH FULL LOAD):	
economical cruising speed	200mph (322kmh)
max. speed at sea level	220mph (354 kmh)
max. speed at 15,000ft (4,570m)	279mph (449 kmh)
max. permissible diving speed	285mph (459 kmh)
stalling speed (undercarriage and flaps up)	70mph (113 kmh)
landing speed	85mph (137 kmh)
climb to 15,000ft	11.5min (at 140mph/225 kmh)
range	1,125miles (1,803km)
service ceiling	30,000ft (9,150m)

aircraft over two years to 8,000 new aircraft over three years. The Blenheim took a dominant position in this scheme. The first Blenheim I, K7033 took to the air at Filton for its maiden flight on 25 June 1936, before going on to Martlesham Heath for official acceptance trials. As a result, it was fitted with improved carburettor air intakes, and controllable gills were soon fitted to the engine cowlings. The retraction gear for the tail wheel was discarded since it added nothing to the performance. Similarly, airscrew spinners, although briefly tried, were found to be of no advantage.

Deliveries finally began in March 1937, with 114 Squadron at RAF Wyton receiving the first production aircraft. Additional contracts for Blenheim Is were signed from July 1936 onwards, and over the next four years a total of 1,242 Mk Is were built. The majority of these, 700, were completed at the Bristol Works at Filton, the last (L4934) being delivered in July 1939. In order to meet the demands of the rapidly expanding Royal Air Force, two other British firms became involved in building the Blenheim I in the new government-sponsored 'shadow factory' scheme. First, A.V. Roe, an established aviation firm at Chadderton, completed a further 250 aircraft (L6594 to L6843) between August 1938 and March 1940. Finally, 292 machines (L8362 to L8731) came off the production lines of Rootes Securities, a motor-car manufacturer at Speke, between November 1938 and August 1939.

The sleek and powerful new aircraft caught the imagination of the public, as the then schoolboy Roger Peacock recalls:

> By the mid 30s one series of cigarette-cards depicted aircraft of the Royal Air Force and I collected them fanatically. I gazed long and devotedly at them all – Harts, Furies, Harrows and Hendons. Later there were Bulldogs, Battles, Whitleys, Wellingtons and one, the best because it was the fastest, plug-nosed and aggressive, the Bristol Blenheim. I could have recited blindfold its vital statistics: 279mph at 13,000ft, two Mercury VIII engines, range 1,000miles, crew of three, two guns and 1,000lb of bombs. The Blenheim was irresistibly fascinating.

Good, but Not Perfect

Despite the fact that the Blenheim was a revolutionary aircraft at the time of its conception, it must be classed as an interim aircraft, bridging the biplane age and that of the modern, all-metal monoplanes. Its engines, for example, lacked constant-speed or airscrew feathering facilities. The hydraulic system, which operated the mid-upper turret, flaps, and landing gear, was very simple. The bomb bay was not hydraulically controlled: bombs were released by gravity. Its doors were smoothly finished on the inside and the bombs hung above on standard RAF racks. These could carry a variety of types: 250lb, 40lb, containers of 4lb incendiary bombs, and from early 1941 even 500lb bombs. Across the

Plug-nosed and aggressive, the Bristol Blenheim was irresistibly fascinating. Frontal view of K7038, the sixth production aircraft, at Manston in 1937. Gp Capt Edwin Shipley

114 Squadron Blenheim Is in a neat formation, 1937. K7038 in foreground, with K7044 next in line. The latter served with 114/AAEE/604 and 54 OTU, before crashing on landing at Church Fenton on 14 February 1942. Douglas McKenzie

bottom were two supports which were held by the bomb-release gear. When the observer (navigator/bomb aimer) or pilot pressed the button for release these two supports fell away and the bombs were free. In the case of the larger types they would fall and strike the bomb bay doors, which were held closed by bungee cords, forcing them open, and once the load was free the doors closed again. However, when light bombs were being used the doors would not open because of the light weight of the explosives and so the doors below the weapons were removed and the load could fall without fear of exploding inside and destroying the aircraft.

In this regard it must be stressed that many valuable lessons were learned by Bristols in building the Blenheim. The aircraft was the company's first modern, twin-engined bomber, and the Blenheim programme in the end enabled Bristols to make a much better job, without undue delay, with the Beaufighter. The Blenheim must be considered as an important part of the company's designers' and engineers' learning process that led to other, better models such as the Beaufort torpedo bomber and the Beaufighter fighter bomber, only three to four years after the conception of the Blenheim. If Bristols had started the Beaufighter programme without the valuable experience gained from building the Blenheim in the mid 1930s, the former would undoubtedly not have been available in 1940. The Beaufighter eventually turned out to be one of the most formidable allied fighter-bombers of World War II. This is, perhaps, an equally important result of the famous, inspired decision of Bristols and Lord Rothermere to make the Blenheim in the first place.

The pilot and observer entered the Blenheim by clambering on to the port wing and gently letting themselves down through the roof hatch, whereas the WOp/AG got into his rather restricted 'office' through an aperture in front of his turret. The turret was equipped with a Vickers K gas-operated machine-gun, pan-fed, with a rate of fire of 650 rounds per minute and a maximum useful range of 400yd. Beyond that distance the angle of trail was so pronounced that, even if the bullets hit something, they glanced harmlessly off. In comparison, the cannons fitted to the new generation of Luftwaffe fighters, the Bf109 and the 110, had a killing range of 1,000m (1,100yd). As soon as war broke out, this became painfully apparent: the Blenheim could not fight back. A few Blenheim gunners did succeed in shooting down the occasional fighter, and any such fortunate gunner was usually awarded an immediate DFM.

Most squadrons converting to the new aircraft had used open-cockpit biplane Hawker Hart bombers, which made the Blenheim I seem a giant leap forwards. Almost all aspects of the aircraft were new, and pilots had to get used to handling the powerful aircraft properly by intensive training. The aircraft, for example, had to be kept in a nose-down attitude immediately after take-off to build up sufficient speed to be able to handle a single engine failure. There were quite a few accidents, usually fatal, with pilots taking off and climbing, then having one engine fail but with insufficient speed to retain single-engine control, the aircraft then turning over and crashing to the ground.

On 3 December 1937, Blenheim K7110 of 'A' Flight 114 Squadron ran into a snow storm near Hinckley, Leicester while en route for bombing practice at Aldergrove. Having lost control, the pilot baled out, with his observer Cpl Tom Barnes and the W.Op/AG still on board. Neither was wearing his parachute. Half-conscious, Barnes climbed into the pilot's seat and managed to level the bomber at 300ft, although he had only had 2-hr dual piloting instruction. The next instant, the aircraft hit the ground, killing a horse in its path, hurtled through a hedge and was wrecked. The two men crawled out, unhurt except for shock. Barnes was subsequently awarded the AFM for his prompt and courageous action. This cartoon was drawn of the incident. Sadly, Sgt 'Barney' Barnes was killed in action on 15 February 1941 while piloting Blenheim T2125 on a weather reconnaissance of Flushing harbour. Derek L. Barnes

18 Squadron Blenheim Mk Is at the underground refuelling point at RAF Upper Heyford, 1938. L1161, on the left, was destined to serve in the RAF for six years with 18 Squadron, CFS, 3FPP and 12 PAFU before being SOC on 17 March 1944. Bryn Williams

Gilbert Haworth's Story

Cpl Gilbert Haworth, observer with 44 Squadron, converted to the Blenheim I at Waddington in April 1938. He flew in this type until the squadron converted to the Hampden bomber in early 1939:

Our Blenheims were of the very earliest type and the transparent glazing which enclosed the crews in their cabins was manufactured from old-fashioned, thick celluloid which had many limitations. It soon discoloured and developed cracks, certain panels had been known to cave in during high-speed manoeuvres. In order to reduce the danger of being trapped in the event of a take-off crash, our instructions were to leave the sliding roof canopy in its open position until a safe take-off was reasonably certain. The Air Observer was then required to reach backwards with his left hand and slam it shut, something that could not be accomplished once the aircraft was fully airborne. On one sad occasion I was surprised to find that the canopy would not budge and I pulled harder only to be surprised much more when the bulky metal handle and front framework came away in my hand, the rest of the canopy disappearing backwards. My arm, on being so suddenly relieved of all its burden, shot forward out of control and the poor old pilot received a terrible blow on the

back of his head when we were racing along at 80mph but not quite airborne. Our large twin-engined monoplane performed some marvellous evolutions as the stunned victim abandoned take-off and miraculously brought the machine to rest a matter of inches from the boundary fence near the public highway.

In this instance too, cracked celluloid had caused a near accident. This could well have been the clue to the cause of at least some of the mysterious fatal crashes which had befallen Blenheims on take-off. The flames would always completely destroy evidence of this kind. Haworth continues the story:

Most of the personnel were very young indeed, and in any case the older pilots were at home only with good, old-fashioned, open-cockpit, single-engined machines which were as different as chalk from cheese. It had always been difficult for old dogs to learn new tricks and many of the so-called highly qualified and experienced men were decidedly at sea when handling a speedy aircraft which had two motors, bothersome retractable wheels, landing flaps and adjustable

airscrews, all factors which exacted stern retribution if mishandled.

Moreover there were some regrettably unsatisfactory design faults which were cruel traps for unwary innocents, things which were never tolerated in more enlightened years. No really thorough instruction was given and a pilot might often be seen furtively consulting a handbook. The scene was well and truly set to provide a fair number of 'ardua', the accident rate was positively high, incidents of varying degrees of gravity were frequent, the sight of a Blenheim resting ignominiously on its belly with wheels collapsed being particularly familiar.

Traditionally, it had always been considered that the use of engine power during the landing procedure was a sign of incompetence, 'dead stick' landings were de rigueur and at some famous squadrons a pilot had to buy drinks all round if he violated convention by resorting to a burst of throttle to get on to the field safely. It soon became painfully apparent that 'dead stick' landings in Blenheims were decidedly traumatic and dangerous. And so, not without reluctance, it came to pass that the practice of motoring the twin-engined machines into a landing was generally adopted.

In fact, over a hundred Blenheims were lost in accidents before the outbreak of war, some 10 per cent of the total deployed. However, among the young aircrew flying the Blenheim, there was a marked tendency to dismiss such things as death and serious injury as being bad luck and all in the game. There were a few incidents which occasioned the raising of eyebrows and when the word 'dangerous' entered the conversation, but even so, the ever-present determination to be light-hearted would come to the surface and the word would be pronounced as 'dangeroos' as if it rhymed with 'kangaroos'. Cpl Haworth explains:

According to my log book it was 10.00hrs on 23 July 1938 when I took off on a high-level bombing exercise. Fg Off 'Pony' Moore, a barrel-chested Canadian, was the pilot. I clambered into the cramped seat at his right side and plugged myself into the intercommunications system. 'Ya got the bomb safety pins removed?', he drawled. 'Sure enough', I replied and soon we commenced a steep climb to reach the required height of 10,000ft over the bombing range. I noted with displeasure that there was enough cloud around to cause a little difficulty in finding the target. We were under orders to drop eight practice bombs and there is nothing more annoying than to be cheated out of an excercise because the target is obscured. At 10,000ft Pony levelled out for me to perform a wind-finding exercise so that I could register the speed and direction of the wind on the bombsight settings. This took only a few minutes and when I gave the word, we attacked the target, which on this occasion was a white triangular structure with sides about 15yd long.

The clouds were now definitely threatening to blot out the area but we applied ourselves to the task and persevered, the Blenheim settled on course, straight and level, and almost exactly where I wanted it to be. 'Left...left', I shouted over our inefficient and badly cracking intercom system, Pony immediately shifted two degrees to the left. The target entered my sighting wires beautifully and began to slide satisfactorily along them. 'Steady – steady', I droned to the pilot, a quick glance confirmed that the bombsight was accurately aligned, another glance showed me that its two spirit levels were as near correct as they were ever likely to be. The target rapidly approached the release point and when it sat neatly in the sights I pressed the firing button and called out 'BOMB GONE'. Those words were the standard expression which notified the pilot that he was free to relax concentration a little but that he must nevertheless maintain his compass heading until a telltale burst of smoke revealed our degree of success. After about 30sec I could see the point of impact, there it was, roughly 70yd short of the target but absolutely in line with our approach, neither to the left nor to the right. This gave me a vital clue.

With that evidence I was now able to appraise the situation very accurately, our bombing run had been straightforward and faultless; moreover we had attacked exactly into the direction from which the wind was coming. I could now confidently deduce that the true windspeed was just a little higher than I had thought, accordingly the bombsight had registered a somewhat low estimate of the aircraft's groundspeed. I well knew that the most common cause of high-level bombing inaccuracies was an error in the wind-finding and whilst Pony was busy turning on to the next heading for attack I confidently added 3mph to the windspeed setting. I reaped an immediate profit, the next attack was rewarded with a burst close to the corner of the target and within about 8min we had launched three more attacks and each time achieved a hit or a very near miss. We were delighted and began fervently to pray that the clouds would continue to be merciful; but alas, on the next attack I was compelled to cry 'Dummy run!' when the target slid out of sight at the vital moment.

Great patience was required before we could manage to complete our exercise and I failed to achieve any more direct hits. Winds are inconsistent, as most people are well aware, and the unwelcome delay imposed by the fleeting clouds had given our particular bombing wind an opportunity to fluctuate. Nevertheless we were far from being displeased with the results we had seen.

Radar surveillance and radio control were unheard of and once our bombing exercise was finished we were free to do as we liked, as free as any of the birds and in the manner of schoolboys newly released from the classroom, we made the most of it.

Those clouds now became our playthings and for some time we cavorted in and out of the towering summits, thoroughly enjoying the exhilaration of very-high-speed flying without the risk of colliding with anything hard and dangerous. When we finally tired of this sort of fun, or perhaps it was because we were getting short of petrol, we brought it to an end by diving steeply through a picturesque chasm in the cloud banks and returning to the airfield at Warmwell in Dorset, which at that time was merely a small, grassy clearance thoroughly hemmed in by trees. We had a splendid excuse

A Blenheim wireless operator/air gunner's restricted space. The radio transmitter and receiver are behind the ammunition tanks. Ken Whittle

The teeth of the Blenheim IV. In an effort to improve the Blenheim's defensive fire power, the single, gas-operated Vickers 'K' gun in the mid-upper turret was replaced by twin, belt-fed, .303 Brownings during the second half of 1940. Ken Whittle

Cockpit layout of the Blenheim IV, the 'office' of the pilot and observer. Blenheim Society

to carry out a very hair-raising low-level circuit because there was no Air Traffic Control in operation and therefore no radio backchat from an interfering authority.

We motored along in fine style, just clearing the treetops nicely until we were about 500yd from the grass landing strip and then, to our dismay, the starboard engine stopped. I must now rely on Air Force parlance to describe our miserable plight adequately, I can only say that I thought we had 'bought it', that we 'had our chips', in other words we were as good as dead. I looked at Pony, his instant reaction had been to apply full rudder to correct the vicious swing that immediately followed the failure and his face betrayed the strenuous effort required of him. He could not afford to give full power to the remaining engine as that would have been really disastrous, but he did open up the throttle a little, just enough to keep our airspeed at the minimum safety level. We experienced a very queasy sensation as the topmost branches scraped our aircraft and it seemed a very long time before we managed to drop heavily on to the open ground. After coming safely to rest I could not restrain myself from muttering 'Dangeroos' into my mouthpiece. 'Ya can say that again', replied Pony.

After sorting ourselves out a little we made our way on foot to the Bomb Plotting Office to inspect the results of our exercise and we were elated to learn that we had averaged a distance of 52yd for the eight bombs dropped from 10,000ft, the best figure ever recorded for the high-performance Blenheim Mark 1 Bomber. Our bombing score was never beaten.

Incidentally, about two days after our exploit, the crew of another Blenheim introduced themselves to some girls at a nearby seaside resort and arranged to give them a quite unofficial demonstration of stunts and low flying at the conclusion of bombing practice. It all went off very well in a way, but the pilot forgot that he was bound to be short of petrol and the girls were all charmed to watch him ditch the aircraft about 100yd from the shore. Rumour had it that he was asked for an encore as the girls had forgotten their cameras on the first occasion.

Despite the high accident rate with the Blenheim I, almost all pilots who flew the aircraft were delighted with its performance and handling qualities. Still, although flying controls were good, the cockpit layout of the essential engine, fuel and hydraulic controls remained problematic. Pilots were easily identified by their 'Blenheim hands' on account of the cuts and scratches on the back of them. These were caused by the springs and screwheads on the fuel-valve controls, the spring-loaded flaps for the undercarriage, and turret hydraulic selector. The general opinion was that the Blenheim had been designed as an aircraft and the pilot was an afterthought, as Flt Lt Arthur Gill, a pilot with 84 Squadron, confirms:

Of the piston-engined aircraft, the Blenheim was one of my favourite aircraft. The Mk1 was the nicer aircraft to fly; it was fully aerobatic and less heavy than the Mk 4, and it rolled

beautifully. My main complaint about the Blenheim was the cockpit layout and the inaccessible positioning of the controls – especially during take-off which was a vital time. For example, the pilot had to hold the control-column 'spectacles' with, first, the right hand, as he opened the throttles; then change hands in order to raise the undercarriage with the right hand. Change hands again to operate the engines' control levers (throttles, airscrew pitch). Change hands again to raise the flaps. Change again – engine-gills, trim, engine boost, aircraft trim wheels, and so on. He needed to be a contortionist!

Wg Cdr H.W. 'Tubby' Mermagen, who was given the job of forming No. 222 night-fighter Squadron in September 1939 with Blenheim IFs, further comments on the aerobatic qualities of the short-nosed Blenheim: 'I found the Blenheim I a very easy aircraft to fly aerobatically. In my squadron such flying was confined to myself! At Duxford, when i/c 222, I could demonstrate loops, rolls, and even a half-roll off a loop. I don't think this was attempted by any other Blenheim pilot.'

By September 1938, a total of sixteen RAF medium bomber squadrons had been equipped with the Blenheim I, six each in No.1 and No. 2 Group, plus four more in No.5 Group. Roger Peacock was trained as a wireless operator and took further training, later on, as an air gunner, being posted to 90 Squadron, 2 Group at Bicester in 1938:

Imagine it, they were flying Blenheims. Suddenly I was free to wander around a hangar stuffed full of Blenheims – I was even given one all for my very own: L1284. I lived in bliss, despite my rank of AC2 (because there was no AC3) and my measly pay of 3s.3d. [16p] per day, later to rise to 3s.9d. [19p], no less, once I had qualified as a gunner and put up my brass flying bullet.

Practical difficulties now arose. I was a hybrid: I belonged both to aircrew and to ground personnel. There were times when I was expected to be in two places at once: in the crewroom being briefed for the day, and busy about my daily inspection. Somehow, we coped – and do notice that 'we': the miracle was produced largely by co-operation between the W.Ops, assisted by the fact that the ground personnel were at the hangar a whole half-hour before the observers (corporals, then) and pilots (about two-thirds officers and the rest sergeants), none of whom had any maintenance work to do.

82 Squadron Blenheim Is taxiing out at Cranfield in March 1939, at the time when Germany occupied the rest of Czechoslovakia. Douglas McKenzie

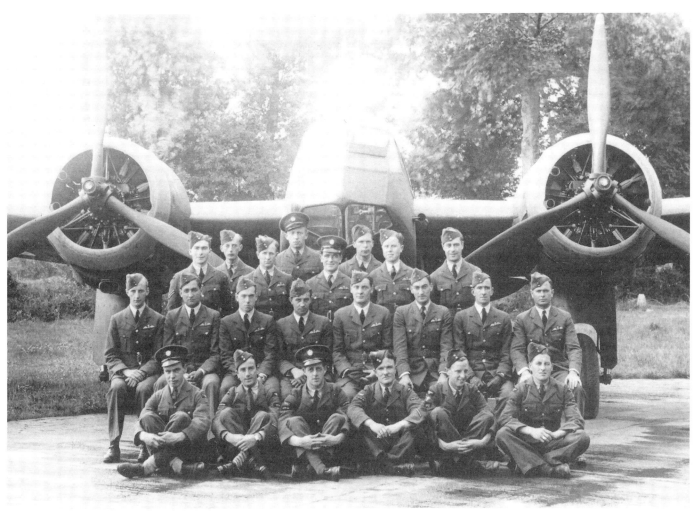

No. 18 Blenheim Delivery Flight, Thorney Island–Heliopolis, 19 July 1939. Hundreds of Blenheim Is were ferried to the Middle and Far East after most home-based bomber Blenheim squadrons had converted to the Mk IV during 1938–39. Gron Edwards

Days were long and work was hard for Peacock and his fellow W.Op/AGs, but:

on several occasions, while riding in the front as a passenger or practising map-reading, I had moments of glory: sitting in the driver's seat and actually flying the Blenheim. It was a very easy kite to fly, which probably says more for the skill of the designer than for any aptitude of mine. In those piping days of peace the RAF was an immense flying club and we were happy in and proud of our Blenheims. We missed no opportunity to land at a strange aerodrome and show off the latest and the best to less-favoured friends, of whom there were always one or two around to greet you. Masterly understatement emphasized the gap between our aircraft and the measly Whitleys, Battles and Hampdens and even Wimpies [Wellingtons] which we met elsewhere. We would always leave with a glorious climbing turn (forbidden by Squadron

Standing Orders, but how were strangers to know that?) within seconds of the wheels being retracted – at a height of some six feet or so.

Design Improvements

With the production of the Blenheim I gaining momentum, Bristols developed the successful design further. The Mk II was externally similar to the Blenheim I but carried more equipment and had an increased loaded weight and a strengthened undercarriage, the Mk III becoming a short-range, long-nosed version; but neither of both these marks was proceeded with. When the Air Ministry issued specification 11/36 in 1936 for an interim general reconnaissance aircraft to replace the Avro Anson, Bristols swiftly came up with Type 149. This design was meant to bridge the gap until the delayed Bristol

Beaufort torpedo bomber (Type 152) programme could gather full speed. Type 149 was structurally similar to the Blenheim Mk I, but was a more powerful war machine. The nose section was extended by 3ft to provide room for a navigation station. Its range was extended to 1,460miles with a 1,000lb bomb load by fitting extra fuel tanks in the outer wing sections, and it was fitted with more powerful 920hp Mercury XV engines. The undercarriage was strengthened and provision was made for bomb racks under the wings. Finally, in order to keep the landing weight within limits, fuel dump pipes were installed under the wings. This aircraft, with serial number K7072, was named Bolingbroke I and first flew on 24 September 1937, but it was unsatisfactory due to the pilot's poor view ahead. The nose was therefore further modified and, finally, the familiar scalloped, asymmetrical shape on the port side of the nose emerged. The aircraft was renamed Blenheim IV to avoid confusion, and the name Bolingbroke was

Schoolchildren inspecting L1112 of 82 Squadron which crashed at Chellaston near Derby, 11 August 1939. Blenheim Society

Specification of the Blenheim Mk IV	
ENGINES	two 920hp Bristol Mercury XV nine-cylinder, air-cooled, supercharged radials
WINGSPAN	56ft 4in (17.16m)
WING AREA	469sq ft (43.57sq m)
LENGTH	42ft 9in (13.03m)
HEIGHT	9ft 10in (3m)
WEIGHT EMPTY	9,823lb (4,519kg)
FULL LOAD	5,200lb (2,392kg)
MAX. BOMB LOAD	1,200lb (552kg)
MAX. ALL-UP WEIGHT	15,682lb (7,120kg)
PERFORMANCE (WITH FULL LOAD):	
economical cruising speed	170mph (274kmh)
max. cruising speed	225mph (363kmh)
max. speed at sea level	230mph (370kmh)
max. speed at 15,000ft	266mph (428kmh)
stalling speed (undercarriage and flaps up)	70mph (113kmh)
initial rate of climb per minute	1,480ft (449m)
range (at 170mph)	1,457miles (2,344km)
service ceiling	23,000ft (7,010m)

'closed' position when ready for taxiing and flight. Little metal rings on the side of the fuselage helped you to climb on to the top of the wing, to reach the sliding roof. Personally, I found the Blenheim a delight to fly, and very smooth on the controls ('Spectacle' control column). In the cockpit a little behind and to the left of the pilot, were the two knobs – one for each engine – which you pushed in, or pulled out, for 'fine' or 'coarse' pitch of the propellor blades of each engine. Never once did the Bristol Mercury engines fail us, even when flying through low mist over the North Sea! Those 'pitch knobs' reminded me very much of the gearbox of a car, and when changing pitch you could hear the distinct change in the sound of the engines. In formation flying, the pilot had a first-class view of the beautiful lines of this mid-wing, twin-engined light bomber.

In early 1938, it was decided to equip overseas squadrons with the Blenheim I, in anticipation of the re-equipping of the home-based Blenheim I units with the more powerful Mk IV. No. 30 Squadron received its first Blenheim Is at Habbaniya, Iraq on 13 January 1938, and one year later the first Mk Is reached India. The Air Ministry also released the Mark I for export, with the Finnish, Turkish, Yugoslavian and Rumanian air forces ordering small batches of the aircraft during the period 1936–39.

War and the First Operations

Political tension meanwhile was building up during the summer of 1938, and war was only just avoided during the Munich crisis with Chamberlain announcing that he had secured 'peace in our time'. It was clear, however, in March 1939 with Hitler marching into Bohemia-Moravia, that the clouds of war were gathering rapidly. British rearmament programmes were stepped up and tension mounted further. On the eve of war, Blenheim Is equipped only two bomber squadrons in the United Kingdom (Nos. 18 and 57), but overseas it equipped eleven squadrons spread between Egypt, Aden, Iraq, India and Singapore. In the meantime, a new role was sought for the hundreds of Mk Is still in Britain, and it was decided to turn them into long-range fighters. This was the standard Mk I bomber with a four Browning .303 gun-pack added under the bomb bay. Nearly 150 were so converted by July 1939, equipping seven home-based squadrons. At the outbreak of war the

transferred to a variant on the model which was later built in Canada.

The observers, particularly, greeted the Blenheim Mk IV with great enthusiasm: now they had a real chart-table at which to work (sitting sideways to the direction of flight), instead of being squashed up on to a small jump-seat alongside the pilot in the Mk I. Due to the extra drag and the loaded weight inevitably going up, from 12,250lb for the Mk I to 14,500lb for the Mk IV, the latter with a maximum speed of 270mph was some 10 mph slower than its older brother (and 37mph slower than 'Britain First'). The Mercury XV, though, could be boosted to 9lb/sq in for 3min when using 100 octane fuel, giving the Mk IV 30 precious extra mph in a combat emergency. Although the Blenheim IV still was a fast aircraft for its day, with the new generation of 350mph and cannon-armed Messerschmitt Bf109 and 110 entering Luftwaffe front-line service in 1937, the writing was already on the wall. Plt Off Guy Avery, a pilot with 139 Squadron, gives an impression of the Blenheim IV bomber:

Some called the Blenheim 'The Flying Coffin', because you got into it by climbing up the side of the fuselage and wing, and through an open, sliding, Perspex roof, which you slid back to the

RAF had 1,089 Blenheims on strength, more than any other type of aircraft. Of these, 899 were short-nosed Mark Is (of which 273 were based overseas) and 190 were home-based Mark IVs.

Hitler's aggression against Poland finally opened hostilities on 3 September 1939, as the twenty-two-years old New Zealander Plt Off Douglas McKenzie, pilot with 82 Squadron, recalls:

Chamberlain's 'we-are-at-war' broadcast began at 11.15am on 3 September 1939; I heard this in the squadron's radio room in the hangar at Watton. Within just a few hours we were in the air to fly – not east against the enemy, but west! All the aircraft went off in a ragged formation (I had no crew, just ballast) and landed at Netheravon on Salisbury Plain. Some anti-climax!

There was no proper accommodation for us. For two nights we slept on the couches in the mess. Then, on 5 September we all flew back to Watton. But the Luftwaffe had not attacked the place while we were away, so I suppose it could be said that the dispersal had been a waste of time. However, better safe than sorry (as they say). Speaking operationally, things were very touchy at the start until it could be seen how the pattern would develop. There were a number of 2 Group Blenheims which had a real smash-up at Wilhelmshaven harbour on the second day of the war.

On the afternoon of 4 September Bomber Command mounted its first bombing raid of the war, on warships at the entrance to Wilhelmshaven. The attack was triggered off by a sighting the day before by 139 Squadron's Fg Off Andrew McPherson and his crew, who were the first members of the RAF to penetrate German airspace during the war in Blenheim N6215, and a similar sighting earlier on the 4th by the same crew. In atrocious weather, five Blenheims of 110 Squadron went into the attack first, catching the Germans by surprise. Although three hits were scored on the pocket battleship *Admiral Scheer*, the bombs bounced harmlessly off its thick armour. The squadron lost one crew, when Fg Off Emden's flak-stricken N6199 crashed on to the training cruiser *Emden*, killing the four-man crew and nine German sailors. By the time 107 Squadron had arrived in the target area, the enemy defences were wide awake, and three out of five aircraft dispatched from Wattisham were shot down by flak, with a fourth blown up by its own bombs. Of the sixteen aircrew lost, only N6240's Sgt G.F. Booth, observer, and AC1 L.J. Slattery, his gunner, survived to become Bomber Command's first prisoners of war in World War II. Five crews of 139 Squadron found nothing in the murk and returned home unscathed. To his great relief, Sgt W.Op/AG H. Robson and his 110 Squadron crew, who had been on stand-by for two days, were stood down for this operation as 2 Group HQ decided that a flight of five aircraft would be more effective than two vics of three: 'There was tremendous excitement when "A" Flight

German officers investigating the tangled remains of N6240, flown by Sgt Prince and crew of 107 Squadron, who were shot down at 18.10hr during the Wilhelmshaven raid of 4 September 1939. Archiv Greve, via Ab A. Jansen

L.J. Slattery, an AC1 W.Op/AG in 107 Squadron (depicted), and his observer G.F. Booth became the first RAF prisoners of war on 4 September 1939. Blenheim Society

returned and consternation when the lone Blenheim of 107 landed. It occurred to us aircrew that if this was to be the pattern of future operations we were in for a very short career.'

Units of 2 Group remained on stand-by status to attack the German fleet at sea, but no further attack was launched. After the initial raid on 4 September, the pace of war slowed down considerably, and the 'Phoney War' became established. Meanwhile, the British government had sent the British Expeditionary Force (BEF) to France, in aid of its French allies. The BEF's supporting Air Component included four 2 Group Blenheim squadrons, Nos. 18, 57, 53 and 59. They became engaged in strategic reconnaissance and photoreconnaissance of the Siegfried Line and the Ruhr, losing eight Blenheims and crews before the year was out. Simultaneously, 2 Group crews were dispatched regularly from East Anglia to fly armed reconnaissance sorties over the North Sea, for the loss of eight aircraft during the first four months of war. At the end of the year, the BEF's Advanced Air Striking Force in northern France, which mainly consisted of vulnerable Fairey Battles, was reinforced by 114 and 139 Squadrons,

equipped with Blenheim IV bombers. On the operational side, it was a case of learning from experience, as Fg Off John Wray, pilot with 53 Squadron, recorded:

On the morning of 30 September 1939 some staff officers arrived from Advanced Air Striking Force HQ and they disappeared into the Commanding Officer's office tent. Shortly afterwards they departed and the CO called us all into a meeting, where we were told that we were to carry out operations over Germany at night with the object of observing any movement of troops and vehicles up towards the Western Front. The tasks were to recce rail and road movement in the areas Hanover–Minden–Hamm and Bremen–Osnabrück–Münster.

Because Plivot was too small to operate out of at night and there were no facilities anyway, each of the sorties was to position at Metz and take off from there. Return would be to Vitry, which was not far from Plivot. Vitry had night facilities. On each night, three aircraft would depart from Metz.

The first night operation over Germany by three 53 Squadron crews was a shambles; Sqn Ldr Clements in L4842 made an emergency landing in a field some 10 miles south-west of Amiens, a second landed on a French fighter field, and only the third member of the flight arrived safely back at Vitry. Fg Off Wray at that time was the most experienced night-flyer on the squadron, with a bare ten hours at night in Blenheims. He continues:

I was in the next party of three to go. We flew to Metz at about midday, had a snack meal, looked at some rather aged French aircraft and then briefed for our night sorties. We were unable to take off that night because of fog, so we went the next night. None of us had any problems other than the fact that we never knew where we were and couldn't see anything. We all received our emergency homings and arrived back at Vitry in good order.

HQ AASF soon realized the futility of what we were doing, so they told us we were to fly to these target areas in daylight. This would allow cameras to be used and would give visual observation a chance also. During our squadron briefing one pilot said, 'If we keep flying back on the same route won't the Germans realize this and start to intercept us?' Although this may seem strange now, at that time I don't think this point had occurred to anybody and it was taken up with AASF. Their answer was that if we felt that way, at the end of the sortie we could fly out over Holland and to the UK, where the photographs could be developed and then the pilots could fly back to France across the Channel. Such an idea immediately brought volunteers from those who were married as it would give them a chance of a fleeting visit to their wives. Whether or not any prearrangement had been reached with the Netherlands I cannot say. I suspect not!

Although the bitterly cold winter weather restricted operational flying, the same pattern of operations continued during early

Together with 40 Squadron, No. XV converted from the Fairey Battle to the Blenheim IV at Wyton during the winter of 1939–40. Here a brand-new aircraft of XV Squadron is being serviced in the snow at Wyton in January 1940. Philip Camp

'Winter in the flat country around the airfield could be a stinker. Imagine a bare windswept airfield, on all sides the flat and monotonous country relieved only by the hangars and aerodrome buildings, and the cold, chilly wind whistling across. That lazy wind is too tired to go round you, so it goes through, causing hands already cold to go numb after a few minutes' contact with equally cold and stubborn metal. Overcoats, scarves and pullovers are merely inadequate barriers to delay the shivering onslaught, a sop to vicious probing fingers.' (Fred Adkin, 'erk' with 17 OTU). Here, each engine of 53 Squadron A Flight's PZ-A has its own, specially-made canvas tent with a small oil heater inside at Poix airfield, as great trouble was experienced in starting the Mercurys in the mornings because the engine oil froze in the extreme cold during the winter of 1939. Peter A. Russell

1940. 2 Group dispatched a total of 250 armed reconnaissance sorties across the North Sea between mid February and the end of March, delivering six successful bombing attacks for the loss of four Blenheims and crews to Bf109s and 110s. On 11 March, Sqn Ldr Miles Delap of 82 Squadron, navigated by Sgt 'Bish' Bareham got another 'first' for the Blenheim, when he sank U-31 in the Schillig Roads, thus becoming the first British aircraft to sink a German submarine in the war. The same U-Boat had been attacked and damaged by Sgt Dickie Gunning in N6183 of 107 Squadron a week previously, which earned Gunning an immediate DFM. Delap was awarded the DFC for his action.

In the second week of April 1940, 82, 21, 107 and 110 Squadrons were deployed to Thornaby, in Yorkshire, and Lossiemouth, in Scotland, to support operations in Norway after Germany had invaded the country on 9 April. Twelve Blenheims of 107 Squadron were the first to be dispatched on 12 April, bravely attacking the *Scharnhorst*, *Gneisenau* and *Hipper*, and other German fleet elements en route to Norway, but no hits were scored. The

attack was pressed home in conjunction with strong Wellington and Hampden forces, but nine of the latter types were lost to fierce opposition from flak and fighters. This signalled the end for the employment of the Hampden and the Wellington in daylight operations, leaving 2 Group as the sole Bomber Command unit to carry the war to the enemy in daytime.

During the Norwegian campaign, 2 Group crews flew 113 sorties in twenty raids against German-occupied airfields, notably Stavanger, and shipping, for the loss of seven crews missing. As a result of these first raids, Wg Cdr Basil Embry, CO of 107 Squadron recommended that the Blenheim's armament should be increased to six Browning machine-guns if the aircraft were to succeed as a daylight bomber. The first combats with Bf110 fighters, which destroyed two of his squadron's aircraft on 17 April, with another Blenheim staggering back to base with 53 hits, had laid bare the painful fact that the Blenheim was a very vulnerable aircraft when engaged by modern, cannon-armed fighters. The 'Wonder Bomber' of only four years earlier had been overtaken by a

technological leap forward in modern fighter aircraft development. The air battles in the Norwegian campaign had also exposed the failure of the self-defending, daylight, bomber formation ('the bomber will always get through'), on which the RAF had relied so heavily during the 1920s and the 1930s. Plt Off McKenzie, a pilot with 82 Squadron, explains:

It was an article of faith before the war that modern aircraft like the Blenheim with revolving turrets were a formidable – even unbeatable – defensive proposition provided that close formation was kept so as to maximize fire power against an attacker.

Someone among the planners and designers must surely have been troubled by the lack of reply to ventral attack on a Blenheim, unless they had the notion that fighters could attack only from above. Later, of course, a back-firing gun was put in to be operated by the observer hanging his head upside down, but, oh, God! The fact is that there was no way that an aircraft the small size of a Blenheim could be given adequate protection underneath. The only answer to this is that they should never have been sent out in formation. The whole concept of a defensive box was a myth. It was a box all right – a box in the sense of a bloody coffin! The trouble with formations was that they looked good. They looked logical, they looked warlike; and everyone was trained to think that close formation-flying was the acme of both offence and defence. Of course, there was a lot of experimenting with aircraft capabilities at the start of the war. The Air Council had to find out exactly what it had in practice compared with the theory of design and the strength of the enemy. This was especially so in the matter of formation flying. Wellingtons from Feltwell went out in formation to test themselves, and found some 110s, and that was more or less the end of that squadron. And this was an aircraft, mark you, with more turrets than a Blenheim. The Wellingtons were hastily put on night work. When the Fairey Battles were given their test they went down like ninepins. But someone had to do the day offensive ops unless the Royal Air Force was prepared to admit that it had nothing for this most visible of its tasks. Thus the Blenheims stood forward as the best of a bad job.

I proved to my own satisfaction that the answer to fighter attack was to get down to hedge hopping. Twelve Blenheims flying singly and hugging the ground when necessary, would have a much greater chance of penetrating to the target and doing the damage they were meant to do, and getting home again, than any unescorted twelve in formation.

CHAPTER TWO

Blenheim Operational Training Units, 1940–44

More than 1,200 Blenheims, over a fifth of the total built, served with one or more of the twenty-six Operational Training Units (OTUs) in the Royal Air Force during World War II. In the United Kingdom the two main Blenheim OTUs were Nos. 13 and 17. In April 1940 13 OTU formed at Bicester from 104 and 108 Squadron, with 265 Blenheim Is, IVs and Vs until April 1944. At Upwood 17 OTU was also established in April 1940 from a merger of 35 and 90 Squadron, operating a total of 184 of all marks of the type until April 1943. These two OTUs provided the replacement crews for 2 Group. Other major Blenheim OTUs in Great Britain were No. 2 at Catfoss (operating a total of 114 Blenheims), and No. 42 using 121 Blenheims for Army Co-operation training at Andover and Ashbourne. Finally, a total of 277 Blenheims served with 51 and 54 OTU, both night fighter OTUs at Cranfield and Church Fenton air bases, respectively.

An OTU course was the last one in aircrew training, where the three Blenheim aircrew trades (pilot, observer and W.Op/AG) all came together. Individual under-training (u/t) aircrew were given short operational courses in their own trades, which was done in separate Flights. At No. 13 OTU in 1941, for example, pupil pilots were under instruction on Blenheim Is in 'A' Flight. 'B' Flight had a few Ansons on strength which were used in navigation training for u/t observers and wireless instruction for pupil W.Op/AGs. In 'C' Flight, sprog (new recruit) observers practised bomb-aiming on the local bombing range in Blenheim IVs with staff pilots.

Finally, when the pupils had successfully passed through their individual courses, they were allowed to sort themselves out into crews and joined 'D' Flight. Here the crews were moulded into efficient fighting teams, flying together on cross-country and night exercises, to be finally posted to an operational squadron.

Roger Peacock's Story

Roger Peacock served as a W.Op/AG in 90 Squadron during 1938–40, and when his unit was amalgamated into No. 17 OTU, started instructing u/t W.Op/AGs:

During the years immediately preceding the 1939–1945 War, some preparations, subsequently proved to be quite inadequate, were being made for the prosecution of that war. One

147 RCAF Squadron Bolingbroke 'M' over the Fraser River, British Columbia in June 1942.
John Muter

Sea Island, British Columbia, late 1942 or early 1943. Fg Off J. Muter, RCAF (on the right) and his 147 (RCAF) Squadron crew pose with Bolingbroke IV 9041. Note the spinners on the aircraft, which served with Nos. 8 and 147 (RCAF) Squadrons and the RCAF's Central Training Establishment between 3 October 1941 and 1 October 1946. This Bolingbroke is the oldest of only six surviving today and is currently on display in Nanton, Alberta, awaiting full restoration. John Muter

Between 1938 and 1943, 626 Bolingbrokes were completed in Canada under licence by Fairchild Aircraft Ltd, at Longueil, Quebec, plus fifty-one spare airframes. The aircraft was similar to the British Blenheim IV, apart from the cockpit being fitted with American instrumentation and the navigator's position being redesigned. Another main difference was in the crew composition: in the Bolingbroke, a fourth crew member was added to work a radio set aft of the gun turret. Eighteen Bolingbroke Mk Is (serial numbers 702–719, all with Bristol Mercury VIII engines), 185 Mk IVs (with Bristol Mercury XVs) and fifteen Mk IVWs (with Pratt & Whitney Wasp Jr SB4G engines) were completed as bomber-reconnaissance aircraft between 1939 and 1943. These equipped eight RCAF squadrons for home defence duties in Canada, serving throughout the war, the last remaining aircraft finally being struck off charge from 122 (RCAF) Squadron strength in September 1945.

Perhaps the most unusual version of the Bolingbroke was the Mk III seaplane. Intended for coastal reconnaissance and fitted with a pair of Edo floats, the prototype No.717 was first flown on 28 August 1940. Directional stability was very good, with the aircraft being capable of a maximum speed of 241mph at 12,000ft. However, it was not a success: the long Atlantic swells and short chop threw too much water into the engines, often making them miss and sometimes die. RCAF 717 reverted to a wheeled undercarriage in January 1942; the aircraft was finally struck off strength on 26 June 1944.

The Bolingbroke, 'Bole' or 'Boly' as it was affectionately called by its crews, mainly saw service in the Mk IVT configuration, as a trainer and target tug for the Bombing and Gunnery Schools in the British Commonwealth Air Training Plan (BCATP) from March 1942 onwards. Thousands

of the things which the top brass of the RAF managed to get right was the provision of a training programme both to replace inevitable losses and to expand the service to many times its peacetime strength. Even before the war was at last upon us, some of our scanty bomber squadrons had been earmarked as training units, to be withdrawn from the line of battle and put to work bringing raw aircrew: pilots, observers, wireless-operators and air gunners, up to operational standard. After a certain programme had been satisfactorily worked through, these men would move on to front-line squadrons.

In 2 Group, Nos. 90 and 35 Squadrons were so designated and by the end of that September they had moved to Upwood and were being filled out with newly-trained aircrew. Very soon

the two squadrons lost their individual identities and had become 17 Operational Training Unit. Initially 'A' and 'B' Flights were exclusively composed of 90 Squadron personnel, while 'C' and 'D' were ex-35. Incoming pupils were evenly spread across all four flights. For screened crews the pace of life and daily doses of fear made us concentrate on the one important question: could we survive the very real dangers of the kind of life which we now lived?

I myself found that daily I had to show 'trained' W.Op/AGs how to use the Blenheim turret (even the use of the 'dead man's handle') and how to manipulate the TR1082/1083. This last was vital: when, not 'if', the pupil pilot and observer became lost, only the W.Op could supply the information necessary for them to

The BCATP in operation: pilots posing with a Boly at No. 6 Bombing and Gunnery School at Mountain View, Ontario in 1942. Vic Thomas

Specification of the Bolingbroke IVT	
ENGINES	two 920hp Bristol Mercury XX nine-cylinder, air-cooled, supercharged radials
WINGSPAN	56ft 4in (17.2m)
WING AREA	469sq ft (43.57sq m)
LENGTH	42ft 9in (13m)
HEIGHT	9ft 10in (3m)
WEIGHT EMPTY	8,963lb (4,065kg)
FULL LOAD	5,200lb (2,364kg)
MAX. BOMB LOAD	1,200lb (545kg)
MAX. ALL-UP WEIGHT	15,000lb (6,818kg)
PERFORMANCE:	
cruising speed	214mph (344kmh)
max. speed	262mph (422kmh)
range	1,950miles (3,138km)
service ceiling	28,400ft (8,660m)

of aircrew were trained in the Boly before passing on to operational units around the world. The last of the 407 Bolingbroke Mk IVTs built were finally struck off RCAF strength on 21 July 1947.

Bolingbroke IV 9031 YO-Y, of No. 8 (BR) RCAF Squadron nosed-over at Cordova, Alaska, in June 1942. It was repaired and finally lost in a sea crash on 8 January 1944. Fourteen Bolingbrokes of No. 8 Squadron spent June 1942 to March 1943 in Alaska on anti-submarine patrols over the Gulf of Alaska, to keep the allied convoy sea lanes safe from Japanese submarines. The Bolingbroke had an exceptionally good record for service in cold weather, and, despite atrocious conditions and lack of spare parts, no aircraft were lost during the Alaska episode. John A. Hill

The first Blenheim IFs arrive with 235 Squadron at Manston, winter 1939–40. L6790, nearest to the camera, served with 242 and 235 Squadrons and was written off in a crash after hitting high tension cables on 12 April 1941 while with 54 OTU. Wijb-Jan Groendijk

pinpoint their position. He could even supply homing bearings which would bring the aircraft directly back to the transmitting station.

As to the training in general, we had a couple of Blenheim Is equipped with dual controls and each sprog pilot was assessed by one of our own pilots – in the case of 90, Tim Partridge. While this was going on, observers were carrying out navigation exercises on the huge chart-table in the crew-room while the W.Op/AGs were attending classes in the armoury and the W/T section. There was, notice, no R/T [voice] communication: all messages were passed by Morse key. We prewar crews worked at speeds of twenty to thirty words per minute; the sprogs were capable of a shaky twelve. This we found quite shocking.

Once all three trades had passed these initial stages, training in the air started. First there were six elementary exercises: P1 to P6. These were largely concerned with testing the skills of the pilots and included circuits and bumps, both by day and by night, short cross-country flights, air-to-air and air-to-ground firing, both from the fixed Browning and from the turret 'K' gun. Once, the pilot of a tug towing the target drogue dropped in to report some hairier-than-usual escapade from one of our sprogs, and we gathered that these Henley pilots were already as frightened as we were slowly becoming.

In due course, on all training flights, each crew would include a screened man whose function was to avert calamity: to dissuade the pupil crew from doing something fatal and to bring them safely to earth somewhere – preferably at base. But 'safely' anywhere, at a pinch. It wasn't always possible, as will be told.

This part of the job over, the survivors started the really difficult bit: exercises O1 to O9: the 'O' denoting an imitation operational flight. Each would detail a target to be attacked (by camera), a route out and a different route home; the exercises would include several night flights and a fair amount of cloud-flying (which real operational flying had shown to be necessary for day-bombers such as the Blenheims). There were also some quite long legs to be flown over sea, out of sight of land and at low level. On all these flights operational conditions were to be observed: W/T silence was the rule except in emergencies. In practice, a fair number of them did result in emergencies: a crew hopelessly lost – perhaps hell-bent for the wide reaches of the Atlantic – and in urgent need of H/F D/F [High Frequency Direction-Finding] assistance.

Eventually the syllabus would have been worked through – or most of it at any rate. The weather largely dictated whether the full programme could be completed and how long this might take. Under optimum conditions, the

whole course could be taken in little over six weeks; in conditions of protracted bad weather even three months was not enough – there were times when the aerodrome was out of use for a week at a stretch. Then there had to be some judicious short-cutting. At the end of the course, the pupils would be posted as crews to operational squadrons: I do not remember that there was any consultation about this; one morning a list announced who would fly, and in all likelihood die, with whom.

As a morbid P.S. to their departure, we instructors would keep an eye on the casualty lists: generally it would be three weeks or less before our ex-pupils would be listed under

64 Squadron Blenheim IF L1478 on the flight line at Church Fenton, August 1939. After the squadron converted on to Spitfires in April 1940, this aircraft went on to serve with Nos. 5, 54 and 60 OTU, finally going to 3484M in December 1942. Eric Watson

'Missing' – which almost always meant the worst. Occasionally an A/G would be listed as 'Killed in action' and we would know that once again a kite had staggered home with a dead gunner. There would be a fair sprinkling of names under the heading 'Killed on active service': this denoted that the best-known invention of the late Isaac Newton had grabbed those sprogs who had managed to emerge intact from their time with us.

After a month or two of all this, I, for one, ceased to feel anything but a mild regret, quickly forgotten. A face, a voice, even a liking – all were erased by the non-stop pressures of our daily lives. I have no reason to believe that any of my screened colleagues viewed the situation any more tragically than I did: after all, only the tap of a typewriter stood between any of us and a similar termination.

You might expect that screened personnel, myself and my prewar friends and colleagues,

would be conscious of relief at being spared the dangers of operational flying. Initially this was the case. Here I must stress that I am speaking of the W.Op/AGs, all of us ordinary or leading aircraftmen: for us there were no automatic tapes – not until it later became necessary to use NCO rank to lure civilians to volunteer for this least-paid and most-dangerous job. Many of the career pilots, especially the officers, fretted at being out of the fray – *quo fas et gloria ducunt*, and all that. Equally, of course, advancement of both kinds – which led directly to myself and a certain reluctant observer 'volunteering' to accompany one of our pilots on a couple of operations during the campaign in France in 1940.

I, for one, had no urge whatever to confront the vile Nazi beast in his lair, to borrow the journalese of the day.

But look back a short way: 'initially' I said; slowly that attitude changed. Flying with sprog pilots was bloody dangerous and sprog observers could confidently be counted on to get you lost – especially over the sea. Life rapidly became an endless series of terrifying experiences. These were augmented by the declining standards of maintenance, the causes of which were twofold. The prewar maintenance schedule was based on units of twenty hours flying; at 120hr, after a series of lesser inspections, each kite was thoroughly stripped down and there were massive replacements. Soon after the outbreak of war these intervals were raised to thirty hours, so that the major inspections did not occur until the kite had done 180hr flying. In addition to this, the work was done in part by men who had not had the same thorough training given pre-

No.26 Air Gunners' Course at No. 13 OTU. In the middle row, fifth from the right is Plt Off Maurice Williams, who joined 21 Squadron at Watton on 26 July 1941, as W.Op/AG in Plt Off Jimmy Corfield's crew. On 12 August he was killed in action on the famous Cologne power stations raid. Mike Williams

war. In the case of operational squadrons, this was of little importance: few Blenheims lasted long enough to see even the first 180hr inspection. Ours, on the other hand, flew by day and by night, as many hours as could be crammed in and they were usually pretty elderly and tired by the time they reached us. It was not at all uncommon for an engine to cut – an event almost unknown in peacetime.

The pilots coming to us from the Flying Training Schools were all highly enthusiastic but often lacking in prudence, experience, skill and commonsense. In addition, they had all been imbibing freely of Biggles and the popular press, so that their self-confidence was boundless. They tried to retract the undercart as they had seen the big boys do, about five feet from the ground, and commonly slithered along on their bellies – or rather, their machines did. A Squadron Standing Order [SSO] went some way to remedy this. They descended through stuffed clouds and made bloody great holes in mountain-sides; another SSO failed to stop this dicing to any great extent – and convinced malefactors were, of course, beyond any human justice. At low level they flew into trees, farm buildings, overhead cables or the ground. In high-level formation they flew into each other. During exercises over the Irish Sea they just vanished, without even an SOS: probably they flew into the drink. If an engine cut either on take-off or on landing, not an uncommon event as I have said, they piled straight into the deck. If there was a way to end a flight by unorthodox and fatal means, they found it.

The only people who were not terrified were the sprogs themselves. We screened crews slowly became frightened men – our numbers shrinking each week. Most weeks we lost one kite, complete with crew. There were many weeks in which we lost two and even weeks in which we lost three. In March of 1940 a signal from 2 Group pointed out that in that quarter the Group had lost more aircraft by accident than by enemy action. It was a deeply unhappy time. When finally I was posted to an operational squadron following my 'rest', I was, if anything, relieved.

In an ironical but fitting end to this account, the LAC who flew in one afternoon to relieve me took my place as from that minute. A quarter of an hour later he took off for a night-flying test with a sprog pilot and the kite crashed on the aerodrome and burnt out. All three men died and if I had not been posted at exactly that minute, I would have been killed. The Grim Reaper doesn't always play fair.

The accident statistics for No. 13 OTU confirm Roger Peacock's observations that life on a Blenheim OTU could be as hazardous as flying on operations in a front-line unit. In the four years between April 1940 and April 1944, at least ninety-three Blenheims from 13 OTU were severely damaged or written off in accidents. A few dozen other aircraft were slightly damaged, mainly in belly-landings due to undercar-

riage failure, with a total of eighty-seven aircrew killed and twenty-nine injured. September and October 1941 proved to be especially bad months in 13 OTU with nineteen accidents and four aircrew perishing. June 1942 was another sad month, with eleven accidents recorded, resulting in one pupil being killed and three others injured.

Stan Moss's Story

The next month, twenty-years-old Sgt Stan Moss, RAAF, was one of the sprog pilots joining No. 58 Pilots Course in 13 OTU. He had crewed up at the beginning of the 'D' Flight course with Sgts Frank Nice and 'Nobby' Edwards, and the three men soon became an efficient team. By the end of August they had advanced into the final course segment, which consisted of long flights over the Irish Sea, the Bristol Channel and eastwards over the North Sea. Because of a cold front rolling in over the Irish Sea, all trainee crews were briefed on 28 August 1942 to do the North Sea trip. The heights and courses they were to fly were left to the discretion of the individual crews. Sgt Moss was detailed to fly Blenheim V6197, a clapped-out aircraft which had seen active service in 18, 226, and 110 Squadron before being relegated to 13 OTU. The aircraft had been patched up after it had bellied in on landing at Bicester in early June through the undercarriage collapsing. Moss had taken it up on a height test on 27 August, but, despite all his coaxings, could not get it above 13,000ft, whereas the official service ceiling of the Blenheim IV was 27,000!

The crew successfully carried out the first part of the North Sea trip, bombing and machine-gunning a sea marker which they had dropped at the end of their first sea leg. That completed, there was nothing more but to turn for home, as Moss vividly recounts:

Plt Off Gifford of 2 OTU lifted off T1945 from Catfoss for a night training flight on 27 August 1941, probably getting lost over the North Sea and belly-landing on his last drops of fuel on the beach of Texel Island at 05.40hr the next morning. Gifford spent the rest of the war in Stalag Luft III. Jaap Bakker

Having settled on the westward course towards England, I decided to check the gyro with the compass and had just pulled out the precessing knob when, on glancing up, I saw that shape hurtling towards me from immediately ahead. We closed at what I have since calculated at 500ft a second. Was it a reflection of my own machine? What large engines! But before brain could register sense, it hit us, flashing only a foot or two above our fuselage. It was Hooker's Blenheim flying on an exact reciprocal course!

Maybe in those brief seconds before we hit, I had subconsciously depressed the stick ever so lightly because the other Blenheim whacked our fin and rudder and sent us zooming up at an acute angle. In trying to correct the zoom, I immediately realized that my rudder and elevator controls were completely ineffective, trimming tabs too. The stick just fell forward, absolutely dead, and the needle of the airspeed indicator was dropping like a stone ...90...80...70...60. Old 6197 was out of control, surging upwards until it would inevitably come to a shuddering stall before falling helplessly to the surface.

During those split seconds my mind raced. I called Frank and Nobby on the intercom to abandon ship. 'What's that?', questioned Nobby in a tense tone, but Frank, who had backcrawled from the nose of the aircraft, answered before I could. 'Bail out', I repeated, 'immediately!' Frank had read my face too, far better than

L1132 OZ-L of 82 Squadron in 1938. When the squadron converted on to Mk IVs in 1939, this aircraft was relegated to Nos. 1 and 2 OTU, until it crashed in a forced landing at Carnaby on 6 April 1942. Douglas McKenzie

A typical Blenheim pilots' course at 17 OTU, September 1941. One wonders what fates were in store for these young men. Bill Burberry

1941 Christmas Greetings from 13 OTU at Bicester, depicting V6027 SL-W, which served with 82 Squadron and 13 OTU and was eventually SOC on 7 March 1944. George Shinnie

words could express and I had read his puzzlement and amazement. Within twenty-five seconds of normal straight and level flying, a man was being told to pitch himself into the sea! My last glimpse of Frank was of his posterior and feet scuttling up the nose of the aircraft where his parachute and dinghy were stored. Both had to be clipped on, but even Houdini could not have performed the trick of hooking on both parachute and dinghy in the time available. The same applied to Nobby.

Almost as 6197 was about to stall before plunging in a headlong dive I unpinned my safety harness and, with an upward and backward lunge that afterwards caused me to wonder greatly what one can physically achieve when in dire emergency, I dragged back the sliding roof hatch and threw myself out of the cockpit; actually, only partly out, because the force of the slipstream immediately grasped hold of me, sucking me out and spinning me over and over so that I had no control over my thoughts or actions whatsoever. In the process, the rear side of my left upper arm struck something, probably what remained of the aircraft fin. As soon as I

was able to control my right arm, I grabbed at the rip cord and the next instant was suddenly and severely jerked to immobility. At once there was an uncanny silence as I hung up there at between two and three thousand feet. Down near the surface, it was far from silent as I watched my aircraft with its two helpless occupants plunge down and hit with an explosive sound that reached me seconds later, by which time two columns of black smoke came spiralling upwards.

A glint of reflected light over to the right diverted my eyes. It was the other aircraft apparently trying to pancake on the water. However, with the sea as smooth and reflective as glass and the hazy glare of the sun probably in the pilot's eyes, it is little wonder that he misjudged, or maybe he had been injured. Whatever the case, the aircraft just slid under the water without so much as a ripple. I was horrified at the tragedy I was witnessing and the cyclonic pace of events over the past few minutes.

Sgts Nice and Edwards disappeared without a trace when their pilotless Blenheim

Many Blenheims came to grief at OTUs. On 31 March 1942, for example, Blenheim IV Z5986 of 42 OTU ran into V6003 of the same unit at Andover airfield. As a result, the latter aircraft broke its back and was written off. Wg Cdr Ted King

plunged into the North Sea, as well as Sgt E.A. Hooker and his u/t crew of Sgts F.L. James and C.W. Free in N6169. Stan Moss had come down in the sea some 26miles north-east of Flamborough Head, and spent the next fifty hours in his one-man dinghy of 4ft by 2ft 9in without any food or water. The second night at sea he had to fight a storm for eight to nine hours, his morale dropping below zero by daybreak. He was sick, wet through, cold, repeatedly drenched, miserable and bitterly disappointed. Miraculously, a few hours later Stan was spotted in the high seas and low clouds by the SS *Southport*, a 600ton coaster on its way to Edinburgh, and was rescued by the ship's crew. Sgt Moss was introduced to another crew at Bicester, and, on completion of the course, they were posted to 464 Squadron at Feltwell, flying the Lockheed Ventura or the 'Flying Pig'. The crew flew their first operation on 6 December 1942, on the famous Philips Eindhoven daylight raid. However, even before crossing the enemy coastline for the

first time, Moss's Ventura was mortally hit by flak and Moss was peppered with dozens of pieces of shrapnel, belly-landing his aircraft in a ploughed field on the Dutch coast to be taken prisoner.

Les Spong's Story
Plt Off Les Spong completed a tour of operations with 139 Squadron between August 1940 and April 1941 and then was posted to 'E' Flight No. 13 OTU at Bicester as a staff pilot. By this time 'E' Flight had been added to give pupils practice in bombing and air firing. He stayed at 13 OTU instructing in Blenheims for the next two and a half years, and in this account gives a fine impression of life at an OTU during this period:

Most of our flying time was taken up with flying a party of two trainee W.Op/AGs with an instructor out to a firing range for firing from the turret at a drogue towed by another Blenheim, a round trip taking 2 to 3hr, or a local trip

taking around an hour with a similar crew practising firing a cine gun from the turret. We had both Blenheim Is and IVs, the IVs being necessary, of course, for the observers, although we used them also for air gunnery.

Our bombing range was at Grendon Underwood, almost within sight of the airfield, so little time was wasted getting there. For air firing, however, we had to go to the Bristol Channel, at Stert Flats. At first we made a practice of flying to Weston Zoyland and making that our base for the day, thus occasionally getting in four trips in one day; but this practice was soon dropped in favour of doing all the trips direct from Bicester. Later we occasionally used a range over Savernake Forest and then Stert Flats was abandoned in favour of a range over the Wash.

The drogues we towed for air firing purposes were let out from the camera hatch of the Blenheim by the air gunners and wound in again by them when the exercise was over. This was a long process and for the winding-in we had to reduce speed to 130 to 140mph (as against our normal 180) to reduce the effort for the lads. The task, judging by the comments of those who did it, was quite a chore.

For cine gun practice we had one Blenheim

Flt Sgt Wesley Newell 'Leslie' Ward, W.Op/AG and instructor with 13 OTU, early 1942. Mollie O'Connell, Ward's fiancée, recounts:
'Leslie was an only child and lived at 9, Sir Williams Lane, Aylsham, Norfolk. After leaving North Walsham Grammar School he volunteered for the RAF. He first went to Jurby, Isle of Man; then I met him in Llandudno, North Wales. He was then stationed at RAF Bicester, Oxfordshire. He spoke very little of his life in the RAF; seemed quite happy and took life as it came. He mentioned a few friends by name and, when he could, visited us in Liverpool. He loved crosswords and chess, and also classical music. He occasionally enjoyed a 'quiet pint' with friends. When free, he would go to the padre at Chipping, Norton, a Jesuit, Fr Webb, and have long discussions about religion. His parents were staunch Weslyans but he was keenly interested in the Roman Catholic faith. He was received into the Catholic Church six weeks before he was killed.

He could not swim and did not wear his 'dog tag', and when I remonstrated with him on this score, was told not to be 'morbid'. I have his last short note, dated 6 May 1942, saying, 'in haste, we are going on dive-bombing practice over the Wash this afternoon, will write tonight'. After that, silence broken by a telegram to his parents, stating 'missing, did not return' then later 'presumed dead'.'

Blenheim L8755 disappeared into the North Sea, dragging down Leslie Ward and his observer, Sgt Donald J. McKenzie. The crew's pilot, Sgt T. Alvin Crawford, was later washed ashore and buried on the Dutch Frisian island of Ameland.

Right: No. 58 Pilots' Course, 13 OTU Bicester, July 1942. Sgt Stan Moss (RAAF) in the front row, second from right. The man leaning over on the right is Sgt E.A. Hooker, who was lost in N6169 on 28 August 1942. Stan Moss

making mock attacks on another until we were given a Hurricane for the purpose, which was, of course, a pleasure for the pilots as well as a better practice for the gunners. Our Hurricane was, however, little faster than the Blenheims, so our attacks tended to be protracted rather than dashing.

I joined 'A' Flight, the pilots' conversion flight, on 22 July 1942. Whereas 'E' Flight was housed in offices in one of the hangars at Bicester, my new flight was stationed at a satellite airfield at Hinton-in-the-Hedges, where I lost the *dolce vita* of life in the brick-built, central heating of the peacetime station for the time being. My recollection is of Nissen huts heated by tall stoves. A month later we were moved to another satellite, at Finmere until 29 April 1943, when we were transferred to yet another, Turweston. Finally we were moved to the main station on 14 May 1943, where we had a Flight Office in a hut on the airfield perimeter.

It was generally a fairly uneventful life in 'A' Flight. We started each new course on a Monday and proceeded, weather permitting, to go through the course curriculum, starting with familiarization and first solo and ending with night flying, with spells of emergency procedures such as engine failure on take-off, of formation flying, and instrument flying, in between. By the end of the second week the course was coming to an end.

Of course, during the war the work of the station went on continuously with no such thing as a weekend break; but if the course finished on a Friday there was the opportunity to get in a 'forty-eight', that is, two days' leave, before the start of the next course.

I was posted to Spitalgate on 1 February 1943 to be an instructor on 12 (P)AFU, converting Turkish pilots on to Blenheims. Some months before we had heard at Bicester that, as squadrons were by then being re-equipped with other aircraft, the sale of Blenheims to Turkey was being considered. Later, 'A' Flight (the pilots' conversion flight at Bicester) was asked to demonstrate the aircraft to a Turkish delegation and Fg Off Mossman and I were detailed to do so. We took off with myself in close formation on Mossman and thus made a number of passes across the airfield. Mossman decided to finish the exercise in style and made a mock attack on Sqn Ldr 'Paddy' Maher (Commander, 'A' Flight) and the Turkish officer standing on the airfield admiring our efforts. I felt at the

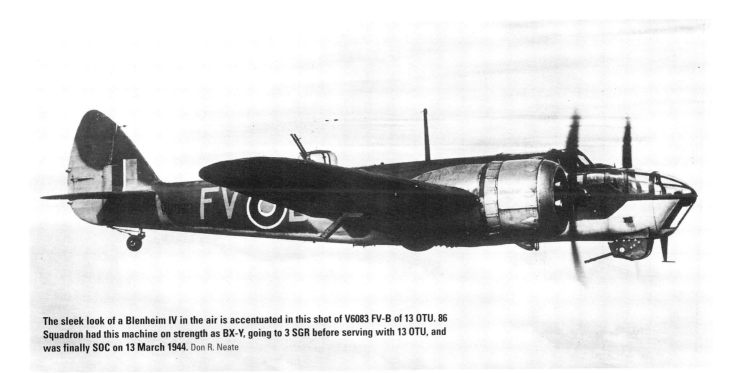

The sleek look of a Blenheim IV in the air is accentuated in this shot of V6083 FV-B of 13 OTU. 86 Squadron had this machine on strength as BX-Y, going to 3 SGR before serving with 13 OTU, and was finally SOC on 13 March 1944. Don R. Neate

time that he was going too low, but maintained close attendance. Had Paddy and the Turk not thrown themselves flat on the ground they would certainly have been decapitated.

Evidently the Turks were not put off by the incident, hence my later posting to Spitalgate, which was the airfield for Grantham. We were not allowed to do our flying from there, however, but from a satellite airfield at Harlaxton, which I recall as being little more than a field with huts.

To make up the unit complement of aircraft, we understood that other Blenheim units had been asked each to loan two or three aircraft. We did not think that they had tried very hard to select their best and ours was an interesting complement of machines.

The Turkish pilots spoke English reasonably well and we had no difficulty in making our instructions understood. There was, however, some scope for misunderstanding. One evening in the Mess there was some light-hearted conversation after a few drinks at the bar. As the chat became more animated, it was perhaps a Turk airing his English idioms who cried 'Attaboy!' Someone (I think it was Fg Off Glen) responded enthusiastically to demonstrate friendship for our guests with 'Attaturk!' In a flash he found himself with a knife presented to his chest. The Turks took a poor view of the name of their national hero being spoken in jest.

The Turks were a mixed crowd. Some were excellent pilots. The names rolled easily off the tongue, Lts Yumlu, Alniz, Konnulu, Iyigun and

Gonluyuce were my pupils. It was Gonluyuce whom I sent off to do a couple of solo circuits at night after he had demonstrated his ability to do so to my satisfaction. As I waited in the flight office for his return, a message came through on the telephone: one of our aircraft with a foreign pilot had landed at a nearby operational aerodrome and would we come and collect it please. Evidently Gonluyuce had been concentrating so hard and long on his cockpit drill for the downwind leg that when he looked up his circuit had extended itself and he found himself looking not at our lights but at theirs and he blithely continued and made a perfect landing. He told his mates that he could not understand why I was so silent on the way back to Harlaxton. He was equally surprised when exactly the same thing happened two nights later.

In fact, after Finland, Turkey was the second foreign country to buy Blenheims. A total of forty short-nosed Blenheim bombers were ordered from Bristols in mid 1937, the first two machines being shipped to Turkey in October of that year, followed by ten Mk Is flown out with British registrations G-AFFP to G-AFFZ between March and June 1938. A second batch of eighteen Mk Is reached the Turkish Air Force between November 1938 and February 1939. The final ten Mk Is for the Turks included L1483, L1485, L1488, L1489 and L1493, which were taken over from 211 Squadron on 21 September 1939. Thus a total force of forty Mk I bombers, with the

serial numbers 2501 to 2540, flew with the Turks in front-line service until 1948, when the type was finally phased out.

In 1942 three Mk IVs (serials 2541–2543, BR8192/93/95) were delivered to the Turks, with Z7986 following on 27 March 1943. Nineteen Bisleys from RAF Middle East stocks (with registration nos. 3901 to 3919) were purchased from March 1943 onwards. Since Turkey remained a neutral country throughout the war, the Blenheims saw no action against any of the belligerents. It is not quite clear when the Turkish Mk IVs and Vs were finally phased out, but this was probably in the early 1950s.

Turkish Air Force Blenheim Service

Operated sixty-three Blenheim Is, IVs and Vs between Oct 1939 and probably the early 1950s.

Rumanian Air Force Blenheim Service

Operated fifty-two Blenheim Is for at least 5 years, 4 months (May 1939–August 1944).

Maintenance Difficulties

Major overseas RAF OTUs using the Blenheim included No. 70 (at Nakuru, Kenya, moving to Shandhur, Egypt in May 1943), 72 OTU at Nanyuki, Kenya (with a total of eighty-five Blenheims), and 75 OTU based at Gianaclis, Egypt (using a

In this 'E' Flight, 13 OTU Blenheim an armourer has replaced one .303 gun with a camera for gunnery training. Ken Whittle

total of twenty-eight Blenheims for general reconnaissance training). Finally, 79 OTU was formed at Nicosia, Cyprus in February with thirty-one Blenheim Is, IVs and Vs, in addition to Ansons and Beaufighters for general reconnaissance training, being disbanded only five months later. When No. 70 OTU operated from Nakuru, of its Blenheims eight were short-nosed Mk Is and the others Mk IVs (a total of 141 Blenheims served in this unit during the war). Due to the altitude of Nakuru, over 7,000ft, the main problems of operating the aircraft there were engines' overheating and cutting on take-off, and tyres and tail wheels bursting due to the long take-off and landing. Spares were hard to obtain or were non-existent in East Africa; at one time only one Blenheim was serviceable at Nakuru; the other aircraft all had burst tyres. LAC Peter Russell served as Fitter IIE in 70 OTU during 1941–42:

The main trouble was low oil pressure due to sand getting into engines in spite of filters.

Changing engines was not easy, getting into the engine crate in the heat was horrible and very often an engine was fitted, taken out to run up and brought back again for another engine due to low oil pressure.

When Jerry got a bit too close to Egypt the unit set sail south on the Salween, arriving at Mombasa and then by train via Nairobi to Nakuru. The train just stopped in the dark, at no station, and we were told, 'Those lights in the distance are your new station, get going.' Our Blenheim replacement aircraft came from a park at Khartoum where they had been standing in sandy conditions. These aircraft came to Takoradi in crates, were assembled and flown across to Khartoum. It was said no navigator was required for this trip, they simply flew from crash to crash across the desert due to their too hasty and inefficient assembly. The aircraft were in a very dirty state, engines and bulkheads covered in oil and sand, difficult to clean properly. We had in the hangar a large portable compressor and we, being of inventive minds, evolved a suitable cleaner. The compressor tank was part filled with petrol and a rubber tube and alloy tube were attached to the drain outlet so that a thin stream of petrol could be sprayed at

the back of the engines and bulkheads. This device, though illegal and dangerous, was ignored by the higher-ups as it meant a quick turnround of aircraft to service.

All went well with this for months, until some sprog who was washing down a newly-arrived aircraft in the hangar and on trestles, turned to talk to an oppo and sprayed petrol on the electric motor, and WHOOSH! The resulting fire burned, as far as I can recall, three aircraft and the hangar. Being on trestles they could not be moved. No more spray cleaning!

One day I was cleaning the oil filters on the starboard engine, which are between the two lower cylinders, head and arms in the exhaust ring, when the prop started to turn. I was out like a shot, to observe that a u/t pilot had climbed into the cockpit and was trying the odd buttons he could find, he was also out very quick but not quick enough for me to identify and report him to my Flight Sergeant.

I managed quite a bit of test flying at Nakuru and in one instance the port airscrew took off on its own as the reduction gear cover had broken. Another pastime on air tests was to find a farmer operating on his harvester and coming up behind when he could not hear us, fly just over his head and down again in front at ground level – very exciting, except for the farmer. Of course, the u/t pilots littered the countryside with Blenheims which had to be rescued by some very clever ex-Italian trailers which could be towed from either end, and sent off to the MU.

On one occasion the whole training programme was halted and the Blenheims grounded. A few crashes were found to be caused by cracks in the airscrew mechanism: when the pitch is changed the piston operates in a slightly curved track to alter the blade angle and cracks were found in these tracks. All aircraft were grounded and I led a gang ordered to strip every airscrew, crack test and reassemble it before flying could resume. I received a Mention [in Dispatches] for this.

Blenheims were gradually phased out and Baltimores took over; these were good aircraft, very strong as well. Then when the unit moved back up to Shandur in Egypt, Marauders joined the unit as well.

Above: **In several parts of the Commonwealth, notably in East Africa, Blenheim OTUs were established. Here, air- and ground-crews of 'A' Flight, 70 OTU, Nakuru, are gathered in 1941 or 1942. Bespectacled LAC P.A. Russell, Fitter 2E, is standing in the middle row, sixth from the left.** Peter A. Russell

Below: **The Turkish Course and their RAF instructors in 12 Pilots Advanced Flying Unit (PAFU) pose for the camera at RAF Spitalgate in February 1943. From the left: Fg Off Stone; unknown; Fg Off Glen; unknown; Lt Gonluyuce; Flt Lt Searles; unknown; unknown; unknown; Fg Off Gilroy.** Les Spong

CHAPTER THREE

Nordic Warriors: the Finnish Blenheims, 1936–58

The Bristol Blenheim formed the backbone of the Finnish bomber force throughout World War II. In all, the Air Force operated ninety-seven Blenheim Is and IVs. The Finns were the first foreign purchasers of the Blenheim, when eighteen Mk Is (BL-104 to BL-121) were ordered on 6 October 1936. The history of the Blenheim in Finnish Air force service can be traced excellently by taking a close look at two Finnish pilots, whose service lives were closely linked with the aircraft.

Armas Eskola's Story

Armas Eskola joined the Air Force in the early 1920s. While serving as an instructor, he initially gained his observer's licence, and then in the late 1920s his pilot's wings. Armas Eskola mainly flew the Fokker CV single-engined biplane reconnaissance aircraft.

Late in 1936 the Finnish Air Force received its first of three Avro Ansons, and twin-engine training was started immedi-

ately. Capt Eskola, then aged thirty-seven, was one of the pilots selected for this programme. In January 1937 Eskola, in the company of an Engineer Lieutenant, travelled to the Bristol works at Filton to inspect the construction of the Blenheim Is which had been ordered by the Finnish government. Seven months later, the great day finally arrived when the first Blenheims for Finland, BL-104 and BL-105, had been completed and were ready for the ferry flight home. Two Air Force

Blenheim Mk I assembly line in the Finnish State Aircraft Factory, Tampere, summer, 1943. Eino Ritaranta

captains arrived for this purpose, but Capt Eskola insisted upon ferrying one of the new aircraft. After four days of conversion training, BL-104 and BL-105 departed from Filton on 27 July and after a 45min flight arrived at Croydon airport for customs formalities. From there, the two flew to Schiphol, Hamburg, Malmö and Stockholm, finally arriving at Helsinki at 14.15hr on 29 July.

In the meantime, a new bomber regiment (equivalent to a squadron) had been formed at Immola and Eskola was appointed commander of the 1st Flight. In November 1937 three more Blenheims were completed at Filton and again Eskola was one of the ferry pilots, taking to the air in BL-106 from Filton at 15.10hr on 26 November. Due to adverse winter weather conditions, it took thirteen days to reach Finland this time.

In February 1938 Eskola ferried BL-109 to Finland in good weather. By this time, the Air Force training scheme on the Blenheim was in full swing: in May 1938 alone twenty pilots were converted to the type by Eskola. Late that month, he was sent to England again as the next batch of Blenheim Is was nearing completion. From Filton he carried out a test dive with a fully-loaded Blenheim I, starting it from 15,200ft at an angle of 72 to 74 degrees and reaching a top speed of 614km/hr, but no fluttering was experienced. When the last three Blenheims left Filton on 26 July 1938, Eskola was piloting BL-121: the Finnish Air Force now had its eighteen Blenheim Is on front-line strength.

With these aircraft, an extensive operational training programme was carried out, including low-level bombing and high-altitude reconnaissance tests. Capt Eskola successfully brought several Blenheims up to a height of 25,000ft, but his camera operator Sgt O. Oinonen was not satisfied with his British Eagle IV camera which froze up at heights above 19,000ft. When, in June 1938, German RMK 20 and RMKS 50 cameras were received, these proved to be better suited for high-altitude reconnaissance.

In the meantime, a production licence for the Blenheim I had been obtained by the Finnish government and preparations for the production of fifteen Mk Is started in April 1939 at the State Aircraft Factory in Tampere. During this month, Eskola was called upon to visit the General Staff in Helsinki, where he was asked to fly a Blenheim on top-secret reconnaissance

BL-135 in the foreground after having collided with BL-131 (on the left) at Luonetjärvi, 27 November 1940.
Eino Ritaranta

BL-142 showing the scars of a strafing attack by Russian fighters on Värtsilä airfield, 3 September 1941.
Eino Ritaranta

sorties over the USSR. Soviet aircraft had violated Finnish airspace on many occasions during the preceding recent months, both at low and high level, clearly reconnoitring Finnish defence lines. Eskola therefore agreed. Back at base, he received orders to fly on special altitude photography tests. His first task was to photograph the eastern part of the Gulf of Finland, from the Estonian border to Leningrad, including Kronstad. His experienced crew consisted of Ensign J. Raty (observer) and Sgt Oinonen, who acted as camera operator in his dorsal turret.

On 6 and 9 May the crew was forced to

return, as clouds obscured the target area. On 10 May, however, two successful flights were made, from 11.50 to12.50 and from 13.50 to 14.50hr. The southern part of the Karelian Isthmus was visited at 25,000ft on these occasions, which was repeated on 11 and 15 May. Although the flights were a success, the Eagle camera gave some trouble. Equipped with a German Zeiss model, Eskola flew BL-118 on 27 and 29 June to the east coast of Lake Ladoga, but was forced to turn back due to worsening weather. On the afternoon of the 29th he made another, and this time successful, attempt. On the next two days he flew

Apart from bombing and intruding, the Finnish Blenheims were also extensively employed in photo-reconnaissance. Groundcrews hauling a camera on board BL-106 during the summer of 1941. Eino Ritaranta

similar sorties, although the crew nearly met with disaster on 1 July. Eskola flew at 18,500ft when, unexpectedly his oxygen tube disconnected: he lost consciousness and slumped forward, involuntarily putting the Blenheim into a steep dive. Raty grabbed the controls, trying to straighten the aircraft while at the same time putting his own mask to his pilot's face. BL-118 plunged down some 10,000ft before Eskola came round and took control of the aircraft again. After climbing back to 23,000ft, Oinonen proceeded to take a series of photographs and the Blenheim safely returned to base. Unfortunately, the incident had taken place on the Soviet side of the frontier: within a few days the Finnish government received an official enquiry from the Soviets, requesting information on the suspect aircraft. It

took the Finns several months to 'investigate' the case, and the Russians finally received an official statement that the suspect aircraft 'was lost during instrument training'.

Following this episode, Eskola flew BL-118 to Onttola airfield in northern Finland, to take photographs of the Lake Onega area. Due to adverse weather conditions, he was forced to break off two sorties on 6 and 7 July. A long wait followed until the morning of 22 July, when the weather finally cleared; he took to the air at 06.30hr and covered the area from 20,000ft. Further abortive sorties were mounted on 24 and 25 July and on 8 August, but he managed to complete two more flights successfully on 9 and 11 August. BL-118 was then taken in for servicing, being replaced by BL-110. In this

aircraft Eskola made an abortive sortie on the 18th, but next day everything went well and pictures were once again taken from 20,000ft. However, immediately after the final camera run was completed, the Blenheim's starboard engine started to cough and had to be shut down, the aircraft gradually losing altitude, and the frontier was crossed at 10,000ft. BL-110 was spotted by the Finnish Frontier Guard, whereupon the local CO drove to the airfield and hauled Eskola over the coals, telling him that an official enquiry would follow. Eskola then took the man aside and confidentially told him the kind of flight he was making. On 29 August 1939, Eskola made one more sortie over the Karelian Isthmus at 20,000ft to end this spell of undercover operations.

Meanwhile, the clouds of war were gathering in the Baltic region. The Soviets claimed territory bordering Finland and also sought to establish fortified bases within the country. Although they had hardly any means of defence, the Finns bravely refused. It was clear, however, that it was only a matter of time before the Soviets would press home their claims with armed force. Before the shooting war broke out, the Finnish Air Force's bomber regiment, Lentorykmentti 4, was moved to a new base at Luonetjärvi. A new conversion regiment, T-LeR4, was formed to train bomber crews, and Capt Eskola was appointed commander. This meant that Eskola would not take part in future operations, a big disappointment for so experienced a man. However, Eskola was promised an operational squadron as soon as more aircraft were received, and for this purpose he was sent off to England in late December 1939 in the company of twenty-three other Finnish aircrew. In expectation of the coming war, two more orders for twelve long-nosed Blenheim IVs (BL-122 to BL-133) and twelve more Mk Is (BL-143 to BL-145) had been placed at the Bristol works in the autumn of 1939. In order to ferry the first batch of Mk IVs to Finland, the aircrew were flown in a Junkers Ju 52 to Stockholm on 30 December, and from there the party went on to Oslo, Amsterdam and London.

The Finns had some familiarization training at Bicester before the Mk IVs were handed over on 16 January. The following morning the aircraft took off, every vic of three Finns being led by an RAF crew. The first vic flew to Perth, while the others landed at Silloth. Next morning, the aft fuselage of BL-122, Eskola's aircraft, broke when the aircraft was towed out of the hangar at Perth because the brakes were still on. This was a bad omen for what was to follow; only eight of the eleven Blenheims bound for Stavanger made the long North Sea haul safely. BL-127 crashed into the North Sea in bad weather, another landing at Kristiansand airfield in Norway and a third touching down on a frozen lake in neutral Sweden. When repairs were completed on BL-122, Eskola reached Västeras in Sweden on 26 January. The other Blenheim IVs gathered there too, after seven of them had been fitted with new bomb racks at Gothenburg. On the day Eskola arrived at Västeras all the Blenheims took to the air for the trip to Finland, but BL-125 suffered an engine failure on take-off and the aircraft was belly-landed in a field. Atrocious weather was again experienced on this trip and as a result the Blenheims were scattered over

many airfields. Eskola managed to land at Artukainen, Turku, but taxied into a ditch, thereby damaging his starboard propellor. It was swiftly replaced and next day he flew on to Luonetjärvi.

Meanwhile, Russian armed forces had finally attacked Finland in November 1939. Throughout the ensuing Winter War, the Finnish bomber force, consisting of two squadrons of Blenheims (Lento-

LeLv 42 running up the engines of its Blenheim Is at Luonetjärvi aerodrome before a raid on Elisenvaara on 8 July 1941. This unit lost twenty-two Blenheims from 1,605 sorties during the Continuation War. Eino Ritaranta

laivue [LeLv] 44 and 46), flew 423 sorties, mainly on bombing and reconnaissance missions. Some 140 tons of bombs were dropped and five Russian fighters were destroyed in air combat. Losses amounted to seven aircraft shot down by Russian fighters, plus four more written off in accidents, nineteen crew members perishing and one losing his life in an accident.

Finnish Air Force Blenheim units
– (Pommitus) Lentolaivue (P)LeLv) 41/Dec 1944–May 1945/Blenheim I & IV
– (Pommitus) Lentolaivue (P)LeLv) 42/Feb 1940–May 1945/Blenheim I & IV
– (Pommitus) Lentolaivue (P)LeLv) 44/Dec 1939–Feb 1943/Blenheim I & IV
– (Pommitus) Lentolaivue (P)LeLv) 45/Feb 1945–Mar 1945/Blenheim I & IV
– (Pommitus) Lentolaivue (P)LeLv) 46/Dec 1939–Jul 1941/Blenheim I & IV
– (Pommitus) Lentolaivue (P)LeLv) 48/Nov 1943–May 1945/Blenheim I & IV

When Eskola arrived back at his home base in late January 1940, an unpleasant surprise awaited him. Although he was

promised the command of a newly-formed bomber squadron, LeLv42, the recently arrived long-nosed Blenheims were instead supplied to the two front-line squadrons LeLv44 and LeLv46 to replace war losses. Once more, Eskola was promised the next batch. This was to have been in a month's time, when the next twelve Blenheim Is (from 2 Group stock at RAF Bicester) would have been ferried to Finland by thirty-six British volunteer 2 Group aircrew. To avoid Russian protests (the Soviet Union was officially allied to the United Kingdom), the Blenheims were repainted as civil aircraft, their armament being completely removed and the British crews flying the four-day journey via Dyce, Stavanger and Västeras in civilian clothing. On 25 February, Eskola warmly welcomed the RAF crews on their arrival at Västeras. The aircraft were flown to Juva ice base the next day, which was a novel experience for the 2 Group aircrew, as they had never seen an ice runway before, let alone landed on one. The memorable secret Finnish adventure came to an end for the British crews when they were flown back, via Sweden, in a Ju52 in early March.

Following a week of intensive training, at last, the newly promoted Maj Eskola led LeLv 42 on its first operation on 4 March. Still, by this time the Winter War was almost over. Eskola's squadron flew only 62 operational sorties for the loss of one

A number of Finnish Blenheims were fitted with retractable skis for taking off and landing on snow and ice runways. BL-129 in the early spring of 1942. Eino Ritaranta

Blenheim before the war came to an end on 13 March. Against all odds, the Finns had been able to retain their independence, although during the peace negotiations they had to yield more territory to the Soviet Union than had been originally demanded.

During the ensuing unstable period of cease-fire, the Finnish State Aircraft Factory started production of the previously ordered 'Series II' (BL-146 to BL-160), the first aircraft being delivered on 14 June 1940 and the last in January 1942. During this period, Eskola flew a successful photo-reconnaissance sortie on 13 October 1940 over Hankoniemi in BL-141, with his old faithful crew of Lt Raty and Sr Sgt Oinonen. On 11 November the crew flew another mission over this area in BL-140. Then, sixteen days later, it was almost the end for the forty-one-years old Eskola. While touching down at Luonetjärvi in BL-135, BL-131 suddenly taxied on to the runway, Eskola's aircraft crashing into the offending Blenheim, its left wing being smashed and the righthand undercarriage

collapsing. Miraculously, Eskola escaped with only minor cuts and bruises.

Peace between Russia and Finland was short-lived and the shooting war broke out again on 25 June 1941. Over three years of fighting followed in the so-called 'Continu-ation War'. In support of the Finnish Army, the Blenheim was subsequently used as a jack-of-all-trades: the crews being employed in daylight bombing, night intruding and reconnaissance. Maj Eskola's squadron, PLeLv 42, used Blenheims throughout the Continuation War, flying 1,605 operational sorties, for the price of twenty-two Blenheims lost. Four of these aircraft were downed by fighters and six by AA fire, forty-four aircrew being killed in action, with only two becoming prisoners of war. On the credit side, two Soviet fighters were shot down by the unit's air gunners. A second squadron, LeLv 44, flew Blenheims from 25 June 1941 until 20 February 1943, successfully completing 723 sorties and destroying one Soviet fighter in air combat, with ten Blenheims being lost. A third unit, PLeLv 48 operated Blenheims between

November 1943 and 4 September 1944, fly-ing a total of 413 sorties for the cost of seven aircraft. To counter the severe war attrition, the Finnish government ordered thirty more Blenheim Is (BL-161 to BL-190), plus ten further Mk IVs (BL-196 to BL-205) from the State Aircraft Factory. The Mk Is were delivered between 28 July and 26 November 1943; the long-nosed Blenheims reaching operational squadrons between February and 15 April 1944. By this time, forty-five Blenheims had been built under licence in Finland, with fifty-two further aircraft purchased in the United Kingdom.

When the Continuation War broke out, LeLv42 was based at Siikakangas airfield, with eight Blenheims serviceable and two more undergoing repairs. The unit flew its first reconnaissance sorties on 29 June 1941, moving to Luonetjärvi five days later. Bombing operations started on 4 July, Eskola leading eight planes to bomb Elisenvaara railway station on the 8th. On the evening of the same day, the raid was repeated with nine Blenheims, followed by an early morning visit to Antrea railway station on the 11th. Four days later the squadron was moved to the beach of Lake Pyhaselka, near Joensuu, and was ordered to keep the aircraft flying, just staggering over the trees at the edge of the airfield. After having laboriously climbed to 600ft, he turned back to the airfield to land, when the windmilling engine came to life again; Eskola decided to proceed to Immola after all. No further mishaps occurred and he returned safely to base the same day, to bid farewell to his unit and his beloved Blenheims.

Reino Pättiniemi's Story

Almost one generation younger than Armas Eskola, Reino Pättiniemi at twenty was one of those few lucky young men who were selected for an Air Force Reserve pilot course in the summer of 1939. He continued training throughout the Winter War, receiving his pilot's badge, No. 720, on 23 July 1940. He was then posted to Lentolaivue 16, a reconnaissance squadron equipped with Fokker X and Lysander aircraft. In late April 1941, he converted on to the Gladiator II, which he flew on operations following the outbreak of the Continuation War. It was in GL-252 on 13 July 1941, that Cpl Pättiniemi was badly hit by Russian flak. Although he managed to reach the Finnish lines, he broke his upper jaw in the subsequent crash landing. Barely recovered from his wounds, he was back with his unit within two weeks and continued flying on reconnaissance and strafing missions in Gladiators throughout the next two and a half years. By the end of February 1944, he had flown 337hr 35min on operations. Pättiniemi then decided to volunteer for further operational duties in the Blenheim, to get experience in a more modern type of combat aircraft. He started converting on the Blenheim in early March, soloing on the 9th in BL-179.

On this very day, the most successful raid in which Finnish Blenheims were involved in the war took place. Russian bomber units at this time were operating against Finland from Gorskaja, Kasimovo and Levashovo airfields in the Leningrad area. Photo-reconnaissance had revealed a force of 133 fighters and bombers concentrated on these Soviet airfields. On the evening of 9 March, Russian bombers struck at Tallinn before heading back east over the Gulf of Finland. In a carefully planned operation, a mixed intruder force of ten Blenheims, six Ju 88s and five Do 17s mingled with the bomber stream under cover of darkness and shadowed them

Maj Eskola (on left) hands over command of LeLv42 to Maj O. Lumiala at Immola airfield, 4 August 1942. Eino Ritaranta

to operate in the area between Lakes Onega and Ladoga. During the night of 21 July, Eskola led six Blenheims to bomb the Petroskoi military installations. The formation was intercepted by Polikarpov I-16s, but the bombers escaped unharmed, one of the Russian fighters being claimed as shot down by a Blenheim gunner.

Having moved to Värtsilä airfield on 1 September, three days later Soviet fighters suddenly swept in at low level and strafed the airfield, which resulted in the explosion of a bombed-up Blenheim and damage to another four aircraft from LeLv42. War attrition soon led to a serious shortage of aircraft and, as a result, LeLv42 was reorganized into two flights in November. During 1942 the Finnish Blenheim crews continued flying bombing and photo-

reconnaissance missions against the Russian forces, LeLv42 receiving new licence-built Blenheims during the winter and spring to bring the unit up to its operational strength again. On 28 February Maj Eskola had another lucky escape. While flying over Vytegra at 23,500ft, a Curtiss Tomahawk suddenly came out of the sun, but the Russian pilot did not fire as his guns were probably frozen. In March, LeLv42 participated in the occupation of Suursaari Island while operating from Immola.

Much against his will, Eskola was appointed CO of the Air Force Signal School on 4 August 1942. Three days later he took off in BL-109 to pay a final visit to a squadron detachment at Immola. At the critical point of take-off his starboard engine suddenly failed, Eskola struggling

back to the Leningrad area. Not suspecting anything unusual, the flarepaths were ignited and the Soviet aircraft came in to land. Then all hell broke loose, the Finnish crews straddling the airfields with their bombs, causing chaos and confusion. At Gorskaja, an explosion and several fires were observed, and later it was seen that at least three fighters and two bombers had been destroyed with two more bombers badly damaged. Four aircraft dispersals at Kasimovo were gutted plus ten bombers destroyed on the field. A large explosion was followed by a smaller one, and the triumphant Finnish crews left several fires raging. At Levashovo several bombers received direct bomb hits and shrapnel damage and a large fire was seen to the north of the airfield.

Following a couple of training flights in dual-control Tupolev SB-2s later that month, Pättiniemi flew Blenheims in solo

night and instrument flying, and in high-altitude training. In April 1944 he received a posting to an operational squadron, PLeLv48, which was based at Onttola. In addition to Blenheims, the unit operated a couple of captured Petljakov Pe-2 bombers. On 9 June 1944 the Red Army initiated a great offensive in the Karelian Istmus, forcing the Finnish Army to retreat. On the 12th the 1st Flight of PLeLv48 was detached for ten days to PLeLv46 (which flew the Dornier Do-17Z bomber) and moved to Mensuvaara airfield. That night, at 23.25hr, Pättiniemi lifted BL-174 off for his first bombing mission. Ens Harri Laakso sat beside him as his observer and Cpl Anders Nynäs manned the Brownings in the dorsal turret. The target for the thirty-eight aircraft was the Kivennapa–Mainila road. On 16 and 17 June Pättiniemi bombed troop concentrations in the villages of Liikala and Hotsola,

two days later attacking shipping south of Koivisto. On the 20th the Huumola crossroads was the objective for a typical mixed formation of three Blenheims, three Ilyushin DB-3s and two Do-17s. Soviet tanks and artillery were bombed again in Huumola on 22 June. There was no rest for Pättiniemi and his comrades: at midnight the following night, eleven Blenheims took off from Onttola for a raid on enemy artillery in Karhusuo. As usual, Messerschmitt Bf109Gs escorted the bombers.

Towards the end of June, Sr Sgt Pättiniemi was granted a short leave to get engaged to his girlfriend, ferrying Blenheim I BL-181 from the State Aircraft Factory at Tampere on his way back to the squadron on 30 June. On arrival, he found his name on the battle order, his crew forming part of a mixed bomber force of thirty-nine aircraft to bomb the road between Viipuri and Ihantala on the night of 1 July. On the 4th, he attacked shipping in the Gulf of Finland, and on the 5th, he flew one of six PLeLv48 Blenheims that attacked tanks and artillery in Tali. Next day Pättiniemi had to abort a sortie due to engine failure; the aircraft was repaired and he test-flew it on the same night.

On 8 July Pättiniemi took part in his regiment's daylight raid on Ayrapaa, again with an escort of Bf109s. After a few days without operational flying, he bombed tanks in Pitkaranta on 14 July, this time with a Brewster B.239 and Curtiss Hawk escort. Over the target his BL-174 was hit by flak, which left the trailing edge of the left wing in tatters. Pättiniemi successfully nursed the aircraft back to base where he carried out a high-speed landing in order to keep the bomber under control.

By this time the advance of the Red Army had been halted, but violent land, sea and air battles were still raging. Only hours after his close escape in BL-174, Pättiniemi once again was called upon to attack a Russian target:

Our bomber squadron, PLeLv48, was based at Onttola airfield near Joensuu. In the morning of 15 July most of we aircrew were having a wash at a lakeshore jetty when we heard the telephone ringing at our quarters. Soon we were told that once more a mission was on. Our Army was fighting bloody battles against the invading Russians and needed all possible help. So we were used to doing two, sometimes even three missions a day.

We collected our personal gear: maps, helmets, goggles, compasses and so on, and walked

Vitska airfield, summer 1943. Sgt Reino Pättiniemi (left) and Lt E. Telajoki (observer). Mrs Pättiniemi

From left to right: Cpl Anders Nynäs, Lt K. Veijola and Sgt Reino Pättiniemi have every reason to put on a broad smile, as Pättiniemi safely brought back flak-damaged BL-174 to Onttola on 14 July 1944. Mrs Pättiniemi

to the headquarters. After briefing, we started to plan our sortie. My observer was Ens Harri Laakso and gunner/radio operator Cpl Anders Nynäs. They were good chaps with whom I had flown many times before. Today my plane was BL-170, a short-nosed Blenheim I. On the previous night, my regular aircraft, BL-174, had been hit by flak in its left wing.

Soon after we were sitting in the plane with the engines ticking over. We proceeded to taxi to the edge of the gravel runway, and one by one we took off. We were airborne at 11.10hr. Our squadron had only five serviceable Blenheims left, but other Blenheims, Junkers Ju88s and Dornier Do17s from other bases were taking part in the raid so we had thirty-three bombers participating.

The heavily loaded Blenheim began her climb to our operational height of 10,000ft, with its Bristol Mercury engines purring properly. I now started to manoeuvre into position in the formation. We flew over Lake Pyhaselka, and in front of us I saw Lake Janis-jarvi, which was our rendezvous point with the other squadrons. Our escort consisted of a gaggle of Brewster B.239 and Curtiss Hawk 75A

fighters. On this raid our objective was a village called Lavajarvi, where the Russians had gathered large troop concentrations. During the flight to the target, however, this was changed to artillery batteries in Nietjarvi village, but the new orders were not received by our leader. So, we and two other Blenheims continued on our original course.

On nearing our target, we saw that it was covered in cloud. We started our descent and only moments before reaching the upper layer of the clouds, Nynäs shouted: 'Fighter on the tail of our number three!' Fortunately, the clouds were close by and within seconds we were swallowed up. By 1944 the Bristol Blenheim was rather helpless when attacked by agile, fast and well-armed fighters. We continued descending and only at 3,800ft did we spot the ground. We commenced our run in to the target and Laakso was crouched over his bombsight. He gave me a course to steer, and then quite suddenly we were surrounded by an infernal barrage of exploding flak shells. 'Keep cool', I said to myself, 'it only takes a minute, and then it will all be over...' But it seemed to last an eternity, the seconds crept by slowly. 'Keep her steady for just one more

second', murmured Laakso, and I felt the Blenheim leaping up at the same instant when he shouted 'NOW!'

I banked left to get out of the range of the flak. With a sigh of relief, I pointed the Blenheim's nose upwards to get back into the cloud cover. Then suddenly Nynäs yelled: 'Fighter left and behind!' His machine-gun fired a short burst. Then a big explosion, and probably more than just one. A Russian Bell Airacobra fighter was zooming by at point-blank range. Our left engine and wing tank were on fire. And what was worse: Anders Nynäs, that jolly young fellow, had fallen from his seat, seemingly lifeless. There was a hole in the cockpit roof and the instrument panel was partly destroyed. Instinctively, I put the plane into a dive. Fortunately, the enemy fighter had disappeared from the scene, and I decided to fly on a westerly heading for as long as possible. I did realize that we would have to bale out before long, and considered it would be better to do this over our own side of the frontline. But we were too low to jump now; I had to gain some altitude before the burning engine would pack up altogether.

It was impossible to go and see in what shape Nynäs was, as the fire soon extended to the fuselage. We therefore decided to get out before it

Obviously rather worn, BL-173 was still in use as a target tug at Halli airbase in early 1958. Eino Ritaranta

was too late. The bottom escape hatch was opened by Laakso and I tried to open the upper one, just over me. However, it was damaged by a bullet in the fighter attack and it didn't open completely. Laakso was already partly outside the aircraft but when he saw me struggling with the hatch he pushed himself up again and came to my aid. By using the instrument panel to support his feet, he pressed hard and the hatch opened up a bit more. Now I tried to get out, but my PAK seat-type parachute pack got stuck (it had long harnesses down to the height of one's knees), and I had to get into the cockpit again. With my left hand I tried to straighten the Blenheim, while, with my right, I unfastened the parachute harness. I then lifted the pack out first, and pressed myself out behind it. By now the flames had enveloped the whole cockpit and I was burnt on my face and hands and the plane was in a violent dive. But I was out, and I pulled the ripcord.

A hard jerk, and my parachute opened over me. My boots almost fell off, but I managed to pull them back on and I felt the air cooling my burnt face. I was wondering where I was, on the enemy side of the front or on our own, and I saw Laakso's chute beneath me. A feeling of safety came over me, but that was soon over, as I spotted an Airacobra banking towards us. Fortunately, a Curtiss Hawk came to our rescue, and the enemy pilot now had something else to turn his attention to. I glanced at my watch, it was 12.05hr. Underneath me, an endless forest stretched out in all directions, and a spruce was waiting to catch me and my parachute.

With my feet on the ground again I took the compass from my breast pocket and started to walk to the west. My back was very sore. I soon spotted a number of wounded soldiers walking on a trail, but they were still too far away and I could not hear them nor see of what nationality they were. I started to follow them carefully and saw them reaching a spot where more wounded soldiers were laying. I slowly sneaked nearer, and what a great relief it was when I heard Finnish words being exchanged! I joined the group and was told that they were expecting transport to take them to hospital. Only moments before a lorry arrived, Ens Laakso appeared on the spot. He told me he had had difficulties with a bunch of frontline soldiers, who had mistaken him for a Russian soldier.

We had proceeded in the truck for only a few miles when two Ilyushin Il-2s, which we nicknamed 'agricultural planes', appeared on the scene and, apparently in the absence of something more worthwhile to attack, strafed our lorry. When they came in at low level, the lightly wounded soldiers ran into the woods, but some were unable to make it and were hiding by the side of the road. A soldier lying there next to me received one more nasty bullet wound during the attack. Fortunately, the truck was not too severely damaged and we continued our journey. Soon we reached the HQ of an Army regiment, where a colonel took us into his sheltering position, as artillery shells were falling close to the spot. Everybody there was obviously having a hard time.

By the evening we had arrived back at

Onttola airbase and the burns on my face and hands were attended to. After that ordeal, a twelve days' leave was very welcome indeed.

The smashed remains of BL-170 and Anders Nynäs were later found just to the west of a small lake in the Katitsanlampi area. Pättiniemi returned to his squadron on 3 August, and immediately was ordered to take off in BL-171 for a raid on a road between Salmijarvi and Kuolismaa. On the evening of that day he headed for the same target in BL-174, but had to abort due to an engine failure. It turned out to be Pättiniemi's final mission against the Red Army: the fighting died down soon after and on 4 September 1944 an armistice was signed. One day earlier, PLeLv48 flew its nine surviving Blenheims and one Pe-2 to Vesivehmaa airport, where Pättiniemi test-flew BL-171 on its arrival.

In the so-called Lapland War of 1944–45, the Finnish Air Force was now forced by the Russians to drive its former German allies from northern Finland, notably the troops of the 20th Mountain Army and Luftflotte 5. On 7 October 1944, Pättiniemi's squadron moved to Vaala airfield, and on the 22nd he took part in a bombing raid of the Muonio–Sirkka road, safely landing at Kemi airfield. Two days later he flew BL-171 back to Vaala. Unknown to him when he touched down at base, this was his last flight with the Air Force, as the Russians had decided to demobilize all

Finnish Air Force reserve pilots. Until the end of the war the by now obsolete Blenheims soldiered on in bombing and reconnaissance sorties and in submarine searches in the Baltic. Losses mounted to three aircraft shot down by the Germans, plus three more lost in flying accidents. The total Finnish Blenheim losses in World War II had so risen to sixty-two aircraft, of which thirty-eight had been lost in action.

After the War

Immediately following the end of the war, PLeLv 41 and 43 still had thirty-one Blenheims on strength. Two more were in use by PLeLv 43 for a period of a few months, and four other aircraft were used by the Air Force Technical School as instructional airframes. Under the terms of the armistice with the Soviet Union, Finland was forced to reduce its Air Force

strength to sixty frontline aircraft, the use of any bomber aircraft being prohibited. By mid September 1948 the last remaining thirteen serviceable Blenheims were put in storage. Three years later, five of these were modified to target tugs; the first was received by the Lentorykmentti 3 on 11 February 1952. These five soldiered on during the 1950s with the 1st. Lennosto (Wing), in 1957 renamed Haemeen Lennosto. The Finnish Air Force's Test Flight, based at Tampere and Halli, took over BL-199, this aircraft being flown for the last time on 20 May 1958, thus ending the long and distinguished career of the Blenheim in the Finnish Air Force.

The longest surviving Finnish Blenheim, one of the batch of twelve ferried to Finland in February 1940 was Blenheim Mk I BL-142. It was damaged in action for the first time on 3 September 1941 by strafing Soviet fighters. While being patched up, an accident caused a fire in the rear fuselage, but the aircraft was

repaired again. It was involved in an extraordinary incident on 20 January 1942. Fitted with skis, one broke off in flight, the pilot decided that a safe landing was impossible and ordered his crew to abandon the aircraft. The three men baled out safely over a large cornfield, and while descending under their parachutes they witnessed the crewless Blenheim performing a perfect belly landing, carefully avoiding all barns and other obstacles in its path. BL-142 was belly-landed again on 1 July 1943 and 12 June 1944. On 9 September 1946 it flew for the last time, finally being scrapped in September 1952.

Today, Blenheim IV BL-200 is the only example of the type remaining worldwide: it was last flown on 5 June 1957, put on to a stand in mid 1960 at Luonetjärvi and served as a gate guard for many years. It is currently in storage in the Central Finland Aviation Museum at Tikkakoski, where it is awaiting a full restoration for static display to the public.

BL-200 guarding the gates of Luonetjärvi in the spring of 1961. Eino Ritaranta

CHAPTER FOUR

Carnage and Raw Courage:

Battles of the Low Countries and France, May–June 1940

Maastricht and the Meuse Bridges

The long-expected German attack finally fell upon the West in the early hours of 10 May 1940. Heralding the Battles of the Low Countries and France, German bomber units struck at over seventy airfields in Holland, Belgium and France at dawn and, with crushing power, the deadly combination of Panzer divisions closely supported by the Luftwaffe swiftly penetrated deep into the Low Countries in true blitzkrieg fashion.

Two Blenheims, one each from XV and 40 Squadron were dispatched at 09.00hr from Wyton to reconnoitre the advance of the enemy into Holland, with L8776 of 40 Squadron falling victim to light flak near the German border. The AASF also came into action with three Blenheims of 18 Squadron taking off from Méharicourt in the course of the day on reconnaissance sorties to the Maastricht area. Only one crew managed to get back safely, although it had to run the gauntlet of both flak and persistent attacks from Bf110s. 57 Squadron lost Plt Off A. Thomas and crew in L9245 during a reconnaissance sortie in the same danger zone during the afternoon.

The home-based Blenheims, however, had brought back sufficient evidence to plan a series of counterattacks against airfields in the heart of Holland which had fallen into the hands of German paratroopers. First, six short-nosed fighter Blenheims of 600 Squadron 'B 'Flight left Manston at 12.30hr to support a Dutch counterattack on Waalhaven airfield just to the south of Rotterdam. Led in at low level by thirty-one-years old Sqn Ldr Jimmy Wells, the Blenheims did one surprise strafing run on Ju52 transports on the aerodrome, causing chaos and confusion. Their luck was short-lived, for a dozen Bf110s of 3/ZG1 patrolling the area came to the paratroopers' rescue and the can-

After being shot up by a Bf 109E of 2/JG1 over the Maastricht–Tongeren road, Fg Off N.E.W. Pepper DFC crash-landed L9416 XD-A of 139 Squadron at Hoepertingen, Belgium on 12 May 1940. Pepper and his observer successfully evaded capture. Bert Beckers

non-armed Zerstörer quickly shot down five out of the six British attackers, Sqn Ldr Wells and six other young men perishing on their first sortie against the enemy. Plt Off Norman Hayes's sole surviving Blenheim 'O' struggled back to Manston with its petrol tanks shot through. 600 Squadron 'A' Flight fared better during the day, claiming two He111s damaged and destroyed during the day.

Next in were XV Squadron, with nine crews successfully bombing clusters of Ju52s at Waalhaven in mid afternoon. Miraculously, they escaped the attention of the dozens of German fighters prowling the area and all aircraft returned safely to Wyton. Another Dutch airfield, at Ypenburg near The Hague, was attacked by four consecutive vics of 40 Squadron around

17.00hr. Although the raid was a success, the last two vics going in encountered Bf109s of 6/JG27 which quickly destroyed three Blenheims, all nine aircrew perishing. The Blenheim actions on the first day of the shooting war were rounded off with a raid by 110 Squadron on large numbers of Ju52s which had landed on Scheveningen beach during the day, the twelve bombers being escorted by six Blenheim IFs of 604 Squadron. The bombing turned out to be ineffective, but low-level strafing runs by the fighter Blenheim crews wrecked seven German transports for the loss of one aircraft.

For these mixed successes, nine home-based and AASF Blenheims had been lost during the course of 10 May. The AASF Battle units had suffered an additional loss

.

Pilots of 235 Squadron posing in the snow at North Coates in January 1940. From the left: Plt Off Hugh Pardoe-Williams (KIA, 27 June 1940); Plt Off Norman Smith (KIA, 12 May 1940); Plt Off Alan Wales (KIA, 27 June 1940); Plt Off Anthony Booth (MIA, 29 May 1940); Flt Lt Manwaring (KIA, 29 May 1940). Wijb-Jan Groendijk

of twenty-two aircraft desperately trying to stem the advancing German columns in the Ardennes and Luxembourg, plus two destroyed on the ground. The outlook of what was in store for the crews looked grim indeed.

At first light next day, 18 and 53 Squadrons both sent off low-level reconnaissance sorties of the Albert Canal and Maastricht. 53 Squadron lost two aircraft, and 18 Squadron's L9255 was shot down in German-held territory, with LAC Davies being killed and his wounded pilot and observer both becoming prisoners. The second 18 Squadron aircraft, R3590, made a successful reconnaissance in the hands of Plt Off M.P.C. Holmes, during which it was discovered that the Germans had already crossed the Albert Canal. In the target area, the Blenheim was subjected to intense light flak and was hit several times on the return journey. A direct hit from a Belgian pom-pom shell put its port engine out of action, and temporarily blinded the pilot in the left eye. Holmes managed to fly the crippled machine back to French territory and force-landed on its belly near Chalons without injury to the crew. Around the same time, the Luftwaffe struck a heavy blow on 114 Squadron when nine Dorniers Do17Zs of 4/KG2 swept across Condé-Vraux airfield at

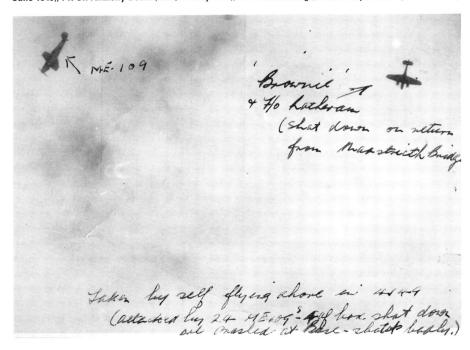

Fg Off Rotherham of 107 Squadron desperately trying to escape from attacking Bf 109s, while speeding home over Belgium after the Maastricht bridges raid on 12 May 1940. A little later Rotherham was forced to crash-land L8748 OM-K near the Belgian Army HQ at Breendonk, Flanders, where, soon after, he was introduced to King Leopold of the Belgians. Together with his observer Sgt Brown he escaped captivity and returned safely to England. LAC Ted Coote, the crew's W.Op/AG, however, was injured in the crash and taken prisoner to spend the next five years in Stalag 357 Kopernikus. Freddie Deeks

A communal grave for the New Zealander Plt Off Claude Frankish and his crew of XV Squadron has been dug at the place where Blenheim P6912 fell. The aircraft was mortally hit by flak on the run in to the Maastricht bridges and crashed near Genk, Belgium around 09.15hr on 12 May 1940. The burnt-out remains of P6912 are still visible in the background. Lucien Bogers

05.45hr, destroying six neatly lined-up Blenheims on the ground and badly damaging several others.

In mid afternoon, L9175 and N6208 of an eleven-strong formation from 110 Squadron fell to withering light flak and a Bf109 of 3/JG27 over Maastricht during an attack on the Meuse bridges, as nineteen-years old Plt Off E. Roy Mullins, flying L9217 recalls:

It was a glorious day. We flew in at about 5,000ft keeping good formation which was the order of the day. We were not bothered until we were a few miles from the target. Then all hell broke loose. I believe the enemy must have had most of their flak guns in defence. We just flew through a hail of shells and machine-gun bullets. Looking through the Perspex I could see clusters of shells surging up like onions on a string. Bits of shrapnel pinged off the plane. It's amazing that more damage was not done. Steadfastly we kept, or tried to keep, formation. It was not easy. Over to my left I saw one plane

get a direct hit and go down in flames. Bombs gone – break, break! We needed no orders for that. The German plan was simple. Hit them with ground-to-air over the target and then let the Messerschmitts come in. Turning, twisting, diving we made our way home. Seeing a convoy of troops below us we loosed off a quick burst of fire. Quite useless, we might as well have used a peashooter. Back home we found that we had not suffered much damage to the plane. Just a few holes in the fuselage. Possibly greater damage was done to our morale.

Three days later, Plt Off Mullins and his crew of Sgt R. Lowe and AC2 Patrick Ahern flew their third sortie (to Sedan), again in L9217, when they were hit by a shell amidships. Mullins and Lowe managed to bail out at 2,000ft and spent the next five years in captivity, but their twenty-years old gunner was killed. 18 Squadron lost a third aircraft, L8861, from another Albert Canal reconnaissance in the late evening of 11 May. The AASF Battle squadrons

suffered further serious losses while attacking troops in eastern Belgium. The German advance had not been delayed during the day, and it became clear to both the British crews and their superiors that a desperate all-out effort was needed to try and stem the irresistibly advancing enemy forces at the strategic Meuse crossings in the Maastricht area.

At dawn on 12 May therefore eight Blenheims of 139 Squadron left Plivot to attack the Maastricht bridges, despite the prospect of having to face both light flak and swarms of Bf109s which were known to patrol the area. Over the Belgian–Dutch border a barrage of flak was thrown at the British crews, and then 109s of Stab I/JG1, 2/JG1 and 3/JG27 bounced the scattered formation before the crews even got a chance to drop their bombs. The German pilots picked off the Blenheims one by one, Oblt Walter Adolph, St Kpt of 3/JG27 claiming three Blenheims destroyed in quick succession.

ACM Sir Basil Embry, who became a living legend in 2 Group. He is depicted here in 1954, when serving with NATO as C-in-C, Allied Air Forces Central Europe. As CO of 107 Squadron this indestructible Blenheim hero led many raids in the Norwegian Campaign during April 1940, the disastrous Maastricht raid on 12 May, and led his squadron into battle at Sedan on 14 May. He was shot down on 27 May, escaping from captivity to England, and subsequently became involved in night-fighting. After a spell of command posts in Operation *Crusader* in the Western Desert and in Fighter Command in the UK, Embry took up the post of AOC, 2 Group, Bomber Command on 27 May 1943. Paddy Embry

Only minutes after the first Bf109 attacks, Wg Cdr Dickens's N6224 (or 6225) was the sole survivor of the formation, nursing his battered aircraft back to Plivot, where it was declared a write-off. This effectively meant that virtually the whole AASF medium bomber force had been wiped out.

With the 139 Squadron massacre taking place over the Maastricht sector, two out of three fighter Blenheims of 235 Squadron, patrolling the Hook of Holland as cover for the expected evacuation of the Queen of the Netherlands, fell victim to eight 109s of II/JG27. Fg Off R.J. 'Pissey' Peacock brought the sole surviving plane back to Bircham Newton. During the Battle of Britain, Peacock and his gunner Sgt W. Wilson (the son of a gamekeeper and a crack at deflection shooting) became a renowned fighter Blenheim team by

destroying two Bf109s plus a Ju87 in air combat. Fg Off Peacock was awarded the DFC but was killed in action afterwards.

While the triumphant German 109 pilots flew back to their bases to refuel and rearm, a second Blenheim formation, twenty-four aircraft strong, left England to try and demolish the Maastricht bridges. Led by the legendary Wg Cdr Basil Embry, CO of 107 Squadron, the two squadrons involved were briefed to go into the attack separately, with XV Squadron bombing first, 107 following a few minutes later. Arriving over eastern Belgium, the crews had to run the gauntlet of an accurate flak barrage for over five minutes which effectively spoiled their aim and no hits were scored on the bridges. The price for their daring was high: in quick succession seven Blenheims plunged out of the sky, mortally hit by flak. A repeat performance of only hours previously, 109s of I/JG1 and 2/JG27 pounced on the scattered formation and another three Blenheims were destroyed in a running battle over Belgium. Only fourteen aircraft struggled back to Wattisham and Wyton, most of them severely shot up. XV Squadron only had two serviceable Blenheims left on strength following this raid. Late in the evening, Flt Lt Watson and his 21 Squadron crew lost their lives when L8739 was blown out of the sky over Tongres. AC1 Jack Bartley, manning the single Vickers 'K' gun in another 21 Squadron Blenheim's turret, watched the crew's demise: 'Butch Burgess [Watson's AG] piled straight in from 15,000ft over Tongres when his machine received a direct hit from flak. I was flying No. 3 to his leader at the time, and after seeing pieces of his tailplane flying past my turret, watched as if hypnotized the crippled machine's devastating plunge down on to the target, culminating in a terrific explosion.'

The loss of L8739 brought the total Blenheim losses on 12 May to twenty. The raw courage of the largely unsung AASF Battle crews culminated in the first two air VCs in World War II posthumously being awarded to Fg Off Garland and his 12 Squadron observer Tom Gray for outstanding courage in leading their section through a curtain of flak while attacking the Veltwezelt bridge at low level, for which they paid the ultimate price. Fourteen Battles were lost in action during this day. Three days of fighting had cost the AASF sixty-three bombers, almost half its frontline strength.

To preserve the remaining stock it was decided to let the hard-pressed bomber crews rest for a day. Only a handful of reconnaissance sorties were flown by 18, 57 and 59 Squadrons during 13 May, the latter units each losing one Blenheim. However, by the end of the day, five German Panzer divisions had secured a bridgehead at the Meuse crossing near Sedan. Therefore there was no choice but to throw the remaining AASF bombers into the gap in a desperate last effort to turn the tide. Wave after wave of British and French bombers attacked the pontoon bridges and troop concentrations in the Sedan sector throughout 14 May, bravely going after their targets despite the viciously concentrated flak and the Messerschmitt fighters covering the bridgehead. The air battle culminated in a loss of thirty-one Battles shot down within an hour in mid afternoon. The remaining handful of AASF Blenheims also made a courageous effort, but it was a fight against overwhelming odds. 57 and 59 Squadrons again each lost two aircraft during reconnaissance sorties. According to one 114 Squadron W.Op/AG, 'the air became black with enemy fighters' on approaching Sedan. 114 Squadron (flying 139 Squadron aircraft) lost four out of six crews to Bf109s of I and III/JG53 in late afternoon, with Plt Off Jordan's L9464

Sgt Jack Bartley, W.Op/AG with 21 Squadron, who was shot down during the massacre over Sedan on 14 May 1940. Jack Bartley

striking the ground during a low-level attack around the same time. Fw Alfred Stark of I/JG53 was killed when flying into the debris of an exploding Blenheim he was attacking. 2 Group came back into the fray in the evening, 21, 107 and 110 Squadrons sending twenty-eight sorties into the Sedan sector. Six more Blenheims fell victim to 109s of III/JG2 and I/JG53, and Bf110s of II/ZG26, five of which came from 110 Squadron, with Fg Off Sarll's P6890 of 21 Squadron written off on return to Bodney because of extensive cannon-shell damage. The day's air battles effectively signed the end of the AASF bomber force: forty-seven bombers were written off at the end of the day, fourteen of which were Blenheims. Over 50 per cent of all bombing sorties dispatched had failed to return, the highest-ever loss during an RAF raid.

Jack Bartley's Story

Nineteen-years-old AC1 Jack Bartley, W.Op/AG with 21 Squadron, vividly recounts the massacre over Sedan:

On the morning of 14 May 1940 we looked up at the clear blue sky with not a little apprehension. We all knew the Germans were advancing with amazing rapidity through the Low Coun-

tries, and we also knew that, cloud cover or no cloud cover, we would be required to attack and bomb some of the enemy columns that day in an attempt to stem their advance.

Throughout the morning we were 'standing by' while 82 Squadron, our sister squadron at RAF Watton made a short, two-hour trip to attack the victorious Panzers in northern Holland, carrying out the raid without loss to themselves. At last the long-awaited summons of the pilots and observers to the Ops Room was announced, and received with the quickening of the pulse that it never failed to effect in me and sighs of genuine relief from all concerned. We had been 'standing by 'since 4am, and activity of any sort was infinitely preferable to that tedious occupation. With assumed nonchalance we trooped into the crew room to receive the 'gen' from our squadron commander.

Our target, as it had been at Maastricht, advancing enemy mechanized columns, with the additional attraction of an important cross-road at Sedan, near the Luxemburg frontier. We were to make a dive attack for accuracy, but to repair quickly to formation after the attack for protection against Jerry fighters whose presence was regarded as inevitable. Twelve sleek and shining Blenheims were lined up on our dispersal field at Bodney awaiting the order to start engines.

We took off at 17.50hr in a cloud of dust, and as I saw the faces of my friends amongst the ground crews rapidly receding, I began to

wonder – but I'd had those doubts before and returned safely, so I fought down that feeling of over-excitement mixed with not a little fear that seems to bring your heart into your mouth and keep it there. My services weren't needed for a little while, so I leaned my forehead on the chin rest of the gun mounting and closed my eyes to allow the excitement to die off, and to get my thoughts into order for the approaching zero hour. When I again looked up we were just about to cross the coast and I watched the chalk cliffs slowly grow indistinct in the summer haze. I'd often had the experience before, yet never before had I felt quite so wistful towards them, nor realized more fully how much they really meant to me as on that lovely warm afternoon in May.

Following the boring flight over the Channel, the French coastline appeared out of the haze, and our presence sent a small convoy of merchantmen zigzagging frantically. We had climbed to 12,000ft so perhaps there was some excuse for their failing to identify us, but the same cannot be said of the ack-ack gunners at different points along the whole of our journey across the continent whose fire, though sparse and rather inaccurate, was at the same time infuriatingly misdirected. However, it served considerably to relieve the monotony of that seemingly endless flight to our targets, for we kept to 15,000ft, and could not improve our knowledge of the countryside from that height.

Plt Off Harriman belly-landed L8856 LS-U of XV Squadron near St. Kruis on the Dutch–Belgian border around noon on 15 May 1940, after having lost his port propellor to flak over his target at Dinant. The crew's observer, Sgt Stanford, was injured and taken prisoner while in a Belgian hospital, but the two other men avoided capture. Hans van Soest

Then I gave him all I had as he neared to 50yd-range, keeping my trigger depressed and seeing my tracers going firstly into his port wing and then raking his fuselage, as clearly as I saw his streams of tracers coming straight at me and seeming to veer off at the last moment. Unwaveringly he kept on until at 30yd he seemed he was intent on ramming us, when suddenly his nose dropped and he was gone. The unorthodoxy of the dive led me to believe I had downed him, and I was leaning out to catch some glimpse of him when I felt a terrible pain in my back as if a red-hot poker had been thrust into it, and turned to see a second Me.109 about to break off his attack made from the opposite beam simultaneously with the first machine. Immobilized with pain for a second or two, I recovered too late to get a smack at him, as, after traversing the turret and attempting to fire the gun with no result, I realized that I had emptied the pan of ammunition in the previous encounter, so with a twist of my turret control I lowered myself into the fuselage, hurriedly removed the empty pan and reloaded before elevating myself again, to be greeted with the sight of a fighter dead astern at 400yd. Jagged holes appeared in the tailplane while I manipulated foot and hand levers till the gun was in position for shooting alongside fin and rudder. He closed in until his machine-guns sounded like a much accentuated typewriter tapping in my ears above the engine noise and in between my own bursts of fire. Attempting to follow him down after his break away, my heart missed a beat or two when I found my turret would no longer respond to pressure on the hand bar – the hydraulics were evidently severed. Desperately I grasped the pillars of the turret and shoved but to no avail, the turret just would not budge. I was, in effect, disarmed. Fortunately at this juncture there was a lapse in the attack.

Placing my hand to my aching back, I brought it away covered with blood, and a feeling of nausea swept over me. Blood was also streaming from a wound in my thigh, so I decided to leave the cordite-reeking atmosphere of the useless turret and have my wounds attended to, pressing the emergency lever that would lower my seat and allow my exit. To my horror I felt no lowering of my seat in answer to my pressure there and realized I was virtually trapped in my turret. I doubled my body down in an effort to slip my seat and fall into the fuselage and was rewarded only by a shower of petrol in my face as it came below the level of the fuselage. It must have been leaking in through the wing roots from the severed feed pipes. I became aware that we were diving steeply and for the first time in the action I had time to be frightened. Feverishly I punched the release button to

Blenheim UX-Y of 82 Squadron is pushed back into a hangar at Watton. This may be P4898, which vanished without trace on the Gembloux raid of 17 May 1940 in the hands of Plt Off S. Christensen. During 1940 82 Squadron was the hardest hit of all Blenheim units with fifty-three aircraft lost on operations. Irene Deeks

At long last Johnny Outhwaite, my pilot, yelled out over the intercom that we were approaching the target area, whereupon I gave the magazine of 'ammo' on the gun a reassuring slap to ascertain its being properly fixed and, forsaking my comfortable pose for a more alert attitude, kept my eyes skinned. I set the turret buzzing around and looked ahead but could make out no sign of activity. It was 7 o'clock and we had 5min before being due over our target. We flew on. I began to have misgivings about our fighter escort (thirty French Dewoitine fighters had been arranged to patrol the target area from 7 to 7.30pm) which were by no means decreased when I caught sight of two machines 2,000ft or so above and flying across our track, their square wing tips almost spelling out the word Messerschmitt. Holding myself in readiness, and watching them like a hawk, I wondered why they made no attempt to attack us, when suddenly the reason was forming all about us in the shape of hundreds of black puffs from exploding anti-aircraft shells, and we were going down in a dive. For a moment I thought we had been hit, but a glance showed me that the rest of the squadron were with us in our descent, though the formation was loosened to go through the flak. We were flying No.3 in our sub-formation and I could see Sqn Ldr Sarll's machine at No.1 with Leo Lightfoot his gunner and Tug Wilson the gunner in the No.2 aircraft. Ack-ack fire is always rather awe-inspiring, especially when you know you are the object of

its attention. Big black blobs appear all over the sky with not a sound to announce their arrival, or so it seems after one's helmeted ears have listened to the roar of the engines for an hour or so, and even those that burst close enough to set the machine staggering drunkenly appear to make as much noise as a penny demon on 5 November, though there is more significance in the sharp report of shrapnel piercing the metal fuselage.

We straightened out at about 8,000ft leaving behind us the large artificial black cloud that was ack-ack. A jubilant shout through the phone compelled me to lower my eyes and see that Sgt Broadland, our observer, had landed his bombs smack on the crossroads. Looking around for the remainder of the squadron, my eyes were arrested by the sight of a Blenheim in flames about 2,000ft below, and going down, but before there was time to watch for the crew's escape my attention was riveted on a 109 fighter approaching from above and on the port quarter. Yelling out the 'gen' to Johnny, I saw that this one had singled me out for attention, and swiftly got him in my sights, until at 200yd he started firing, giving the appearance of blowing smoke rings from his leading edges. Tracers were zipping a little over my head and I gave a short burst in reply to see where my tracer was going. He closed in further and I held on until I really had the weight of him, as he evidently had of me, for I felt a couple of slaps on my legs and holes were appearing in the fuselage around my turret.

relieve myself of my parachute harness, tore at the strings of my Mae West and fumbled with the Irvin suit zip, finally managing to extricate myself from these encumbrances and then with a manoeuvre worthy of a contortionist I at last managed to squeeze myself between the turret seat and its side down into the fuselage.

With the machine still roaring earthwards, I donned my harness, this time with parachute attached in readiness, replugged my phones in the midships socket, and, wondering whether Johnny had given the order to jump, or indeed whether he were still alive, yelled down the mike, 'I'm out of action Sarge, I'm out of action Sarge.' There was no reply, but my increasing fears were allayed by the gradual straightening out of the machine and through the camera hatch I saw we were flashing over forest land, only a couple of hundred feet from the tree tops. Then my hopes of survival recently cherished were dashed to the ground as more jagged rips appeared in the already riddled fuselage, bullets whipped inside the machine clanging against metal, and above it, nearer and nearer, the terrifying tapping of those lethal typewriters.

A couple of bullets smacked into the parachute fastened to my chest, and, deciding I had not much longer to live, the mortal fear I had of being wounded in the stomach forced me to double up and point my head towards the tail, resignedly hoping for a mercifully quick end. The fact that I presented a small target in that position was purely incidental, though it was probably responsible for saving my life, for, though I received two ricocheting splinters in my side during the next few seconds, live

through the inferno I did, much to my surprise, though the ache from my wounds and the infuriation at my inability to retaliate knew no bounds. The firing stopped as suddenly as it had begun and all went comparatively quiet. I fervently hoped that was the last of the fighters to pay us its unwelcome attentions.

My wishes in this respect were borne out, though we were still not out of the wood, as, wriggling over the bomb well and peering over the pilot's seat I could see that Johnny was having one royal time endeavouring to keep the machine on some sort of course and to check her pitching, the difficulty arising, as we afterwards found, from the fact that half the tailplane was non-existent and the rudder resembled a tattered rag fluttering in the breeze. I managed to attract my observer's attention and he placed a shell dressing over my worst gash in the back from which blood still oozed in a steady stream.

Johnny yelled out that he would have to force lob her before the remaining fuel supply gave out and, after flying over seemingly endless forests covering the slopes of the Ardennes, we perceived through the cabin Perspex, which had not escaped the onslaught unscathed, a comparatively flat stretch of grassland. Banking steeply, Johnny prepared to put her down and, realizing that even if the attempt were successful the landing would be a very bumpy affair owing to the unserviceability of the undercarriage from both tactical and practical points of view, I rolled myself up in the bomb-well, the strongest part of the aircraft, and gripped the nearest fuselage rib as if my very life depended

on it. I saw the ground approaching through the rips in the metal fuselage, heard the swish of air as the flaps lowered and a crash that shook every bone in my body as I was thrown from my grip of the rib, dashed against the ceiling of the fuselage and down again two or three times, till with a scraping and rending, the battered machine came to a halt, and all was curiously quiet. Here let me pay tribute to Johnny's grand show in landing that crippled machine on that rough and steeply sloping grassy stretch in the Ardennes mountains without so much as scraping a wing tip, though of course the propeller tips and bomb doors were somewhat buckled.

The possibility of the kite firing spurred me in my opening of the hatch and scrambling on to terra firma, over which I stumbled for 20yd or so, followed by Johnny and Sgt Broadland, until my injured leg refused to carry me any further and buckled beneath me, and I fell to the ground, weak, sick and exhausted, but with that triumphant feeling of exhilaration that only those who have passed through the Valley of Death and survived can ever know.

Blenheim L8738 had come down in woods to the west of Givonne in the Ardennes, to the north of Sedan. Jack Bartley was hospitalized at Rheims, Epernay and finally Bordeaux, and soon lost touch with his pilot and observer. Operations followed to remove the bullets from his body, and on the day France fell, 21 June, he was shipped back to England.

The Retreat to the Channel

Following the devastating bombing raid on Rotterdam by fifty-seven He 111Ps of KG54, the Dutch government surrendered on 14 May. The rapidly advancing German armies forced a relocation of the AASF units further to the south and west. Although their numbers were depleted, the hard-working crews kept up pressure on the German forces as best they could, aided in their effort by home-based 2 Group squadrons. In the course of 15 and 16 May, a further thirteen precious Blenheims were lost over the frontlines with the majority of the thirty-nine crew members being killed or taken prisoner. When a new, bright day dawned on 17 May, twelve aircraft of 82 Squadron were dispatched from Watton with orders to strike at a concentration of Panzers in the Gembloux area. As had already happened so many times before, the promised fighter escort did not materialize, but the crews

Remnants of 82 Squadron in Spangenberg Castle, Oflag IXA/H, near Kassel, 1941. Between brackets are the dates in 1940 on which these men became prisoners of war. Left to right: Plt Off Biden (13 August); Flt Lt Syms (same); Plt Off Newland (same); Flt Lt Ellen (same); Flt Lt McKenzie (8 June); Flt Lt Toft (17 May); Flt Lt Keighley (29 July); Sqn Ldr 'Rusty' Wardell (13 August). Douglas McKenzie

248 Squadron fighter Blenheim pilots having fun, spring 1940. Sitting in the pram is Plt Off Sam McHardy.
Sally Goldsworthy

pressed on regardless in clear weather at 8,000ft. On their arrival over Gembloux, an unbelievably intense curtain of fire was sent up from hundreds of flak guns which scattered the formation and, within seconds, the first Blenheim crashed in flames. Emerging from the flak cloud, ten of the remaining aircraft fell victim to six Bf 109s of 1/JG3 prowling in the area, Ofw Max Bucholz claiming four Blenheims destroyed. Of the thirty-three aircrew, twenty-two perished. One lone Blenheim, P8858 of Sgt Morrison and crew, staggered back to base to bring home the terrible news. His aircraft was so badly shot up that he could not taxi it in. AASF squadrons lost a further five Blenheims in action the same day, wellnigh bringing the AASF Blenheim effort to a halt for lack of aircraft and crews. For all practical purposes, 82 Squadron had ceased to exist as a fighting unit, but its indomitable CO, Wg Cdr the Earl of Bandon, fought the Group decision to have his squadron disbanded. He won the day and had the squadron up to full strength within three days, resuming operations on 20 May.

Chaos was complete by this time, the allied HQs having lost track of the rapid German advance. The BEF was rapidly pushed back towards the Channel in the Dunkirk area, and both Bomber and Coastal Command Blenheim units were employed in covering the retreat, as Plt

Off E.H. Sam McHardy, pilot with 248 Squadron recorded:

On 18 May we were again called to provide three aircraft to go to the coast just to the north of Dunkirk, to escort an armed trawler, purported to be carrying the Dutch Royal family back to Britain. Penny (Flt Lt Alan Pennington Legh, 'A 'Flight Commander), Alfie Fowler and I would make up the small formation and again Plt Off Morris was my navigator and LAC Heavyside the air gunner. We duly flew out with Penny leading and found the trawler among what seemed like thousands of other ships fleeing the continent. It was an incredible spectacle.

Plt Off McHardy at the controls of his 248 Squadron Blenheim IVF, 1940/41. New Zealander Sam McHardy flew two consecutive tours of operations in fighter Blenheims with 248 and 404 (RCAF) Squadrons during 1940–42, amassing an impressive 137 operational sorties with a total of 487 flying hours. In 248 Squadron he scored a Bf 110 shot down and a shared He 111 destroyed off Dunkirk on 18 May 1940, and another Heinkel damaged off Norway on 3 November that year. In 404 (RCAF) Squadron, McHardy claimed an He 115 float plane probably destroyed in air combat off Norway on 15 January 1942 and a Ju 88 damaged off the British east coast on 22 April, which made him the top-scoring fighter Blenheim pilot of the war. When he was finally taken off operations in autumn 1942 for a rest, he had risen to the rank of Wing Commander, commanded 404 (RCAF) Squadron and been awarded the DFC and Bar and the _Croix de Guerre_.
Sally Goldsworthy

While circling the trawler we noticed a large passenger ship in nearer the coast just north of us, being bombed by a squadron of Stuka dive bombers. As they dived down one after the other, there were huge explosions in the sea close around the ill-fated passenger ship and the situation looked terrible. We were just about to move over and have a go at the Stukas, thinking they were more our match, when I observed a strange aircraft not far from me, so zeroed in on it to investigate.

When I was almost in close formation with it, I suddenly saw the crosses on its fuselage and an air gunner in the upper dorsal turret, looking at me. As I repositioned to attack, the pilot obviously reacted to my presence and dived. I followed him down at a speed that I felt would pull the wings off the Blenheim, firing whenever I got a good sight on him. It was one of the old models of Heinkel 111 bombers. As I continued to chase it at sea level, I was joined by Penny who also got in some bursts of fire at it. At this moment we were joined by some Me 110s which came in to attack us. I broke away and repositioned to attack the nearest Me 110 and, after a bit of jockeying for an advantageous position, I came up underneath the belly of the Me 110 and got in a good burst of fire from my five Brownings. As I fell out from the steep climb, the Me was gliding down and ahead of me, so I closed to get in another burst. At the same time the gunner in the Me had a potshot at me and hit my starboard engine. A few seconds later the Me suddenly hit the sea in a great cloud of spray and was gone. As I looked around there was an Me109 out to my starboard side, so I started to manoeuvre to take him on before he had a go at me. He did not seem ready and continued to climb away and I saw no more of him. Meanwhile, Penny had been attacking the other Me 110 and succeeded in shooting it

down in flames. The Heinkel also was seen to crash into the sea. By this time we were out of ammunition, so set course for Bircham Newton. That night Penny and I celebrated the loss of three German aircraft between us in a pub in King's Lynn.

While the British and French armies withdrew towards Dunkirk, the Blenheims kept attacking enemy troop columns, motor transport and Panzers at every possible opportunity. In an effort to impede the supply of reinforcements, bridges and roads to the rear of the battle front were also bombed. In the course of these operations during the week after the Gembloux debacle, 2 Group and the AASF lost thirty-four more Blenheims, the majority falling victim to the deadly efficient light flak. XV Squadron was hit especially hard, with eight aircraft lost, four out of six being destroyed by Bf 109s of 3/JG2 on 18 May, the remaining two returning to Wyton with battle damage. 40 Squadron had the misfortune of losing its second commanding officer, Wg Cdr Llewellyn, within eight days on 23 May. He was on only his first Blenheim operation, leading an attack against enemy forces near Arras. His predecessor, the immensely popular Wg Cdr 'Kekki 'Barlow had been killed in a Bf 109 attack in the Dinant area on the 15th.

The Belgian armed forces surrendered on 27 May, at a time when the main body of the BEF with its back against the wall had been pushed back inside the Dunkirk perimeter, while the few survivors of most AASF units were being withdrawn to Britain. Still, instead of launching an all-out ground and air offensive to crush the trapped British troops, Hitler ordered his armoured divisions to halt. At Göring's request, the Luftwaffe was given a free hand to bomb the concentrated and broken BEF forces to destruction. This overconfident decision gave the British seven precious days in which to evacuate the bulk of their forces, some 338,000 men, safely before the trap closed completely. Throughout the epic evacuation, the RAF mounted hundreds of sorties to try and keep the German forces close to the salient at bay. Remarkably, losses among 2 Group Blenheim units were relatively light over Dunkirk, although the unthinkable happened to 107 Squadron on 27 May, when their CO, Wg Cdr Basil Embry's L9391 fell victim to a heavy flak barrage during a raid on troop

248 Squadron fighter Blenheims on patrol over the North Sea, 1940. Sally Goldsworthy

concentrations near St Omer. Happily, this indestructible Blenheim hero turned up again at Wattisham ten weeks later after escaping from the Germans and surviving many hair-raising adventures.

Aubrey Lancaster's Story

Sgt Aubrey Lancaster, observer, and his 235 Squadron crew were detached to Detling aerodrome near Maidstone in late May, to protect the Dunkirk evacuation:

The morning of 29 May dawned bright and sunny. After a cup of tea and some breakfast we tried to find out what was happening. We were told that we were to fly a protective role, from Calais to Dunkirk for the full duration of our fuel, say 4hr. This was in an attempt to protect our troops from dive bombing Ju 87s, etc.

One flight was already on station with the next ready to go, then we were to follow. It was not long before the first crews landed and reported that the trip was 'a piece of cake': apart from the men on the beach, nothing else was happening – no air activity at all. This, of course, helped to lift our spirits in spite of the continuous roar of artillery and bombs which could be clearly heard.

Eventually our time came and off we went to Calais where we turned north along the coast to Dunkirk. As soon as we turned north we could see the columns of smoke from the burning oil tanks at Dunkirk. We seemed to be there in minutes and soon we spotted lots of aircraft circling, silhouetted against the black background

of the smoke. We had been warned that we may expect to come across some Spitfires and that is what I hoped these were. Almost as soon as we saw them they must have seen us because they came screaming towards us and turned behind our tails. I was trying to see where they were when out of the corner of my eye I saw an aircraft sweeping across our bows with the obvious Jerry black markings of a Messerschmitt.

Almost immediately I looked across to our No.1 man and he had a Messerschmitt on his tail and, as I looked, what seemed to be a solid sheet of flame shot from the nose of the Me and hit our colleague. John Cronan, our pilot swept across and just poured everything we had into the attacker's fuselage, but at that moment we also had a 'friend' on our tail. John went into a tight turn to starboard and, while we were in that steep bank, I looked down at the sea and saw what I am certain were two splashes – one of ours and one of theirs.

But I had little time to bother about that as we had another on our tail. John went into a steep dive (with the plus 9 boost in operation); but we were sitting ducks at that speed and soon we were being riddled. I remember seeing one of my instruments floating in mid-air a couple of yards in front of me when it suddenly disappeared, having been hit with a bullet which must have gone just past my ear. We were now heading for the water at a faster speed than I had ever done in a Blenheim when John started to try and pull out. In the end he had both feet on the instrument panel to try and get some leverage. My head was getting heavier and heavier with the pull of gravity. At last his efforts bore some results and we started to level out and finished up only a few metres off the water.

We now found that our port engine had stopped and we were going round in circles. John tried to adjust it but found that all the trimmers on the tail section had been shot away. His only resort was to put both feet on the port rudder to try and force the aircraft on to a straight course. In the end I sat on the floor and got hold of the starboard rudder pedal and pulled with all my strength to try and help. I gave John a course to steer which would bring us somewhere near home. A mental calculation to hit England – anywhere.

It was about this time that we both realized that we were still losing height and John told me that we would not be able to make it. He shouted to the gunner Phil Lloyd to get the dinghy ready as we were almost certainly going to ditch. From my position – I sat on the floor – I could see the water getting closer and closer. I was not worried unduly since I thought we were on a nice, shallow approach and visualized a condition similar to throwing a flat stone and getting it to bounce. However, it was nothing like that, instead as we hit the sea the large flat windows in the nose suddenly burst and flew back into my face. I shot forward into the nose and was immediately under water.

I can't swim...

I thought, well, I have only been shot forward and all I have to do is to take a few steps backwards and stand up. This I tried to do but could not move backwards. Alright, I thought, go forwards but I couldn't do that either. By this time I was short of breath and breathed in with dire results. Eventually my hands found a hole which in hindsight were the holes where the front windows had been. I pulled myself through but came up by the guns which were, of course, on the belly. By this time I was almost bursting for fresh air. I did a couple of swimming strokes or dog-paddles and this time got entangled in the undercarriage which had dropped down on impact. One last despairing paddle and I was under the smooth wing and with a final desperate swirl came up about 5m from the aircraft, which was still afloat but nose down with its tail in the air. John and Phil were in the dinghy wondering what had happened to me and, in fact, John was just preparing to get on to the aircraft and look for me.

Again using my newly-found ability to swim, I got to the dinghy and got in with their help. We now found that the dinghy was still fastened to the aircraft by parachute cord but luckily I had a penknife in my pocket and cut ourselves free only seconds before the plane went down. As we were sitting in the dinghy we could see a cross-channel ferry which was on its way to take the men off the beach. They had spotted us and it wasn't long before they came and took us aboard the ferryboat. They must have radioed Ramsgate, for it didn't seem long before a motor launch came alongside and took us off and back to Ramsgate and a hero's welcome from the crowds lining the dock side. My only injury – apart from being waterlogged – was a very badly bruised stomach and shoulder muscles.

As Lancaster recounts, the first 235 Squadron Dunkirk patrol on 29 May had been completed without incident. A second vic then took off from Detling, but it got off to a bad start when Flt Lt Dick Cross's P6909 crashed into a tree through engine failure, killing the crew. When the two remaining Blenheims had returned, the squadron mounted a third patrol, which turned into a black affair. No

aircraft survived the encounter with six Bf 109s over the Dunkirk beaches. Apart from Lancaster's L9260, Flt Lt Manwaring and his crew of P9401 fell to the concentrated fire of a Messerschmitt, killing the whole crew. Plt Off Anthony Booth and crew vanished without trace in L9397, which was last seen going down in flames. As a slight consolation, Plt Off Cronan was credited with a Bf 109 destroyed.

Less than a month after this episode, on 27 June, history repeated itself during a reconnaissance of invasion barges over western Holland. This time, four out of six fighter Blenheims of 235 Squadron fell victim to Bf 109s of 3/JG21 and I./JG76, Sgt Lancaster being the only crew member to escape alive to be taken prisoner. The 27 June carnage brought the total of 235 Squadron's losses to seventeen fighter Blenheims in six weeks of operations.

235 Squadron was not the only Blenheim unit active in the Dunkirk area on 29 May. 2 Group's 21, 40, 107 and 110 Squadrons harassed German troop concentrations in the battle zone without loss, although P6886 of 21 Squadron was written off on return to Watton, having

235 Squadron fighter Blenheim before taking off in December 1940. Photograph taken from crew room window at Bircham Newton. Geoff Brazier

sustained severe punishment from a Bf 109 during an operation to Dixemunde. AC1 Jack Guest, gunner, claimed a Bf 109 destroyed with his Vickers 'K', a rare achievement.

Douglas McKenzie's Story

82 Squadron was also in the thick of the action over Dunkirk, as Plt Off Douglas McKenzie graphically recounts. Together with his crew of Sgts Cooper, observer, and Crozier, W.Op/AG, Douglas completed eleven sorties in nineteen days against troop concentrations and roads in northern France during late May and early June. On 3 June, while the BEF withdrawal was coming into its final phase, the crew was one of eighteen from 21 and 82 Squadrons to patrol over Dunkirk:

Someone devised the notion that it would help the last hours of the evacuation if a standing offensive patrol of Blenheims were maintained over the beachhead. This was set up to run from soon after daybreak and went on through the morning at least, as far as I know. Blenheims were there singly, each for 15min. We carried four 250s. We were to present ourselves along the defensive perimeter dropping a bomb outside this 'line' every few minutes. This was presumably meant to terrify the attacking artillery, making them continuously seek cover and thus frustrating their shelling. I have no idea whether the plan worked but this seems very unlikely. It was theory born of desperation, I think. I have no recollection how I was to have identified the 'line'; thus I can only hope now that I didn't bomb the BEF. My spell over the beach was quite early – something like six or

seven o'clock in the morning.

My predominant memory from the whole thing was the smoke cloud. That summer of 1940 had outstandingly good weather, so that in the unbroken blue skies of all my operations there was never once even a tiny cloud which could be scurried to in the event of attack by fighters. But Dunkirk had the smoke cloud. This was a great, black mass put up by burning oil installations. It rose straight for several thousand feet before breaking and drifting. At last I had somewhere I could hide! I gratefully flitted in and out of the lower fringes of this Messerschmitt haven as often as I could in the course of my patrol.

When my turn over the perimeter was finished I swooped down over the beach itself on my way home. The now famous fan of small marine craft was stretched out towards England. In the water, up to their waists, were lines of men waiting their time to board. I roared over them, quite low, imagining that I was giving their morale a boost from the sight of one of their own aircraft. I was never more wrong; or perhaps my dive looked to them just like another Luftwaffe attack. Anyway, the faces just stared blankly up and swivelled with me. Not one wave. I felt shamed.

No Blenheims nor crews were lost on this final day of the Dunkirk evacuation. There were still 140,000 British troops fighting in France, and the Blenheim squadrons continued to provide close support. On 6 June thirty-eight Blenheims supporting the 51st (Highland) Division still fighting at St Valéry, ran into trouble. 40 Squadron was badly mauled with five aircraft shot down, Plt Off B.B. James and his crew perishing in L9410 and eight men were taken

prisoner. The 2 Group slaughter in the Battle of France was not over yet. Promoted to Flying Officer, Douglas McKenzie's next operational sortie came on 7 June, when he had to do a lone reconnaissance in the Abbeville area:

I remember the roads and villages that the Abbeville reconnaissance was to cover as a loose oblong of country with the long, south side bounded by the Somme river. This date of 7 June was just at the start of the final German push to Paris. The German Army was believed to be thick in this area.

We reached the designated region and, sure enough, found a road full of German transport. I had adopted a cruising height of about 4,000ft, this because it was considered to be a level too low for heavy flak and too high for light flak. We duly started noting the type and number of vehicles (Cooper was writing it down). At once we began to be engaged by flak and the sky was soon dotted with black puffs, but we had expected this and were not particularly worried. Then, as on a signal, the flak abruptly ceased. I knew what this could imply: the arrival of fighters.

For a few seconds I was cogitating what I might do about this when Crozier's voice yelled down the intercom: 'FIGHTERS!' Instinctively I looked out the window on my side. Directly opposite me, travelling parallel, a 109 was scudding past in the same direction. I registered two things almost simultaneously: one was the unbelievable sight, at such close quarters, of the ragged black cross on the fuselage; the other, that the pilot was staring straight at me (as I was at him).

Without any conscious thought I rammed the control column right forward and held it there. From 180mph cruising we must have got up to about 250 before we reached the ground – pretty fast for a Blenheim. I estimate that it would have taken not much more than 10sec to get down.

When I was a small boy I used to think it interesting to generate a deafening racket by running at full tilt alongside a vertically-corrugated iron fence and pressing the end of a stick on it. This caused a fast and satisfying b-r-r-r-r-r. A similar sound now briefly filled my aeroplane. What I hadn't known at first about the 109 was that he had a companion, although I suppose I could have guessed it; otherwise why would he just look instead of doing. It was surely the other 109 which now got the burst in on us: just as we were well into our wild dive there was this shattering noise through the aircraft and the stench of cordite.

We were not hit again. As I was reaching the end of my near-vertical plunge, I noticed some

The Blenheim was defenceless against fighters attacking from below and behind. Here the Messerschmitt's favoured tail-end view of the aircraft is demonstrated with a 235 Squadron plane. Wijb-Jan Groendijk

Plt Off Len 'Mad' Trent sitting on his XV Squadron Fairey Battle at Bétheniville, France in September 1939. After the squadron had converted on to the Blenheim IV bomber, Trent survived thirteen sorties during the Battles of France and Britain and was awarded the DFC on 9 July 1940. During his second tour in 487 (RNZAF) Ventura Squadron, Trent won the VC during the ill-fated Amsterdam power-station raid of 3 May 1943. Hugh George

of lack of respect which obviously could not be tolerated. Accordingly I came round in a large arc, approaching the road from the other side and could see my dispatch rider still speeding along. On the right wing of the control column head was a button to be pressed by the thumb to trigger the single .303 in the leading edge. I turned the button to 'fire'. To aid accuracy in the use of this weapon the designers had even provided a ring-sight ahead of the front Perspex. Unfortunately, I had made my turning arc too tight – no doubt to get this matter over as quickly as possible because my heart wasn't really in it. My burst flew too far in front of my quarry and my attempted skid could not compensate. If my motor-cyclist could seem to overlook the roar of two engines he must still have heard the machine-gun and seen the tracer. How did he respond this time to evident direct danger? He simply hunched his shoulders, thereby drawing his coalscuttle down around his neck, as a turtle's head might seek protection below the rim of the shell. And he carried right on. A good man. My only credit in this miserable and absurd manoeuvre was that I didn't try to repeat it.

After the return to Watton a few of us went down to the maintenance hangar to look at this slightly honeycombed Blenheim. There was much black humour. We counted forty bullet holes in the fuselage.

2 Group lost just one aircraft, R3686 of 107 Squadron, during the day's operations, with Fg Off Pleasance escaping to England. Sgt A.E. Merritt's P6915 'A' from 82 Squadron returned to Watton so badly shot up by 109s that it was declared beyond repair. Next day Fg Off Douglas McKenzie lifted R3618 into the bright sky from Watton at 10.22hr for his seventeenth operational sortie:

On the morning of 8 June 82 Squadron put up a formation of twelve, of which I was a member, to bomb enemy concentrations on a road near Poix, south of the Somme river. Having formed up over Watton we went to North Weald to collect a fighter escort of Spitfires, I think twenty-four. This was our first experience of cover. I had never felt safer on an operation: enemy fighters would clearly represent no problem and I had developed a kind of contempt for flak. This overconfidence may have contributed to my being shot down.

We were armed with four 250s. Over the target I followed the notion of making four separate, shallow, dive-bombing attacks, I suppose with the dotty idea of planting my contribution the more accurately. I was too cool by half and

German soldiers right below. They began looking up and running. It must have seemed to them that I was headed full pelt into the ground beside them. Or perhaps even on them! The last I saw of this group, as I pulled out, was two men in a frantic, prancing run which even at that time struck me as comic.

Once at ground level I hugged the tree tops. I had the belief that if I could prevent the fighters from getting under us we would be all right. After all, my air gunner had his dorsal popgun. I thundered along, hoping for the best. One good look back through my blister showed me two 109s weaving in the distance. How long this chase lasted I can't really say. There was no attack during it. Then Crozier was on the intercom again: 'They've gone, sir!' This was indeed true. We came up, as it were, for a good look round – and the fighters were nowhere to be seen.

The burst of fire we had taken might, for all we knew, have had serious structural consequences – a partly severed fuel line or control cable, for instance. I don't recall that we even thought about it. All these moments were terribly

exciting. We ended in a mental turmoil of relief and swagger.

There seemed no good reason not to try to complete the reconnaissance. Cooper 'found himself' on the map, he thought; and we chased along roads and noted what we saw – which wasn't much, I'm afraid. For the rest of the time on the recce we stayed at the lowest reasonable height: at least we were not attacked again. At one point we surged across a large clearing in a forest. It was packed with vehicles, men and horses. We were as unexpected to them, no doubt, as they were to us: so we picked up no ground fire. I yelled to Crozier for attention and he left behind a satisfying burst which might have frightened the horses if doing nothing else.

I then came up at right angles to a road, and on it, directly ahead, was a solitary motor-cyclist in a German coalscuttle helmet. Ah-ha! I thought – dispatch rider. I came at him very low expecting the minimum courtesy from him of a leap into the ditch. Instead he ignored me completely, just as though we were not there at all, as we passed over him with only metres to spare. I was shocked. This was a demonstration

equipment designed to self-destruct in a crash or to be fired by a switch. It was kept near the wireless operator's seat. Crozier said it had gone off okay.

We were moving to get Cooper out when a strange noise began. It struck both of us as ominous. It was something like a crackle. In a second each had acted according to his individual belief. We both jumped to the ground. Crozier had assessed the noise as the petrol tanks fizzing before blowing up; therefore he ran into the open. To me the noise sounded like continuous rifle fire (directed at us) and I was preparing to take cover. Crozier yelled, dropped to the ground, and writhed there clutching his leg. It had indeed been rifle fire. We were, of course, in 'enemy territory'. To the troops coming up to take us it could justifiably be concluded that we were up to no good around the aeroplane – like trying to destroy it. One look at Crozier and I was under the wing, where there was just enough clearance; and whence, very soon, I was encouraged to emerge by the pointed barrels of half-a-dozen rifles, and associated coalscuttle helmets, coming round the tail.

I displayed as much of the palms of my hands as was possible consistent with lying face to the ground and wriggled out. There was a lot of shouting in the Germanic way; and I am sure that if I had known anything of the language then I should have recognized the classic: 'Hände hoch!'

Twenty-years old Sgt Joseph H. Cooper, a prewar regular, was buried in Eplessier churchyard in the Somme district, where he still rests. Over the next eighteen months, McKenzie was operated on his

R3594 LS-D of XV Squadron revving up its engines before departing from Wyton for an operation during the summer of 1940. Philip Camp

paid for it. I think everyone else quite properly loosed off everything in one 'stick' and cleared out. Flak was moderately heavy and persistent throughout. On my fourth and last run, at the very moment of starting the pull out from the dive, a colossal noise enveloped the aircraft: a flak explosion had carried away most of the nose. I was conscious of being hit in both arms. The instrument panel must have saved the worst.

Cooper, who had been sitting at the table in the nose, was thrown back on the floor beside me. He had lost the right side of his head. This I saw as I looked down while recovering from the dive. A very loud gale of well over 200mph was funnelling through the fuselage. Cooper's left eye was open but already, I think, sightless. The cockpit was, in the fullness of the term, a bloody shambles. What would I do? I could get back to England without a navigator – there was no difficulty about that. But I don't think I even considered the option (if I had tried it I must, for a start, have been beaten by the cold to finish in the Channel). The immediate thought was one of survival. As you can imagine, I have already relived this moment a million times and will continue to do so until the day I die.

My arms were stiffening. Blood was trickling into my eye: I hadn't realized at first that a fragment of something had lodged in my forehead. Even in level flight again the controls felt sluggish and unresponsive. I sensed a failure. It came to me that the plane was unflyable. This was probably a bad decision. It grew out of shock, noise, wind, fear and an instinct to seek amends (if that makes sense) in getting on the ground as soon as possible. Captivity, and its consequences, failed to enter my mind.

I had already had one experience of belly-landing a Blenheim 'without benefit of airfield' when both engines failed during take-off at Weston Zoyland, in Somerset [19 September 1939, P4861 written off]. This experience was about to be repeated. In the distance I could spy a large, clear area alongside a forest; this became the target. The last moves were to throttle back, switch off the ignition, and hold off. We slithered to a dusty halt. This was (as a sidelight) the last time I ever flew as a pilot.

In no time I had got rid of my harness and parachute straps, slid open the hatch, and climbed out on the wing. Crozier appeared from the back and climbed up beside me. It's funny how duty and training come to the fore: even in these smash-up conditions I remembered to ask him if the IFF box had blown. This was secret

Under a reassuring cover of clouds, XV Squadron Blenheims are on their way to bomb roads and rail targets around Abbeville and St. Valéry on the evening of 6 June 1940, in support of the 51st (Highland) Division. Of the thirty-eight Blenheim sorties dispatched on 6 June, five Blenheims, all of 40 Squadron, failed to return. Philip Camp

Having bombed its target in northern France on 11 June 1940, 82 Squadron's P6925 'Z 'was attacked by Bf 109s. During the fight the blister and windows were shot away by cannon fire and all the maps and navigation kit blown out. Undaunted, Sgt Jack 'Bish' Bareham, an exceptionally skilled navigator safely guided his pilot, Sqn Ldr Theo 'Joe' Hunt, back to Watton, while exposed to a howling gale and with his legs lacerated by pieces of Perspex. Bareham was awarded the DFM for this and other Blenheim sorties in 82 Squadron during the first half of 1940. During raids in the St. Valéry area on the evening of 11 June 21 Squadron lost a whole section of three aircraft to Messerschmitts, plus one badly shot up. In all, 2 Group lost seven Blenheims and thirteen crew members during supporting operations on this day. Blenheim Society

right arm many times and came close to losing it through medical neglect in the early stages. He concludes:

From prison camp I wrote to Sgt Cooper's mother – a letter of sympathy and explanation – and said I would come to see her after I got back. This meeting took place in May 1945. It turned out to be a *mauvais quart d'heure* for me. Mrs Cooper wanted the fullest possible details about her son's death, and insisted. I found, though, that I was altogether unable to describe the state of the boy's head, for example. I had to try to satisfy her by saying that he had died instantly in the explosion through being hit in the head, and had not suffered. In the next stage Mrs Cooper appeared to be arriving at the position that I had killed her son, to which I could only point to the common risk and claim that it was the war, and the war alone, which had killed him. Happily for me, Mrs Cooper's daughter and son-in-law were present at this interview and became pretty embarrassed at the turn of events, trying to deflect their mother's accusation.

Apart from Fg Off McKenzie's Blenheim, 21 Squadron's L9023 was lost near Abbeville (Somme), with Fg Off H.D.S. Dunford-Wood and crew perishing. Later the same day the hard-pressed 82 Squadron suffered another blow, when Plt Off Robertson in R3709 'F' failed to return from a bombing raid on a petrol dump near Abbeville (which was blown up) and Plt Off Percival in R3754 crashed on return to base with his air gunner Sgt Byatt dead. With the evacuation of most of the BEF successfully completed on 4 June, the end of the Battle of France was now drawing near. 2 Group and the few remaining Battles of the AASF were flying at maximum effort in support of the retreating British forces during the remaining days of June, taking horrifying casualties at times. The crews' dedication and raw courage, however, could not compensate for the inadequacies of their machines in the

forty-seven days of the battles for the Low Countries and France. The overwhelming superiority of the German light flak and Messerschmitt fighters, both in number and performance, was simply too much for the British crews to match. By the time France fell on 25 June, 2 Group had lost ninety-two Blenheims or 5.7 per cent of the 1,601 daylight sorties dispatched. This was the equivalent of six and a half complete squadrons from the nine in 2 Group during this period. In all, 178 RAF Blenheims had been lost on operations since 10 May. The majority of the crews were missing, killed or prisoner of war. The precious cadres of prewar professional airmen had been decimated, irreplaceable losses which were deeply felt at squadron and group level. Their places were taken by hastily-trained, green and vastly more vulnerable crews. Britain now stood alone, facing the prospect of invasion by a vastly superior enemy. The future looked black indeed for the free world.

CHAPTER FIVE

On the Offensive and the Defensive:

The Battle of Britain, July–October 1940

Following the outbreak of war, it was found that Fighter Command's Spitfires and Hurricanes, with their limited range of only 400 miles, were unable to give British shipping in the North Sea sufficient protection from Luftwaffe attacks. Consequently, four fighter Blenheim squadrons, Nos. 254, 235, 236 and 248, were transferred from Fighter to Coastal Command in early 1940, and employed on these 'trade protection' duties. From May 1940 these squadrons were used as highly mobile units, with detachments moving around the country to wherever they were most needed. Their crews flew defensive and offensive fighter patrols by day, by night and in bad weather; and convoy-escort sorties and offensive escort missions for bombers and seaplanes. Two other

Victim in the 2 Group cloud-cover offensive. On its way back from a sortie to north-west Germany on 4 July 1940, Flt Lt Ivor C.B. Worthington-Wilmer's L8866 of 18 Squadron was intercepted and shot down at 12.15hr by two Luftwaffe fighters. The Blenheim crashed in the Brielse Maas near Oostvoorne, Holland, with the loss of the crew. Here, the wreckage is salvaged by German soldiers two days later. Archief gemeente Westvoorne, via C. Wind

Blenheim squadrons, Nos. 53 and 59, were released by Army Co-operation Command in June 1940 to take up vitally important anti-invasion reconnaissance duties from Detling and Thorney Island. They formed the 'eyes' for Britain, keeping a close watch on the Channel ports from which the Germans were preparing to launch a large-scale invasion of the Sussex and Kent coasts. The crews of 53 and 59 Squadrons also mounted anti-shipping attacks whenever the opportunity arose.

The Norwegian Raids

In order to monitor a possible invasion from Norway, 2 Group sent 21 and 57 Squadrons to RAF Lossiemouth in Scotland on 29 June. Almost daily, the crews ventured out to the Norwegian fiords in co-operation with their fighter Blenheim colleagues of 248 and 254 Squadrons in search of invasion vessels and also to attack any shipping they encountered. Cloud cover was of prime importance on these sorties, because of roaming Messerschmitt Bf 109 and 110 and Ju 88 fighter aircraft, notably in the Stavanger area. Sgt Harry Huckins, observer with 21 Squadron, has vivid memories of the Lossiemouth detachment:

After being completely 'bloodied' from May 11 onwards at Maastricht, Dunkirk and points south, the squadron was removed to Lossiemouth. After having to make my way back from the aftermath of the largely ineffective Les Andelys raid on 11 June, where we lost three out of nine Blenheims (including my own aircraft L8743) to fighters, it was a relief to rejoin my crew again to make our way into relatively peaceful Scotland and Lossiemouth – a picturesque fishing village near Inverness whose inhabitants were surely the most friendly people in the world. What a relief it was to enjoy the long evenings of summer and bask in the sunshine on the beach! It seemed so far away

from the disastrous battles over the Netherlands and France.

As for the squadron itself, our flight personnel had been replaced two or three times and my own crew (Plt Off Dick Rogers and Sgt Bill Bradshaw) were just about the sole survivors from the outset of the blitzkrieg (indelibly stamped 10 May 1940). At this time most of our Blenheim crews were probably unaware of the vital period the 'free world' was going through. As I had miraculously survived over two months of air combat and approximately twenty raids, the 'sprog' crews used to look up to my crew somewhat. Suffice it to say that the morale of 21 Squadron continued to be high. New crews seemed to be looking forward to the initiation into aerial warfare.

Our flying at this time, over a period of ten days, seemed to consist mainly of practice formation flying and we lost two Blenheims at this time which just 'tucked in' too closely, with disastrous results. The word went out that there was going to be a big raid. On 8 July we were confined to camp and could not go to our favourite 'stamping ground' at Elgin. The next

Not shrapnel but seagull! Bird strikes were a real problem during low-level, anti-shipping patrols. Depicted is a 57 Squadron aircraft, probably at Lossiemouth in the summer of 1940, together with Sgt James Dunnet, observer. James survived seventy operational sorties in Blenheims with 57, 211 and 11 Squadrons during 1940–41. James Dunnet

day twelve Blenheims (six from 'A' Flight, 21 Squadron and six from 'A' Flight, 57 Squadron) took off at dawn and aimed to get to Stavanger airfield. We got only sketchy reports on this raid. Three Blenheims of the other squadron managed to get back unscathed. Apparently the formation of twelve Blenheims was intercepted out to sea by a positive swarm of fighters at their normal bombing altitude of 6,000ft. Our rear gunners were equipped with only a single Vickers 'K' turret gun. This was no match for the horde of fighters. It seemed like a repeat of the Maastricht raid, 'business as usual' for the poor old Blenheim Boys!

On the 9 July raid against Stavanger airfield, the formation of twelve Blenheims bombed the target despite a heavy flak barrage. As the crews recrossed the coast, a mixed group of Bf 109s and 110s attacked them from all sides and

within five minutes, 21 Squadron lost R3619, R3876 and L8872 to their fire. A further two aircraft from 57 Squadron, R3750 and R3847, also went down in the sea with the loss of Plt Off Hopkinson and Sgt Mills and their crews. Sgt James Dunnet, observer in one of 57 Squadron's Blenheims, and his crew survived the ordeal and were struggling to make it back:

I remember vividly, limping back over the North Sea on one engine, and hoping that we would not have to ditch. As we were gradually losing height, I gave the pilot a course for Dyce (now the civil airport for Aberdeen), as I was certain that we would not make Lossiemouth. Coming in to land, some fool in an Anson started to take off right in front of us. My pilot yanked down the emergency nine boost lever and hauled back on the stick. There was no way that he could control the tremendous torque

from the one engine, and the Blenheim just rolled over. It was a strange experience for me. Just before we hit the ground, my pilot shouted 'Goodbye' and crossed his arms over his face. Sitting beside him, I watched the ground rush up, and the now well-known, slow-motion effect materialized. I watched the nose of the plane hit the ground, and the Mk 9 bombsight crumble towards me. I thought, 'This is how I am going to die.' I had no fear. It was a total disassociation of personality, complete detachment. Then I was conscious of being racked from side to side, tremendous noise, stones, dirt, all sorts of rubble flying about, then nothing but the realization that I was still alive.

Fortunately, the three men were able to walk away from their wrecked Blenheim. Meanwhile the three 21 Squadron survivors had broken for cloud cover over the North Sea, but R3822 with Plt Off

In full flying gear, this crew is ready to board R3821 UX-N at Bodney for a sortie early in the Battle of Britain. From the left: Sgt Don McFarlane (observer); Sgt Peter Eames (W.Op/AG, later awarded the DFM, who died during a shipping strike off Schiermonnikoog on 26 April 1941, while serving in the crew of 21 Squadron's CO Wg Cdr Bartlett, DFC); Plt Off Donald Wellings (pilot, killed in 1944). This 82 Squadron crew scored a chance hit attacking Haamstede airfield on 7 August 1940, when their bombs straddled a line of Bf 109s of 4/JG54, effectively putting this Luftwaffe fighter unit out of action for the final month of the Battle of Britain. R3821 crashed on Aalborg airfield on 13 August, with Plt Off E.R. Hale and his crew being killed. Don McFarlane

Heath-Brown and crew were never seen again. Wg Cdr Bennett's W.Op/AG, Sgt Burt in R3732, sent a ditching message at 11.45hr and RAF Kinloss followed the Blenheim's progress on IFF until it finally disappeared at 12.31hr. Bennett's body was later washed up on the Danish coast and was buried at Lonstrup. No trace was ever found of his crew nor of the other twelve crew members of 21 Squadron that were lost on this raid. Plt Off Rogers nursed his sole surviving and bullet-riddled aircraft back to base and managed to get it down in one piece, although both tyres had burst.

Wg Cdr Miles Delap, DFC, ex-Flight Commander in 82 Squadon, was posted to command 21 Squadron on 10 July, replacement crews and aircraft were received and soon the crews were in action again. Sgt Huckins continues:

21 Squadron from then on did 'feint' raids and U-boat searches which went to within 50 miles of the coast of Norway and then returned to Lossiemouth. Some time after our Stavanger raid the Luftwaffe showed us 'how to do it' by mounting a low-level raid on Lossiemouth airfield (on 26 October). The two Heinkels came in at 50ft and, as I was good at aircraft recognition, I immediately recognized the elliptical tail structure on the Heinkels. I was strolling down to the local pub in Lossiemouth at the time and rushed towards a nearby Lewis gun, but they had dropped their bombs and departed by the time I got there. The two Heinkels destroyed a Blenheim of 'B' Flight. Two crew members were killed in one Blenheim which was about to take off. The Heinkels were using instantaneous fuses on their bombs and one Heinkel blew itself up.

Blenheim T2233, which was prepared for a night flying exercise together with five other aircraft, received a direct hit, instantly killing Plt Off Slater, Sgt Jones and Cpl Holland. Wreckage strewn around damaged T1878 and L8744, injuring three more ground crew. The starboard wing of He.111 6854 from I/KG26, flown by Oblt Georg Imhof, was blown up by its own bomb blast; it did a slow roll and went in, the whole crew perishing. Harry Huckins concludes: 'At the end of October 1940, 21 Squadron were sent back to dear old Watton to continue our efforts against the Luftwaffe by night raids on their airfields. We lost a lot of aircraft simply because we were not sufficiently well equipped for night ops. Altogether the

Bill Magrath, shot down and taken prisoner on the 13 August 1940 Aalborg raid. Bill Magrath

Blenheim Boys took an awful beating.'

On 5 June 2 Group was ordered to mount hit-and-run daylight attacks under cloud cover on selected military targets in Germany, the Low Countries and Denmark. This was aimed to tie down Luftwaffe fighter units in these regions and thus to prevent them from being used on offensive operations over southern England. Due to the brilliant weather which prevailed throughout the summer of 1940, however, many of these cloud-cover sorties were subsequently aborted. When the Blenheim crews 'pressed on regardless' they usually paid a heavy price.

Bill Magrath's Story

This was painfully illustrated by the train of events on 13 August, the day that has gone down in history as 'Eagle Day' (Adlertag), or the Luftwaffe's (failed) all-out air assault on Britain as a direct prelude of invasion. Nineteen-years-old Sgt Bill Magrath was observer to Sgts Donald Blair (pilot) and Bill Greenwood (W.Op/AG), both aged twenty. They had been posted to 82 Squadron as a replacement crew after the 17 May Gembloux disaster and had survived a few cloud-cover raids as a single aircraft or in small formations:

The powers-that-be, not content with this sort of affair, wanted to have a bigger and better raid.

They wanted this idea of formations of a full squadron or two squadrons of Blenheims, more or less doing what the Americans did later on in the war, and that is the carpet-bombing of a target. The theory behind this was that you could do a fair amount of damage that way. Secondly, there was a reasonable chance that, if you kept a nice tight formation, that everybody had the benefit of the other fellow's guns to defend them from the fighters. Frankly, it may have worked in other squadrons, but I never really saw it being a particularly great success in anything I was in. The most incredible thing is that the Blenheims with 1,000lb of bombs on board were not aeroplanes that could climb very rapidly or very high. Nevertheless, we practised this type of op, would you believe it, by climbing to 20,000ft to drop our bombs!

We were going to go and attack Aalborg, which we did on 13 August 1940. Twelve Blenheims took off at about 9 o'clock in the morning, a nice August morning, to set off for Aalborg. From the time I served on the squadron, I had got – from I suppose the nervous tension of dealing with the day-to-day living there, as life expectancy was only a very few weeks on the whole – almost like what you would call second sight. I was able to look at a member of the aircrew, and so to say, 'He'll not be home tonight, he'll be getting a one-way ticket.' And in ninety-nine cases out of a hundred I'd be right. But the one thing I never had was the thought that it might happen to me, that I might not come back! However, funnily enough, getting airborne on that particular morning as we were steadily climbing up in formation, and I could see the Norfolk coast disappearing in the murk, it came to me as an absolute certainty, there was no question about it, that I was not coming back. That was good-bye to the Norfolk coast for the last time.

And, funnily enough, it never occurred to me to get excited about it. The only thing I made quite sure was that I ate my goodies – the aircrew when they went on an operation were issued with a little bag of goodies to eat, I suppose to keep morale up, like a Kit-Kat, a little chocolate wafer biscuit, and an apple or an orange and one or two nice little things like that. So I sat in the Blenheim – there was not much navigation to do because we were at the tail-end of the squadron and really all we were doing was following our leader – and I ate my chocolate and had a sort of little picnic lunch while we flew along our outward track. We flew there at I suppose 6 or 7,000ft and actually flew between two layers of cloud. It was a very uneventful trip.

One thing about this trip which I think ought to be recorded was that we had recently had a

The wreckage of R2772 UX-T of 82 Squadron in Limfjord, Denmark, 13 August 1940. Incredibly, Sgts Blair, Magrath and Greenwood all survived the crash. Ole Ronnest

new Squadron Commander. Our Squadron Commander initially had been Wg Cdr the Earl of Bandon, 'Paddy' Bandon, and he was a very charismatic character and a marvellous leader. However, by the time August had come we had lost him. He had got a well-earned DSO and had gone to higher things, promoted to Group Captain. We had a Wg Cdr De Lart as our new Squadron Commander. Now I must admit, as an older man, I can understand how that chap must have found life very difficult at 82 Squadron, because he was having to replace as leader a very charismatic one, and De Lart, while he was a good, conscientious officer, he certainly was not of the same quality. So I think that he tended to try to be almost braver than the brave, which makes life difficult. He also had the feeling that an officer was an officer and other ranks, the NCOs and so on, came from 'below the salt'. Our lead navigator had with Paddy Bandon been a Flt Sgt King, who was a very experienced prewar navigator and so knew his way about. He certainly was the right man to put in the Squadron Commander's aircraft to lead the rest. However, with Wg Cdr De Lart taking over command, he felt that the lead aircraft should have an officer in it. So he took a Pilot Officer as his navigator. This had the snag that the chap hadn't very much experience.

This, I think, is germane to what happened next, because what we had planned to do was to hit the coast to the west of Aalborg – which is up on the north-eastern corner of Jutland, so we would have a quick run over the short portion of land into Aalborg and then rush out again and fly home. Now that was the plan, but the other sobering thing that we had been told was

that we were on the extreme range of the Blenheim's fuel endurance. So if there were fighters or any problem where we had to use plus nine boost we wouldn't have enough fuel to get home. So we were told that anyone who found himself in this sort of problem would have to head for Newcastle, which was the nearest point of England to aim for. So that wasn't exactly the most promising start to the whole thing.

Anyway, we flew out in between these two layers of cloud until we got close to the Danish coast, which unfortunately, the navigation not having been quite up to the standard we'd hoped, we hit not very far north of Esbjerg, so we were down in the south-western corner of Jutland with a fair amount of land to travel across to find a way to Aalborg. Not only that, but the cloud cover which had been plentiful while we were over the North Sea suddenly disappeared and there were we, motoring our way across Denmark at a height of about 5 or 6,000ft in a clear blue August day without any cloud cover whatsoever. Well, I don't need to tell you that that really wasn't very clever. So we waited; we thought, well, our leader will surely turn back shortly, because normally we attacked with at least some cloud cover, and this didn't look too promising. However, he ploughed on, so we ploughed on, with the exception of one aircraft that pulled out of the formation at this stage and headed for home.

So we were plodding our way across Denmark with presumably every Observer Corps in the land there reporting to the Germans that these Blenheims were probably heading for Aalborg. So it was small wonder that the Aalborg defences were waiting for us. The first thing we got was an attack from fighters, 109s. I didn't see it because, of course, I was in the bomb aiming position which is looking forward, but I gather that one of our aircraft was hit and just blew up there and then. But most of us seemed to survive

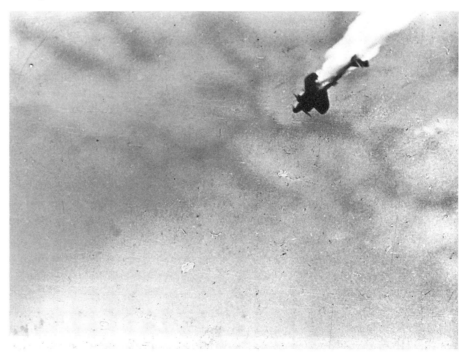

R3800 UX-Z plunges down in flames over Limfjord, south of Egholm Island, after being mortally hit by the Aalborg flak defences. Flt Lt Syms and his observer Sgt Wright managed to bale out to be taken prisoner, but Sgt Turner was killed. Ole Ronnest

The eleventh and final Blenheim of 82 Squadron going down during the Aalborg raid was T1889 UX-L, which Sgt Oates crash-landed at Vust, to the west of Aalborg. He is lying in front of the wreckage, having suffered a fractured skull and a broken back. Oates was paralysed for life from the waist down. Ole Ronnest

those first few minutes of fighter attack, and they pulled away to let the anti-aircraft guns have a go at us as we got near Aalborg. I had the job then of getting on with dropping my bombs on the airfield. At 5,000ft it wasn't really a difficult feat frankly, because on a clear blue day at 5,000ft an airfield looks very big. So I got off the bombs, two 250lb general purpose bombs and two small bomb containers with 40lb anti-personnel bombs and incendiaries. As I was looking down my bombsight at 5,000ft, I seemed to be looking down the barrel of an anti-aircraft gun pointing up at me, I could really see the flame and fire coming up, it was quite exciting!

It wasn't very long after that I heard the rattle of the fire from fighters attacking us again, and very shortly after that we were hit and lost an engine. It went on fire and it was pretty obvious that we weren't going to go home. So I sort of worked out a little contingency plan; I knew Sweden wasn't very far away so I was thinking, well, alright, if the worst comes to the worst, Sweden is neutral and we will head for Sweden. However, we never even got that chance because before very long our second engine was set on fire and we started to head down towards

a fiord there at Aalborg. Don Blair, our pilot, put us down in the water alongside a small island, Egholm. He put us down alongside it, fairly close in. What, of course, none of us knew, although the water looked nice and calm down there, it was very shallow and there were rocks close to the surface; indeed, as soon as the aircraft went down, it smashed to pieces.

The airplane broke up and we were thrown out of it into the water and by sheer good luck didn't hit anything hard. So all three of us survived. I was the most severely injured of our crew, although I wasn't to know that at that stage. I obviously went unconscious in the crash and I woke up in the water with my Mae West inflated and could see my pilot Don Blair not very far away from me with his face covered in blood, and he looked in a hell of a mess. So I thought, God, I wonder whether he is still alive? And I could see the gunner further back and he didn't look too good either. So it looked as if I was the only one very much living at that time. In fact, the other two had only superficial injuries.

A farmer and his eleven-years old son had been at Egholm and had been standing on the

beach watching the action and when they saw us crash they waded out and pulled us ashore. Then a little boat came along from the harbour at Aalborg to take us to hospital. I was in and out of consciousness all the time and discovered later that, in fact, I was concussed, I was blind in the right eye and still am; I had a smashed shoulder and right arm and a smashed right hip. That and, of course, any amount of bits of Perspex and bits of Blenheim stuck in me when I was thrown out of it. So you can imagine that I wasn't in good shape at this stage. However, when they put us in the boat to take us back to Aalborg they laid me in the bottom and I can remember quite well that at one period of consciousness I opened my eyes and was looking straight up at a very nice pair of legs of a young lady who was sitting in the back of the boat. I couldn't help but be naturally interested a little bit, and I was thinking, 'It's alright, if you can still think like that Magrath, you're alright, you're going to live!' They put us in the emergency area of the Aalborg hospital and patched us up as best they could.

We lost the entire squadron, Wg Cdr De Lart and his crew were actually killed when their aircraft crashed on the airfield. I think the last one to be flying was Sgt John Oates, who managed an amazing piece of manoeuvring, dodging the fighters and so on down below roof level in Denmark for about 20min, but he was riddled with bullets and eventually had to put the thing down in a field, which broke his back, and he has been a paraplegic for the last fifty-odd years. Still, he is a wonderful chap with a wonderful spirit. Anyway, there it was, twenty of our young people were dead that day and the rest, thirteen of us had survived, of whom John Oates was the most grievously wounded with his broken back.

Including the 82 Squadron losses on 13 August 1940, seventy-eight Blenheims from 2 Group were lost on operations during Britain's 'Finest Hour' (July to September 1940), in their determined effort to hamper the German invasion plans, plus dozens of Coastal Command Blenheims. 53 Squadron, for example, lost seventeen aircraft between mid July and the end of October 1940. Flt Lt Dick Maydwell, Flight Commander in 53 Squadron recalls:

During July and August 1940, the squadron flew a large number of low-level daylight cross-over patrols fairly close to the Dutch coast to ensure that enemy forces could be located and attacked in the North Sea. On 13 August I was returning from one of these patrols near

Holland and had just crossed the coast of Kent at 200ft, when I saw large clouds of black smoke rising from the direction of Detling. The closer I flew towards the airfield the more obvious it became that it had been bombed by the Luftwaffe. When I flew overhead all the squadron Blenheims in dispersal were in flames and the concrete Operations Room had been completely destroyed. The enemy raid was carried out by twenty Stukas and twelve Me 109s. I was lucky not to have been shot down myself. If I had flown over the coast two minutes earlier I should have met the returning Me 109s head-on, and that would have been certain death.

Indeed, five Blenheims were destroyed at Detling after being set on fire by incendiary machine-gun fire, causing their bomb loads to explode, and two more were severely damaged. Nine squadron personnel were killed and ten injured. Still, despite the widespread damage and disrupted communications, Detling was operational again before 'Eagle Day' was over.

Raids on the Invasion Barges

With the real threat of invasion, attacks on barges and shipping in Holland, Belgium and France and reconnaissance of the German invasion forces assembling in

these regions was given high priority by mid July. Using cloud cover and under cover of darkness, the main task of the hard-pressed Blenheim squadrons of Coastal and 2 Group Bomber Command became the bombing of the growing accumulation of invasion barges in the Channel ports. One of the young 2 Group aircrew who was in the thick of the action during the 'Battle of the Barges' was Sgt W.Op/AG Mike Henry. He was posted to 110 Squadron on 19 August 1940 at Wattisham, in the crew of Flg Off Powell (pilot), and Sgt Richmond, observer:

Our first three operations were St Omer (23 August); Deauville (27th) and Emden on the 30th. It was after this overture to the Battle of Britain that we began to pulverize the gathering invasion fleet of barges in the Channel ports: Calais, Dunkirk, Boulogne, Ostend and Antwerp.

On the night of 7/8 September, the crew bus dropped us off at our aircraft. 'Sandy' made his way up the port wing and into the cockpit, closely followed by 'Rich'. I heaved myself up to the hatch, just behind the turret, and lowered myself into the body of the aircraft. Packing my parachute, signals satchel and thermos, I waited at the open hatch for the ground crew to hand me the pitot head cover and the undercarriage links. The former, if not removed, would prevent the airspeed indicator from registering. The links prevented the undercarriage from being retracted – neither desirable.

I slammed the hatch cover and crawled into the confines of my turret. Plugging into the intercom system, I told the pilot that the pitot cover and links were stowed. He answered, 'Thanks, all OK in the back?' 'Yes sir, intercom OK.' 'What about you Rich?' 'Fine, can hear you both. Your first course is 064 magnetic.'

Taxi-ing out to the flarepath, the usual butterfly feeling began to stir in my stomach. Although the target was on the French coast, which meant that we had no long overland journey, we thought of the warning given at briefing, that light flak at the height we were going to bomb from (between 6,000 and 8,000ft) would be at its most lethal. We were soon to find out what the night sky over Dunkirk would look like.

A green light from the Aldis lamp cleared us for take-off. Bumping over the uneven turf, we set course for the Suffolk coast. In my back-to-the-engine position, I saw the single line of flares disappear into the haze. Our route took us across the coast north of Ipswich and Harwich and their attendant balloon barrages. Eventually we turned due south towards France. The

The face of the enemy. These fighter pilots of 5/JG77 claimed eleven Blenheims of 82 Squadron destroyed in the one-sided air battle over Aalborg between 12.15 and 12.25hr. From the left: Oblt Friedrich (St.Kpt. 5/JG77, who led the action, two claims); Gefr Esser (one claim); Gefr Brunsmann (no claim); Fw Petermann (three claims); Uffz Fröse (one claim); Uffz Schmidt (two claims); and Uffz Eissler (two claims). Not included in this picture is Fw Menge (5/JG77), who claimed four Blenheims shot down. After careful examination of the combat reports, eyewitness accounts and the wrecks of the Blenheims littering the countryside around Aalborg, the pilots of 5/JG77 were credited with six Blenheims destroyed. The flak defences were credited with the remaining five. Heinrich Brunsmann, via Jorn Junker

18 Squadron 'B' Flight aircrew at West Raynham, 1 August 1940. Sqn Ldr Maxwell, Flight Commander is seated in the centre of the photograph; he later rose to AVM rank. Note the spinners on the Blenheim's propellors, which were fitted as an experiment to try and improve the aircraft's performance. This was no success and the experiment was not extended. John Douch

Dunkirk episode came to mind as we approached those very beaches. Swivelling my turret and looking forward I could see the searchlights clawing the sky – one or two master searchlights standing out in contrast, their vivid blue fingers seeking a target. There were other aircraft ahead of us, this becoming obvious when a fierce barrage of light flak joined the searchlights. As we approached this fearsome scene, I felt a mixture of excitement and fear and my imagination began to build frightening pictures until, looking down when finally over target, I became fascinated to watch the flashes from gun batteries – wondering whether they were aimed at us and had they got the right height. Colourful tracer and flaming onions, the latter levelling out at about our altitude and then exploding one by one. The streams of tracer coming from many points and forming a cone nearby was quite terrifying, although when it left the ground it seemed so slow and its wavy trajectory whipped by at its true velocity. We were over the target only a short while, but it seemed an age before we got rid of our bomb load and turned towards the

coast and home. How anybody could survive in that ferocious showing of defence was my uppermost thought – to be repeated every time we bombed a similar target. However, on landing at base we looked all over the aircraft for signs of damage – not a scratch!

On our way back from Dunkirk, I noticed an ominous glow in the west, from the direction of London, my home town. At first I thought it might be the moon, but the BBC told us that the blitzkrieg was replacing the dogfights over Kent and the home counties. The Battle of Britain had been joined by the Battle of London.

The next night (8/9 September), Ostend and Boulogne docks were bombed, but the attackers paid a heavy price. Five Blenheims (of 40, 101 and 107 Squadrons, with all fifteen aircrew perishing) and two Wellingtons of 149 Squadron fell victim to the ferocious flak defences. Mike Henry continues:

On 9 September we were briefed to straddle the

dock area of Boulogne with our bomb load. I was flying with another crew just for that night. We took off at 19.00 and received the usual reception. The same fascination and fear seeped through my bones. But, again, we came out of that hellish cauldron without a scratch. On these operations enemy fighters fought clear of their own defences, therefore I sat there without recourse to my machine-gun. Mark you, my eyes were everywhere, with furtive glances at the parachute stowage. Also, radio silence was the order of the night until we reached the East Anglian coast, when we had to get a bearing before crossing it. We had lost one or two aircraft which mistakenly flew up the Thames Estuary and were lost to balloon barrages.

On the 11th, back with my regular crew, we took off for Calais. This target didn't differ in reception to Dunkirk or Boulogne. It was Calais again on the 14th when our take-off was moved from late evening to early morning – this time we got off the deck at 04.15. We were wrong to assume that the Germans manning the defences were sleeping, for there came up millions worth of Reichsmarks in ammunition, and the candle-power must have consumed a few million kilowatts.

On the 16th, at 04.00, we took off for Dunkirk. As a matter of interest, the Calais return trip took a little over two hours, while

Plt Off Leonard Joseph 'Paul' Dejace, an experienced pilot who amassed some 3,000 flying hours, both as an airline pilot and in the Belgian Air Force during the 1930s, posing with his fighter Blenheim of 236 Squadron at St. Eval on 25 August 1940. Dejace was one of several Belgian escapee pilots who flew with 236 Squadron from August 1940 onwards. He was killed in action during a meteorological reconnaissance over Norway on 26 July 1942, aged thirty-three. Gerry Holder

Boulogne was over three hours, and the Dunkirk about the same as Calais. So we didn't lose too much beauty sleep.

Unknown to Henry at the time, he had participated in an outstandingly successful raid on the harbour of Dunkirk in the early hours of 16 September. Under a full moon, twenty-six barges were sunk or badly damaged with a further fifty-eight being lightly damaged. Additionally, 500 tons of ammunition were blown up. Sgt Henry continues his story:

The next on the Channel port 'milk run' was to Boulogne on 18 September (three days after the official climax of the Battle of Britain). The sky over the port was a repeat performance of German anger, if anything a little brighter (contrary to popular belief, one couldn't hear much against the noise of our two engines – except for a very close heavy AA shell burst). Nearly a year later, still in a Blenheim turret, I was part of a daylight 'circus' over Boulogne – we had the comfort of six squadrons of Spitfires and Hurricanes as escort. This operation differed in that the sky was littered with hundreds of dirty black smudges without any useless searchlights. It made a change!

Moving into October 1940, our targets were

still on the Channel coast. On the night of 7th/8th, I was flying with a different crew –'Sandy' Powell had been promoted and posted to Boscombe Down for test pilot's duties. My new pilot was a Flt Lt Lyon (who hadn't tasted enemy aggression). He lifted me off the ground at midnight, and with four 250lb HE bombs in the belly of Blenheim IV L9310, we set course for Boulogne.

Over the target at a not very amusing height (6,000–8,000ft) for light flak, we flew through a frightening storm of 'pyrotechnics' which seemed innocuous when leaving the gun barrels far below, but demonstrated their lethal velocity when arriving at and passing by the aircraft. We came through unscathed – the age of miracles hadn't passed – and, turning on to a course for home, left behind the searchlights and flak storm. Exhilaration followed but vigilance remained for the W.Op/AG because fighters on night-intruder patrols were a potential hazard, especially in the airfield areas.

With permission to approach the glim path (gooseneck paraffin flares) and land, I looked forward from the turret and saw the flarepath ahead and, with still some distance to go, noticed that the angle of glide indicator was showing red. We were too low, and in the surrounding darkness I could just discern trees whipping by beneath us. The pilot, who by this time was obviously not an experienced night-flying type, switched on the port wing light and crossed the boundary without hitting any trees. But the aircraft wasn't lined up with the flarepath. He opened up to go round again but

made no attempt to climb out; we crossed the flares at nought feet which prompted my fervent prayer that he wouldn't retract the flaps. So many crews had been killed when their aircraft hit various obstructions – lifting flaps at below 500ft was potentially fatal as an aircraft sinks when 'cleaning up', and at that time we were about 25ft, if that. However, I sensed impending disaster as he was still skimming the grass; was he heading for the hangars or woods at the far side of the airfield? Before that threat materialized the port wing started to drop – he was turning too low. The wing hit the ground and the aircraft was thrown on its back and with a horrible sound of screeching metal the fuselage came to a stop.

Silence. It had become lighter, the reason becoming horrifyingly clear as flames were licking their way down the twisted remains of the fuselage. Through the turret Perspex I saw bits and pieces of wreckage burning outside my 'prison'. I was trapped. The ladder was wedged across my back, preventing any exit through the camera hatch (the main hatch being on the ground). There was no way out aft. My immediate thought was, 'The only chance I've got is for somebody to start cutting from the outside – but pretty damn quickly.'

Looking around to my left I saw a jagged hole in the fuselage side. It was big enough for my head to go through. Through it I went, and with strength lent by desperation I braced my feet on the fuselage side and pushed. A gallon of Guinness wouldn't have bettered my efforts. My shoulders were, fortunately, protected by a thick

53 Squadron Blenheim IV at Detling, September 1940, with, from the left: Sgt Doug Smart (observer, killed on D-Day), Plt Off Dick Muspratt (pilot) and Sgt Reg Cole (W.Op/AG). Dick Muspratt

Irvin jacket and parachute harness webbing. The metal skin gave and after wriggling furiously, I fell out into the night air which was lit by the raging fire.

I saw two men running towards me: the duty medical officer and one of the ambulance crew (they and the fire crew were on the spot very smartly and went about their work without thought for their personal safety), grabbed me by the arms and hurried me towards the gaping doors of the ambulance. At any moment the fuel tanks would explode and throw their blazing contents in all directions, as would the oxygen bottles and the ammunition. Before getting into the 'blood wagon' I noticed the pilot staggering from one side of the blazing wreckage and the navigator from the other side. They had both been thrown clear from the front section; both had bloody faces, but they were alive and on their feet. The ambulance moved off quickly and, as we pulled away, we heard the bang and whine of an oxygen bottle getting airborne; my ammunition started to go off in fits and starts. 'Keep your heads down', said the MO. As we drew further away from the airfield, silence returned, broken only by the soft purring of the Albion engine.

Sgt Henry was shepherded into sick quarters, while his crew were taken to a civil hospital in Ipswich. Henry was lucky to get away with only a deep cut on the back of his head and a torn thigh which he had picked up when squeezing through the jagged hole in the fuselage. He concludes:

Just four nights after the crash I sat in the turret of Blenheim IV T2253 with my fourth operational pilot. Destination Boulogne! We took off at 18.30 and landed, after the usual reception from below, at 21.00, in time for a few nerve-calming drinks in the mess before going to bed.

Our trips to the Channel ports came to an end: apart from one night-intruder operation over France, we began to turn our aircraft's nose towards Germany. So that short interlude of colourful enemy aggression over the French Channel ports came to an end. The threatened invasion was called off and we reverted to other targets. I must add that, while we survived those hectic nights over Dunkirk, Calais and Boulogne, we weren't at all sorry to climb higher into the night sky and just remain prey to the heavier flak.

Notwithstanding the at times heavy losses among the Blenheims and their colleagues in Wellingtons, Whitleys, Hampdens and even the Fairey Battles that were thrown into the Battle of the Barges, their crews at least had the satisfaction of inflicting serious damage on the assembled German invasion fleet during September. By the 21st the incessant pounding had put twelve transport ships, four tugs, and fifty-one barges out of action. A further nine transport vessels, one tug and 163 barges were damaged. One week later, 214 out of the assembled fleet of 1,918 converted Rhine barges had been temporarily or permanently put out of commission, a serious loss of some 12 per cent. This undoubtedly contributed to Hitler's decision to break off the invasion preparations on 12 October.

Night Fighting

Great Britain had no specialized night-fighter units on strength when hostilities began. To fill this gap in the early months of the war eight squadrons of Blenheim IF fighters (Nos. 23, 25, 29, 145, 219, 600, 601 and 604) were assigned to night-fighting duties. These fighter Blenheim aircraft were converted Mk I bombers, fitted with an underbelly gun pack of four Brownings and with their bomb doors sealed. Following intensive night-flying training, the units were employed in night and North Sea patrols and convoy escort duties. 25 and 601 Squadrons had the distinction of

TR-J of 59 Squadron 'A' Flight at Thorney Island, October 1940. Alec McCurdy

being the first RAF fighter units to undertake an offensive sortie over German territory when twelve crews, led by Sqn Ldr J.R. Halling-Pott (OC, 25 Squadron) in L1437, struck at the seaplane base on Borkum island on 28 November 1939. At 15.25hr all Blenheim IFs attacked the base out of a rainstorm, blasting away at seaplanes and buildings with their front guns. As many as 3,622 rounds were expended, wounding two Germans and damaging three aircraft, a few hangars and administration buildings. All the British aircraft returned safely to Debden at 17.50hr. Soon after this episode 601 Squadron converted to the Hawker Hurricane, just as did 145 Squadron.

At this time night fighting still largely relied on the old formula of intercepting enemy aircraft with the aid of the 'eyeball Mark One' in moonlight conditions or in co-operation with searchlights. But by 1935 various successful experiments had already been conducted in Britain on the detection and location of aircraft by radio direction finding (RDF). These led to the development of both ground and airborne radar sets over the following years. 25 Squadron broke new ground in August 1939 when it received four Mk IF Blenheims with mysterious, black metal boxes containing AI radar sets fitted amidships in the aircrafts' fuselages. A handful of fighter Blenheims (both Mk IFs and IVFs) of 604 Squadron, the Fighter Interception Unit (FIU, at Tangmere) and the Special Duty Flight (SDF, at Martlesham Heath) were soon after also equipped with the top-secret airborne radar, which was clearly recognizable by the aerials projecting from the aircrafts' wings and nose. Specialists were added to the crews to operate the sets.

The radar-directed night fighting trials that followed, often carried out in co-operation with radar stations on the ground, were very much a trial and error affair. The first and eagerly awaited success finally came for Flt Lt Christopher D.S. Smith, DFC of the SDF, who was successfully guided by the CH radar station at Bawdsey towards an He 111 in daylight over the North Sea around noon on 12 May 1940. Smith shot down the bomber into the sea off the Hook of Holland, but was injured by return fire and only just managed to nurse his burning Blenheim IVF P4834 back to base.

A few months later, on the night of 23 July, a Dornier Do 17Z of 2/KG3 was

Sgt Mike Henry, W.Op/AG with Blenheim SR-R of 101 Squadron at Wattisham, winter 1940. Mike Henry

plotted by the CH radar at Poling and Fg Off Ashfield, flying a Blenheim IF of the FIU, was guided on to an interception course. His radar operator, Sgt R.H. Leyland, succeeded in picking up the enemy bomber on his Mk IV AI set which, in fact, was one of the first of these improved sets delivered to the RAF. With the aid of the crew's observer, Plt Off G.E. Morris, Ashfield lined his Blenheim up on the bomber and poured a ten-second burst of machine-gun fire into the fuel tanks of the Dornier, which plunged in flames into the Channel south of Brighton. This historic feat of arms was the herald of a revolution in air combat at night and in bad weather which was to take place in the coming war years. AI radar had finally demonstrated its potential.

Yet many a frustrating and fruitless sortie would follow, with fighter Blenheim crews groping around in the darkness and with operators cursing away at their rudimentary and unreliable AI sets, without being able to get at the Luftwaffe bombers 'blitzing' London and other major cities during the second half of the Battle of Britain. Nevertheless, many valuable lessons on the techniques and tactics of night fighting were learnt during these months, and the Blenheim crews worked

hard to come to terms with the difficulties of night interception. This is clearly illustrated by the story of Plt Off Noel 'Paddy' Corry, who finished fighter pilot training during the battle of Dunkirk before joining 25 Squadron:

There was too little time for anything. Wg Cdr 'Bull' Halahan and Sqn Ldr Walker had been brought home from No.1 Squadron in France to start up No.5 OTU at Aston Down. It was a Fighter OTU, but there were not enough Spitfires for every pupil, so some of us had to make do with Blenheim Mk I fighters. 'Jock', my close pal on the training course, got a Spitfire and I got a Blenheim. (There was no appeal, it was simply a matter of arithmetic, but of great consequence for our careers.)

After just over two weeks, Jock and I parted company; he to No.19 Squadron on 'Spits' and me to No.25 Squadron on Blenheims, as fully operational pilots and ready for battle, we thought (but boy, were we green!). No.25 Squadron, 11 Group, Fighter Command, was split in two, with 'A' Flight at Martlesham Heath and 'B' Flight at North Weald. It was principally a night-fighter squadron, but when I joined 'A' Flight, 25 (F) Squadron, at Martlesham Heath on 26 June, I had not flown a Blenheim at night.

When I joined the squadron not all of the air-

"BRISTOL BLENHEIMS" RAID AN ENEMY SEAPLANE BASE AT BORKUM.
REPRODUCED BY PERMISSION OF THE BRISTOL AEROPLANE CO. LTD.

Borkum seaplane base under attack. This impression was probably drawn after the Borkum raid by 25 and 601 Squadrons on 28 November 1939. Rodney Armstrong

craft were fitted with serviceable AI sets and many of the set operators were specially trained 'lowly' Aircraft Hands, not even Leading Aircraft Hands. Indeed, a few operators were still in civilian clothes – which must have created headaches for the Admin. staff in the event of a fatality.

On a number of occasions as early as July 1940, I flew on 'RDF trials' – a cover title for the work being done at that time, in secrecy, on the development of radar. I did training AI flights in daylight on three occasions in July (5th, 22nd and 29th), on four occasions in August (3rd, 14th, 22nd and 26th), and used AI on defensive patrols on two occasions in August (28th and 30th), but without success. After the night patrol on the 30th, using AI, I did a second patrol that night without an AI operator (3hr 55min in all).

We had, of course, much work to do other than on AI development and training, for instance, on Army and Navy Anti-Aircraft Co-operation and calibration work, and convoy patrols off the east coast because our duration/range far exceeded that of the single-engined fighters. It was on a convoy patrol of 2-hr duration on 10 July that I had my first combat with a Luftwaffe fighter, the pilot of which must have been as green as I was, otherwise I would have been a dead duck!

600 Squadron received its first Blenheim IVFs equipped with AI sets in November 1939, and these were detached to Manston in an unsuccessful attempt to catch Heinkel He 59 and He 115 seaplanes of KüFlGr 106 and 906 mining the Thames Estuary. First contact with the enemy came for the Squadron in the early hours of 10 May 1940, when Plt Off Anderson was vectored across the Channel, encountering two He 111s and attacking one without visible results. He returned to base with his hydraulics shot away. Later the same day, Anderson and his 'B' Flight found their Waterloo over Waalhaven airfield in Holland (see Chapter 4). 600 Squadron was further employed in night-fighting operations, but had a frustrating time during the Battle of Britain with only one He 111 probably destroyed.

604 Squadron met no enemy aircraft during its first eight months of operating the Blenheim IF at night. The squadron's first action came in daylight, when six crews destroyed seven Ju 52s on Scheveningen beach in Holland on the late afternoon of 10 May. The Dunkirk beaches were patrolled during the evacuation of the BEF, and then finally the unit

was lucky on the night of 18 June. While patrolling over northern France, Fg Off Alistair Hunter and his gunner Sgt 'Tommy' Thomas encountered an He 115 seaplane with its navigation lights on and shot it down into the sea off Calais. While the new AI sets and aerials were installed and tested during daytime, day and night patrols off the south coast continued. During one of these, on 11 August, two crews found an He 59 (of the air–sea rescue flight based at Cherbourg) on the water some 30 miles off the French coast. It was quickly sunk, the German crew escaping unhurt.

23 Squadron opened its score on 18/19 June 1940, when seven crews were dispatched on interception patrols. Plt Off Duke-Woolley, on patrol near King's Lynn in YP-L, pursued an He 111 which had only minutes previously shot Sgt Close's L1458 YP-S down in flames. Duke-Woolley revenged the loss of his colleague by sending the Heinkel down in flames into the sea at Blakeney Creek, Cley in Norfolk after prolonged combat. Later that night, Sqn Ldr O'Brien shot down a second He 111 near Newmarket; but his L8687 YP-X was badly hit by return fire and fell in an uncontrollable spin. O'Brien managed to bale out safely, but his radar operator Plt Off King-Clark jumped into the starboard airscrew and was killed. Cpl Little, the crew's gunner perished in the crash.

On the same night 29 Squadron had its first taste of success with an He 111 destroyed by Plt Off John Barnwell in L6636. However, Barnwell, one of the sons of the designer of the Blenheim (who had himself been killed in a flying accident a few years previously), was probably hit by return fire and failed to return. His parachute was picked up from the sea on the following day. Plt Off Dave Humphries in L1375 had an indecisive combat with an He 111 over Bury St. Edmunds, the adversaries departing with their aircraft damaged. During August the unit added an He 111 H-3 of II/KG53 to its tally on the night of the 17/18th. After a GCI-controlled chase of nearly two hours, Plt Off Rhodes in L6741 finally got within range of the 'bandit' and expended all his front gun ammunition into the aircraft from a range of 400yd. His gunner, Sgt 'Sticks' Gregory emptied another pan of ammunition into the slowly circling Heinkel and saw it land gently on the water ten miles west of Cromer Knoll.

Sir Samuel Hoare, Secretary of State for Air, accompanied by AVM Welsh, about to shake hands with Fg Off John Cunningham during a 604 Squadron AAF parade at Northolt, April 1940. 'Cat's Eyes' Cunningham flew Blenheim night fighters for about a year, before converting to the Beaufighter and later the Mosquito and gaining national fame as a night-fighter pilot with 20 kills. 604 Squadron Assocation

Among the six-man crew killed by their combined gun fire was Maj Tamm, CO of this Gruppe: a fat scalp for 29 Squadron. Rhodes was killed in action only one week later. The combined gunfire of Plt Off John 'Bob' Braham and his W.Op/AG Sgt Wilsden destroyed another Luftwaffe bomber, this time a searchlight-coned He 111P of III/KG55 over the Humber at 01.30hr on 24 August. Braham was destined to become the RAF's most decorated fighter pilot with twenty confirmed night and nine daytime victories in the war.

Crews of another Blenheim night-fighter unit, No. 219 Squadron, were thrown into the heavy day battles in the south during August. The squadron had its finest hour on the 15th, when its crews were scrambled to intercept a large enemy raid just after noon. Sgt F.G. Nightingale probably destroyed a Ju 88 in a large formation at around 13.30hr, but he was forced to break off his stern chase on account of being fired at by first a Blenheim and then by three Spitfires. The last he saw of his opponent was its front gunner trying to beat out the flames in the Junkers' starboard wing and engine with his hands. Flt Lt H.G. Goddard damaged one Do 17 from a formation of four around the same time. Sgt Dupee in L8698 fared

quite differently: he was seriously wounded in the right arm by return fire while intercepting the enemy raid. With the assistance of his gunner Sgt Banister, he brought the machine back from over the sea, force-landing at Driffield. Both men received the DFM for their brave action.

Due to its somewhat similar appearance, the Blenheim IF was at times mistaken for the Ju 88 during daylight operations by friendly fighter aircraft, which led to a number of tragic encounters. 235 Squadron from Thorney Island, for example, lost T1804 when it was shot down (Plt Off D.N. Woodger and Sgt D.L. Wright both being killed) and Z5730 was badly damaged, when a vic of three were bounced near Portsmouth by 1 Squadron Hurricanes at 17.05hr on 24 August. This unfortunate incident was repeated on 3 September when three 25 Squadron aircraft, while carrying out 'X' raid patrols over North Weald, were attacked out of the sun by Hurricanes of 46 Squadron. Two Blenheim IFs were shot down by pilots claiming them as Ju 88s. The pilot of one aircraft, Plt Off D.W. Hogg, died at the controls, his aircraft crashing one mile away from North Weald, but luckily the three other crew members escaped unhurt. However, the following night 25

Sgt Harry Stewart manning the Vickers 'K' gun in his fighter Blenheim of 236 Squadron at Aldergrove, September 1940. Harry Stewart

Squadron drew first blood. Three crews were scrambled to intercept a force of some eighty He 111s and Do 17s heading for Liverpool. Plt Off Noel Corry had an uneventful flight, but his two colleagues fared quite differently. Plt Off Bernard Rolfe sighted a bomber and went into the attack, but, on opening fire, his Blenheim was hit in the tail by friendly ack ack, causing it to spin twice, and Rolfe only just managed to nurse his crippled aircraft back to base. The third night-fighter crew had more luck: Plt Off Mike Herrick and Sgt Pugh in ZK-J intercepted and destroyed an He 111 H-3 V4+AB of Stab I/KG1 at 02.15hr, Maj Maier and his four-man crew all perishing. Thirty minutes later, Plt Off Herrick came across a second He 111; this was 1H+AM of 4/KG26, which was also sent down in flames with Fw Ewerts and his crew posted missing. Herrick went on

to bag a third Heinkel on 14 September and was awarded the DFC. Plt Off Corry continues:

In September and October, when business involving night patrols was indeed brisk, I did not carry AI operators in my aircraft – it seems that training with the AI sets had to give way to the old fashioned 'use your bloody eyes'. The additional weight of the early AI set and the AI operator affected the operational performance of the aircraft and reduced the service ceiling (up where the enemy aircraft were known to operate) to a significant extent: alas the poor, old, tired Blenheim!

When the Luftwaffe switched their raids from the airfields to the City of London, we flew our hearts out in the inadequate Blenheims, desperately trying to close with the enemy aircraft at night. We could see London ablaze – the AA concentrations and the searchlight cones: they

rarely coincided – indeed, there were times when I was so angry at what I saw that, ignoring courses and heights given over the R/T, I flew into the airspace between the AA bursts and searchlight cones, cursing with rage, in the forlorn hope that I would come upon a hostile aircraft in there somewhere.

As winter with its bad weather drew nigh, I felt that the generators in the Blenheims were hard pressed to cope with the demand for electricity for their pitot-head heating, R/T, etc., and often one found the pitot-head icing up and the R/T petering out. This could leave one in heavy cloud at night with no contact with the ground and no airspeed indicator… This situation was not helped by the extra drain on the electrics imposed by the AI sets. If the generator failed to cope and the batteries went flat, the intercommunication system packed up: this meant getting the gunner to squeeze his way up forward to the cockpit with his parachute in

Plt Off Noel 'Paddy' Corry at the controls of his 25 Squadron fighter Blenheim. Noel Corry

case it became necessary to bale out.

Then it all happened: 25 Squadron got its first kill at night. On 4 September 1940, a pal of mine, Mike Herrick, flying in a Blenheim with Sgt Pugh as gunner, intercepted and destroyed an He 111 at 02.15hr. Thirty minutes later, on the way home to base, they destroyed another Heinkel. As far as I know, no airborne AI was employed and this contact in each case was pure chance. Mike suddenly found himself right up the backside of a big fat Heinkel (as a result of guidance from the ground controller) and did everything just about right. Then, on his way home, he nearly collided with a second Heinkel – which fell to pieces after a burst fired at less than 30yd. I believe it was the first of the two enemy aircraft which gave Mike a bad time; during his attack Mike's windscreen was shattered and he had Perspex debris in his eyes – which made his second visual contact and attack all the more remarkable. I was airborne at the same time as Mike that night on a three-hour defensive patrol, but without success.

When we landed back 'on' and had supper, we decided to seek the crash site of one of Mike's Heinkels. It turned out to be the first of his kills and we were rooting about on the scene of the crash looking for a souvenir for Mike to take home to New Zealand (Mike had a grandiose idea of mounting a souvenir machine-gun on a tripod on either side of the entrance to the family homestead, similar to the old Civil

War cannons at the entrances to homes in the USA), when someone let out a cry of alarm, the urgency of which took us away from the scene like scalded cats. The bloke concerned had found himself standing in smouldering wreckage amidst a stack of hot, German, potato-masher hand grenades. This explained Mike's shattered windscreen – when attacked the upper gunner in the Heinkel tossed out the hand-grenades. This information was, of course, passed immediately to the 'powers' at 11 Group HQ. Mike didn't get his guns – but he did get a well-earned, immediate DFC for his night's work, which did wonders for the morale of the Squadron. Sadly, after an illustrious career during which he went on to serve in the Pacific with the Yanks before returning to Great Britain to fly Mosquitos, Mike was shot down during a two-plane sweep over Denmark on 16 June 1944 by an Fw 190. Mike and his observer baled out but were too low to survive.

Since operational results with night-fighter Blenheims continued to remain disappointing, 25, 29, 219, 600 and 604 Squadrons began converting on to the Bristol Beaufighter by September, although 25, 600 and 604 Squadrons still operated a few Blenheims, with their gun turrets taken out, into early 1941. 23 Squadron received its first Douglas Havocs in October 1940. Though the actual number of enemy aircraft destroyed by the night-hunting Blenheims may have been

small, their great merit was pioneering the radar-guided, night-fighting techniques. Through trial and error, they sowed the seeds which the better-equipped Beaufighter, Havoc and Mosquito crews could later harvest. Plt Off Noel Corry concludes:

While all the pilots in the squadron hoped that AI would prove successful, I think it is true to say that by September, when we got our first Beaufighter from Bristol, we felt that the old experimental sets fitted to the Blenheims had probably had their day. The new Beaufighter, as a purpose-designed night-fighter with new improved AI sets, the Mk IV, and with much heavier armament, four 20mm cannon and six .303 Brownings, had caught our imagination. We took quickly to the Beaus – provided you treated it with great respect at low altitude (no steep turns on take-off). We came to appreciate the great power of the two Hercules engines and the great punch of the four cannon and six machine-guns. It was to become a great fighting machine. The first operational patrol in a Beaufighter was flown by 25 Squadron on 10 October 1940 and the first Beaufighter victory came about mid November. In the spring of 1941, 25 Squadron really got going with the Beaus (too late for me – I was posted away to Special Duties at the end of January) and, having eliminated many of the 'bugs' from the new AI sets installed in the Beaus, they began to claw the enemy bombers out of the sky.

Night-fighting pioneer: Plt Off Don Anderson, pilot with 29 Squadron, boarding his fighter Blenheim at K3, a satellite to Wittering, for a night patrol during September 1940. Don Anderson

CHAPTER SIX

Shiphunters, Circuses and Fringe Raiders, March–June 1941

R3594 of 114 Squadron crashed at Catton Deer Park, Norwich while returning from a Cologne raid on 27/28 November 1940. The Blenheim was on its landing approach to Horsham St. Faith when it flew into a tree, due to faulty readings of the pilot's altimeter and ice forming on his windscreen. Incredibly, Sgts Waigh and Rook in the completely smashed up cockpit section, and Sgt Murray in the gun turret survived the crash, although all three men were severely injured. *Dickie Rook*

During the exceptionally cold winter of 1940–41, 2 Group Blenheim units were mainly employed on cloud cover raids by day and the bombing of strategic targets in Germany as part of the Bomber Command Main Force at night. It was a period of retrenchment and of building up the depleted forces following the heavy losses during the Battles of the Low Countries, France and Britain. As a result, losses were relatively light during this period; in the six months between October 1940 and March 1941 2 Group's operational losses amounted to only twenty-six Blenheims. A further forty-nine were written off during training flights and in crashes and accidents in the United Kingdom.

Guy Avery's Story

During this period, Plt Off Guy Avery served as a pilot in 139 Squadron, and tells of a new type of operation which was devised for the Blenheim crews:

It was in January 1941, when the Blenheims were put on to daylight formation raids on the Channel ports. In a formation raid on Boulogne on 2 February, I was flying as No. 2 to Hughie Edwards (on his right). I remember him as a Flight Lieutenant when I first joined 139. He had a slight limp due to having injured his leg when baling out of a Blenheim. On this raid our six Blenheims set course at 16,000ft over Dungeness, for Boulogne. We dropped our bombs in

unison, having met no opposition. Then, as we turned for home – and even with the French coast left two miles behind, a very heavy and accurate barrage of flak was directed at us: four black puffs to the left, four to the right, four behind, four in front. Then 'wumpth'! My Blenheim was hit and bucked like a bronco (I had first seen No. 3 [Sgt Farmer's Blenheim] dive down, and I thought they had got him), and I thought the bottom of our Blenheim had been blown off. I found we were alone over the Channel, and wonder to this day why we were not picked off by some German fighter. Due to the coolness of my air gunner (who had a rear view), he guided me back to the formation, which was behind and above us a little. I had to throttle back, ask to rejoin on the R/T ('Come in, Red 2', said Hughie), and climb gratefully back to the formation. We got back to Norwich at 8,000ft, in broken, sunny cloud, formed echelon, and landed in turn. Later, when I saw my Blenheim in the hangar for repair, there was a hole one inch in diameter just a foot behind Ron Dews's turret, and small perforations at each wing-tip. Sgt Farmer had also got away with it, and returned with us.

This type of operation developed into the so-called 'Circus' raids, the first being carried out on 10 January 1941. Six crews of 114 Squadron, heavily escorted by Fighter Command, bombed an ammunition dump in the Forêt de Guines, south of Calais without loss. The main purpose of these 'circuses' was to lure German fighters into battle with the escorting Hurricanes and Spitfires, with a small formation of Blenheims acting as 'bait'. A second reason to mount these operations was to prevent the Luftwaffe from renewing daylight bomber and fighter-bomber attacks on Britain, by raiding their airfields. The first circus was followed by three similar raids in early February against the Boulogne docks, the snow-covered airfield of St. Omer and the docks of Dunkirk. It was an auspicious start to the circus campaign: all the targets were hit, no bombers were lost,

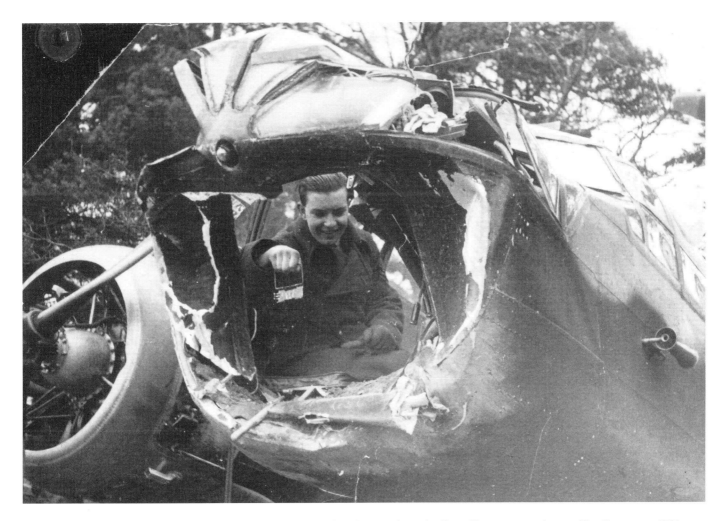

'T' for Trixie of 21 Squadron overshot on landing at Watton on return from a raid on Hannover on 23/24 March 1941, and had its nose crushed in. The crew's W.Op/AG, Sgt Bonnett, is seen inspecting the damage. Tommy Mann

and on all occasions the German fighters had risen to the challenge. These first four raids would be followed over the next ten months by another 106 circus operations, with Blenheims from both 2 Group and Coastal Command being involved. The majority of these raids, however, were carried out during the second half of 1941, as another offensive task received absolute priority in March.

The War at Sea

By early 1941 the strategic situation for Great Britain looked bleak indeed. Although the RAF had emerged as the victor in the Battle of Britain, the country's armed forces were still fighting with their backs against the wall. In a renewed attempt to force Britain to its knees, Hitler had launched a blockade during February. His U-Boats, surface raiders and long-range Focke-Wulf Condors threatened to cut off Britain's vital life-lines with the United States. Merchant shipping, loaded

with supplies which were critical to Britain's needs, were sunk in the Atlantic on such an alarming scale that, if allowed to continue unchecked, would in the long run signal certain defeat. By the end of 1940 1,281 British, allied and neutral ships had been sunk, with a total tonnage of 4,745,033. In January 1941 a further 320,240 tons of shipping were sent to the bottom of the Atlantic and 403,393 tons more in February.

Although the Royal Navy tried its best to counter this stranglehold, it clearly could not cope alone. Prime Minister Churchill therefore issued a new directive on 6 March 1941, giving the war at sea absolute priority. Seventeen RAF squadrons were among the units diverted to maritime attack duties, with 2 Group Bomber Command contributing 21, 107 and 139 Squadrons to the force. These were ordered to halt the enemy iron-ore

convoys sailing from Scandinavia to northern Germany and Rotterdam. Over the next four months 18, 82, 88, 110 and 226 Squadrons joined the maritime strike force, bringing the Bomber Command Blenheim anti-shipping strike force up to a strength of some hundred aircraft and crews at the height of the campaign.

Earlier in the year the decision had been made to establish an anti-shipping strike force in Coastal Command consisting of twelve squadrons, equally divided between bomber, torpedo bomber and long-range fighter units. The bomber component of this force consisted of 53, 59 and 114 Squadrons, the last being loaned from 2 Group, and all equipped with Blenheim IVs. The long-range fighter squadrons were Nos. 235, 236, 248 and 254, all equipped with fighter Blenheims and further reinforced by 404 (RCAF) Squadron in July 1941. This force laid the foundation of what in later years grew into the concept of the mighty Beaufighter Strike Wings and the ultimate answer to combat German coastal shipping. Photo-reconnaissance for this Bomber and Coastal Command Blenheim anti-shipping force was provided by No. 1 PRU Spitfires, Hudsons and Blenheims from RAF Benson.

For the purpose of attack the enemy-occupied coastlines were divided into six so-called 'beat' areas (soon extended to fifteen and later to nineteen beats), starting in southern Norway and stretching south to the Bay of Biscay. Blenheims were to patrol these beats at low level for some five minutes or for 20miles, and attack and sink any shipping they encountered, at any cost. The new operations order signalled the start of a maritime daylight campaign that was to prove to be every bit as savage and demanding as that fought in the Low Countries and France during May and June 1940. The big difference was that that campaign had lasted only two months, whereas the anti-shipping campaign was to last four times longer. From Sgt Jim 'Dinty' Moore, W.Op/AG with 18 Squadron in the crew of Sgts George Milson (pilot) and Ron Millar (observer) we learn of the tactics used by the Blenheim crews on shipping strikes.

Jim Moore's Story

On the morning of 27 April we flew south to Chivenor in north Devon to refuel and to patrol a shipping beat off the French coast. At 1.20pm we took off again with five other Blenheims heading south until we reached a point 30miles from the enemy coast where we split up into three pairs to sweep a larger area. We and our partner flew on until close to the coast when we saw the tell-tale smoke of a small convoy of two merchant ships escorted by a patrol boat. There was no hesitation as we headed for our target, each aircraft heading for a different ship, George jinking our kite to present a more difficult target. We remained at nought feet until at the last moment George hauled us up just over the masts of our target while Ron dropped our bombs. As we hurtled over the top of the mast I found I was looking up at the belly of the other Blenheim which had just bombed but, fortunately, we did not collide. We returned to nought feet immediately and I was able to fire several bursts at the unfortunate seamen who, together with the patrol boat, had sent up a terrific concentration of flak through which we

had to pass, but without managing to hit us. As we flew away, looking back I'm afraid I was unable to report any dramatic hits on our targets although it must be remembered that the fuses on our bombs had an 11sec delay. We called in at Chivenor to refuel, after a flight which had taken 3hr 50min, stopping about an hour before flying back to Oulton.

On each shipping patrol you took off with your desire to find a convoy to attack, which you knew would be defended by a murderous curtain of flak, fighting with your natural desire to stay alive. You would fly alone or in company mile after mile over an empty, cruel looking sea searching continuously for an elusive target. If your search was successful, or unsuccessful depending on your point of view, the whole action would be over in a matter of moments. I submit that the manner in which this campaign was carried out, in aircraft ill-suited to the task, showed a high degree of courage and determination on the part of the crews involved.

It might be appropriate to mention that not all aircrew were, due to nerves, able to complete a tour. It wasn't just the operations on which we flew but also the briefings we attended when, after a long wait, the mission was cancelled, all of which affected us in our different ways. There was always a queue for the toilets after a briefing and we used to refer to this as 'operational twitch'. Those unfortunate souls whose nerves

cracked were immediately grounded by an unsympathetic hierarchy on the grounds that they lacked moral fibre, another way of labelling them as cowards. I must emphasize that there were very, very few aircrew who fell into this category.

Len Hunt's Story

Sgt Len Hunt, observer with 59 Squadron, further comments on the start of the Coastal Command maritime campaign:

59 Squadron in 1941 was stationed at Thorney Island near Portsmouth but detached flights to Bircham Newton near King's Lynn and Detling near Maidstone. Bircham Newton was used for recces along the Dutch coast both by day and night, searching for enemy shipping, but although I was involved in some twenty operations of two to three hours' duration there was very little to report.

There appeared to be more action for us further south in the Channel. Operating from Thorney Island and Detling on the south coast we attacked shipping and harbour installations at Calais, Boulogne, Cherbourg, etc. On a few occasions we attacked targets further inland with large fighter escorts, the Blenheims acting as 'bait' to draw up the 109s. Losses, of course, were fairly high at that time, as strikes on shipping

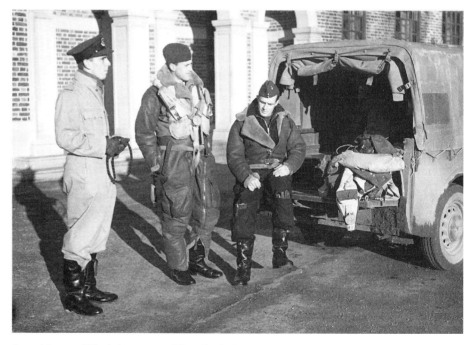

Coastal Command Blenheims were mainly active in the anti-shipping and maritime reconnaissance roles during 1941, both by day and night. Here 59 Squadron aircrew are waiting by the crew bus at Thorney Island to be transported to the dispersal aircraft in early 1941. Left to right: Plt Off H.D. Norton (pilot, taken PoW off the Hook of Holland, 28 April 1941); Plt Off Eric Moore (observer, missing off Katwijk on 23 March 1941 when T2433 was shot down by Oblt Paul Stolte's Bf 109 of 3/JG1); Flt Lt Tony Fry, DFC (missing off the Hook of Holland on 28 April 1941). Alec McCurdy

Cannon-shell riddled TR-A of 59 Squadron rests on its belly at Hawkinge, after the shoot-out with Bf 109s off Calais on 30 March 1941 Len Hunt

were always carried out at very low level with 11sec delay fuses.

I relate one incident in 1941; it may give an idea of the hectic life on a Blenheim squadron in those far-off days. On Sunday afternoon, 30 March 1941, a formation of three Blenheims from 'A' Flight, 59 Squadron based at Thorney Island were briefed to bomb a convoy of enemy ships sighted near Calais. We were airborne at 16.30hr. The promised escort of fighters did not materialize (not unusual in early 1941), so we set off alone across the Channel at low level in tight formation.

The ships were sighted in the reported position and so, unfortunately, were numerous Me.109s, probably from nearby Calais Marck. The attack, however, was pressed home and the bombing carried out, but in the melee that ensued the formation was split up and our aircraft TR-A was singled out for a series of individual attacks by the fighters, Jack Munt our W.Op/AG desperately fighting them off from the turret.

John Griffith, the pilot, put in the emergency 9 boost and turned north for Dover and home.

The attacks continued – cannon shells penetrated the fuselage just below the turret, seriously injuring Jack Munt who was unable to take any further part in the fight. I came back to assist the pilot in keeping the aircraft straight and level – another shell passed between us exploding behind the instrument panel which disappeared in a mass of bits and pieces. I received cannon shell splinters in my left leg and John Griffith a grazing to his right shoulder. Another shell entered the port wing just below the engine which continued to function at full revs.

With Griffith and I exerting all our strength on the control column, the aircraft was kept a few feet above the water and more or less straight and level. We were relieved that both engines on full boost gave no heart-stopping noises but kept running perfectly. However, we were more relieved when halfway across the Channel two Spitfires of 91 Squadron saw our predicament, dropped down and covered our retreat. The welcome cliffs of Dover presented the next problem – most of the controls had been shot away and the aircraft needed to be climbed. This we achieved with brute force and

desperation by Griffith and I both pulling back the column, closing our eyes very tightly and praying hard. The combination of all these methods resulted in TR-A finding itself above green fields – at maximum revs (the plus 9 boost had jammed and it simply was not possible to withdraw it).

One of the Spitfires (W/O Jackie Mann) appeared ahead and directed our Blenheim towards Hawkinge. Without hydraulics and throttle control John Griffith belly-landed the aircraft on the fringe of the airfield. Jack Munt was lifted out through the hatch and sent to hospital in Folkestone – he later recovered but was invalided out. I was treated in Medical Quarters – John Griffith required only repairs to his flying jacket and uniform tunic. Tragically he was posted missing the following year in the Middle East.

Coastal Duties

One day after Sgt Hunt's narrow escape, 2 Group's sphere of daylight operations was extended to the coastal areas of the beat lines. These coastal or 'fringe' attacks were aimed at any German military targets

This fighter Blenheim of 248 Squadron somersaulted on landing at Castleton in early 1941, fortunately without injury to Plt Off Wright and his crew. 248 and 254 Squadrons, both equipped with Blenheim IVFs, were active on coastal patrols off Norway during the first half of 1941. On these long-range patrols aircraft regularly fell victim to the German defences and bad weather: at least nine Blenheim crash locations dating from 1940–41 have been identified in the Bergen area. Ronny Wright

encountered, in the hope that these roaming hit-and-run raiders would force the Germans to disperse their flak and fighter defences. On 31 March 1941, eight crews of 21 Squadron carried out the first fringe raid in the Dutch Frisian Islands area (Beat 9), with much chaos and confusion being created on the islands of Ameland and Terschelling. Sgt Peter A. Adams's R3884 and Plt Off Dennis A. Rogers's R3900 fell to the concentrated gun fire of two Vorpostenboote or flak-ships which were skip-bombed off Texel during the initial phase of the attack. There were no survivors.

Just as during the Battle of Britain, detachments of 2 Group Blenheim units were sent to Scotland for operations off Norway during 1941, usually for a stint of two weeks. An exception to the rule was 114 Squadron, which was loaned to 18 Group, Coastal Command, in early March. Its base was at Thornaby for east coast convoy-escort operations and for reconnaissance and strike operations against enemy shipping off the Norwegian coast. On 19 July the squadron returned to 2 Group for further daylight raids from West Raynham. One of the young aircrew involved in the Norway operations was Sgt Terry Staples, an experienced pilot,

who had served with 114 Squadron from September 1940. He gives a graphic account of one particularly memorable day:

On 18 April 1941 attacks had been made during the day on a convoy off the coast of Norway. As a sergeant pilot I would not have been aware of or closely involved with all that was going on, but I believe orders came through in the afternoon for a further attack to be made by 114 Squadron. I can recall its being said at the time that we had only four sufficiently experienced crews available for this additional attack: they were the Squadron Commander (Wg Cdr Elsmie), the 'A' Flight Commander (Sqn Ldr Robins), Flt Lt Myers and myself. At briefing I was detailed to fly in the No.3 position on the port side of the Wing Commander, who was leading the formation, and that Sqn Ldr Robins would fly in the No.4 position behind the Wing Commander and move into a port echelon position for the attack. From the beginning there was some urgency and everything was hurried to enable us to reach the target in time for a low-level attack to be made in daylight.

We flew at about 2,000ft for most of the way across, and began to lose height when the coast came into sight. The Wing Commander had no difficulty locating the ships, which were at anchor close inshore in a small bay. However, as

we approached the ships and at about the same time as Sqn Ldr Robins began to take up his position on my left, we were intercepted and attacked by Me.110s. Afterwards, my air gunner said that there were five 110s to begin with, and we were told that they came from the German airfield at Stavanger. Sqn Ldr Robins was hit in the first attack as I saw him peel away with an engine on fire. Apart from this and the sight of one of the 110s that came almost abreast of us and very close indeed as it completed its attack, I could not see anything going on astern. There was just the noise of the guns.

As we approached the ships I had to keep close formation for defensive firepower while we were under attack, and then open out for our low-level attack on the ships. At the same time, each of us had to select our target. In the event, there was one ship substantially larger than the others. The Wing Commander had obviously selected this ship as his target. There was no other ship to the left of it that I could have attacked, and so I was committed to attacking it as well. As we came close to the ships, the 110s broke off their attack and I dropped slightly back to avoid colliding as we bombed.

All my attention was taken up now by the ship which was my target, and just before I released my own bombs I saw one or two bombs from the other aircraft splash in the water ahead of me, very close to the side of the ship. We each carried four 250lb bombs fused with an 11sec delay so that the aircraft were clear of the target before they exploded. As soon as I had dropped my bombs I turned to follow the other two air-craft, which had wheeled away to the right and were heading out to sea for the flight back. My No.3 position had somehow been taken up by the other aircraft and I found myself rejoining the formation on the right. About this time the 110s resumed their attack, but they did not come in as close as they had done previously.

I saw one of the enemy aircraft making an attack on the port quarter. Our air gunners were returning fire, but I do not know how successful this was. The Blenheim in the No.3 position must then have been hit because it peeled away to the left and I did not see it again. Shortly after this the Wing Commander suddenly gained height and broke away towards land with a thin trail of smoke coming from his aircraft. As I was now on my own, I was able to turn to see him in the distance, and at the same time to see that there was still one Me.110 astern and firing. As a single aircraft I was able to fly lower than we had been in formation and I reduced my height to just a few feet off the water. As we were primarily a daylight bombing squadron, there had been opportunities to practice low flying in training and I was now glad that I had always

Early victims of the daylight anti-shipping campaign. Sgt W.Op/AG John MacIlwraith, second from right, went missing off the Dutch coast on 10 April 1941. Flt Lt Ralph Tallis, DFC (second from left) and his crew of Sgts Doug Shayler (observer, on left) and Frank Davis (W.Op/AG, on right) were killed during a convoy strike off Sola, Norway on 29 April 1941. 82 Squadron, Bodney, early 1941. Ralph Tallis

made the most of those occasions.

The remaining 110 was not closing in. It was not in effective range of the .303 twin Brownings in the rear turret, but we were nevertheless in effective range of its heavier calibre 20mm cannon. In view of his tactics there was not much to be gained from taking evasive action and I concentrated on keeping as low as I could to make it as difficult as possible for him to sight his guns on us. In the event, this may have been our saving grace, as I could see the splash of shells hitting the water just ahead. We were hit quite a number of times, including once through the gunner's turret. We were also holed in the wings and fuselage but, incredibly, we did not sustain any very serious damage to the aircraft, R3891 'W'. This continued until quite suddenly my air gunner told me over the intercom that this remaining 110 had broken off the engagement. I turned and saw that we were on our own and that we were out of sight of land. I naturally wondered how badly we had been hit and what damage had been done to the aircraft that could still affect our airworthiness. I gained height and the navigator gave me a course to steer for home.

It was about midnight when we arrived back at Thornaby, only to be told that we would have to divert as the visibility at the airfield was not sufficient for landing. There must have been a moon as I can remember seeing half the airfield covered in a low-lying industrial haze, with sufficient of the flare path clear for me to land. I did not want to divert if it could be avoided after all that had happened, and at my request I was given permission to make one attempt to land which I did successfully. The debriefing took some time and there was great sorrow at the loss that the squadron had suffered.

No one in the three crews shot down escaped alive from the sharp encounter with Bf.110 'Zerstörer' of III/ZG76. Sqn Ldr Augustine S.Q. Robins, Plt Off Michael S. Proudlock (observer) and South African W.Op/AG Sgt Stephen A. Du Plessis were the first to go down in Blenheim V5650 'A'. The Canadian Flt Lt Thomas H. Myers and his crew of Sgts Reginald E. Williams and Ronald Mann in T2272 'F' crashed in the North Sea a few minutes later. Twenty-years old Sgt Mann was washed ashore and was buried in the Sola Churchyard cemetery. Last to go down were thirty-one-years old Wg Cdr George R.A. Elsmie, DFC and his crew of Flt Sgts Michael B. Appleby (observer) and Clifford Jennings, DFM (W.Op/AG)

in V5954 'T'. These three men are commemorated on panels 28, 35 and 36, respectively, of the RAF Memorial for the Missing on Cooper's Hill, Runnymede. Lt Helmut Viedebannt of 8/ZG76 claimed two of these Blenheims destroyed.

In fact, the 114 Squadron attack was the last in a series of strikes made during the day on this strongly defended convoy off Stavanger. Eight Blenheims of 21 Squadron went in first in the early afternoon, claiming two large merchantmen sunk and one flak ship on fire. However, the price for their daring was high, as Plt Off H.K. Marshall and his crew in T1814, and Sgt J. Dunning and crew in V5855 fell to the ships' gun-fire and to Lt Viedebannt's Bf110. Following this strike, six aircraft of 107 Squadron (on loan to Coastal Command) were dispatched from Leuchars for a repeat attack. They raced in at wave-top height to be met by a wall of flak, which shot R3873 of Wg Cdr Arthur M.A. Birch and his crew, and R3740 in the hands of Flt Sgt Jack Hickingbotham out of the sky. The names of all six men are also honoured on the Runnymede Memorial. Another 107 Squadron Blenheim, V5516 'P', limped home with its W.Op/AG, Flt Sgt John Brown, DFM dead.

Lt Helmut Viedebannt was the hero of the day with three Blenheims destroyed in two sorties. These were his first victories in the war, to be followed by at least twenty

Sq Ldr Atkinson, DSO, DFC and Bar of 21 Squadron. By May 1941 'Attie' was the most experienced anti-shipping pilot in 2 Group, having led the first Malta detachment, the first fringe target raids and dozens of convoy strikes. Portrait by Eric Kennington, via Ralph Fastnedge

more on the eastern front. He was awarded the Ritterkreuz in December 1942 and continued operating fighter-bombers over southern England and Italy before he too was killed in action on 1 May 1945 near Berlin. The only Luftwaffe loss in the massacre off Stavanger was Uffz Kind's Bf 109 from I/JG77, which was shot down by Blenheim return fire, killing the pilot.

In addition to the losses off Norway, R2787 of 110 Squadron collided with a tree on take-off from Wattisham for a shipping sweep at 03.35hr, killing Sgt H.W. Wright and crew. 53 Squadron's V6302 PZ-W of Plt Off Edward W. Thomas and his crew were shot down on a sortie to Brest with the loss of the whole crew. Finally, Z6050 of 500 Squadron crashed near Detling, Kent, killing all four men on board. It had been another cruel day for the Blenheim crews.

Meanwhile, Blenheim operations from bases in East Anglia and southern England went on unabated. By 22 April 482 sorties had been dispatched by 2 Group on coastal sweeps and fringe targets between Norway and Bordeaux, the majority going to the Beat lines off Holland, the Frisian Islands and the Heligoland Bight. Of these, 161 were effectively completed. Another 118 aircraft had been sent to attack industrial targets and shipping in port, with sixty-eight sorties completed, and forty-eight crews had been dispatched in circus-type operations (all completed effectively). A total of thirty-seven ships were claimed to have been hit during these five weeks of operations. Considering the hazardous nature of the daylight operations, losses during the initial stages of the maritime campaign were considered to be surprisingly few with only twenty-three 2 Group Blenheims lost and fifty-two crew members killed, and the operational results quite promising. Coastal Command units lost an additional forty-seven Blenheims (about half of these failing to return from operations) during the same period of mid March to 22 April 1941. These were mainly from 53, 59 and 235 Squadrons, with at least seventy-one crew members killed or missing. The often truly exhilarating nature of the low-level maritime daylight operations is vividly illustrated by Plt Off Charles Sherring, W.Op/AG with 18 Squadron. The crews were able to see what they were actually bombing, usually at close quarters, and even seeing the face of the enemy, as

Dreaded target: five big merchantmen, escorted by several flak ships, are sailing up the Dutch coast. An average of eight to ten such convoys sailed to and from Rotterdam each month during 1941, transporting 7 million tons of essential war materials over the year. Helmut Persch

Sherring recounts of a shipping and fringe beat in the Heligoland Bight on 25 April.

Charles Sherring's Story

Six crews were briefed for a shipping sweep in pairs at the very top of the Frisian Islands, and, as Group particularly wanted a diversion, if there was no shipping available we were to go in and bomb on land.

About 40miles off Texel there was a squealer boat – a wireless boat apparently harmless that flashed through our numbers, course, etc. to the Jerry fighters. So our last pair peeled off to try

and sink it – which they failed to do. A little further on our own other aircraft, flown by little Jacky Fisher, peeled off and went home with a dud engine. Jenkins and his other aircraft broke off from us as they were to patrol the top beat behind Heligoland, and we went on on our own trying really hard to find a ship. As we couldn't see a thing on the horizon there was nothing for it but to turn in towards the land. It was one of those hot still days with a sea almost like glass.

Low on the horizon we could see a square-looking building, and Buckner said, 'That's the biggest hangar I've ever seen in my life, we might as well have a crack at that.' Land appeared and we could see part of three low

pier – quite a long one which ran out on our right and parallel to our run; as we reached the pier our bombs went off. One bit of roof went up in the air; for a few seconds nothing more happened, then smoke and debris poured out of all the windows facing me (as I sat in the turret) and a plume of smoke drifted vertically upwards. I had been firing hard at the people leaving the building, who were now out of range, and at the end of the pier was a cluster of about ten or twelve white motor launches – lovely looking boats- and about four small fishing smacks. I fired a lot of rounds into the motor boats and saw splashes and strikes.

Hawkins was taking violent evasive action, bouncing and skidding the aircraft, and then we turned hard to starboard to follow the main channel round and get back to the sea again. There was a boat coming from the next island, a small tramp or ferry boat, about three-quarters of a mile away, too far for me, so I didn't fire, and as we rushed between the two islands, but much nearer our own, I could see men running to their gun posts on the sand dunes and shot them up.

There was a big black ball of smoke hanging above our building and we were rushing out to sea 'flat out' and the land got low down on the skyline. Jenkins, from 30miles further north, saw the column of smoke from our bombing. We were flying very low and the next thing we knew – dead ahead was a convoy heading north-east-wards along the coast. There was no time to dodge – the convoy must be full on the alert as they couldn't have helped hearing our bombing. The leading ship fired a five-shell cartridge into the air and they opened fire. The biggest boat was about 4,000 to 5,000 tons and there were five in all. The biggest one heavily camouflaged in white and green, the others were all black. We went straight through the middle – getting a lot of light flak from pompoms, Bofors and machine-guns.

I could see the tracer passing the turret and wing tips like little electric sparks showing red and yellow. On the deck of the nearest boat a man was running up to a gun with his arms full of shells. It seemed ages and Hawkins was skidding low all over the place. It can't really have been long and we were clear and heading for home, which is along the coast from there. We held this course for a couple of minutes at the most and then Buckner had an inspiration and turned half back on our course and right out to sea. We were going well and 'flat out' for a bit, and then low down on the skyline I saw about a dozen fighters, too far away for accurate counting, sweeping along on our original course. We remained in +9 for some time, and at last eased down and headed for the English coast. I got a wireless bearing a bit later on, and we finally

islands; working from right to left there was a town at the end of an island, then some sea, then a smaller island with what we thought was our hangar on it, then more sea and another island with a sort of village and a church at our end of it. We were flying very fast by now and very low and as we came in the water changed colour and became sandy-looking as it shallowed. The water was dead smooth, and Hawkins was flying very low indeed – our two props were leaving two little wind trails stretching far out behind us on the sea.

As we got nearer we could see our building wasn't a hangar as we had thought but a brand new, concrete building with big factory-type

windows – all metal frames and rectangular. There were two longshoremen digging worms out on the sandy foreshore, and they both lay down flat when they saw what was about to happen. We rushed over the beach and Hawkins began to fire his front gun at the building, the next moment we climbed steeply and Buckner let the bombs go in a salvo, and we pulled up to go over the roof which we missed by about six feet I should think. There were six ridges of roof – all most carefully camouflaged – and a lot of men trying to get out of the back. Behind the building was a cluster of new little houses with bright red roofs, all spotlessly clean with wee gardens on some, and beyond that a

came in just by Cromer.

Altogether I fired 1,200 rounds, 600 from each gun, and could have fired much more, but was keeping them in case of fighter reception. We all felt on the crest of the wave, as it had been a really good op. We had bombed Baltrum, between the German islands of Nordeney and Langerooge. We had done a solo low level on Germany. I think this was my best and most exciting trip.

Coastal Activity Becomes More Dangerous

In late April it was decided to send 2 Group squadrons on two-week detachments to Manston, a few miles north of the Straits of Dover, to close the Channel for any German shipping trying to force its way through. 'Channel Stop' was inaugurated on 24 April, when Sqn Ldr R.O.M. Graham led nine 101 Squadron aircraft down to Manston. In the early afternoon of 3 May, Plt Off C.D. Brown sank a 2,000-tonner off Ostend as the first Channel Stop success. He only had a few hours left to enjoy this, as at 20.00hr on the same day he and his crew perished in T1825, together with Sgt C.H. Deane and his crew in T2234 during a similar strike off Boulogne. The six surviving 101 Squadron crews returned to West Raynham on 9 May to convert to Wellingtons in 3 Group, being relieved at Manston by 110 Squadron. Its crews mounted only a handful of sorties, losing the almost tour-expired Flt Sgt Arthur E. Guesford and his crew in V6375 on the 15th.

At this time, 21 Squadron's Sqn Ldr 'Attie' Atkinson led the first anti-shipping detachment to Malta to suppress Rommel's supply lines in the Mediterranean. It was the first of many 2 Group Blenheim detachments which were sent there during the next eight months (see Chapter 8).

During late April and May the Blenheim daylight offensive was stepped up even further, with dozens of aircraft swarming out on coastal sweeps to the continent on nearly every day. In an effort to keep losses down to an acceptable level, moonlight anti-shipping sweeps were also mounted by 2 Group during the second week of May, but these proved ineffective and were soon abandoned altogether. But Coastal Command Blenheim crews remained active at night, hunting down German coastal shipping, but to little

effect. It was no mean feat to find, let alone hit a ship in complete darkness at night.

As a direct result of the mounting pressure on their coastal shipping during April and May 1941, the Germans systematically reinforced their coastal defences. Convoys were now usually flanked by a number of Kriegsmarine *Vorpostenboote* (heavily armed converted fishing trawlers) and minesweepers, and escorted by standing patrols of Bf 109 and 110 fighter aircraft. These measures had an immediate effect on the effectiveness of the anti-shipping campaign. Statistics covering the 2 Group effort for the six weeks between 22 April and 3 June clearly illustrate the difficult position into which the Blenheim crews had been manoeuvred: the effectiveness of their sorties steadily declined while their operational losses went up at an alarming rate. During this period 470 sorties were dispatched on coastal sweeps and fringe operations, of which only 141 were effectively completed. Another 249 were directed against industrial targets and shipping in port, with 139 effective, and finally forty-two sorties were flown on circus operations with fighter escort (eleven effective). In the two weeks between 22 April and 6 May, a total of twenty-eight ships were claimed hit, dropping to fourteen in the following two weeks, and to only ten in the fourteen days ending 3 June. 2 Group HQ admitted the operational loss of thirty-four Blenheims destroyed, crashed or missing in these six weeks, with eighty-seven crew members being killed or missing. Due to the dangerous nature of the low-level, high-speed shipping and fringe target attacks, only ten aircrew survived their crashes to be taken prisoner.

During the same six weeks, Coastal Command Blenheim squadrons lost twenty-two aircraft, with thirty-two crew members killed, missing or taken prisoner of war. Again, 59 and 235 Squadrons suffered the heaviest casualties, with eight and five Blenheims lost, respectively. A disastrous convoy strike off the Hook of Holland took place on 28 April, when a complete formation of four 59 Squadron Blenheims (N3615, V5520, V5687 and V6097) were shot down at 12.20hr by escorting flak ships. Only two crew members, Plt Off H.D. Norton and his observer Sgt W. Flury, from V5687 TR-H, were picked up from the North Sea to be taken prisoner. Sgt Ian 'Robbie' Robinson, observer in the crew of Plt Off 'Foss' Foster, SAAF and Sgt

'Ozzie' Osborne (W.Op/AG), reflects on the first six months of 1941, when he served with 59 Squadron:

> We were all very proud when we were posted to a Blenheim OTU and experienced flying in such a sleek-looking aircraft. However, when we learned later of the heavy losses the Blenheim squadrons were taking, we realized what we were up against. I got my first shock when I first joined the squadron. My good friend, who had been with me throughout training, had preceded me to 59 a week before. He was posted missing on his first operation.
>
> Losses were very heavy and we were soon getting to be one of the more experienced crews remaining on the squadron. At the beginning, I had been quite shocked when crews I knew did not return from an operation, but had, by June, grown accustomed to it. We learned that so and so had 'gone for a Burton' or 'got the chop' with a laconic resignation that I would not have thought possible a few months before. I should add that, in spite of the losses, morale was always very high while I was on 59 Squadron.

Alarmed by the rapidly mounting losses and obvious decline in effectiveness, strong voices were raised at squadron command and 2 Group level to halt the Blenheim daylight offensive against the strongly-defended enemy shipping temporarily and to resume the offensive once the American Mitchell and Boston aircraft and the De Havilland Mosquito would become available in numbers during the following year. Nevertheless, AVM Donald Stevenson, AOC 2 Group, wanted to hear no more of it, and remained determined to make the Blenheim anti-shipping and fringe targets campaign a decisive success. He did make a concerted effort though to get long-range Spitfire fighter protection for his vulnerable Blenheims on the shipping beats, but this would be forthcoming only in mid August. Thus during June 1941 the hard-pressed Blenheim Boys were kept busy on the shipping beats, fringe attacks and circus operations, with 2 Group mounting 558 sorties. About half of these were completed effectively.

Dickie Rook's Story

The story of air warfare in World War II is mostly a grim tale of killing or being killed. At times, however, there was still room for chivalry, as Sgt Dickie Rook, observer with 114 Squadron, experienced:

Another victory is chalked up on the bridge of *Vorpostenboot* Vp1304 in early 1942. This was one of several dozen flak ships escorting convoys between Cuxhaven in northern Germany and the large transhipment port of Rotterdam during 1941. Most of this ship's seven kills were Blenheims. Helmut Persch

Daylight Coastal Attacks

On 9 June 1941, while 114 Squadron was based at Leuchars, an incident alerted my mind to the fact that, although much hate and bitterness pertained during wartime, there continued to exist within some people of both sides a certain suppressed chivalry. This I believe was the case particularly with airmen, perhaps because it was they alone who confronted one another in a win or lose contest, albeit the odds at times were heavily stacked on one side or the other.

This was exemplified by a chance encounter while on an anti-shipping patrol in Blenheim Z5797, over the Skagerrak, south of Kristiansand. Flying low in poor visibility we suddenly sighted a Me.110 and, being a very long way from home, a certain anxiety arose as we took some evasive action. Thinking that we had managed to lose him, we started to relax somewhat when, suddenly, for some

unknown reason, the fighter came in very close and formated on our starboard wingtip momentarily. The pilot, wearing a broad smile, saluted and suddenly swung away to starboard and was lost to view. The reason for such behaviour has puzzled me ever since and I have theorized along three main lines. First, the fighter may have been low on fuel; secondly he may well have been out of ammunition or, thirdly, was this a fellow aviator, albeit an enemy, who felt no desire to destroy another crew, as he most certainly could have done? We are most unlikely to ever know but I have always felt the last to be a very strong possibility and, should this be the case, I wonder who that pilot was and whether, like myself, he survived the war. I can remember well the sight of that smiling pilot, and his almost frivolous salute.

This day, 9 June, was a typical one in the first phase of the daylight campaign. Twelve aircraft from 18 and 107 Squadrons swarmed out to the German and Dutch coasts during the day with orders to attack and sink any shipping encountered in their allotted Beats. No shipping was found in Beat 10 (off the mouth of the River Scheldt), but two 18 Squadron crews came across and attacked a 1,200-ton vessel in a convoy off Terschelling. Sgt Ian Bullivant's V6428 WV-M was repeatedly hit in the curtain of flak coming up from the convoy and finished off moments later by Fw Ahnert's Bf 109F of 3/JG52 at 17.57hr. Before reaching its beatline, Sgt Leslie Box's V6427 WV-B had disappeared in a fog-bank off Texel with the loss of the whole crew. Coastal Command lost no Blenheims on operations this day,

Sgt pilots of the prewar RAF VR being mobilized in September 1939 and awaiting a posting to an operational squadron. Front row, left to right: John Tilsey; 'Tich' Newell; Johnnie Maple. Back row, left to right: Jack Irvin; 'Scottie' Grant; Jack Barker; John Blackmore; Terry Staples. Apart from Sgts Staples and Barker (who died in a flying accident), all these pilots went missing on operations while flying Blenheims, Hampdens, Whitleys and Wellingtons in Bomber Command during the early days of the war. Staples completed a tour flying Blenheims in 114 Squadron during 1940–41 and finished the war as Wing Commander, OBE, DFM. Terry Staples

although Z6025, flown by Plt Off Werner, crashed at Geragh, Londonderry, fortunately without injury to the crew.

Terry Staples's Story

During June 114 Squadron was still on loan by Coastal Command, its crews mainly operating off Norway from Leuchars. On the afternoon of the 12th, Sgt Terry Staples, pilot, and his experienced navigator Jerry Ingham were summoned to the Operations Room. They were told that they and another crew were to do an urgent night reconnaissance off the Norwegian coast as intelligence had been received that a German pocket battleship and its escort were on their way into the North Sea from the Baltic, presumably to break out into the Atlantic to attack the allied convoys.

They were to be sent out to locate the ships undetected, ahead of a force of Beaufort torpedo bombers, and transmit the position report. Staples picks up the story:

I was detailed to lead the section of two aircraft to a point on the west coast of Norway where I would turn south and search as far as the most southerly point of the coastline; the other aircraft would turn north to search. We must have taken off about nine-thirty in the evening. I can remember flying at about 1,500 or 2,000ft to enable my navigator to take the necessary drift measurements for his dead reckoning navigation as we had no other navigational aid or facility. When we were about 50 nautical miles [nm] from the Norwegian coast I descended to a lower level to avoid detection, and then, at the prearranged point off the coast, we separated. It was about eleven-thirty; there was low cloud

with the base about 1,000ft, the sea was choppy and the visibility was not good in the midnight twilight of northern latitudes at that time of year. It seemed that the Germans had chosen favourable conditions for the movement of their ship.

My navigator was convinced that the battleship and its escort would not be found in the coastal shipping lane just a few miles offshore but was more likely to be sailing in open waters further out to sea. I respected his judgement, and we began our search flying parallel to the coast about 25nm out to sea. We flew on this south-easterly course until we had almost reached the end of our patrol line and I was beginning to wonder if we had done right in being so far out to sea when I saw ahead of me a float plane heading towards the land. I should have connected it with the presence of the enemy ships, but I did not and my initial

First victims of Channel Stop: three aircraft from 101 Squadron with an escort of six 74 Squadron Spitfires took off from Manston at 10.54hr on 27 April 1941 to attack enemy trawlers in the Straits of Dover. In the face of heavy opposition from shore batteries and ship's flak, nine trawlers were attacked off Calais, with V5493 SR-G of Sgts R. Ridgman-Parsons and his crew of Sgt G.W. Hickman (observer) and H.T.H. Downes (W.Op/AG) being shot down into the sea. Blenheim Society

reaction was to attack it. Bearing in mind the purpose of our reconnaissance, this would have been a mistake; but given a few moments to think about it, I am sure I would have reached that conclusion and would have turned to fly back up the coast to continue the search closer inshore. By a stroke of good fortune, combined with my navigator's good judgement, the situation resolved itself before I had time to think any more about the float plane.

Ahead, and slightly to starboard, the pocket battleship and its escort of five destroyers – two either side and one ahead- suddenly came into view. The ships were not much more than a mile away. It was a most impressive sight – a capital ship under way at sea with its attendant escort in battle order is always a majestic sight, and this was no exception. It was clearly visible to me as I looked down on it at a slight angle. I could see fighter aircraft overhead at about the same height as that at which I was flying. The sea was rough and the ships blended into the seascape so that at first sight in the half-light they gave a false impression of waves breaking on the shore. Events move rapidly at times like this and thoughts pass quickly through one's mind. I was incredulous of my first impression as I knew we were far from land, then within seconds the reality of the sighting was apparent. The illusion of waves breaking on the shore was, of course, created by the ships steaming in line astern, three abreast, at speed in choppy water.

The ships did not open fire on me and I was not attacked by the fighters because I turned away to port into the cloud as soon as my navigator had made his necessary observation. As I turned away and entered the low cloud I alerted my wireless operator/air gunner to the job ahead of transmitting our sighting report. To do this he had to lower himself from his turret to operate his set in the fuselage to the rear of his position and wind out a trailing aerial. During this time there was no rear look-out and no defence against fighter attack. I do not think I was detected. This view is reinforced by the fact that the Germans did not seem alert to the fact that they had been located because they clearly continued on their course, 25nm or so offshore. We did not shadow the ships which was in keeping with our operational briefing.

The report prepared by my navigator was that we had sighted the ships 30nm south of Lister steering west-north-west at a speed of 22 knots. This was at midnight on 12/13 June. We learned later that the pocket battleship was the Lützow. We naturally wondered about the accuracy of our sighting report as our navigation had been entirely by dead reckoning. The Lützow was torpedoed at 2.18am on 13 June off Eggersund, having sailed roughly 50nm since we saw it. That is almost exactly where we would have expected it to be on the basis of our sighting – 25nm out to sea.

In fact, the Lützow was torpedoed by Flt Sgt Ray Loveitt in a Beaufort of 42 Squadron, who approached the ship unseen and secured a hit amidships. His torpedo blew a 7m-wide hole in the battleship's port side. Aided by Loveitt's attack report, other Beauforts soon appeared on the scene, but the escorting destroyers had laid a smokescreen immediately after the first attack and no further hits were scored. Four days later the Lützow was in dry dock at Kiel, out of action for six months in a crucial phase of the Battle of the Atlantic.

During the second half of June gradually more emphasis was being laid on the circus-type operations, both by 2 Group Bomber Command and by Coastal Command. During the mid-morning of 14 June, twelve strongly escorted Blenheims of 110 Squadron bombed the airfield of St. Omer in Circus No.12. A Staffel of Bf 109s from III/JG26 managed to break through the close escort near the target and Uffz Oemler shot down V6334 with the loss of Flt Lt P. Windram and his crew. The next circus, No. 13, was mounted in the late afternoon of 16 June against the Boulogne docks and gasworks. It was a dreaded target, being very heavily defended by both fighters and flak. The bomber force on this occasion comprised six 59 Squadron Blenheims with the escort provided by six squadrons of Hurricanes and Spitfires. The orders were that three Blenheims were to bomb from 6,000ft and three from low level in order to confuse enemy defences. The meteorological briefing confirmed that there would be a clear sky over the target, with little chance of any clouds to hide in if the German fighters rose to intercept.

The bombing force made a successful rendezvous with the escorts, and the flight across the Channel was uneventful. Plt Off Foster and crew were among the three to go in low and, as their aircraft was fitted with a camera, they would be the last in. Sgt Ian Robinson, 'Foss' Foster's observer, takes up the story of his twenty-second Blenheim trip, when they were approaching Boulogne.

Ian Robinson's Story

It is an exhilarating feeling flying low over the water but I did not have the time nor inclination to enjoy it on this day. I was looking for landmarks to guide us into the target. We flew in over the harbour and over the roof tops, down what seemed to be a main street. Passing over the harbour, I could see tracer coming at us but we got through it without being hit. Then Foss shouted, 'There's the gasworks ahead on the port!' Simultaneously I saw it and gave him a quick 'left, left'. He made a slight turn and I called 'steady' as I saw the target coming down the parallel wires of the bomb sight. As it came to the release mark I pressed the button and yelled, 'Bombs away!'

As I shouted, Foss started throwing the aircraft from side to side taking violent evasive action. Lifting my head from the bombsight I could see the tracer coming at us and several black puffs. Fortunately they all seemed to be going high. Then a 'crumph' followed by a sound like pebbles thrown on a tin roof. My God, we'd been hit. Trying to get up from the floor back into the navigator's position I found impossible to do so. The force of the turns was holding me down. I looked back at Foss. He seemed to be in his element. Then we were out of the town and flying over the countryside like a snipe as Foss zigzagged from side to side. He made a turn and we crossed the coast and went out over the sea. We seemed to have left the flak behind. I got back into my navigation seat in the nose and over the intercom Foss said, 'I'm going to stay down on the deck, Robbie, it's safer down here. Is this course OK?' I had given him a course to steer before going in and I answered, 'It's OK skipper.' Then he said. 'Watch out for fighters, Robbie, Ozzie's been hit.' It was at that moment I realized that there was a pool of blood over my maps on the nav. table and I saw blood oozing from my right hand. I felt no pain at this point. Later it was discovered that a piece of shrapnel one-quarter inch square had gone into the back of my right hand and broken two bones. I told Foss that I had also been hit but it didn't appear too bad. Two or three minutes later, I realized that the right leg of my pants was wet and I thought I had experienced an accident of another kind. Looking down I saw my trouser leg was soaked with blood.

All the way across the Channel I was looking out for enemy fighters but fortunately none had spotted us, neither were we seen by any of our own fighters who should have been watching for us as we left the target area. I had been pressing the wound on my right hand with my left and the flow of blood seemed to have abated. However I had not had an opportunity to examine the wound in my leg.

Soon, Foss put the aircraft into a slow climb and we crossed the English coast at about 1,000ft. I was able to check our position and give a slight change of course to return us to Detling. We had not seen any of the other five

aircraft and I wondered how they had fared. As I was able to relax a little, the pain from my wounds began to manifest itself and I seemed to have lost the feeling in my leg. Later I was to learn that there were also superficial wounds in my back. As I felt that my leg would not bear my weight, I told Foss I would stay in the nose for landing rather than moving back to my normal position for landing, alongside the pilot.

Soon we sighted Detling and Foss was making his approach for landing. I thanked God we would soon be on terra firma again. My feeling of safety turned out to be premature. We were about 200yd from the end of the runway when Foss yelled, 'Get back Robbie, I can't get the wheels down. The shell must have hit the undercarriage.' I crawled back and, just as I strapped myself in, we hit the ground. Foss had landed off the runway to soften the impact. My 'greenhouse' was completely demolished. The navigator's seat and table where I had been sitting seconds before had been forced back by the scraped-up earth. There is no doubt that if Foss had not called me back to the co-pilot's seat I would have been 'never more'. His call had saved my life.

Sgt Robinson and 'Ozzie', his gunner, were sent off to the Chatham naval hospital; Robinson continues:

A few days later we received a message from our pilot Foss, telling us he would come and visit us in the hospital on his first weekend pass. Alas – he didn't live long enough. He had been sent on a bombing raid with a new crew and they failed to return from their first operation together. Poor Foss, he had travelled so far, from South Africa, to join the RAF. I remember that I was devastated when I heard the news, but so many had died during the past few months it just seemed part of the pattern. We had worked well together, he was an excellent pilot, his coolness under pressure had saved my life.

I was pronounced fit for flying again and returned to the squadron in September. It was being converted to a Hudson squadron. I had flown my last Blenheim flight and I was not sorry. It was ill-equipped for the operations it was expected to perform. I was assigned to a new crew and I flew another eighty-eight ops with my new pilot.

What Robbie Robinson did not mention was that his pilot brought their crippled Blenheim V6386 TR-D back on one engine on 16 June, after having been damaged by flak and in a Bf 109 attack (from JG26). Of the high-level force, Z3073 TR-G (Plt Off Villa and crew) and

Z3339 TR-Y (Plt Off Kennedy and crew) were bounced by Hptm Rolf Pingel, Kommandeur of II/JG26, and by Oblt Josef Priller of I/JG26 after having successfully evaded the 54 Squadron high-cover Spitfires. Both Blenheims were shot down in the target area. Plt Off Laughland's TR-L, the only remaining aircraft in the high-level vic, was also engaged by Bf 109s from JG26, but his assailants were driven off by 258 Squadron Hurricanes providing close escort. Plt Off Griffiths, flying TR-H in the low-level vic, belly-landed his badly shot up aircraft at Hawkinge. Laughland and Sqn Ldr Aitken in TR-M were the only pilots to bring back their Blenheims and crews to base in one piece. Circus No.13 had turned out to be a black affair for 59 Squadron.

2 Group anti-shipping operations on 16 June also suffered heavily, with three Blenheims from 18 and 139 Squadrons being lost to fighters and flak during convoy strikes off the Dutch coast. Furthermore, 21 Squadron's V6034 in the hands of Flt Sgt Rex Leavers, DFM hit the mast of a 'squealer' vessel in Beat 7 (off Borkum) and cartwheeled into the North Sea minus half a wing, with the loss of the whole crew. Leavers and his crew were some of the most experienced ship-hunters in 2 Group, and were almost tour-expired when they met their fate. Four aircraft lost from twenty-five anti-shipping sorties dispatched was a high price to pay and one which set the trend for the remaining months of the 1941 daylight anti-shipping campaign.

Next day, it was 2 Group's turn to supply a force of twenty-three Blenheims from 18, 105, 110 and 139 Squadrons for Circus No. 14 to Choques. It was the most ambitious escorted bomber mission yet mounted by the RAF in the war, with no fewer than nineteen squadrons of Spitfires and Hurricanes providing close escort, high cover, forward support, target support and Channel patrols. From the moment the formation crossed the French coast near Cap Gris-Nez, they came under continuous attack from small groups of Bf 109Es and Fs from III/JG2 and Stab, I, II and III/JG26, making beam and stern firing passes. The British fighter pilots fought hard to keep the Messerschmitts away from the bombers, which they did successfully, but they paid a grim price. In a running battle lasting some 20min, fifteen German pilots claimed nineteen victories for only three Bf 109s lost (with

A fine shot of a 235 Squadron fighter Blenheim on patrol, April 1941. Doug Pole

Many Blenheims came home with severe battle scars. Apart from a peppered fuselage and wings, the left aileron of V6525 WV-G of 18 Squadron, flown by Fg Off Tudge has been shot away by Bf 109s during a Circus on Z437 (the marshalling yard at Hazebrouck). Horsham St. Faith, 22 June 1941. Dennis Denton

two pilots killed). True RAF fighter losses amounted to thirteen aircraft.

Jim Moore Continues His Story

Sgt Jim 'Dinty' Moore manned the mid-upper twin Brownings in one of the 18 Squadron Blenheims on Circus No.14.

On 17 June we were briefed to take part in what was to prove to be a very eventful operation and one which we would never forget. In order to attend this briefing we flew over to Horsham' St. Faith where we found we were to take part in a 'Circus' attack on the Kuhlmann Chemical Works at Choques near Bethune in northern France, accompanied by a large fighter escort. We were to fly in one large formation of twenty-four aircraft in eight vics of three stacked up slightly below and behind the other. We also

discovered that we had drawn the 'short straw' in our position as we would be the last aircraft in this large and unwieldy formation. Later in the war, no matter how many bombers took part in a raid, we never flew in boxes of more than six aircraft, which could manoeuvre sufficiently to carry out evasive action in response to attack by flak or fighters.

At 5.45pm we taxied out, with my excitement having some difficulty in overcoming my fear, taking off, the last in the queue, gaining height and getting into formation. Flying down to our rendezvous with our escort, looking behind me I could see this enormous formation of Blenheims while, looking forward over the tail, there was an empty sky. Whenever I see a flock of birds I am always reminded of that moment. On meeting the Hurricanes, who were our close escort, they closed in around us while the Spitfires flew high above carefully forming a

protective umbrella. They certainly were a most comforting sight.

We droned on towards the French coast, having climbed to our operational height of about 10,000ft, being met by a heavy barrage of flak. We carried on towards the target by which time our vic was lagging behind the main formation and we attracted the unwelcome attention of a number of German fighters who had managed to avoid our escort, who themselves were also under attack. The sky was full of fighters whirling around in combat while we were under constant attack. One determined character actually flew up between ourselves and the number two in our formation but, although I was surprised, I was astounded to find I immediately reacted and managed to fire a burst as he went past. My instant reaction must have been due to the training I had received.

The fighters were armed with cannon so, on

occasions, they could stay off out of range of our machine-guns and take pot shots at us, hitting us in both wings and putting our port engine out of commission. If that was the bad news, the good news was that the power for the landing gear and the turret was supplied by the starboard engine which, thankfully, was undamaged.

Losing power on the port engine initially made our kite swing to the left although our pilot George Milson somehow managed to manoeuvre underneath our colleagues for mutual protection. Sadly, they gradually pulled away, leaving us with an unfriendly and persistent Messerschmitt for company, with a heavy flak barrage as we crossed the coast at Cap Gris-Nez to speed us, if that is appropriate in this instant, on our way. Fortunately, one of our escorting Hurricanes came to our aid and we heard later that he had shot down our German friend near the English coast.

The Blenheim was not noted for its ability to fly on one engine and George had to fight with the controls to keep us in the air and on course. Apart from sending a message back to base notifying them of our problems there was little I could do but cross my fingers. We could have landed at any aerodrome, once we crossed the coast, but George was determined to get us back to Horsham St. Faith, which he not only did but he also brought us in for a perfect landing. It

was, by any standard, an example of marvellous flying so there was no wonder that our observer Ron Millar and I were happy with our pilot. The flight actually lasted for 3hr 10min although it seemed a great deal longer.

At our debriefing I was credited with shooting down one of the enemy fighters, a distinction I had to share with three other W.Op/AGs. Later we were to learn that the attack on the chemical works had been successful, our bombs causing a great deal of damage. Further, if the object of the exercise was to tempt the Luftwaffe to join battle with our fighter escort then this had been a huge success.

More Circuses

Before the month of June was out, thirteen more circus raids had been launched (on 18, 19, 21 [two], 22, 23, 24, 25 [two], 26, 27, 28 and 30). Losses among the Blenheims on these raids were relatively light. Sgt P. Brown's V7450 of 21 Squadron was shot down in flames on 21 June near St. Omer by Obstlt Adolf Galland in his Bf 109F of Stab/JG26, as his sixty-ninth victory. Although the German ace caught a glimpse of parachutes, Sgt Brown and his crew of Sgts L.R. Wilson

and M.D. Brooker all perished and were buried at St. Omer. 107 Squadron lost V5517 and V6195 to Bf 109s in the Dunkirk area on 23 June, with one crew being killed. V6381 of 21 Squadron crashed on return from Circus 22 at 13.30hr on 25 June, while 18 Squadron's V6259 fell victim to flak on Circus 23 to St. Omer airfield a few hours later, with the loss of Sgt W.H. Mounser and his crew.

In four weeks of intensive operations between 3 and 30 June, a total of twenty-two Blenheims from 2 Group had been lost, mainly on anti-shipping strikes off the Dutch coast, the Frisian Islands and in the Heligoland Bight. Only two crews (107 Squadron's Fg Off E.T. Fairbank and crew in V5517 on 23 June, and Sgt C.M. Chown and crew in V6139 on 30 June) survived to be taken prisoner, the other fifty-six aircrew perished with the majority of them missing. Coastal Command suffered an additional loss of thirteen Blenheims (about half due to non-operational causes), with twelve crew members killed, missing or prisoner of war. The vulnerability of Coastal Command's Hudsons and Blenheims in the anti-shipping role is illustrated by the fact that of 143 attacking aircraft, fifty-two, or 36 per cent, were shot down between 1 April and 30 June 1941. By mid 1941, most Blenheim-equipped Coastal Command units were busy converting on to the Beaufighter, the Hudson or the Beaufort.

Hitler's launch of Operation *Barbarossa* on 22 June led to a great strategic upheaval in Europe. Britain's single-handed opposition to Nazi Germany was finally at an end, and the German armed forces were now irrevocably committed to a war on two fronts. As a direct response to Hitler's thrust towards the east, a new Bomber Command directive was issued, which came into effect on 9 July. The dreaded anti-shipping beats were downgraded as of secondary importance. 2 Group was now to spearhead British aid to Russia, by launching the maximum number of circus operations in the Pas-de-Calais. Further emphasis was laid on raiding key ports in north-west Germany and the Low Countries, and on the execution of deep penetration raids into the Ruhr Valley, all in daylight. All these initiatives were taken in an effort to tie down as many Luftwaffe fighter and flak units in the west of Europe as possible. A daunting new array of tasks lay ahead for the hard-pressed Blenheim crews.

Relieved to have survived another shipping strike, Flt Sgt Arthur Asker (observer, left), Flt Sgt John Brett (W.Op/AG, middle) and Flt Lt Shaw Kennedy (pilot) light up. 226 Squadron, summer 1941. Arthur Asker

CHAPTER SEVEN

The Charge of the Light Brigade:

The Cruel Summer of 1941

The shift in strategic aims, brought about by the new Bomber Command directive of 9 July, led direct to a series of famous Blenheim raids during July and August 1941. First, although it does not strictly fall within the period of the new directive, a daring daylight raid was mounted by 2 Group against Bremen in the early hours of 4 July. Six and four days previously daylight raids had already been tried against Germany's second largest port under the codename of Operation *Wreckage*, but due to various circumstances, which took away the vital element of surprise, the main Bremen force had turned back. Before a third attempt was undertaken, AVM Donald F. Stevenson, AOC 2 Group made it perfectly clear to the Australian Wg Cdr Hughie I. Edwards, CO of 105 Squadron at Swanton Morley who was chosen to lead *Wreckage*, that there must be no turning back.

Edwards's Squadron contributed nine crews, plus six crews from Wg Cdr Lawrence V.E. Petley's 107 Squadron, based at Great Massingham. On the long North Sea crossing, racing over the wavetops at less than 50ft to avoid radar detection, three aircraft turned back with technical problems. Despite the perfectly clear weather with not a cloud in sight in which to hide from fighters, the remaining four vics of three pressed on, even after encountering enemy vessels on three separate occasions. By 08.05hr, the loose formation, now in line-abreast, raced in over the outskirts of Bremen at about 50ft. Within minutes, the crews had to plough their way through a lattice of crossfire, which was hosed up in an unbelievably intense curtain by thirty batteries of 20 and 37mm flak from the section of the city which the Blenheims had penetrated. Exposed to a combined fire-power of an estimated 62,400 rounds per minute, all the aircraft were repeatedly hit but none turned about. Avoiding collision with all kinds of hazards such as balloon cables,

Wg Cdr Hughie I. Edwards, VC, DFC, CO of 105 Squadron, leader of the 4 July 1941 Bremen raid.
Portrait by Eric Kennington, via Ralph Fastnedge

pylons, cranes, buildings and ships' masts, the crews accurately dropped their bombs in the industrial area between the main railway station and the docks. Losses, however, were inevitable, and four aircraft were destroyed by the withering fire, two from each squadron which included Wg Cdr Petley's V6020. Just one man, Flt Lt F. Wellburn who piloted V6193 from 107 Squadron, escaped alive to be taken prisoner.

226 Squadron, in the meantime, flew a diversionary sweep towards the seaplane base on Nordeney with the purpose of drawing Luftwaffe fighters away from the main Bremen raid. Although this attack was successfully executed, light flak hit the leading Blenheim, Z7291, in the hands of the Squadron Commander, Wg Cdr R.G. Hurst, and moments later it exploded in a sheet of flame and smoke. His NCO crew, Flt Sgts T.C. Davies, DFM and R.W.J.

Green, DFM were both veterans of the French campaign of May–June 1940. Later the same day 226 Squadron was struck another blow when Sgt A. Smith and his crew in V6365 crashed near Dunkirk at 15.13hr during Circus No.32 against a chemical plant at Choques.

Wg Cdr Edwards's highest standard of gallantry, leadership and determination was duly recognized by the award of an immediate Victoria Cross, the first air award to be made to a Blenheim pilot in World War II. It had been an outstandingly heroic raid, but the cost was high. A third of the attacking force had been lost, and almost all of the surviving Blenheims returned to base badly battered and many with wounded crew members.

Twelve days later, in accordance with the new directive, another ambitious and daring daylight raid was mounted by 2 Group. This time the target was the strategic transhipment port of Rotterdam. In late afternoon two successive waves of seventeen and eighteen Blenheims thundered in from low level and wrought havoc in the docks area. A wide range of ships, harbour installations, storage buildings and railway lines were bombed and machine-gunned. The first wave achieved almost complete surprise and suffered the loss of only one aircraft. At 16.55hr, Sgt Bevan's V6240 of 21 Squadron fell to gunfire from Vp1107. When Wg Cdr Tim Partridge, DFC, CO of 18 Squadron, led in the second wave only three minutes later, the flak defences were wide awake. V6267 WV-M for Mother, Partridge's aircraft, completely disintegrated in a failed ditching on the Noordsingel at 17.00hr, with the loss of the whole crew. Sqn Ldr Sidney-Smith successfully belly-landed his stricken 139 Squadron aircraft into the bombed-out centre of the city after a 13th VP-flotilla flak ship had knocked out his port engine. A few minutes later, 18 Squadron's Sgt Ronald J.B. Rost, RAAF tried to crash-land Z7497 near Delft but failed. Dutch

Even though the Blenheim's defensive fire had been considerably improved by fitting its Bristol B4 gun turret with belt-fed twin Browning .303 machine guns, by the summer of 1941 the aircraft was no match any more for the strengthened German convoy defences and Messerschmitt fighters. Note the open turret entry hatch on this 139 Squadron Blenheim IV. Ken Whittle

civilians dragged him and his crew away from the burning wreck, but the three men succumbed to their wounds later in the day.

The crews' sacrifices were not in vain this time. Jubilant statistics were proudly issued by 2 Group HQ's War Room the day after the daring raid. Thirteen German vessels with a total tonnage of 65,650 were assessed as total losses, with a further six ships totalling 39,800 tons damaged. Four vessels were believed possibly damaged, totalling 22,800 tons. These figures were not far off the mark, as twenty-two ships were in fact damaged during the raid, but none was sunk. Most of the vessels were repaired within a few weeks to sail another day. With hindsight one must conclude that the Blenheims with their puny 250lb, 11sec delay bombs simply did not have the decisive striking power necessary to

demolish ships of more than two or three thousand tons.

Although the daylight anti-shipping campaign was officially downgraded as of secondary importance in the new Bomber Command directive, the majority of 2 Group's sorties were still directed towards the dreaded shipping beats. Statistics from 2 Group HQ reveal that in the fourteen days ending on 15 July, 222 aircraft were dispatched, of which 131 effectively completed their tasks. For the loss of eighteen Blenheims, thirty-one ships were claimed hit. In the following two weeks ending on 29 July, 176 sorties were flown, 118 of which were effective. Seventeen Blenheims failed to return, but thirty-seven ships were claimed damaged or destroyed (mainly in Rotterdam). The large majority of Blenheim losses were incurred while they were engaged on

maritime attack duties: thirty-three of these aircraft and their crews failed to return during July.

One of the crews joining 2 Group during this eventful month consisted of Sgts Bill Brandwood (pilot), Jock Miller (observer), and Tony Mee (W.Op/AG), who had been posted to 82 Squadron at Bodney on 1 July. On the 30th they were to get their baptism of fire in a cloud cover attack against shipping in the Kiel Canal. In all, forty-three Blenheims from 18, 82, 114, 139 and 226 Squadrons swarmed out during the day to sweep the German and Dutch coastal shipping lanes and the Canal.

Tony Mee's Story

Just past 13.00hr, twelve crews of 18 and 82 Squadrons bound for the Kiel Canal rendezvoused and set out for the North Sea crossing, as Sgt Mee vividly recounts:

The formation descended to sea level and looking ahead I saw that No.2's tailwheel was every now

Sgt Leonard Mynott, a twenty-six-year old W.Op/AG with 21 Squadron, who came from Clapham Park, London. During 2 Group's first low-level daylight raid on Rotterdam harbour on 16 July 1941, Blenheim V6240 YH-B was hit by flak from Vorpostenboot Vp1107 at 16.55hr and crashed into Waalhaven harbour. The whole crew perished in the high-speed crash. Nineteen-year-old Sgt James Bevan, pilot and Plt Off Ralph Slade, a married man of thirty from Prestwick and the observer in the crew, were retrieved from the wreckage and buried in Rotterdam. No trace was ever found of Mynott, his name is honoured on Panel 49 of the Runnymede Memorial. Rusty Russell

Flt Sgt Edmund Caban, DFM, twenty-one-years-old W.Op/AG in 139 Squadron. He was awarded a DFM on 7 March 1941 for shooting down a German fighter with his single Vickers 'K' gun, and completed a tour of operations in 18 and 139 Squadrons during 1940–41. Although screened from ops by July 1941, Caban was crewed up with Sqn Ldr Eric Sidney-Smith, DFC and observer Plt Off Adrian White for the 16 July Rotterdam docks raid. Over target, their Blenheim Z7362 XD-V suffered a direct hit from a flak ship of the 13th Vorpostenboot Flotilla and Sidney-Smith belly-landed the stricken aircraft in the bombed-out centre of Rotterdam. The whole crew escaped alive, although Caban had been hit by shrapnel in his foot and was given medical treatment in hospital before being transported to Stalag Luft 357 Kopernikus. Sybil Caban

and suddenly a heat haze followed by a fine mist appeared inboard of the starboard engine from the wingroot containing the inner fuel tank. I did not see the igniting of the remaining 100 octane, Bill had already switched to 'outers', as my attention was on the ship. Fortunately, the gunners lost interest as we bore down on them and Bill dropped the two 500lb armour-piercing bombs with their 11sec delay fuses just before passing low over the vessel.

As we drew away from the area, sounds of alarm came over the intercom. Bill and Jack had seen the fire but I had other worries. Two Messerschmitt 110s were overhauling us slightly above and at starboard astern. I informed Bill and asked for 'plus nine'. The boost came in and with it came a great increase in thrust from the propellers. This power, however, could be held for only 5min before the engines would be put at risk. The fighters were not gaining on us for the moment, when after some hesitation they banked to port. They had evidently spotted something over the horizon that we, flying 'on the deck', could not see. The enemy having left the scene, Bill throttled back and we found that during the emergency, the fire had burnt itself out.

Indeed, four Bf 110s of II/ZG76, which had scrambled from Leeuwarden and De Kooy airfields, had found a very worthwhile target in the form of a four-aircraft formation of 139 Squadron. Returning from a shipping beat off north-west Germany, the bombers ran into the cannon-armed, heavy fighters, at some 180km north of Texel. In a running battle starting at 16.18hr, all the British aircraft were destroyed, the last crashing into the North Sea at 16.32hr without survivors.

After touching down at Bodney again at 17.00hr, Mee and his novice crew were informed that two aircraft from their squadron had been shot down on the raid. Sgt P. Stocks and his crew in R3803 UX-N and V6513 UX-S of Plt Off J. Bell and crew crashed into the sea in the target area with the loss of all six men. 18 Squadron suffered the loss of L9240 WV-G on the Kiel Canal raid, but Sgt H.D. Cue and his NCO crew were very fortunate to survive and were taken prisoner.

Dickie Rook's Story Continued

Despite the often horrendous losses that were incurred by the Blenheims, by mid 1941 it still was a versatile aircraft, as is illustrated by Sgt Dickie Rook's story. Rook, a twenty-three-years old observer in

and again touching the peaks of the heavy swell. Our Blenheims would have been trimmed to give a nose-up attitude as a precaution against flying into the sea. The lowering sky lived up to the Met. Officer's forecast and gave us some cover against attack. This was my first operational sortie, as it was with some of the other crews, and I was very conscious of leaving 'home' and facing the unknown. We flew on steadily towards the Heligoland Bight, keeping a sharp look out for fighters. When still some time from landfall, a line of small fishing boats, or 'squealers', appeared lying across our path. These were anchored equally spaced into the distance, port and starboard, and were flying Danish flags. On the nearest, to starboard, a seaman leant against the mast smoking his pipe.

Events started to speed up rapidly as the cloud cover gave out and we were flying under a blue sky towards a sun-drenched coastline some miles ahead. The element of surprise was gone

and Wg Cdr Burt opened up his throttles and headed for the nearest coastal vessel. This he proceeded to attack four times, dropping a 250lb bomb on each occasion. His wife and children had lost their lives in a German air raid, I had been told. In the meantime, the flight had broken up with each Blenheim looking for a target. Bill turned to port and flew parallel to the coast and soon a large group of small, grey, naval craft, probably minesweepers, appeared out to sea moving in the same direction. Two flakships, vessels with tripod structures surmounted with gun platforms, escorted the convoy. Bill headed for the one near the front and a coloured, four-star recognition signal rose into the air soon to be followed by red tracer from the gun positions. I watched with fascination as these blobs of cannon fire slowly climbed to a point in their trajectory and suddenly snapped into a rapid acceleration towards us. They flew all around our aircraft,

Sqn Ldr Alan Judson's crew ('B' Flight commander, 114 Squadron) was sent out as one of twenty-four crews to sweep the coastal shipping lanes between Cherbourg and Texel on 2 August in Blenheim V5875:

Offshore between Ameland and Borkum we sighted, at great distance, aircraft which I reported to Sqn Ldr Alan Judson as Me.110s. It is here that I have to reveal a rather worrying characteristic of my pilot. He once confided in me that he had a theory that if we encountered enemy aircraft, of whatever type, if we turned into the attack this would both surprise and demoralize the enemy and give us a psychological advantage. How do you convey to a senior officer, even if at that time you were able to speak, that you think that he is talking rubbish? I did not follow up on the topic and just hoped that should the occasion arise he would think better of it if they were fighter aircraft.

No sooner had I reported the sighting of the Me.110s than, consistent with his theory, Alan Judson wheeled towards them, climbing as he turned. As we closed I suddenly realized, to my relief, that they were not Me.110s but four reconnaissance seaplanes and at a distance I had taken the floats for twin engines. This was one occasion when I was delighted to have made a mistake. The nearer we came the easier identification became and they were, in fact, four Arado 196 aircraft. I immediately advised Alan Judson that many of such aircraft had cannons fitted in the floats and it was therefore inadvisable to make a head-on attack. He heeded my information and made the initial attack from below and astern.

Unfortunately, one of our other aircraft did make a head-on attack, was hit by cannon fire and the crew suffered severe injuries [Sgts Locke, Hindle and Johnstone in V6378 'B', landed at Bodney at 15.50hr]. Ivor Broom, who was the third member of the formation, made no such mistake and suffered no damage. We continued our attack on one particular aircraft for what seemed a very long period of time, but despite our efforts the only visible sign of success was smoke coming from his engine as he headed east into the mainland of Germany. By this time we were at a very vulnerable height around 3–4,000ft in a clear sky to the north-west of Groningen and decided that to prolong the encounter further would be folly. When we broke off our attack all other aircraft had disappeared and we headed for home. After landing we inspected the aircraft and found a number of bullet holes in the fuselage and damage to the bombsight.

Channel Stop

Apart from the low-level shipping strikes off the enemy-occupied coastlines, coastal target raids and fighter-escorted circus attacks, the dreaded *Channel Stop* campaign also continued during the cruel summer of 1941. On 17 July, it was 21 Squadron's turn for a two-weeks' stay at Manston. Its crews were on the receiving end almost immediately. At dusk the next day, Sqn Ldr D. Graham-Hogg led off three Blenheims, with a Hurricane escort to silence the ships' flak. Off Gravelines a convoy was sighted, consisting of a 6,000-ton freighter and no fewer than six flak ships. All three Blenheims raced in for the merchantman at zero feet, but Graham-Hogg's Z7502 and Sgt J.R.M. Kemp's V5595 were mortally hit by a curtain of flak, crashing into the sea and on the beach short of their quarry, surprisingly with the loss of only one crew member. Sgt

Blenheim 'S' of 21 Squadron skimming over the Waalhaven in Rotterdam harbour on 16 July 1941. The 10,547 tons MV Oranjefontein can be seen burning in the background. Pieter Bergman

Maguire's V6369 YH-N was badly shot up on the run in; the shaken crew struggled back to Manston safely but their aircraft was beyond repair and never flew again. Five days later the Squadron suffered even more grievously when four out of six attacking Blenheims were shot down within two minutes in mid afternoon in a hail of fire off Ostend. The target this time was a 4,000-ton tanker, escorted by four *Vorpostenboote*, which escaped unscathed. Only three men were picked up from the sea to be taken prisoner. It was another black day for 2 Group with 18 Squadron losing R3666 and V6250 to Bf 110s of 5/ZG76 off Den Helder during an early afternoon shipping sweep. On 25 July 18 Squadron relieved the hard-hit 21 Squadron, which returned to Watton to lick its wounds. Replacement aircraft and crews were flown in and within a week 21 Squadron had regained operational strength. These terrible losses earned Manston the doubtful nickname in 2 Group of 'Hell's Half Acre'. 18 Squadron had a luckier spell at Manston, as only Flt Lt W. Hughes in V6038 WV-H for Harry and his crew were lost after hitting the mast of their target ship and crashing into the sea off Le Touquet on 20 July. 139 Squadron suffered the loss of a very experienced NCO crew in the same area that afternoon, when Z7499 was hit by flak while attacking an 8,000-ton tanker and crashed into the sea. Sgt Norman Baron, DFM was buried in Blankenberge, whilst Sgts K.W. Hopkinson and Robert W. Ullmer, DFM found a last resting place in Boulogne.

226 Squadron left Wattisham on 4 August to replace No. 18. One of the green crews flying into Manston in 'A' Flight that day was Sgt Bill O'Connell, RCAF and his crew of Sgt Peter Saunders, observer and Plt Off Les Harrell, W.Op/AG. Amazingly, after five days of waiting without any action, O'Connell's fellow Canadian pilot and friend Sgt 'Ossie' Osborne, with whom he had done all his training in the RCAF, walked into the crew room. 'Ossie' had been posted to 'B' Flight, 226 Squadron only that day, as O'Connell recounts:

The next morning, 10 August, when I met Ossie in the crew room he was not his usual cheerful self. He was worried. I asked him what was wrong. He explained that he had a problem. He had been in both Ramsgate and Margate the evening before, and he had met a fine young

After receiving hits from ships' flak, V5595 YH-P of 21 Squadron crashed on the beach at Gravelines during a *Channel Stop* operation on 18 July 1941. Miraculously, Sgt Kemp and his crew got away from this tangled mess with only a few cuts and bruises and were taken prisoner. 21 Squadron lost Z7502 on the same operation, and V6369 was so badly shot up that it never flew again after landing back at Manston. Cynrik de Decker

lady whom he was certain that he would one day marry. By Ossie's account, it was a case of mutual love at first sight and he had made a date to meet this girl again at 6pm that evening to take her to dinner. Being his first day on the squadron, he thought when he made the date that 'B' Flight would be stood-down around 3pm, as they had yesterday. He had not found out until breakfast time in the Sergeants' Mess that, being in 'B' Flight, he would not be stood-down until about an hour before sunset. It would be impossible for him to meet his date. Worse still, the girl was out of reach for the day and he had no way that he could get a message to her. He was very depressed. Had there been a spare crew in 'B' Flight it might not have been much of a problem, but each flight had no more than a full complement and no reserves.

He asked me if I would switch places with him for the day. I thought for a moment, then said that I couldn't. I looked upon crewing-up as a trust with my crew, and switching to another crew seemed to smack a little of a breach of faith. Anyway, I didn't think the flight commanders would like the idea because a casualty in a possible operation would create problems for the flights and the surviving crew members concerned. Ossie knew he had erred in asking the question and he apologized. He was grasping at straws. We sat together in silence at one end of the crew room. Ossie was in no mood for talking. Finally, I said, 'Look, Ossie, if you can get your crew to agree, and I can get mine of the

same mind, it may be that our crews could switch flights for the rest of the day. It's a chance, but the flight commanders might be receptive.' He brightened a bit and asked, 'Would your crew do it?'; I said, 'I don't know. But it's worth a try.' I told him to go and check with his crew first, then I would check with mine.

He was off immediately to talk with his crew and was back in less than a minute to report that it was OK with his crew. It was my turn. When I explained Ossie's problem to my crew, they were less than enthusiastic about changing flights for the day because it would mean three consecutive, long and boring, afternoon stand-by stints. But, they were very understanding and after a little discussion they agreed. I reported to Ossie and said, 'All you have to do now is tell the flight commanders about your love life. I'm not going to do it.' He was off to the flight offices, and when I saw him returning in about five minutes, he was beaming. No need to ask questions about how it went. Ossie was going to have lots of time to meet his date. His crew would get a bonus too: they would have three consecutive early stand-downs. Now in 'B' Flight, I wasn't exactly excited about three successive, long, afternoon/evening stand-bys.

Apart from being almost fawned on by Ossie for a couple of minutes, I saw very little of him for the rest of the morning. When we got on the squadron bus with 'B' Flight to go to lunch, Ossie, who would be going to lunch with 'A'

Late in the afternoon of 20 July 1941, Flt Lt W. Hughes led three aircraft of 18 Squadron and three of 139 Squadron on an attack against the 6,900-tons tanker *Karabishes-Meer* off Le Touquet. During the strike Flt Lt Hughes in V6038 WV-H clipped the mast of the ship and is seen here crashing into the sea with the loss of the whole crew. The tanker was beached, but after being refloated was towed into Le Havre. Public Record Office: Air 37/47

A 139 Squadron aircraft banking away steeply after having straddled a 1,500-tons vessel in a six-ship convoy in the Heligoland Bight, 30 July 1941. On this black day, seven out of forty-three Blenheims dispatched were lost off the Dutch and northern German coasts. Don Bruce

the doorway from down the hall and asked for our attention. We were all ears. He said that 'A' Flight had been scrambled to attack a German coastal convoy just minutes after we had left for lunch and that they had fared badly. It was what we had feared. Five of their six aircraft had been shot down by two squadrons of Me.109 fighters which had been escorting the convoy and had broken from their escort flight pattern to intercept the Blenheims several miles from the convoy. A squadron of Hurricane fighters which was escorting the Blenheims couldn't handle the situation. The Hurricane pilots reported that they were overwhelmed and had to spend all their time looking after themselves. The Blenheims thus became fairly easy prey for the extra Me.109s that the Hurricanes had been unable to engage. All the Hurricanes had returned. Some of the Hurricane pilots who had been in the dogfight scoured the area of the engagement off Dover at low level immediately before returning to Manston, looking for survivors. There were none. My heart sank when the flight commander said that only one of 'A' Flight's six aircraft had returned. Ossie and his crew had been shot down. After answering a few questions and announcing that 'B' Flight had been ordered to stand-down status, he returned to his office.

There was a heavy silence in the crew room. Several of the 'B' Flight aircrew patted me on the back, and one shook my hand. But no one said a word. There was nothing to say. In a matter that seemed only seconds, almost half the 'B' Flight crews had melted away, and there were only three or four of us left in the crew room, saying nothing. I didn't ask myself, 'What if?'; I knew. And my crew knew. But, at the same time, I was sad. And I did think how ironic it was that fate seemed to mock Ossie cruelly when 'B' Flight was ordered to stand-down status that day before 1pm. I had planned to do Ossie a friendly favour by agreeing to switch flights with our crews for the day. Instead, I was left to mourn his loss because fate had other ideas. Ossie and his crew had been on 226 Squadron for less than one day.

According to official records, at 11.50hr, three 226 Squadron aircraft had taken to the air from Manston with a fighter escort for an attack on a reported 2,000-ton ship, escorted by two flak ships off Fort Phillipe. Braving a curtain of both heavy and light flak, Sqn Ldr Waddington in V5854 'L' hurled his bombs at the merchant vessel from zero feet, but they fell short of the target. V5854 then received the full attention of the flak; it stalled and crashed into the sea. On the run in to the merchant

Flight when we returned, was in high spirits. He could hardly wait to meet his date. As we boarded the bus, he slapped me on the back and said, 'I'm going to buy you guys a drink, you know, but I owe you a lot more than that.'

When we returned from lunch on the bus an hour and a half later to take up our long stand-by status until late evening, we found the crew room empty. The atmosphere was eerie and ominous, but no one dared wonder out loud. We

could hear voices coming from down a short hallway off the crew room down which were the offices of the flight commanders, with the squadron CO's office at the end of the hall. The voices were coming from behind the closed door of the CO's office, but we couldn't make out what was being said. The whole flight was silent until a voice said, with more hope than optimism, 'They'll be back shortly.'

One of the flight commanders appeared in

Sqn Ldr Martin Waddington of 226 Squadron with his newly-wed wife. Waddington went missing on 10 August 1941 while leading a Channel Stop convoy strike. James Waddington

ship, Sgt Osborne in Z7280 'M' was attacked from the rear by a Bf 109 and shot down in flames. Sgt Chippendale and his crew in the sole surviving Blenheim Z7304 'S' returned to Manston, having scored two direct hits amidships on the camouflaged main target ship. This is the official story. Several 226 Squadron survivors are convinced, however, that not two but five Blenheims were shot down on this operation and that none of the aircraft got within a mile of the convoy. They therefore claim that the official story is incorrect and that someone, somehow recklessly lost the records of three aircraft and nine aircrew.

A detachment of 139 Squadron stayed at Manston between 27 August and 7 September, losing Sqn Ldr Kevin H. Walsh and his crew in Z7274 to ships' flak off Zeebrugge on the 2nd. 88 Squadron took over responsibility for Channel Stop on 7 September, mounting a costly operation on the 18th. Three crews with a strong Hurricane and Spitfire escort attacked a 5,000-ton tanker, which was escorted by no fewer than ten flak ships, off Blankenberge. Suddenly, during the run in, Fw.190s and Bf 110s jumped the bombers. V6380 'G', flown by Plt Off Bruce E. Hislop, RAAF on his first operation, was destroyed by Ofw Roth of 4/JG26 at 11.15hr. Z7488 'F' fell foul to Lt Koenig

of 5/ZG76, Plt Off T.E. Cooper, RNZAF and his crew disappearing without a trace. The Canadian Sqn Ldr Harris, in his badly shot-up Z7353, struggled back to Manston to make a belly-landing, his observer, Flt Sgt Woolbridge, succumbing to his wounds in Margate hospital. On the credit side, Hptm Walther Adolph, Gruppen Kommandeur of II/JG26 an ace with twenty-eight victories, was killed while dogfighting with the Blenheims' 91 Squadron Spitfire escort. This Ritterkreuzträger, who had destroyed three Blenheims during May 1940, fell victim to either Fg Off Labouchere or Plt Off Slade.

Fighter Command finally took over the Channel Stop operations on 9 October. 402 and 607 Squadrons' Hurricane IIB fighter-bombers, equipped with 20mm cannons and 250lb bombs, proved much more effective and less vulnerable than the Blenheim in this deadly work.

Due to the heavy losses incurred during June and July, the average life expectancy for fresh crews joining 2 Group had been reduced to as little as two to three weeks. Blenheim courses in 13 and 17 OTU, officially lasting twelve weeks, were even cut back to only four weeks to keep the seriously depleted Blenheim squadrons in 2 Group nominally up to strength. During July losses reached their peak during the 1941 daylight campaign, with forty-four

aircraft lost on operations, plus five in training. Twenty-seven crew members were taken prisoner; the other 109 men were posted as killed or missing. When these losses were compared with 2 Group's first-line strength of nine squadrons with 101 aircraft and eighty-nine operational crews in mid August, it was quite clear that the Blenheim's days as an effective daylight bomber in the west were finally over. The hard-pressed crews, finally getting long-range Spitfire fighter escorts on anti-shipping sweeps from 18 August, did not conceal this fact, nor that it became increasingly clear that the Blenheim, with its small payload, was unable to inflict major damage on enemy coastal shipping.

The Cologne Raid

Before the month of August was out, however, two further spectacular daylight raids were planned by 2 Group HQ, the first for Sunday, 12 August. Virtually all shipping sweeps were suspended for one week and the crews were kept busy practising low-level formation flying. With his four months on 114 Squadron, the twenty-years-old pilot Flt Lt Charles Patterson was already a veteran. He flew as Wg Cdr Nichol's (114 Squadron's new CO) number two in the practice flying preceding the large-scale raid:

As deputy leader to him I was taken into the operations room on Friday, 10 August, to look at the target and at what this operation was to be. The atmosphere throughout the whole group was very tense as to what the target was. It had been rumoured that it was to be a factory outside Paris, which, without a fighter escort, sounded terrifying enough. I'll never forget the sight that met my eyes when I went into the operations room. There was a huge map on a table laid out in the centre of the ops room. And there, leading absolutely straight, was a red tape from Orfordness straight across the North Sea, right through Holland and right down to Cologne. At first I just didn't believe that this was the target. I assumed it referred to something else. But then I realized that it must be. And the truth, the reality dawned on me: that I was going to have to take part in a low-level daylight attack on Cologne, with no fighter escort, in Blenheims. Well, I can still feel the sense of shock now.

However, it was no use panicking or doing anything about it at the time. So I listened to the briefing and instructions I was given. Of

Wg Cdr Charles Patterson, DSO, DFC, taken on completion of his third tour of operations in Blenheims and Mosquitoes with 114 and 105 Squadron. Charles Patterson

course, the target was not Cologne itself but the Knapsack power station which Gp Capt Bandon told me was the biggest in Europe. I was shown a photograph of it. It had twelve chimneys on one side and eight on the other; 114 Squadron was to lead the operation. Wg Cdr Nichol was to lead it although he'd never operated before. But, of course, he had probably the best navigator in the Group to go with him, Flt Lt Tommy Baker, DFM. The navigator was the key man for this sort of operation. We were to fly down between these chimneys and then turn round and come back again. Well, I accepted that at the time.

I went out and thought about it. I of course couldn't communicate what the target was to anybody else. I had to carry this secret about with me with my fellow air crew for two days. Then I had to make up my mind – could I do this? The chances of surviving an operation like that appeared negligible at that time. Well, how was I, a fundamental coward who'd managed to skate past up to now, to make myself do this operation?

The next two days were spent in wrestling with myself as to how I was to do it. And I evolved an attitude, a philosophy, peculiar to myself. I found that the only thing to do was to stop worrying and say to yourself: you're not coming back. You've just got to go. You're caught in this situation. The alternative is to just completely funk it and not go at all. That – I don't know why, I can't explain it – to me seemed of the two the more impossible. So I just

resigned myself to the fact that I was not coming back. And I had to live with that for two days. Well, life goes on. One did live with it.

Finally, in the early hours of 12 August, the crews were briefed that their targets were the two large power-generating stations of Knapsack and Quadrath on the northern outskirts of Cologne. In all, fifty-four Blenheims would be engaged, 36 of 18, 107, 114 and 139 Squadrons heading for Knapsack, with Wg Cdr Nichol in the lead. Another eighteen from 21 and 82 Squadrons, led by Wg Cdr Kercher of 21 Squadron, were to bomb Quadrath. Once the bombs had been released the crews were to retake low-level formation and follow a reciprocal course to the coast where, if all went well, a strong fighter escort would await them. The targets were 150miles inland from the coast which would entail flying unescorted over enemy territory in daylight for at least two hours. There would be the coastal defences and enemy fighters to contend with and finally the North Sea to cross. It was indeed a daunting prospect for the crews. Patterson continues:

I spent a pretty poor night's sleep the night before, and I do remember when I woke at half-past six, suddenly remembering that this was the morning when I was just not going to come back. And still saying, well, it's got to be. When all the crews in the squadron gathered into the operations room and they all realized what the target was – hardened though some of them

were, even the most hardened ones – there was the most terrible sort of gasp of disbelief. And unlike me, of course, they hadn't had the opportunity to prepare themselves. Well, the operation was very comprehensively planned. We learned that there were to be diversionary bombing attacks in northern France. There were to be two Flying Fortresses flying at great height who were going to attack northern Germany. Everything was being done to mislead and divert the enemy fighter defences.

The great dread was not only the tremendous light flak that we assumed would surround the target, but, of course, the assumption was that we could hardly expect to get into Germany, and we certainly couldn't get out, without all being shot down by fighters. All the experience showed that when a formation of Blenheims was actually intercepted by 109s it was unusual for more than one or two out of six to get away. Sometimes none got away.

Well, it's the only time in my life that I can recall seeing some of my fellow air crew literally grey and shaking. My own air gunner who was a pretty imperturbable type – I can see his face now absolutely grey and looking at me with a wry look. Curiously enough, seeing all the others looking so frightened rather bolstered me a bit. Because I'd already dealt with the situation psychologically, and come to terms with what the outcome was going to be. This lifted a certain amount of the load.

So the full briefing went through. Then we all went up to the airfield. We had to take off at about eight o'clock. We'd been advised to rendezvous with various other squadrons over Orfordness and then set off across the North Sea

Funeral of Plt Off Rolland and his 82 Squadron crew in Strijen cemetery. They were shot down by flak in T2437, crashing at Strijensas near Moerdijkbridge as the first Blenheim to go down on the 12 August 1941 Cologne raid. Henk Nootenboom

at low level. We all took off, formed up and I formated on Wg Cdr Nichol. We all rendezvoused on time and came down to low level over the North Sea. Although I thought I was going to certain death, as I actually got involved and we were really off, somehow the scale or the element of the adventurous aspect of it began to take over. And the involvement in the actual operation and the flying. Here I'm glad to say I found I was not as panicky as I had expected.

Then I'd always wondered what on earth enemy territory looked like. And it was when we suddenly found ourselves flying over these flat, sandy Dutch islands and actually entering enemy territory and nobody had shot at us as we came in... Everything looked so normal and real that it was in some extraordinary way reassuring – just the normality of the surroundings, of the countryside. And being so low and able to see ordinary Dutch people in the fields. And the

Twenty-seven-years old Wg Cdr James 'Nick' Nicol, here depicted hunting off duty from Upwood in July 1941. Later that month Nicol, a prewar regular, was posted as CO to 114 Squadron, being awarded a DSO for leading Strike Force 2 on the Cologne raid of 12 August 1941, his first operation. Nicol was married to Pip: 'I did see Nick just after the Cologne raid. He told me they found an unexpected new chimney in the way at Knapsack, so they had to blow that up first. One of his crew had his jaw hit so he was in Ely Hospital when they were shot down later on. Group had said they weren't going in close enough so I suppose that's what they did the next week.' One week after the Cologne raid, a complete vic of three 114 Squadron aircraft which Nicol was leading fell to three Bf 110s of II/ZG76 during a shipping strike off Vlieland. There were no survivors. Pip Wray

little houses and everything just underneath us. It all looked so normal. It was reassuring.

Well, we flew down south of a German fighter airfield called Woensdrecht, down the Schelde estuary into the heathland of Holland which was all new to me, this sort of countryside. I was formating closely on Wg Cdr Nichol, at the same time keeping one eye ahead, at any moment expecting these fighters. We went on mile after mile, not a cloud in the sky, and still no fighters. I asked my navigator, 'How long?' He said, 'Not long now.' And then I remember on the RT, Wg Cdr Nichol saying: 'Turn to starboard.' Which meant, of course, a very, very gentle turn because we were only just above the ground. As I turned slightly to starboard, there, away up on the top of a long, long slope about two or three miles away – unmistakable – was this enormous industrial complex with these chimneys. I realized this was Knapsack up on the top of the hill there.

We turned to starboard, and I thought, well, we've just got to go now. There'll be a big bang, and that's all I'll know. We'll just have to get on with it now. And we climbed up the hill. As we went up this long slope for the last two or three miles to the target, we had to climb up a bit to avoid the increasing maze of pylons and wires. The electrical grids and everything started long before we got to the target, which made one realize what an enormous place it was. Then the chimneys came unmistakably into view. We got closer and closer until the chimneys were coming right up to us. Wg Cdr Nichol swung in between the chimneys. And I followed him. Then I became enveloped in mist and steam from the complex. I was in it now. There was nothing I could do about it now except concentrate on flying the aeroplane properly. We had been told not to release our bombs on the attractive-looking watercoolers but to keep them for the actual power house at the far end. And so we flew on down between these chimneys. As we did so, I saw a lot of blue flashes from the ground which would be machine-gun fire. But I was past caring about that now. At the far end of the power station I could see the great thing now in front of my eyes and the steam and the smoke and everything. I pressed my tit and let the bombs go. As I did so, I saw Wg Cdr Nichol just ahead of me swerve sharply to starboard. I did the same; I realized that he was about to fly into a chimney which he just missed.

Then, out the other side – a lot more blue flashes and sparks and tracer. We dived down to the ground. Wg Cdr Nichol was there. He'd survived. I formed up on him. We raced away across the cables again down past the other side of the power station, started to turn to starboard

to fly on the course back for England or the Dutch coast. To my amazement, all of the other five members of the formation emerged safely and formed up with us and we set off for the journey home. Well, despite the fact that we covered the target, I didn't feel any particular sense of relief, because it was the journey home which seemed the most impossible part of it. We were bound to be intercepted.

Well, I settled down in formation. The other chap who was on my starboard settled down to formate on me and the whole formation got together. We set off for home. We flew on and on over the heath of western Germany and into Holland. Still we went on and on. No interception yet. And then we flew into a rainstorm. For one wonderful moment I thought we were going to get cloud cover, but it was only a shower and we emerged very shortly afterwards out into the brilliant sun again. No cloud above us. On and on over these fields, past little villages and hamlets, with the occasional individual diving into a ditch beneath us. Then just before we got to the German border, we flew over a typical German industrialist's Victorian, semi-baronial mansion with turrets and a garden. I just got a glimpse beside a cedar tree of a table with a large white tablecloth, all laid out for lunch because it was about midday. A group of people were standing round it. As we whizzed over the top of this my gunner let fly and broke up the party. He felt that any rich Germans who were living like that while the war was on deserved to be shot. Now that sounds appalling, but at the time it seemed right and proper.

Well on across now into Holland, further and further on. Then suddenly it seemed to me we were going to make it. Nothing was going to happen after all. But it's always when that psychological moment comes that you're brought down to earth. Suddenly ahead of us just as we were coming up to the estuary of the Schelde black dots appeared ahead of us. For a moment my navigator thought they might be Spitfires which had come out to escort us home. And, sure enough, the leader, Wg Cdr Nichol called out, 'Snappers.' I was flying on straight into these Messerschmitts which were circling around about a thousand feet above us. Wg Cdr Nichol told us to close in tight. He led us right down on to the water. The water was racing underneath, sparkling in the sun. We couldn't have been more than ten, fifteen, occasionally perhaps twenty feet above it. And I got as tight into him as I could. I knew this was life or death. Frankly, the concentration on the flying side of it was able to drive out most of the fear of the fighters – the sheer concentration of flying so close, so low. With my wing tip practically inside his wing tip, at that height. It took all the

With great flying skill, Plt Off F.M.W. Johnstone belly-landed his flak-riddled and burning Z7289 MQ-R of 226 Squadron in the typically flat Dutch countryside near Kethel, located in the area to the north of the Rotterdam docks, 28 August 1941. Wim Hermans

flying concentration and skill I possessed to do it. And the others closed in.

Then Wg Cdr Nichol handed over, as was the tactical drill, to the leading gunner, Plt Off Morton, who was a very experienced second-tour air gunner. He then directed the formation because the gunners looking back could all see the fighters coming into the attack. Also, he had to decide when was the right moment to open fire and when was the right moment to take evasive action. Evasive action consisted of turning into the attack, as is well known. As the fighters dived down to attack at the right moment – which was up to his judgement – the leading gunner would say: 'Turn to starboard/port', according to the angle at which the fighters were coming in. It's the starboard turns I remember. Wg Cdr Nichol would begin his gentle turn, and I would have to concentrate on turning with him with my wing tip practically inside his. Then I heard the rattle of machine-gun fire – I realized our guns were firing. I could see every now and then the water between Wg Cdr Nichol's Blenheim and mine, and the water between my Blenheim and the one on my starboard being ripped with white froth, which, of course, was the cannon shells of these 109s.

Then, on one turn to starboard, out of the corner of my eye out of the starboard Perspex

window of my cockpit, I caught a glimpse of a 109 right in front of my eyes, peeling off its attack, so close that I saw the pilot in the cockpit – let alone the black crosses and the yellow nose of the 109. Even then my reaction was simply one of interest in seeing a 109 so close. Then we straightened up. Of course, I knew, we all knew, that the only safety was to be out to sea, out of the range of these 109s. And we would make it. After each attack one just had to crouch down and prepare for the next. And this carried on all the way up the Schelde estuary; they made several attacks of this same nature. Yet we still seemed to survive them. And I do remember thinking, by Jove, the gunners must be doing a wonderful job.

Then, unbelievably, the islands to each side of us suddenly ceased and we were in the open sea. We'd hardly gone any distance out to sea when the leading gunner told us over the RT that the fighters had broken off the attack. I suppose they were running out of ammunition. And we still didn't feel it was all over yet. So one didn't relax. But we carried on out to sea.

The first reaction of realizing that I had survived was a sort of numbness. Then the leading Blenheim climbed gently up; we were sufficiently far out to sea. He climbed up to about five hundred, six hundred feet. And I realized we'd survived. I suppose when I think

about it, it was the greatest moment of elation I've ever experienced in all my life. Even with all the operations that were to come, nothing was quite like that. We'd survived, and all seven in the 'vic' had survived.

Then it was just a matter of flying back, waving to each other through the cockpits and through the Perspex. Waving at the other pilots and the gunners. And we'd all seven survived. We'd made it. It was just marvellous, happy relief. Just joy, sheer joy, flying back across the North Sea. And then the cliffs came up: England, we're back. Then the rather basic but perhaps human realization that we were returning as national heroes. Because we knew this would cause tremendous headlines. It would be the headline thing. We felt at the time that we'd done something so astounding that it would live for ever and ever as one of the greatest operations there'd ever been.

Well, we came in and landed, one after the other. I can't remember anything more than the haze of relief and excitement, joy and everything. I don't remember the debriefing now, it doesn't matter. There was a general opinion that we'd all hit the target. Then reports began to come in that we'd got away with it, but it hadn't been quite the same for many of the others. By the afternoon word got round that we'd lost twelve and that several others had been badly shot up and crash landed. And that the two Blenheims which had navigated the Spitfire fighters out to meet us, to escort us home, had both been shot down. Which seemed very tragic and unfair, and a terrible waste. And then, of course, the inevitable relaxation – we were all to go to Norwich, the whole group for a party and a beat up. We all met up with all the squadrons, the other crews. And drank away. All great excitement, great fun. We felt very heroic and wonderful. We never gave a thought to the future. We thought, this is it. We've done it. We forgot there was any future.

In all twelve Blenheims were lost on the Cologne raid. Three (from 21 and 82 Squadrons) fell to flak on the way in; V5725 and Z7448 of 139 Squadron were destroyed over the target; and in a fierce air battle over the Schelde estuary on the way out, seven more were shot down (of 226, 18, 21, 139, and 114 Squadrons). But, considering the odds on the biggest low-level daylight raid of the war, with the deepest penetration into enemy territory yet undertaken, the 22 per cent Blenheim losses were considered to be acceptable. Deservedly the raid made big headlines in the national press, and a few days later, the AOC AVM Stevenson offered his personal congratulations to the assembled survivors. He went on to announce that the pilots of the leading formations had each been awarded the DFC and, in recognition of their leadership in the two separate attacks, DSOs went to Wg Cdrs Kercher and Nichol.

The Attack on the Submarine Pens

During the following two weeks 2 Group was employed in the usual mixture of anti-shipping sweeps and circus operations to northern France. One of the most controversial operations during the second half of the 1941 daylight campaign took place on 24 August. On that day Wg Cdr Lascelles, DFC, a cousin of the Royal Family and 82 Squadron's new CO was ordered to lead six of his crews on a daylight raid to attack the passenger liner Europa, reported as docked in Bremerhaven. Take-off from Bodney was at 12.25hr, but, owing to lack of cloud cover, Lascelles decided to break off the raid and head back for home. To 'press on regardless' would have been suicidal. On the way back, Plt Off Robinson bombed a 300-ton vessel but no hits were observed, all aircraft returning to base safely. It was rumoured at Bodney next day that AVM Stevenson was

Another view of the ruined Z7289 MQ-R of 226 Squadron in the Dutch countryside, so expertly landed by Plt Off F.M.W. Johnstone. After the crash-landing the three-man crew were all taken prisoner, remarkably suffering only cuts and bruises. Wim Hermans

displeased with Lascelles's decision not to press on to the primary target during the previous day. It therefore came as no surprise when orders were issued that the same crews were to be briefed for a similar operation on the next day, 26 August. This time the crews were ordered to make low-level attacks on the submarine pens at Heligoland. Wg Cdr Lascelles (in T2165 'W') led the formation off from Bodney shortly after 10.30hr for the long haul eastwards. T2162 'Y', in the hands of Plt Off Bartlett, was forced to abandon its task owing to engine trouble, returning to base at 13.07hr. V6454 'H', flown by Plt Off Robinson, lost touch with the formation nearing the target area and returned alone at 15.35hr. The other four aircraft all failed to return: they were shot down into the North Sea by three Bf 109s of I/JG53 prowling off the island of Juist, with no survivors. Plt Off Walter S. Robinson had joined 82 Squadron earlier that month with his crew of Plt Off Kenneth Pike (observer) and Sgt Attenborough (W.Op/AG). He takes up the story:

It was common knowledge that the submarine pens at Heligoland were not only heavily defended but also protected by heavy layers of concrete. Even if we were successful in bombing it is doubtful whether our 500lb bombs dropped from 50ft with 11sec delay fuses would do more than scratch the paint on the pens.

However, 'theirs not to reason why…', so we set out on the morning of the 26th in the same two vics of three aircraft with Wg Cdr Lascelles leading the formation in the starboard vic, on

course for Heligoland. The route was virtually identical to that of two days earlier. We flew, of course, by dead reckoning, as no direction-finding beams then existed and we ourselves observed strict radio silence. Due, probably, to an incorrect wind forecast, we did not sight Heligoland. Some minutes after our ETA for Heligoland we sighted an island straight ahead which my navigator identified as Neuwerk. Lascelles, at the same moment, also apparently realized that the island in view was not Heligoland and commenced a turn to starboard. He did not, apparently, identify the island as Neuwerk as, in that case, he would have called for a turn to port in the direction of Heligoland.

We were, by that time, flying almost line abreast as, in any case, our formation flying in Blenheims was pretty loose at best. Consequently, in order not to close in on the formation leader, I could turn only very slowly, to the point where I was going to cross in front of Neuwerk in a belly-up attitude. I decided that, to avoid becoming such an easy target for flak, to fly across the island, only some few hundred yards wide, before turning to starboard. This I did but found myself chasing behind the others, now some miles ahead. They were, in fact, four aircraft, as one of our flight had turned back over the North Sea with engine trouble.

After a few minutes we sighted the German coast near Cuxhaven and I lost sight of the rest of the flight in the coastal haze. There seemed little point in hanging around so decided to return to base. We set course north-west and, after some time, actually sighted Heligoland off to starboard. I was not so foolish as attempt a lone strike at the island and contented myself with dropping our bombs on a small ship that appeared in our path just off the island.

We arrived back at Bodney after a flight time of 5.05hr. After recounting our experience to the Station Group Captain, who had come over from Watton, we waited, and waited, but no other aircraft appeared. The atmosphere in the mess that night was strange and no further mention was made of the operation. I was not debriefed in the normal meaning of the term.

Our participation in that operation was never recognized. It was as if the powers that be wanted to draw a blind over the whole affair. I had the impression that they would have preferred if we also had not returned. If, in fact, Lascelles was sent out on 26 August to atone for his 'cowardice' it is shameful that eleven other aircrew also were condemned to death. As a novice pilot officer, twenty years old, I could hardly be expected to be au fait with high-level intrigue, but I could certainly feel sad over the loss of my friends and comrades.

Rotterdam Again

In an effort to repeat the success of the Rotterdam docks raid on 16 July, 2 Group HQ decided to mount a similar operation two days after the controversial 82 Squadron effort, on 28 August. Thirty-six crews of 21, 88, 110 and 226 Squadrons

were briefed for the raid, which was to be executed on broadly similar lines to the raid of six weeks earlier, with two exceptions. This time the aircraft were loaded with 500lb bombs, which were much better suited to cause lasting damage to larger ships. Secondly, a strong escort of long-range Spitfires were to keep any intruding Luftwaffe fighters away from the bombers. The whole concept of the raid was looking very promising, but things went wrong from the start. A first attempt was recalled in mid afternoon after Sgt Bill O'Connell, RCAF, in Z7299 of 226 Squadron, had crashed on take-off from Wattisham and after the leader of the raid had to abort with engine trouble.

It was decided to make another attempt in the early evening with half of the original force, seventeen aircraft of 21, 88 and 226 Squadrons. This time the formation set off without mishap, but, due to a small navigational error, landfall was made over a heavily defended stretch of coastline at the Hook of Holland. The approaching bombers were swiftly reported to the Rotterdam defences and the shore batteries and flak ships at the Hook immediately opened up. Z7447 of 21 Squadron (with Sqn Ldr Dick Shuttleworth, the leader of the raid, at the controls) and L9379 of 88

Squadrons crashed in flames in the Scheurpolder with the loss of all on board. The remaining fifteen Blenheims hedge-hopped to the east towards the line of harbour cranes and ships' masts on the horizon. Braving a hail of flak, the crews selected their individual targets and at least three large ships were hit. The 12,150-tons *Zuiderdam* and its sister ship the *Westerdam* were severely damaged, as was the 10,574-tons merchantman *Oranjefontein*. The decision to use 500lb bombs on this raid clearly paid off. The harbour defences were on full alert, however, and three of the attackers were shot down by flak in the target area. Z7445 of 88 Squadron, flown by Flt Lt Alexander, crashed into the slaughterhouse at Schiedam and Plt Off Frank Orme's V6436 exploded at Maassluis, with the loss of all six men on board. Plt Off Johnstone skillfully belly-landed his burning Z7289 at Kethel and together with his crew was fortunate to survive with only cuts and bruises.

In the meantime, Bf 109s of JG53 had scrambled from Katwijk airfield and rushed to the scene. Its pilots were soon entangled in fierce dogfighting with the Blenheims' Spitfire escorts. Still Lt Hans Müller of 6/JG53 managed to evade the British fighters and destroyed 21 Squadron's Z7435 and V5825 at 20.15 and 20.25hr, respectively. Two crew members of the latter plane survived to be taken prisoner. Just ten out of the original seventeen Blenheims, many of them with shaken crews and severe battle-scars, made it back to their bases in East Anglia. The raid inspired Winston Churchill to write his famous message to the crews: 'The devotion of the attacks on Rotterdam and other objectives are beyond all praise. The charge of the Light Brigade at Balaclava is eclipsed in brightness by these almost daily deeds of fame.'

Z7359 'R' for Robert of 18 Squadron with Sqn Ldr Lerwill, DFC and crew, plus five groundcrew, before a shipping strike off Ijmuiden on 12 September 1941. This veteran Blenheim is sporting a bomb log of thirty-two operational sorties completed in 18 Squadron during the summer of 1941. The two swastikas represent two Bf 109Es destroyed by the crew's previous air gunner, AC1 Jack Guest (14 May 1940 over Sedan) and LAC Bill Bradshaw (who is depicted second from the right) on 11 June 1940. 'R' for Robert went on to serve in 105 and 11 Squadrons, finally crashing in a forced landing on 25 January 1942. Harry Huckins

End of the Daylight Raids

During August, the gallant 2 Group Blenheim crews had flown a total of 494 operational sorties, mainly on fighter-escorted shipping sweeps and on ten circus operations (half of which were directed against St. Omer airfield). About half of these sorties were completed successfully, but the fight had been more and more against all the odds. At the end of the month, it became clear that out of seventy-seven aircraft attacking coastal shipping, no fewer than twenty-three had been shot down. Total operational losses for 2 Group during August amounted to thirty-nine aircraft lost, with ninety-two crew members being posted as killed or missing in action, plus eighteen taken prisoner. A further nine Blenheims were lost in training, with ten aircrew perishing. For these grievous losses no decisive operational results had been gained. These facts did not pass unnoticed by Bomber Command HQ and the Air Ministry. On 30 August Stevenson received direct orders to conserve his Blenheim force in the United Kingdom, as it was deemed to be more suitably employed in the Mediterranean hunting Rommel's supply ships (see Chapter 8).

In consequence losses were drastically reduced during September. From 266 sorties (just over half the number mounted during the previous month), eleven Blenheims failed to return, with thirty-two aircrew killed or missing. Only one man, Sgt Pilot D.G. Adams, of 18 Squadron, was taken prisoner during Circus 93 on 4 September. A further five aircraft were written off in training accidents in the United Kingdom, with a total of eight men perishing.

The Blenheim daylight offensive was dwindling in October, with Circuses 104 to 108 being mounted and a handful of shipping sweeps undertaken. However, from 198 2 Group sorties (170 effective), eighteen Blenheims were lost without a single man surviving. Five more aircraft were destroyed in training flights, with twelve crew members dying. The most eventful day of the month occurred on the 15th. Before dawn, twelve crews of 114 and 139 Squadrons were briefed for unescorted shipping sweeps in Beats 7 and 8, the coastal shipping lanes off the Frisian Islands where so many Blenheim crews had already met their fate during the year. Although large convoys were successfully attacked off Schiermonnikoog, Ameland and Heligoland (albeit with no sinkings), the crews paid a high price. Two 114 Squadron crews (Plt Off William Davidson, RCAF in L9382 and Sgt Christian Balzer, RAAF in V5875) were intercepted and shot down at 12.05hr, some 130km west-north-west of Den Helder by Bf 110s of 5/ZG76. Ofw Siegfried Goebel and Lt Hans Heinrich Koenig were the victorious Zerstörer pilots. A vic of 139 Squadron, led by Sqn Ldr Richard T. Stubbs, DFC in

A formation of fighter Blenheims of 254 Squadron patrolling over Northern Ireland in the summer of 1941.
Gerry Holder

V6249, found and attacked an eastbound convoy in the eastern half of Beat 7 (south-west of Heligoland), but one of the Blenheims immediately fell victim to the withering ships' flak. The remaining two aircraft were then bounced by a flight of Bf 109s from 3/JG52, which had been called in by the convoy, and both were quickly dispatched.

In mid afternoon, the slaughter continued, when offensive Ramrod No. XII on shipping in Le Havre harbour was mounted. Plt Off O'Connell, pilot in 226 Squadron flying Z7455 on this raid recounts:

This operation involved one of the sharpest and most spectacular dogfights of the entire war. It was a mixed operation in which two squadrons put up twelve aircraft: eleven from 226 and the others from 110 Squadron. Sqn Ldr J.S. 'Ken' Kennedy of 226 Squadron led the operation in the first box of six and was followed by the second box of six, which was to be behind, and slightly above the first box. I was flying No.2 to Sqn Ldr Kennedy. We were escorted by many fighter aircraft which, bear in mind, at that range had very limited fighting fuel. At that time, the Spitfires could give us escort (high, intermediate, close and bottom cover) to any target on the French coast between Ostende and Dieppe, and have ten minutes' fighting fuel. Le Havre was well beyond this limit, so the Spits would have had only a couple of minutes' fighting fuel.

Our target was shipping in the harbour, and, as I remember, we started our bombing run roughly from west to east at 8,000ft (I think if we had asked the German flak gunners which altitude they would like to have us fly, they would have said, as one man, '8,000ft, please'). Anyway, just before we bombed, we were aware that there were German fighters in the area, with some of them above our top cover, which

would have been something in excess of 18,000ft. The flak was coming up in great quantities on our bombing run, and I was flying very close to Sqn Ldr Kennedy in my No. 2 position (much too close, in retrospect). We bombed on the leader (the leading bomb aimer transmitted his corrections by radio, and the rest of the aircraft in the formation dropped their bombs at the same time as the leading aircraft).

We had just dropped our bombs, when, in a matter of a fraction of a second, I was aware that the second box, which was supposed to be behind us, was simply a few feet above us, and not behind. The leader of the second box had become too anxious, and the second box had dropped their bombs through our box. I was aware at approximately the same instant that Sqn Ldr Kennedy had an ugly-looking 500lb bomb, which had been dropped by the second box, in the middle of his right wing, just a few feet from my face, and it was rolling towards his wing tip. This had turned his aircraft into an uncontrollable steep turn, which I could not avoid. My left wing tip punctured and locked into his fuselage directly behind the turret. I did

a drastic 'last resort' effort, and hammered on right rudder, and both aircraft parted company.

On recovering after a few seconds, I took stock and saw that there was no way that I could rejoin the formation, and I realized that we would have to go it alone. The incident seemed to have triggered the dogfight. We were several hundred feet below, behind and to the right of the formation, and I decided to head for ground level. Still heading east, I went into a very steep dive to put a little distance between us and the dogfight I now knew was going on; then we turned right so that we would return on our way home at low level over the water and south of the city, and continued in the dive. My observer, Peter Saunders, said to me on the way down in the dive that he thought the aircraft was going to stall because the airspeed indicator showed only about 70mph. But Peter hadn't been watching the airspeed indicator closely enough, because the indicating needle was by that time on its way around the dial for a second time. We had far exceeded the airspeed limitation of the aircraft.

After turning westbound, we passed a Blenheim that was on fire from nose to tail, and I watched the observer of that aircraft bale out from the observer's escape hatch, but, in a panic, he had forgotten to buckle on his parachute. I couldn't do anything for him except say a short prayer. An Me.109E chased us down and made several attacks, but he was not a very good shot and it took only minor evasive action to make sure he missed, and he gave up long before we had reached the water of the harbour. I watched six or eight fighter aircraft go down in smoke, and I could see a number of open parachutes high above us. When I started to check our dive at 800 or 900ft, I watched a Spitfire going down absolutely vertically, with no smoke coming from it, just a few hundred feet directly ahead of us. We felt the 'whoomph' as we passed through its slipstream. That was the last I saw of the dogfight.

When we landed at Wattisham, we saw that the aircraft was riddled with flak holes, but no bullet holes. Then I noticed that the rear half of the exhaust stack on the outboard side of the left engine was missing. It had been cleanly cut and there was a telltale black smudge along the length of the cut. A projected line of this cut (indicating the path of the shell) in both directions, showed clearly that this one 88mm shell must have gone through the disc of the speeding propeller before it contacted the exhaust stack and then left its final calling card, a dirty 88 mm size rut about 1-in deep in the top of the leading edge of the port wing. I have often wondered about the odds of a shell of that size (about 3-in in diameter and 12in long) going

through the speeding propeller and hitting the aircraft twice without going off. Whatever the odds, a near-miss didn't count.

Indeed, very accurate fire was encountered from flak ships off Le Havre and heavy flak from the shore on the run up, which accounted for V6371 'Z'. A shell was seen to burst on its port propellor; the machine jettisoned its bombs and dived into the sea, killing Sgt Paine and crew. Braving the hail of exploding flak, Wg Cdr Butler in V6511 'B' successfully led the Blenheims over the target, which was bombed from 7,000ft. A warehouse, two large vessels, including the ex-British tanker *Canadolite* and one smaller ship received direct hits. At least twelve Bf 109s then bounced the box of bombers. The fierceness of the encounter with the German defences over Le Havre is clearly illustrated by the fact that only three Blenheims returned to base without battle-scars. During the combats raging over Le Havre, five Bf 109s were claimed shot down by the five squadrons of Spitfires escorting the Blenheims, with one probably destroyed and four damaged. On the debit side, one Spitfire and pilot were missing.

The Circus raid of 15 October signalled the end of 226 Squadron's Blenheim operations, and it soon re-equipped with Douglas Bostons. The last shipping sweep mounted in the 1941 daylight offensive was carried out by six crews of 114 Squadron in the afternoon of 27 October. Off Texel, one vic attacking a convoy was intercepted by Bf 109Fs of 4/JG53, flown by Lt Fritz Dinger and Uffz Fritz Muschter. Within the space of one minute, at 15.06hr, they shot down V5888 of Sgt James W. Bradley and crew, and Plt Off Walter G.C. Beatson's Z7309. The leader of the vic, Wg Cdr Jenkins, was badly shot up, but was able to shake off the fighters and, escorted by Sgt Johnson's Spitfire of 152 Squadron, he nursed his crippled Blenheim back to West Raynham. As a slight consolation, the 1,396-tons Danish merchantman *Gunlog* was sunk in the attack. At the end of the month, the crews in 2 Group were very relieved to hear that the dreaded anti-shipping operations were finally halted. The final two Blenheim circuses were mounted in November against Lannion and Lille, both without loss. Officially, Bomber Command was relieved of all responsibility for anti-shipping operations on 25 November. The 'Bloody Summer' of 1941 was over at last.

CHAPTER EIGHT

Malta Crusade:

Hunting Rommel's Supplies, 1941–42

The small rocky island of Malta, measuring only about 10 miles by 5 miles and lying isolated in the middle of the Mediterranean some 60 miles south of Sicily, was a strategic focal point for the British forces in this theatre. It was a springboard for the Royal Air Force and the Royal Navy to attack the vital Axis supply shipping lanes off Sicily, Tunisia and Libya, and coastal targets in the area. It also served as a staging post for aircraft flying from Britain to Egypt, where the Desert Air Force was being built up in 1940–41. Very accurate navigation was required to find the small island, especially for the Blenheim IVs with their limited range of 1,460 miles. During 1940 the aircraft flew straight from Thorney Island (near Portsmouth), via France to Malta, which led to inevitable losses. At the end of the year it was estimated that one in four ferry aircraft had been lost on the long, eight-hour journey. The Blenheim ferrying record was probably set by Plt Off Richard 'Herby' Herbert and his 57 Squadron crew on 24 September 1940, who touched down on Malta after having survived a violent thunder storm over France and having been in the air for 8hr 55min. In order to cut down the high rate of losses on the ferry trip, the route to Malta was changed in early 1941 from the direct flight to an indirect one via Gibraltar. Les Clayton, a member of 18 Squadron's ground crew, has vivid memories of the long and arduous flight from Portreath to Malta.

Les Clayton's Malta Trip

In the bomb bay were two overload tanks. These were fed into the main tanks by a zwicky pump that was operated from the cockpit by the extra ground crew who was carried. On the morning of our take-off, 12 October 1941, we collected our rubber money bags – these were filled with the different currencies of the coun-

tries we passed, to help us escape if we were forced down. We needed all of the runway to take off as we were carrying a heavier load than a normal bomb load. We rumbled along and at the end of the runway it dropped over the edge of a 250ft cliff; we went over the edge and dropped like a stone until we picked up flying speed, by this time we were just above the sea. A most nerve-racking experience.

There was a place on the journey that was called, 'the point of no return'; if you had trouble before it you could turn back as you would have enough fuel, but if after that you just carried on and trusted to luck. On our first journey we had trouble and had to turn back. The second take-off and journey were more successful. When we had picked up flying speed we settled ourselves down for about an eight-hour journey. We knew that we had very little fuel to spare so this called for spot-on navigation. Maximum observation was needed on this leg as there was danger from the German

ship-raiding aircraft and also from aircraft that patrolled off the Spanish mainland.

The approach to Gibraltar was very hazardous; you had to signal in the right order and a circuit of the rock was necessary before they gave you permission to land on the old race track that acted as a runway, before the extension was built out into the bay. It was touch and go as to whether you made this leg with the amount of fuel carried. We were there a week waiting for the weather to change to take off for our second leg to Malta. While we were there we witnessed many accidents on take-off owing to the short length of the runway (1,300yd); these resulted in wreckage piled up at the end of the runway, this was pushed in to the sea and eventually formed the base for the extension which forms the modern runway.

The hardest part of the journey was now to come, owing to the enemy being on both sides as we flew through. The Med is notorious for its sudden storms. On take-off the aircraft was

Many Blenheims ran out of fuel on the last lap of the ferry flight from Britain to Gibraltar and ditched off Gibraltar or crash-landed in Portuguese territory. Here Sgt Farmer's Blenheim 'A' of 139 Squadron is about to put down on the water off Gibraltar on 11 May 1941, a Norwegian boat picking up the crew after the successful ditching. Wilf Hepworth

Sgt Tommy Thompson and his 18 Squadron crew are feted on port and sponge biscuits in the Sergeants' Mess of the Military Flying School at Aveiro, Portugal. Due to problems with their long-range tank, Thompson had been forced to belly-land Z7678 on the local beach on their way to Gibraltar on 27 August 1941. Before being taken into custody, Thompson had set his Blenheim on fire by firing Verey lights into the fuel-soaked aircraft. During their short stay in Portugal, the crew met colleagues from 107 Squadron who had experienced the same problem, putting down their plane on the beach near Estoril. The Portuguese Air Force operated a few of these force-landed Blenheims. L8837, for example, a Mk I crashed in a forced landing at Cintra while on a ferry flight on 15 September 1943. Other ex-RAF Blenheim IVs (N3544, R2775, R2781, R3830, T2434, V5429, V5434, V5501, V5883, Z5760, and Z6035) were purchased by the Portuguese Air Force and were flown over during the autumn of 1943. Finally, AZ986, an ex-RAF Mk V went to Portugal on 30 August 1943. Tommy Thompson

---

Portuguese Air Force Blenheim Service

Operated at least twenty-three Blenheim Is, IVs and Vs between 1940 and 1945.

---

drawn back to the very edge on the Med side, 9lb boost was put on and then the brakes let go and we rumbled towards the bay end with our fingers crossed. We just began to lift as we reached the end and we had to wallow between the masts of ships and so out over the Med. The whole of this journey had to be done at sea level owing to enemy radar. On the early part of our journey we had two very bad storms and as we were flying low down and not able to see; the strain on the crew and especially the pilot was enormous. When we were level with Pantellaria we saw some CR.42s going in to land; they had missed us because we were flying so low, low enough to bring up spray from the sea with wind from our props. We were getting very tense as we noticed that our fuel was going down rather quickly and we still had a long way to go to get to Malta. This leg called for extreme spot-on navigation as we would have no reserve by the time we got to Malta.

The sequence for getting to Malta was such that should you make one wrong move, they would have shot you out of the sky. Our navigation was such that we entered exactly over the small island of Pilfa on the west coast of Malta with our fuel gauges showing empty. We had got permission from Malta control to bypass the necessary procedure as our fuel was so low. As we flew over Malta we noticed the guns following us round and we knew that one wrong move on our part and we would have been shot out of the sky. With the island being so small we could easily pick out the airfield at Luqa where we were to land. As we landed we noticed aircraft burning on either side of the runway and others that had belly-landed during an enemy

bombing raid that had just ceased. It looked just like Dante's Inferno. As we reached the end of the runway both engines gave a cough and stopped, I think we must have been the luckiest men alive.

While the Blenheim anti-shipping campaign was gathering momentum in the United Kingdom in March 1941, it was decided to strengthen the meagre anti-shipping strike forces in the Mediterranean by sending a 2 Group Blenheim detachment to Malta. It was to test out the feasibility of combating supply shipping bound for the Italian forces and Rommel's Afrika Korps in north Africa. Under the command of the experienced ship-hunter Sqn Ldr L.V.E. 'Attie' Atkinson, six crews of 21 Squadron were selected as the first to test the feasibility of such operations, leaving Portreath on 26 April for the long haul to Malta via Gibraltar. Half a dozen shipping attacks were successfully carried out by these crews during May, with only one aircraft lost in an air raid: a promising start.

Following this inaugural detachment, Air Cdr Hugh Pughe Lloyd, MC, DFC, the much respected SASO at 2 Group HQ, was ordered by ACM Sir Charles Portal, Chief of the Air Staff to take command of the RAF units on Malta on 1 June, with the words: 'Your main task is to sink Axis shipping sailing between Europe and Africa.' A man of action, Lloyd wasted no time devising a new scheme in which squadrons of 2 Group would, in rotation, equip with 'tropicalized' Blenheims, fly out to Malta and operate there for about five weeks. These aircraft were painted in Middle East colours, with a bright duck egg green underneath and brown on top, and were fitted with special Vokes filters over the air intakes (protection against sand and dust), plus other modifications. At the

Blenheim 'J' of 139 Squadron in the 'dead engines' phase during a convoy attack south of Pantellaria, 22 May 1941. On this occasion two hits were scored on a 6,000-ton vessel. Wilf Hepworth

Crippling Rommel's supply fleet. A somewhat blurred, but interesting action shot taken by 139 Squadron's Sgt Ullmer from his gun turret, of the successful bombing attack on 22 May 1941. Wilf Hepworth

time, living and operating conditions were very primitive on Malta, the island being on the receiving end of daily bombing raids, but Lloyd did everything he could to get Luqa airfield ready to receive the next Blenheim detachments, from 139 and 82 Squadrons. Five aircraft and seven crews from the former unit arrived at Luqa on 16 May (two Blenheims having been lost at Gibraltar), while 82 Squadron, now commanded by the newly-promoted Wg Cdr Atkinson, dispatched three consecutive small groups of aircraft on 19 May, 4 and 11 June.

Operational tactics for the Malta-based Blenheims were laid down as follows: Marylands were daily to make individual reconnaissance flights around the Mediterranean in order to spot the movements of Axis shipping which might be heading for Tripoli, either by way of the Tunisian coast or through the Ionian sea. As signals to or from these aircraft were monitored in Sicily, wireless silence was to be maintained during these flights, the Marylands making a beeline for Malta to give details of any sightings to the Luqa Operations Room. Their sighting reports were to trigger off Blenheim strikes against the south-bound convoys carrying essential food, ammunition, fuel, guns, armoured vehicles and spares. If no ships were sighted, individual aircraft or small formations were to be sent out to look for them in wide zigzags down to the coast of north Africa. If the crews should fail to come across any shipping, they had orders to beat up the main road that led from Tripoli to the Axis frontlines.

The first six-aircraft detachment from 82 Squadron lost one aircraft on the way to Malta on 21 May, with Sgt L.H. Wrightson and his crew perishing. After two uneventful anti-shipping patrols on 23 and 25 May, the squadron found its first convoy, as Sgt Ken Collins experienced to his cost. He had served with the squadron since December 1940 in the crew of Sgts Ted Inman (pilot) and Ron Austin (W.Op/AG), and had completed thirty-four sorties before being posted to Malta:

27 May 1941. Our five Blenheims (plus one from 139 Squadron) attacked a large convoy of merchant ships, escorted by four Italian destroyers, sailing to Tripoli. I dropped my bombs from mast height and our aircraft and that behind us were blown up. I was unconscious but must have landed in the sea as my watch was rusty. I was picked up by the destroyer *Cigno*, and taken to

Tripoli as a prisoner of war. My right leg was amputated and my left leg badly damaged. I was a prisoner for two years and repatriated in April 1943 together with other seriously wounded prisoners.

Sgts Inman and Austin in V6460 were posted killed in action, as was the crew in the aircraft behind them, Flt Lt G.M. Fairbairn's V6427. But their sacrifice had not been in vain: the Italian steamer *Foscarini* was left on fire and had to be towed into Tripoli.

For the loss of one crew, which fell victim to escorting Fiat CR.42 biplane fighters, five crews of 82 Squadron attacked another convoy on 2 June northwest of Lampedusa.

Left to right: Flt Lt Sidney-Smith (PoW, 16 July 1941) and his crew of Sgts Shepherd and Fox with Blenheim 'V' at Luqa. Eric Sidney-Smith earned a DFC for his successful anti-shipping attacks from Malta during May–June 1941. Wilf Hepworth

Wilf Hepworth's Story

During its stay at Malta, 139 Squadron flew a total of thirty sorties, with most aircraft being seriously damaged by enemy fighters and flak, but the squadron suffered only one aircraft and crew lost. Sgt Wilf Hepworth, observer in Flt Lt Thompson's crew, remembers:

Shortly before 3 June 1941, the AVM had 'decreed' that Axis convoys escorted by more than five warships were not to be attacked by

the six remaining serviceable Blenheims operating from Malta – five on a short tour from 139 Squadron and one from 82 Squadron. This was because any heavy losses suffered by these remaining aircraft would temporarily suspend the ability of the RAF to continue offensive strikes against Axis shipping.

In the late morning of 3 June, a Maryland landed at Luqa with the information that a convoy of five vessels was moving south off the Tunisian coast not far from the island of Lampedusa, escorted by three cruisers and six destroyers. When this news was given to Wg Cdr Pepper he referred the Maryland pilot to the new decree, concerning the fact that convoys with such a heavy naval escort were not now to be attacked. Apparently, on being reminded of this, the Maryland pilot inferred that Wg Cdr Pepper was mentioning this as a means of avoiding having to make an attack on the convoy. If this was intended to incense Wg Cdr Pepper it succeeded; without further ado he called together the Blenheim crews (who were sunbathing near a battered shack loosely described as the crew room), gave them details of the convoy and its last known location. He would lead the loose formation of six Blenheims and the attack would be carried out in two stages – he leading the first vic in line abreast and about 30sec later the second vic would follow, led by Flt Lt Thompson, my own pilot; the aircraft to

While awaiting news of any shipping sighted, twenty-three-years old Wg Cdr N.E.W. Pepper, DFC, CO of 139 Squadron, relaxes in the Luqa crew room, 18 May 1941. Pepper was killed during the 3 June convoy strike. Wilf Hepworth, via Blenheim Society

select their own vessel in the convoy. Each aircraft carried four 250lb bombs, fitted with an 11sec delay, and the formation took off at 13.00hr, flying in a loose box about 50ft above sea level.

About 14.10hr the convoy was sighted almost 170 miles due west of Malta about halfway between the Italian island of Lampedusa and the Tunisian coast, steaming on a course for Tripoli. Although the sky was clear above, there was a slight haze at sea level which gave the vessels in the convoy a wraith-like appearance. Circling the convoy at about 500ft was a Cant flying boat, which, on sighting our formation at sea level, moved over the convoy, away from us, obviously advising the naval commander of our imminent arrival. We had maintained wireless silence throughout the flight, so it was rather confusing to those in the second vic when the Wing Commander's flight, instead of going straight in to attack, as we had expected, turned on to a southerly course, which we flew for a matter of seven or eight minutes, passing the convoy about 800yd on our port side. We in our aircraft naturally wondered whether, because of the strength and size of the naval escort, the Wing Commander had decided that discretion was the better part of valour and was breaking off the attack. Having lost the initial element of surprise to the Cant flying boat (which was still airborne), it had seemed to us that the best thing to have done was to attack

on sight, in the hope that the warships were not entirely ready for us. However, we concluded that we were not going in to attack and I started working out the course back to Malta. The Wing Commander then indicated a turn to port and turned almost 180 degrees on to an almost reciprocal course, which wasn't much different from the homeward course I had just worked out and which initially seemed to confirm that we were heading back for Luqa. After several minutes on this course, the convoy suddenly reappeared out of the sea mist and the Wing Commander's vic, in line abreast broke away to attack at mast height. We gave his formation a few seconds start and then turned in to lead our formation into the attack from a line rather more northerly than that of the Wing Commander.

This was the last I remember of the action, for as we made our choice of target, bombs from the starboard aircraft of the first vic (piloted by Flt Lt Sidney Smith) hit an ammunition ship and this exploded as we went in. We started the run in at 50ft with the sea flashing by at about 200mph and my next conscious awareness was of the sea going by below us in what seemed to be slow motion, with a massive cloud of smoke coming from the blazing ammo ship below and Axis naval vessels cutting white wakes in the sea nearby. On looking at the altimeter I realized that we had been lifted up to over 1,000ft (as also had the rest of our vic) by the

force of the explosion.

In our own aircraft (J) the bombing position for the observer was in the Perspex nose. The explosion had shattered the lower Perspex windows and lifted me back about 5ft to a position alongside the pilot; at the same time the Perspex blister beside the observer's take-off/landing seat had been blown out. This I discovered when I tried to look out of the blister, forgetting that my flying helmet was unfastened and it blew out in the slipstream like a small parachute until it was arrested by the intercom cords impinging on my throat. I also realized that all my navigation maps and charts had been sucked from the chart table and out through the blister. My knees were all bloodied by shattered bits of Perspex from the nose window (I was in khaki shorts) but it was nothing serious when cleaned up later.

I shouted to Flt Lt Thompson the course home I had worked out before the attack and the remaining four aircraft formated on us as the airgunner on our starboard (Sgt Ullmer) took a photograph of the smoke cloud from the convoy with a Leica camera. He also pointed at our aircraft and his pilot advised us by intercom that our fuselage was all corrugated where earlier it had been smooth. One of the two remaining aircraft of Wg Cdr Pepper's vic advised us that his aircraft had gone down in the sea – it had either been hit by AA fire or had struck a ship's mast as it went over the convoy. He was flying parallel to a leading Italian destroyer, his engines were trailing smoke and it looked as if he was ditching.

Fortunately, our aircraft stayed airborne and our five crews reached Luqa at about 16.00hr. 'J' landed first and much to our relief the undercarriage went down and held for the landing, but the flaps would not retract on landing and the rudder controls were somewhat sick. None of the aircraft of the second vic dropped its bombs on the convoy – they were jettisoned into the sea to prevent accidents on landing. The other two aircraft in our section, although caught in the blast and lifted, had not sustained the same damage.

We later learned that the Wing Commander had been killed; the observer Eric Hyde died of injuries in a Tripoli hospital and the air gunner Leslie Pickford after a long spell in hospital was sent to a PoW camp. We were later also told that the exploding ammo ship had severely damaged other ships in the convoy, possibly sinking one other.

Two Italian merchantmen were lost during the strike on 3 June 1941. The *Montello*, a 6,117-tons vessel carrying ammunition blew up with no survivors. A second ship,

Left to right: Sgts Turner and Hepworth and Sqn Ldr Thompson have just returned from a convoy attack 70 miles off Tripoli in Blenheim 'J' of 139 Squadron, 27 May 1941. Wilf Hepworth

pilot struggling to maintain control. In spite of his efforts we descended rapidly and crashed into the sea. I had previously opened the escape hatch and, before the aircraft sank, managed to vacate the aircraft. We climbed aboard our rubber dinghy which had been launched by the air gunner. I had a severe head injury and quickly lost a lot of blood but remained conscious. We were picked up some five hours later by an Italian destroyer and taken prisoner.

More Anti-shipping Attacks

On 24 June, Wg Cdr Atkinson led his 82 Squadron crews on a daring low-level strike against the same convoy in Tripoli harbour, a raid which was successfully repeated on 3 July without loss. Two further squadron aircraft and five crew members were lost on 29 June and 5 July. Though small in numbers, the initial Blenheim detachments made their presence felt immediately and inflicted serious losses on the Axis shipping, with their own losses being relatively small. Three merchant vessels totalling 11,188 tons were sunk in May, with a further seven (13,353 tons) during June.

Seventeen crews of 110 Squadron left Wattisham on 29 June for a stint of anti-shipping operations from Malta, relieving the 82 Squadron survivors. They were soon in action, seven crews attacking Tripoli harbour on 9 July, claiming four large merchant vessels damaged. Losses, however, were heavy on 110's maiden raid: four Blenheims (Z6449, Z9537, Z9553 and Z9578) were shot down in the target area, with only Sgt W.H. Twist and his crew becoming prisoners. After losing Z9551 in a crash landing on the 14th (fortunately without harm to the crew), the squadron was struck another blow four days later. The CO, Wg Cdr Theo Hunt, DFC, led six Blenheims on a low-level raid against the power station at Trapani. Direct hits were scored on the objective but, while speeding home, 'Joe' Hunt's aircraft came under attack from a CR.42 fighter and was seen to crash into the sea immediately. There were no survivors. Undaunted by these heavy losses, 110 Squadron remained a thorn in Rommel's side, four crews sinking the ammunition ship Preussen and crippling the Italian 6,996-ton tanker Brarena in a surprise dusk attack off Pantelleria on the 22nd. Next day a similar force attacked cargo ships in the hornet's nest of Trapani harbour, the

the 6,135-tons *Beatrice Costa* (with a cargo of petrol) was set on fire and, after taking off its crew, was later sunk by a destroyer. The 3 June attack left only two serviceable Blenheims at Malta, and the surviving 139 Squadron crews were flown back to the United Kingdom.

Replacement crews from 82 Squadron carried out successful convoy strikes on 11 June (Sqn Ldr M.L. Watson and crew in Z6426 were lost), and on 22 June, when six crews severely damaged the supply ships *Tembien* and the German *Wachtfels* off Lampedusa. During the latter strike, violent opposition from both escorting fighters and flak was encountered, Flt Lt T.J. Watkins's aircraft being extensively shot up with one of his legs all but severed by a flak shell bursting in his cockpit. While in excruciating pain, and aided by Sgt J.S. Sargent his observer, he managed to bring back his Blenheim to Luqa, where he was awarded an immediate DSO and Sargent the DFM. Their gunner, Sgt E.F. Chandler, was credited with a Fiat CR.42 destroyed during the battle, which earned him a DFM.

Philip Felton's Story

Another aircraft did not make it back home, as Sgt Philip Felton recalls. He had served with 21 Squadron as observer in Fg Off Harrison-Broadley's crew during May

and early June 1941, when they received a sudden posting:

My crew were detached from 21 Squadron at Watton and transferred to 82 Squadron for operations in the Egyptian war theatre. On our way to Egypt we arrived in Malta on 18 June 1941. We were in our thick serge uniforms and the temperature in Malta was about 30° C. The Navy helped us out with an assortment of lighter clothing. The following day, in company with one other Blenheim, we attacked a ship off the coast of Sfax in Tunisia. We had been shanghaied by the authorities of Malta to enhance their offensive activities!

A few days later, on 22 June (the day the German Army invaded Russia) a reconnaissance Maryland found a convoy of enemy ships just south of Lampedusa. We and five other Blenheims of 82 Squadron took off to attack this convoy at 11.30am. We found the convoy at about midday and attacked. The convoy consisted of four merchant ships escorted by two Italian destroyers. We selected one of the merchant vessels and flew towards it very close to the water, encountering intense ack ack fire. We were armed with four General Purpose 250lb bombs. We really needed semi-armour-piercing bombs but there were none in the Malta armoury. Then, at the last possible moment, we pulled up over the ship releasing our bombs as we did so. As we were flying over the ship we were hit in our port engine and wing. We staggered up to about 500ft with the

Casualty of war: Portuguese medical orderlies helping Sgt Ken Collins, observer, from the train at Lisbon railway station to a hospital ship on 18 April 1943. During a strike on a Tripoli-bound convoy on 27 May 1941, Collins lost his 82 Squadron crew and, due to his severe wounds, he was repatriated after two years as a PoW. Ken Collins

leader Z7409 (flown by Sgt N.A.C. Cathles) falling to a CR.42 of the 23rd Gruppo. These 110 Squadron strikes contributed decisively to the total of eight merchantmen sunk in air attacks during July, their tonnage amounting to 22,717.

Ten tropicalized Blenheims of 105 Squadron, led by Wg Cdr Hughie Edwards, VC, DFC, arrived at Luqa in the last week of July, to relieve 110 Squadron, Sgt W.A. Williams and crew of the original batch of twelve having landed in neutral Portugal and another having belly-landed at Gibraltar through hydraulics failure. Almost daily the crews ventured out in search of enemy shipping and coastal transports during the next few weeks. The aircraft of Flt Lt A.B. 'Ben' Broadley, DFC (Z9605 'U') fell victim to flak on the squadron's first convoy strike on 1 August, but revenge was had two days later with two merchantmen set on fire in Tripoli harbour without loss. A very successful attack took place on 7 August on a six-ship convoy: the 6,813-ton freighter *Nita* was sunk and a tanker was

beached near Lampedusa where it burned out. Severe losses, however, were also soon incurred on 105 Squadron: the experienced flight commander Sqn Ldr George Goode, DFC and crew in Z7503 were shot down and taken prisoner during a fringe raid at Crotone in southern Italy on the 11th, while four days later Plt Off P.H. Standfast's Z9604 'D' exploded and Fg Off H.J. Roe and crew in Z7522 'E' collided with the mast of a tanker and spun in during a convoy strike in the Gulf of Sirte.

By the end of August, British Intelligence assessed that 58 per cent of all seaborne supplies intended for the Axis forces in Africa had been lost at sea. Although this assessment was somewhat inflated, a record number of eleven merchantmen, totalling 35,196 tons, were sunk by air attack in the Mediterranean during the month. About half of this

tonnage was destroyed in Blenheim strikes. Average losses among these aircraft, however, had mounted to 12 per cent. Yet it looked as if the balance in the grim war of attrition against the supply convoys would turn in favour of Malta's strike aircraft. This was confirmed when the Axis convoys ceased sailing west of Sicily during September. Their shipping now took the longer easterly route, hugging the Balkan coastline. RAF sorties hunting these convoys were longer and faced the danger of more fighters and strengthened destroyer escorts.

107 Squadron, at full battle-strength with twenty-six crews, arrived at Malta in the first week of September, where it joined forces with 105 Squadron. The might of the strengthened enemy convoy defences was hammered home painfully on the 12th, when eight crews of 105 and

107 Squadrons found and attacked a large convoy consisting of five heavily armed merchantmen some 40 miles north-north-west of Tripoli. The Axis vessels were strongly escorted by seven destroyers and six MC 200 and CR 42 fighters of 23rd Gruppo. As expected, the price the Blenheim crews paid for their daring, almost suicidal, attack on such a heavily defended target in broad daylight, was high. 107 Squadron's Flight Commander, Sqn Ldr F.R.H. Charney, DFC, and his crew perished when Z9603 'F' was hit by the hail of the destroyers' gunfire on the run in and was seen to cartwheel into the sea in flames. Sgt Q.E. Mortimer and crew in Z7504 'G', Charney's No.2, were also shot down into the sea by the destroyers. It was almost curtains too for Sgt Bill Brandwood's Z7367 of 105 Squadron shortly after they had hurled their two 500lb bombs into a large liner. Sgt Tony Mee, manning the twin Brownings in 'L' for Leather recorded:

> Suddenly a line of tracer rose from the escort moving parallel to our Blenheim. It flickered behind the tail like flashing water from a garden hose on a sunny day. The cannon fire moved steadily with us and slowly moved up the fuselage with a plunking sound as it passed through the thin skin. Fortunately, the cannon mounting gave the shells a vertical spread. As they were deflected off the armour plate behind the wireless equipment, I shouted to Bill over the intercomm. for evasive action. The aircraft's nose went down slightly and the port wing dipped a little. This manoeuvre added just enough speed to send the shells back down the fuselage and beyond the tail. The gunners seeing our aircraft lurching towards the sea couldn't resist watching the end and stopped firing. We levelled out above the waves and flew out of range.

Following the few minutes of concentrated action during the convoy strike, the surviving aircraft formed up again. However, Sgt Brandwood's Blenheim 'L', with a fire raging in the bomb-bay, had to be ditched about 12 miles from the convoy at 14.25hr. Sgts Brandwood, Jock Miller and Tony Mee were very fortunate to be picked up by HM Submarine *Utmost* (N19) early the next day, having survived a large shark's attack shortly before their rescue. Finally, returning from this attack, 105 Squadron's Sgt J. Bendall bellied his badly shot-up Z9606 'V' in at Luqa with his hydraulics shot away and his observer

Wg Cdr Theo Hunt, DFC, CO of 110 Squadron. 'Joe' Hunt and his W.Op/AG Flt Sgt Freddie Thripp, the squadron's Gunnery Leader, had remarkably survived fifty-five Blenheim operations in 82 and 110 Squadrons during 1939, 1940 and 1941, before they finally fell to a CR 42 fighter off Tripoli on 18 July 1941. Irene Deeks

Sgt Hindle wounded. As a meagre compensation for all these losses, a 1,000-ton merchant ship was confirmed sunk on this occasion. On 17 September 105 Squadron lost two out of four aircraft and crews during a dawn attack on Tripoli harbour. The squadron was struck another blow when Wg Cdr Don Scivier, AFC in Z7423 'H' (who had replaced Wg Cdr Edwards as CO on 31 August) collided with Sgt Tommy Williams's Z9606 'T' and crashed to his death, minus tail unit near Homs on the 22nd. Amazingly, Sgt Williams successfully flew his badly battered Blenheim back to Luqa, a distance of 218 miles. Twenty-two-years old Williams was

so severely shocked that he became completely grey, then white-haired a month later. His W.Op/AG, Sgt Alan Tuppen, never flew again. Only one day previously, Scivier had nursed his Blenheim back to Luqa with one engine on fire after a daring and brilliantly executed two-aircraft strike on a 24,000- ton troop-carrier off Lampedusa. 105's spell of duty at Malta was over on the 28th. The handful of crews that had survived the slaughter were shipped back home, only to arrive at Greenock in the middle of a dock strike.

As a direct result of these and subsequent high casualties, aircraft serviceability was becoming a problem at Malta and consequently operations were seriously curtailed. By mid September, the Blenheim crews hardly ever flew an anti-shipping operation without loss. This was made up by 'press-ganging' transit crews, but the continuous turnover was sapping the very identity of the squadrons involved, which in turn started to affect morale. 107 Squadron was decimated within a month, with two flight commanders, the CO and most of the officers lost. The South African Wg Cdr F.A. Harte and his crew failed to return from a shipping sweep by four aircraft off southern Italy on 9 October, together with Fg

Destroyer escorts to Rommel's vital supply convoys were gradually strengthened during the summer of 1941 due to mounting pressure from the Malta-based, anti-shipping strike force. This Italian destroyer was abandoned in shallow water, 60 miles from Malta after a Blenheim attack, possibly in May 1941. Wilf Hepworth

Off N. Whitford-Walders and crew. Only two days later two out of six Blenheims failed to return from a convoy strike in the Gulf of Sirte. This brought 107's losses to seven aircraft and six crews in less than a month, plus scores of other aircraft having returned full of holes. But the sacrifices had not been in vain: during September, the hard-pressed Mediterranean Axis merchant fleet lost a further eleven vessels with a total tonnage of 23,031 (or 28 per cent of all cargoes shipped to Libya). In an effort to reduce losses, the Blenheim crews started night attacks, the first being mounted by 107 Squadron on 7/8 October. A 2,000-ton merchantman was attacked from low level in moonlight off Tripoli, with two direct hits scored.

Sixteen crews from 18 Squadron relieved their colleagues of 105 on 14 October. Initially, operations, often in the company of 107 Squadron, consisted of medium-level formation bombing raids by twelve aircraft in support of the 8th Army against targets in Italy, Sicily and north Africa, the main targets being Italian Army units in Africa. During one of these raids, against Homs on 22 October, a new type of parachute bomb was used by 18 Squadron. Accidentally, one parachute opened immediately on being dropped and was blown back into the aircraft of Sgt J.D. Woodburn, DFM, destroying the Blenheim and its crew in a blinding flash and damaging the aircraft on either side in the formation. During November the crews mainly carried out low-level shipping strikes in the face of withering flak and determined fighter attacks, and surprise raids on enemy troops and transport on the main coastal road in north Africa. Losses in air crews remained horrendous. On 19 November, for example, three out of five 18 Squadron crews (Sgts D.W. Buck, J.H. Woolman and H.L. Hanson and their crews) were killed during a shipping attack on a destroyer and three merchant ships in the Gulf of Sirte. One ship was thought to be sunk.

Towards the end of the year, Luqa, home of the Blenheim detachments, was on the receiving end of a mounting number of Axis raids, as twenty-year-old Sgt Bill Bradshaw testifies. He was on his second tour of operations in 18 Squadron, as W.Op/AG in the crew of Sqn Ldr George Lerwill, DFC:

On one occasion, we landed back at Luqa towards dusk, in the middle of a major air raid.

Left to right: Sgts Tony Mee (W.Op/AG); Bill Brandwood (pilot) and Jock Miller (observer), a 105 Squadron crew who were shot down off Libya during the 12 September 1941 convoy strike. They were rescued next day by HMS Utmost and taken to Malta. Fg Offs Brandwood and Miller were killed in action when their Mosquito XVI ML975 of 571 Squadron received a flak hit during a bombing operation against Gelsenkirchen on the night of 15 June 1944. David Brandwood-Spencer

As we touched down on the runway, a Ju 88 appeared, flying head-on towards us, at low level, releasing its bombs. As it seemed likely that the bombs would fall on us, we had to abandon the aircraft as it was still travelling along the runway. Fortunately, the bombs missed us. I remember lying flat on the ground next to the runway, wishing I could sink into the surface, with the noise of the battle going on all around us. I gradually became aware of someone standing over me and on looking up found it was the Air Officer Commanding (AVM Hugh Pughe Lloyd). He had been driven across the airfield to pick us up. He calmly and quietly invited us to get into the car, then driving us back to the operations room; all in the middle of a pretty hectic air raid. From that moment, my respect and admiration for Air Vice-Marshals improved considerably!

Despite the high losses and deteriorating living and working conditions under siege, the Blenheim crews kept hammering the Axis supply convoys and ports. Braving fierce flak, three crews from 18 and 107 Squadrons badly damaged the 3,363-ton tanker Volturno off Greece on 29 November, which earned the formation leader Flt Lt E.G. Edmunds, RNZAF (of 18 Squadron) an immediate DFC. However, whereas during October eleven Axis merchant ships (totalling 24,691 tons) had

been sunk in direct air attacks (the majority by Fleet Air Arm aircraft), this number fell sharply during November. Only nine small ships (with a tonnage of 8,910) were sunk by the Malta-based strike aircraft. During that month, on the other hand, Royal Navy units ravaged the Axis shipping lanes with some 57,000 tons of shipping destroyed. This amounted to a staggering 63 per cent of all Axis cargoes bound for Libya.

Operational Blenheim results at the beginning of December were promising: on the 1st, six 18 Squadron Blenheims sank the 3,476-ton freighter Capo Faro, and damaged the Iseo without loss. Next day, the 10,540-ton tanker Iridio Mantovani, loaded with 7,000 tons of fuel, was attacked through a curtain of flak from the escorting destroyer Alvisa da Mosto by three 18 Squadron crews, leaving it badly damaged and stationary. It was subsequently sunk by the British cruiser Aurora, which also dealt with the Italian destroyer. This, however, was the only real success for the Blenheim crews from Malta during the month, their strike results falling dramatically with only three further, small ships sunk, totalling 2,148 tons. On 8 December two bombers from 18 Squadron collided in bad weather during a raid on Catania, while following attacks by two

Groundcrew of the 18 Squadron detachment at Malta, October 1941. A high rate of injury was sustained by these men by the end of 1941 due to mounting Axis bombing raids against the island. Les Deadfield

CR 42s of 23rd Gruppo, Flt Lt Edmunds, DFC was seen to crash into the sea with one engine ablaze during a shipping strike at Argostoli on the 11th. During raids on the same target over the next two days, four Blenheims from 18 and 107 Squadrons were shot down into the sea with the loss of all on board. Further losses were incurred during the remainder of the month: when 107 Squadron was finally relieved from operations in Malta in early January 1942 there were only three of the original twenty-six crews left.

Enemy raids on Malta were reaching a crescendo in consequence of the continuing pressure from Malta's anti-shipping forces during the last week of December 1941. In a matter of a few days over 500 sorties were flown against the island's airfields. At this period the losses were such that many aircraft and crews destined for the Middle and the Far East were commandeered to make up for the losses. One of those crews was Flt Sgts Dave Bone (pilot), Jim Martin (observer) and Ken Girling (W.Op/AG). They had joined 110 Squadron at Wattisham in the late autumn of 1941, but the crew had not really settled in when all 2 Group squadrons had to send three crews on the Reinforcement Flight for Malta, Egypt, Iraq, India and Burma. On their arrival at Malta on 8 November, the crew was ordered to stay at Luqa, together with three other crews, to replace losses in 18 Squadron. Three of those four crews were lost within a month, Bone and his crew being lucky to survive twenty-seven

operational sorties during the next three months at Malta, with Bone being awarded the DFM. The crew witnessed the demise of at least fifteen Blenheims and crews during the raids they were on. Jim Martin comments on his Malta days:

In Malta morale kept up very well among the servicemen, most of whom were young and buoyant. If the aircrew were not flying they could usefully help to check aircraft; if not, I can recall sitting with my mates under a sheet of corrugated iron (shrapnel-proof) and discussing coastal landmarks, aircraft recognition, etc. or playing bridge. If colleagues failed to return it was taken philosophically – something beyond our control. The Squadron Adjutant was meticulous about collecting the personal effects of those missing, but thought it reasonable if X's service equipment was taken over by needy Y (no stores on the island). Because we flew very low there was little chance of survival or being taken prisoner. Very much later, on a Lancaster squadron, the tension was much greater – all having the hope of completing thirty trips for a tour. Then there was general dismay when a crew was lost with twenty-five or more done.

The Raid on Castel Vetrano

Perhaps the most effective and memorable raid by 18 and 107 Squadrons while at Malta was one carried out on an Italian airfield at Castel Vetrano on the western tip of Sicily on 4 January 1942. The object was to destroy a virtual armada of some seventy-five bombers, torpedo-bombers

and transports, Z1007s, SM 79s, SM 82s, Ju 52s and Ju 88s, which were lined up wing tip to wing tip. They were being loaded with supplies of fuel, to be flown over to Africa to resupply the Afrika Korps, which badly needed fuel for its tanks and transport. The raid consisted of twelve Blenheims, which was all the two squadrons could muster. Sqn Ldr George Lerwill, DFC of 18 Squadron led the formation off from Luqa at 15.55hr. Bradshaw continues:

When approaching Sicily, we saw a group of fighters in the distance, but they turned away and we saw nothing more of them. We crossed over the Sicily coast at about 50ft and followed a valley which led to Castel Vetrano. The airfield was situated at the end of a valley, up on a plateau. We approached the target, therefore, below airfield level. I remember turning my turret round to look ahead as we approached the target and we had to climb suddenly in order to pass over the airfield boundary. As we passed over the boundary, I saw a mechanic sitting on the wing of a Ju 52, looking up in horror at us as we passed over him, at what seemed only a few feet. The route had been perfectly planned and Harry Huckins had guided the formation to exactly the right spot for the attack. All twelve Blenheims flew down the line of the runway, dropping our 250lb bombs with the gunners firing at the aircraft as we passed over them. The bombs were set for an 11sec delay, to avoid blowing ourselves up! The raid was followed that night by Wellington aircraft from Malta. Subsequently I learned that over forty German aircraft, Ju 52s and Ju 88s, were destroyed. Fortunately, much to our surprise, all our aircraft returned safely. The surprise element was such that there was no fighter opposition or flak.

One 18 Squadron pilot was wounded in the knee by a machine-gun bullet but otherwise there was no apparent opposition. The operation was a great success with thirty aircraft destroyed and many buildings damaged or destroyed. In a follow-up raid on the next night by Wellingtons, another fourteen enemy aircraft were smashed. What gave the Castel Vetrano raid that extra zest was that the Blenheim crews had been able to hit back in answer to the continual bombing they had been enduring, and finally had managed to give Sicily some of its own medicine. However, by this time German air raids on Malta's airfields had become so severe that it was decided to move 18 and 107 Squadrons. A week later, on 12 January 1942, seventeen

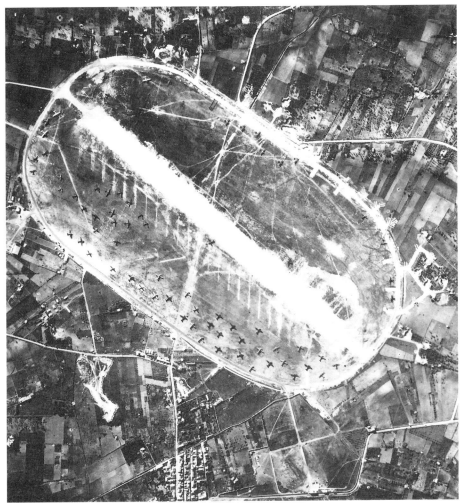

This photograph was brought back from a reconnaissance of Castel Vetrano airfield on 3 January 1942, and triggered off the brilliant raid next day by twelve Blenheims from 18 and 107 Squadrons. It was issued to the crews as a target map. Jim Martin

west of Palermo. On leaving the area, the Blenheims climbed away up a steep narrow valley with cloud on top. Only two emerged to fly back to Malta – three aircraft either crashed into the hillsides or fell victim to Italian flak. Z2734, in the hands of Sgt Matthew C. Houston, crashed at Palermo harbour at around 11.15hr. The others lost were Z9812 of the Australian Plt Off Workman and crew, and Z9824, flown by Flt Sgt Jack Ibbotson, RNZAF. None of the aircrews survived.

Two days later, Sqn Ldr Russell Stewart, RNZAF led a trio of Blenheims on a shipping sweep off Buerat. Returning to the island, they were bounced by Bf 109s of JG53, which shot all three down into the sea near Filfla. A similar tragedy unfolded on 11 February, this time one Blenheim, Z9823, was sent spinning into the sea off Malta. This brought the total losses of 21 Squadron to eleven aircraft and crews in just over three weeks of operations. The unit was so severely weakened that it was disbanded on 14 March 1942 to reform on the Lockheed Ventura in England, thus bringing the Blenheim era at Malta to a sad end.

Flt Sgts Harry Huckins (observer, on left) and Bill Bradshaw (W.Op/AG) in Cairo, on completion of their second tour of operations in March 1942. Huckins was responsible for the perfect navigation of the Blenheim force on the Castel Vetrano raid. Note the small silver-winged boots; these were awarded to aircrew who got shot down in enemy territory and managed to walk back to rejoin their units and marked them as members of the 'Late Arrivals Club' (they had been shot down by a Bf 109 in Blenheim L8743 while serving in 21 Squadron, near Damville, Normandy on 11 June 1940, and made their way back to Britain). This club was not officially recognized and they had to take the insignia down when they got home later in 1942. Harry Huckins

battle-weary, surviving aircrews left Malta and flew to Egypt, where they were dispersed to other squadrons such as No. 55 in the western desert and to units in the Far East to fight the Japanese assault. Sqn Ldr Lerwill and his crew were one of only two left of the original sixteen crews from 18 Squadron who had arrived at Malta three months before.

The final 2 Group Malta detachment came from 21 Squadron, arriving at Luqa on Christmas Day. By this time, the Luftwaffe's all-out air offensive against Malta had reached such proportions that it was hardly possible any more to mount offensive operations and many aircraft were destroyed on the ground. However, anti-shipping and coastal attacks were carried out whenever possible. These operations often turned out to be suicidal with only few results gained in the face of daunting odds. The desperate position for Malta's strike aircraft is clearly illustrated by the fact that throughout January its crews were unable to sink a single Axis ship. 21 Squadron, on the other hand, was decimated. From the squadron's first convoy attack, 50 miles east of Kerkenah Island by four aircraft on 13 January, two Blenheims failed to return. Flt Lt H.F. Dukes-Smith and Sgt Ken Coakley and their crews were all killed. On 4 February six Blenheims were despatched to attack shipping in Palermo harbour. Approaching the coast at zero feet, high ground was suddenly encountered with tragic results. Wg Cdr Bill Selkirk, CO of the squadron, banked Z9806 steeply to climb over this, but clipped the water and his aircraft was seen to cartwheel into the sea. The remaining five Blenheims missed their primary target and instead attacked railway targets to the

CHAPTER NINE

Blenheim Wireless Operator/ Air Gunner at War

Very few Blenheim aircrews in 2 Group, Bomber Command were fortunate enough to complete a tour of twenty-five to thirty operations during 1941. Losses on the low-level daylight shipping strikes were so high that by November only three crews in 2 Group had been able to complete fifty sorties, or 200 hours, on operations in Blenheims.

Monty Scotney's Story

One of the handful of young men who succeeded in completing a full tour in 2 Group during this period was Sgt Monty Scotney. He takes up the story of his war in Blenheims:

Our crew, comprising Sgt 'Jeff' Jefferson, Sgt Millns and myself, were posted from No.17 OTU to 18 Squadron at Oulton on 29 June 1941. I was twenty, Jefferson was older, about thirty, almost elderly to us youngsters, but a superb pilot. Sgt Ralph Millns was a quiet personality and a very efficient navigator/bomb aimer.

The next day we did our first op. – a power plant at Pont a Vendin, near Lens. Take-off time 17.10hr, duration 2hr 35min, bomb load four 250lb HE, plus four 40lb incendiaries – weather, a beautiful, calm summer evening. For me, sitting in the turret behind twin Brownings and a sense of wonderment rather than fear, an innocent abroad kind of feeling, not really knowing what it was all about or what to expect. We were given a steel helmet to take on these raids: I sat on mine. Most air gunners did.

We crossed the French coast at Point de Gravelines, height anything from 12 to 15,000ft (oxygen turned on at 10,000ft), clear blue sky, and no sign of our escorting Spitfires. But we knew they were there, mostly well above us as top cover. Then the first awareness that this was not a Sir Alan Cobham five-shillings pleasure trip – the heavy flak appeared: unpleasantly close, slightly behind or just in front, more or less the same height, nasty puff balls of black smoke with a vicious orange flash in the centre.

I remember putting my head forward and to one side so that the the the thick metal gun mounting acted as a shield. After the coast no more flak, but once or twice a sense of apprehension as the nearest Blenheim in our vic of three drifted in perilously close, the whirling Mercury propeller threatening to sheer off our tail. At times I was on the point of telling Jeff to take avoiding action, but the offending pilot always saw the danger and pulled away.

'Approaching the target', the voice of the leading observer could be heard giving instructions to his pilot, 'Left, left-steady, steady-right-steady, steady-bombs gone!' Then a sight which I always found awesome, twelve Blenheims disgorging a total of forty-eight 250lb HE bombs and forty-eight 40lb incendiaries, at first keeping up with the formation, then slowly falling behind, and downwards. I don't ever remember watching them all the way to the ground, presumably as I realized I should be keeping a sharp look-out to the rear.

Then the whole formation wheeling about and heading for home, still without a Spitfire in sight, nor, for that matter, any 109s. Again the coast crossed at Point de Gravelines, with this time a valedictory salute rather than a welcoming one, but of the same variety, nasty, black, smoke balls with orange centres. I can't ever remember hearing shells exploding, although some bursts were close. Over the Channel a sharp descent, eventually in the circuit over our home base of Oulton, then landing, debriefing and a good meal. That evening, a look at the mess notice-board for the next day's battle order. Were we on? Yes. Arrive on the squadron 29 June, first raid the next day, second one the following day. Truly a speedy baptism of fire – 18 Squadron must have been very short of crews.

Most circus raids followed the same general pattern, but some were memorable because of particular incidents. Our second sortie (after two recalls) was an attack on marshalling yards at Hazebrouck on 3 July. Again twelve of us in four vics of three, and again heavy anti-aircraft fire at Point de Gravelines. But this time a 109E of Adolf Galland's famous squadron managed to break through the Spitfire protective screen.

Meet the crew. Left to right: Sgt Montague 'Monty' Scotney (W.Op/AG); Sqn Ldr T.G. 'Jeff' Jefferson (pilot) and Sgt Ralph Millns (observer), 18 Squadron, Oulton, August 1941. Monty Scotney

Wartime graves of Wg Cdr Tim Partridge, DFC, OC 18 Squadron, and his crew at Rotterdam. Douwe Drijver

was not attacked, there was a danger from enemy fighters. I was always apprehensive about meeting up with Me 110s which were armed with cannons and could stand well away while producing devastating fire.

I do recall that for long flights, when it was important to remain alert for possible fighter attacks, we were given little, round, white 'pep' pills to take – an amphetamine drug, Benzedrine. We were also supplied with fruit drops to suck.

During the morning of 7 July, Sgt Jefferson and crew in V6519 ventured into the Heligoland Bight, attacking a sea-going tug towing two barges, but no results were observed. A few hours later, a combined force of 105 and 139 Squadron attacked a convoy off Scheveningen and were hit badly, with three Blenheims shot down by escorting flak ships and a standing patrol of Bf 109s of 2/JG52. All nine aircrew perished. Three days later, the Jefferson crew did a low-level bombing trip of 3 hr 30min against shipping in Le Havre harbour, landing back at base at 14.10hr. Twenty-three other Blenheim crews were dispatched on coastal sweeps off France and on a circus raid to the docks at Cherbourg, the latter force losing V6398 of 21 Squadron, with Sqn Ldr Tudge and crew becoming prisoners of war. Sgt Jefferson lifted V6519 off the grass field at Horsham St. Faith at 09.15hr on the 12th for a sea sweep near Borkum, as part of a strong force of thirty-eight Blenheims roaming

Painted a vivid yellow from the tip of its propellor back to the cockpit, it flashed through our formation at great speed, firing as it went. I didn't see the approach, and caught no more than a glimpse as it whipped past. My guns were pointing in the right direction and as a shock reaction I fired a short burst. Much too late, completely ineffective, and more a danger to other members of our formation than to the German fighter. This method of attack was difficult to counter. Sitting thousands of feet above the Blenheims, having sneaked up, unobserved, the 109 would go into a vertical dive, build up formidable speed, pull out behind firing continuously, flash through, and break away. This time none of our aircraft was hit, but this was not always the case.

Scotney is not quite right with his assessment of the losses on Circus No.30. In fact, Blenheim V6452 of 139 Squadron was lost, Sgt J.A. Cormack, RAAF and crew all perishing. The next operation for the crew was a shipping sweep off the Frisian Islands on 5 July, in Blenheim V6519. Take off from Oulton was 19.10hr:

> The weather was fine, and I have a clear recollection of ten R-boats which we saw off the Frisian Islands. They fired at us, the bullets making splashes in the sea, but none of us was hit, nor did we attack. It was not our brief to do so. We were looking for merchant ships, and it would have been unwise to take on ten well-armed naval vessels. Had there been a cargo-

carrying ship which the patrol boats were protecting, we would have attacked. On our return (and we all came back safely), an aircrew Squadron Leader who had not flown this sortie, remarked in my presence, 'I'm surprised they all got back, I thought we'd have lost at least two.' I remember thinking that it was an unfeeling, not to say callous remark to have made. I can see why he made it; flights to the Frisian Islands were mostly lengthy, and without fighter protection. Even if heavily-defended shipping

V6519 has come to grief in a field near Oulton, 5 August 1941. Plt Off Jefferson and his crew escaped with minor injuries. Monty Scotney

Veteran. L9240, Ben My Cree had chalked up forty-six sorties when depicted at Horsham St. Faith in early July 1941. The aircraft, having survived more than a year of operations with 18 Squadron, was finally lost on the Kiel Canal raid of 30 July, on its fifty-third sortie. Bryn Williams

I fired a long burst at him, and then suddenly realized that while my attention was being concentrated on him, we could ourselves be the object of attack from behind. This proved to be the case. On swinging the guns rearward, I found another 109 on our tail doing a copybook quarter attack. It was close, but as far as I could tell, not firing – no tracer, no smoke. I fired a long burst and the left-hand Browning jammed. Using the toggle provided, I recocked the gun. This briefly diverted my attention, and when I looked again the 109 was nowhere to be seen.

At debriefing, on our return to base, crews of other Blenheims said that one of the 109s (either the one on our port beam or the one behind) had dived into the sea. This was not seen by me. I've always had the feeling that these 109s were on a training flight, perhaps from an OTU and possibly even unarmed. I don't know, but in any event, how else to explain the naivety of the Luftwaffe pilot who flew alongside us? No experienced pilot would have done so.

Although the Blenheims escaped unscathed on this occasion, a 139 Squadron force directed to sweep the coast off Le Havre fared less well. Bf 109s intercepted the shipping raiders in the Beat area and wasted no time, shooting down R3704 and V6253 into the sea. Plt Offs Wilson and Galt and their crews all perished.

All 2 Group squadrons were kept busy in low-level formation flying practice during the second week of July. Scotney recorded:

There was a definite air of apprehension and expectancy among the crews of something big and different about to take place: engendered, no doubt, by the knowledge that our aircraft had been fitted with balloon-cable cutters on the wing leading edges. Briefing on 16 July confirmed the target: Rotterdam docks, low level, two waves, each of eighteen Blenheims. Our commanding officer, Wg Cdr Tim Partridge, to lead the second wave, and our crew to fly number two to him.

I clearly remember waiting for the transport to take us to our aircraft. The weather was fine, and some crew members were lolling around on the grass, others standing in small groups. One of them was Fg Off Smith, who was the W.Op/AG flying with the CO. I spoke to him, but I can't remember the actual conversation. Whatever his reply was, the words were among the last he spoke – two hours later he was dead. Sgt Davies was the CO's regular air gunner, but he had been called home urgently to his critically ill father. Fg Off Smith replaced him. I also

the shipping lanes off the Dutch coast. 107 Squadron suffered a serious blow when its CO, Wg Cdr Arthur Booth, and his crew were shot down in Z7487 while attacking a convoy off IJmuiden at 12.35hr. In contrast, the Jefferson crew had an uneventful, four-hour sortie; but one incident did occur which nearly resulted in the loss of the aircraft and crew, as Scotney recalls:

We always kept low (about 50ft), to avoid detection by enemy radar. Jeff trimmed the aircraft so that it would climb should pressure on the control column be relaxed. I remember watching the sea slipping underneath at a constant distance away for mile after mile. Suddenly we went down to within inches of the water. I thought we were about to hit – but then we rose again. On landing I mentioned the incident to Ralph, who told me that Jeff leaned forward to accept a sandwich. In doing so he pushed the control column forward – hence our dip forwards. At 50ft or less such incidents can be disastrous.

On 16 September we flew another long North Sea sweep near Borkum, during which nothing was seen, but one of our aircraft failed to return. Sgt Tracey was formating on us on the way out. At some stage he just disappeared, and

no one saw him go. It was assumed that for some reason he hit the sea. This was easily done at low level when turning steeply – a loss of concentration during the turn, perhaps aggravated by fatigue and constant watching of a dull, grey surface for hour after hour – wing tip touching, and that's it.

In the late morning of 14 July, Sqn Ldr Roe led twelve Blenheims of 18 and 139 Squadron on a North Sea sweep off IJmuiden. Five crews successfully bombed shipping in the Beat area, a large merchantman being attacked by both Roe and Jefferson. It was hit in the bows with a large explosion being observed. Their victim was the 1,308-tons Swedish *Aspen*, which was sunk. Escorting Bf 109s then came to the rescue of the convoy, as Scotney vividly recounts:

After bombing, the Blenheims were strung out and all heading the same way, parallel to the coast. One Me 109, intent on pursuing a Blenheim ahead of us and off to our port side, seemed quite oblivious to our presence and flew alongside our aircraft no more than 50yd away. I clearly remember being astonished by the pilot's lack of awareness of his vulnerability.

recall, when we got to our plane, looking at the small, evenly spaced protuberances on the wings' leading edges. These were the cable cutters, and they looked very inadequate for the job.

On the run in to the dock area I traversed the turret to port and took a photograph, over our port engine, of Wg Cdr Partridge's aircraft. This could only have been a minute or two before he was shot down. Over the target I took a second photograph, looking rearwards, of several bomb bursts. One of them must have been our two five-hundred pounders. Both these shots were published in the *Daily Sketch* for Saturday, 19 July 1941.

The flak was intense by the time the second wave of Blenheims appeared over the docks. The first eighteen alerted the defences and suffered one loss, the second eighteen lost three (two from 18 Squadron). Although we were flying very close, I didn't see Tim Partridge's plane go down, but Jeff and Ralph did. On the way back Ralph came over the intercom and said to Jeff: 'Did you see the Wingco go? He turned over and was on fire underneath.' Tim's aircraft hit the side of a canal.

Immediately after this raid our crew went on leave. I was home when the newspaper accounts appeared on the Saturday following the Wednesday on which the raid took place.

On return from a well-deserved leave, newly commissioned Plt Off Jefferson and his crew became involved in Army co-operation exercises, starting with mock attacks on armoured columns at Newell Wood, south-west of Bourne and north of Horncastle on 4 August. However, things went wrong on the crew's third sortie on 5 August, when they came back from a low-level attack on infantry near Candlesby in V6519. Scotney continues:

The weather had not been ideal, and strong, gusty winds were blowing as we were making our final approach on return. Some distance before crossing the aerodrome boundary the port wing suddenly lifted, quite markedly and violently, and just as quickly went back to a normal position and we continued the approach. I thought something might be wrong but nothing was said over the intercom, and when I looked up the length of the aircraft to the cockpit area, everything appeared to be normal: I could see the back of Jeff's head, and Ralph was in his usual position. Everything OK it seemed.

In a Blenheim, just before touching down, the air gunner had to get out of his turret and disconnect a lead to a large accumulator on the floor of the aircraft. This minimized the risk of fire should something go wrong on landing – and on this occasion it certainly did. I had just

bent down, with hand outstretched towards the accumulator, when there was a violent impact with the ground. I was thrown heavily forward towards the main spar, on to my back, and tossed about wildly from side to side. My mind went back to the wing tipping episode – something had been wrong, and we had crashed.

But how had we gone in? I didn't know, since I wasn't looking out at the moment of impact. Had we hit wing tip first, nose first, was everything about to disintegrate? I have a strong recollection of lying on my back, waiting for a decisive, obliterating blow, a coup de grace. And then, what I can only describe as an extraordinary sensation – a feeling of complete and utter peace, came over me as I looked up at the 'roof' of the aircraft. I can only describe it thus – sublime contentment, calm, and acceptance. Others have undergone this experience in times of extreme danger and a conviction of certain death. It is a phenomenon known to medical science, but not able to be completely and satisfactorily explained. I have wondered since, is this Nature's way of softening the blow, the shock of the moment of death? Does everybody, at the very instant of dying, have the same easy slide into oblivion? I don't know, but I do emphatically know that I underwent this extraordinary moment of peacefulness.

There followed a realization that I had survived and my first thought was to get out as

Sqn Ldr Jefferson at the controls of his Blenheim somewhere over England, August 1941. Monty Scotney

quickly as I could. The top flap door had not jammed and a quick exit was possible. We had landed in a field studded with upright poles and lengths of wire to prevent German aircraft and gliders landing (fears of invasion were still alive). Two car-loads of 18 Squadron personnel soon appeared – they had seen us in difficulties and obviously about to crash. Jeff was alright, Ralph had a gash on the head and was whipped off to the sick bay, and I was uninjured apart from extensive bruising. For a week or two afterwards I was constantly finding new sore and painful spots.

The trouble had been a broken flap, caused by having sustained undetected flak damage on one of our previous sorties – V6519 had been on six. Jeff had just managed to maintain level flight by holding maximum opposite aileron, but he could not maintain height nor could he change course. We were heading straight for the side of a bungalow, and there was nothing to be done except cut both engines and drop out of the sky from perhaps twenty or thirty feet – which is what happened. We completed our Army co-operation exercises in L9390 and then went on leave. While on leave 18 Squadron lost three crews attacking Cologne in daylight. It's an ill wind....

Due to the serious casualties in 18 Squadron during July and August, 'Jeff' Jefferson was promoted straight from Pilot Officer to Flight Lieutenant while away on leave. On 16 August, Flt Lt Jefferson and crew were detailed to fly to Manston for a dreaded *Channel Stop* detachment:

At Manston, each day three crews were on shipping strike stand-by. The rest of the squadron was either stood down or taking part in a circus raid. On call in the mess was a nerve-racking business. *Channel Stop* shipping attacks were synonymous with a high casualty rate, and the waiting aircrew sat nervously, hoping that the telephone remained silent.

On 17 August we were waiting when the 'phone rang – a call for briefing. A tanker, heavily escorted by flak ships and a standing patrol of 109s, was attempting the narrowest part of the Channel. Three torpedo Beauforts made an initial attack – unsuccessfully – only two returned. Now it was our turn, we were to lead a vic of three. I was advised to wear a thick leather Irvin flying jacket – 'good against flak'. I was also to be given an Aldis lamp with which to signal to the leader of an accompanying group of cannon-firing Hurricanes. Their role was to shoot up the flak ships immediately before we attacked – my Aldis signal was to be sent a few minutes before reaching the target area. Incidentally, I can still see the kindly concerned look on the face of the wireless technician who handed me the black, bulky lamp. He was a middle-aged civilian and probably had a son as old as me – I don't think he expected to see me, or his lamp, again.

But things went wrong. Ralph told me when to contact the lead Hurricane pilot, which I did, but it was all too late. We were on the German ships before the fighters had time to nullify the flak. Realizing this, I vividly recollect shouting over the intercom to my pilot, 'Don't attack Jeff!' Ralph joined me in exhorting Jeff not to go

in. He was persuaded, and wheeled our small formation in a tight turn to port, and away. As we turned, I saw a Hurricane fail to pull out of its vertical dive on the flak ships and go nose-first into the sea.

Back at Manston all hell let loose. The fighter boys were furious. I believe they lost more than the one aircraft I saw go in, and refused to accept our reason for not pressing on. Nor would our CO, Wing Commander Smythe, although I think he was trying to appease the Hurricane squadron commander. The following morning we left the squadron, and proceeded to London on immediate posting to the Middle East. The Adjutant, a friendly flight lieutenant, tried to jolly us along by saying we were better off not being with 18 Squadron – casualties were high, survival expectations low, etc. He was somewhat embarrassed when, after reaching London, we were recalled to rejoin the squadron and actually went back to Manston the same day. A change of heart by whom? The CO, the Hurricane CO, Air Ministry postings? I never found out. I believe this incident was instrumental in Jeff not being awarded the DFC, although he did finish up as Wg Cdr Jefferson, DSO, AFC.

Indeed, the escorting Hurricanes of 242 Squadron lost two aircraft and pilots: Z3845 of Plt Off Hicks, RAAF and Sgt Redfern's Z3454 both fell victim to the murderous flak of the German convoy. Plt Off Quillian of 242 Squadron encountered two Bf 109s and shot both down, but that was scant comfort for the hard-pressed fighter boys at Manston. Scotney continues:

Next day, 18 August, our crew was on shipping stand-by when the others took part in a raid on St. Omer. Bader's legs were delivered to him on this occasion. They were packed in a crate which was pushed out of the camera (and escape) hatch of Sgt Nickelson's Blenheim. The air gunner who did the pushing was Sgt Pearson, rather older than most of us, a family man in his early thirties. I got to know him well, and was sorry when he was shot down on a shipping strike off the Dutch coast on 20 September. I was also on this raid and took a photograph of his wing tip sticking out of the water. We were given Leica cameras to record low-level bombing results.

On this circus raid, a very young, fair-haired W.Op/AG, Sgt Stevens, was not so lucky while negotiating the flak at Point de Gravelines. His aircraft was hit and damaged while coming out of France, but made it across the Channel before crash-landing just over the coast. Sgt

LAC Les Deadfield took this snapshot of his 18 Squadron groundcrew colleagues posing with the crate containing Wg Cdr Douglas Bader's artificial leg, before it was stowed into R3843 at Manston and parachuted to Bader during Circus No.78 on St. Omer, 18 August 1941. *Les Deadfield*

14 September 1941; (i) Sqn Ldr Jefferson is jinking Z7308 'Y' madly while running in on a 10,000-ton merchantman in a strongly defended convoy off The Hague.

(ii) After hurling his two 500lb bombs towards the ship's side, Jefferson pulled up steeply to avoid hitting the vessel's superstructure. At this instant, the aircraft was hit by flak in its starboard wing, but the pilot brought the aircraft safely back to base. Monty Scotney

Stevens had been hit by a shell fragment which entered his anatomy in the place which sitting on tin helmets had been designed to protect. He was rushed to hospital but died shortly afterwards.

Stevens's Blenheim was V6175 'G', which his pilot Sgt Vickers crash-landed one mile north-east of Rye in Sussex at 18.45hr. Both Vickers and his observer Sgt Lowe were injured. Another Blenheim was lost on Circus No.78: V5491 of 110 Squadron was hit by flak and crashed into the Channel, Sgt N.W. Berg and his crew being killed.

The last operation carried out by the 18 Squadron detachment at Manston was a circus raid to Lille in northern France, as Sgt Scotney recalls:

On 27 August, the target for twelve Blenheims was the Lille power plant. Take-off time was earlier than usual, five past seven in the morning. Weather fine, but some patchy cloud about. We crossed into France and flew on, and on, and still on. It seemed to be taking an interminably long time to reach the target. In fact we never did. Incredible as it may seem, the lead navigator had lost his way. We were not allowed to off-load bombs just anywhere in France, so back they all came. It turned out to be an early morning cruise around northern France, but not entirely abortive. If the object of circuses was to entice up German fighters, success was achieved.

I remember watching the demise of a 109. It suddenly appeared behind our formation, being closely pursued by a Spitfire which it evaded by diving into a large, billowy cloud. Very shortly afterwards the 109 reappeared, but this time in two halves. It had been completely cut in two, the fuselage severed just behind the pilot's cockpit. The main plane was descending in a leisurely flat spin, rather like a slowed-up sycamore seed, the tail unit was acting similarly a short distance away, and the German pilot? He was going down in his parachute some distance below, and between the remains of his aircraft. Perhaps not an entirely wasted morning.

Wg Cdr Stapleton, leading the Hornchurch Wing as escort for the Blenheims on this circus raid, and Plt Off Wood, both of 403 Squadron, each claimed a Bf 109 destroyed. In mid afternoon on 27 August, the 18 Squadron crews flew back to Horsham St. Faith to resume high-level circus raids and shipping sweeps at zero feet:

On 4 September we attacked a synthetic oil plant south-east of Bethune. We were leading the last vic of three, below and behind the first three aircraft; a position not beloved by aircrew. It was what was commonly referred to as the 'arse-end Charlie' position – somewhat exposed and vulnerable. Flying number three to us (to my right, as I looked out of my turret) was a crew on its first operation. The wireless operator/air gunner was a pleasant, young, Jewish lad by the name of Koranski. He was billeted in a room next to mine in comfortable aircrew quarters at Horsham St. Faiths, just outside Norwich. We had swapped airfields a few weeks previously with our sister squadron, 139. Koranski played 'Amapola', a popular tune of the day, constantly on his gramophone. Being 'old hands' by now we were often asked by new crews, 'What's it like?' Koranski was no exception. I can't remember what my reply was, but undoubtedly it was reassuring even though I didn't feel that the overall situation was quite as rosy as I made out. I probably mentioned that, while we detested low-level attacks on shipping, which had a high casualty rate, we considered circus trips a 'piece of cake' – nothing much to worry about.

On this particular raid, I was sitting on the small, padded seat of the turret, feet on the pedals, hands on the crossbar controls, watching Koranski close in to my right, another Blenheim equally tucked in to my left, and gazing at the empty sky beyond our fin and rudder. Quite suddenly it was empty no longer. Immediately behind, on a level with us and closing rapidly, was a small, grey, fighter plane with wispy smoke blowing back from alongside its engine cowling. I still have a vivid recollection of this. Equally vividly I remember the doubt in my mind, was it one of our close escort, or a 109? This momentary hesitation was a fatal inhibitor of action. I didn't fire, the enemy aircraft streaked through straight over the top of Koranski, and away. I looked at Koranski's plane, and saw that there were large rips in the upper surfaces of the tailplane and both wings. Thin lines of black smoke trailed from both engines. I quickly looked away and rearwards in case a second 109 was attacking, but the sky was clear. I looked for Koranski again, but he was no longer with us. His Blenheim was two thousand feet below, curving away downwards in a wide, gentle sweep which had put him on a reciprocal course. The plane seemed under control but was on fire with thick, black smoke coming from the engines. No chutes appeared. The attack was over in seconds. I don't know to this day what happened to that crew. The plane seemed to be riddled, which didn't augur well for its unfortunate occupants.

Sgt M. Koranski perished together with his observer Sgt F. Woodcock, whereas the pilot of Z7296 'P', Sgt D.G. Adams, RAAF was taken prisoner. Scotney continues:

I clearly recollect another happening while on this same raid. There was always a sense of relief, almost, in fact, of peacefulness and well-being, about going home. It was a beautiful September evening, no cloud, just clear blue sky. The steady drone of the engines was almost soporific. Away on the port beam, a few thousand feet above, its distinctive, elliptical wing shape just discernible, was an escorting Spitfire, flying straight and steady, keeping station. I imagined the young pilot anticipating landing back at base, a meal in the mess, and perhaps an evening out with the lads in some congenial pub. As I watched, a small, grey shape descended vertically and seemingly so slowly downwards on to the Spitfire, it exploded in a great orange flash. One moment man and elegant machine in an almost peaceful and beautiful setting, the next, a mass of incandescing metal. Once again, an incident indelibly seared into my memory.

Sgt Charles Tracey's V6339 in formation with eleven other 18 Squadron Blenheims on an anti-'squealer' sweep in Beat B (off Texel), 16 September 1941. Moments later, this aircraft hit the surface of the sea and disappeared, Sgt Tracey and his crew all perishing. *Monty Scotney*

over farmhouse rooftops, fields and trees. A peaceful scene and in complete contrast to what we were about to do. I really do recall envying the occupants of those houses and the fact that they were probably enjoying a quiet afternoon cup of tea while I was speeding by sitting on top of two 500lb SAP bombs.

The weather was overcast and dull, almost dark, in fact. On the approach to the convoy off The Hague Jeff kept very low, literally skimming the sea and using the rudder to do a kind of flat zigzag; we were jinking madly. Strung out in a line to our starboard were six flak ships, and the tracer from their guns showed up clearly in the gloom. A strong impression I retain is the apparent slowness of the projectiles – like strings of fairy lights reaching out lazily towards us. At the moment of attack, when we had already released the two 500lb bombs, we were hit in the starboard wing by flak. Six aircraft attacked and, although an attack was made by three Me 109s, none of our aircraft were lost and no hits were achieved on the target.

During the second half of September, the usual practice bombing and photographing exercises were flown and, in between, Flt Lt Jefferson and crew flew four further operations. The shipping lanes off Borkum were visited on the 16th (with Sgt Tracey disappearing off Texel Island) and shipping was attacked off IJmuiden and Zandvoort on the 18th and 20th. 18 Squadron escaped further casualties on 18 September, but 88 Squadron lost V6380 and Z7488 off the Belgian coast on that day. 18 Squadron's Flt Sgt Nickleson and crew in R3843 fell victim to ships' flak while attacking a convoy off Zandvoort on the 20th, whereas Flt Lt Jefferson successfully bombed a 3,000-ton merchantman before speeding back home in Z7308. 226 Squadron lost two further aircraft, with all six crew members perishing, while attacking a convoy off the Hook of Holland on this day. Finally, the Jefferson crew rounded off a busy month with a circus raid on Gosnay power station on the 21st.

The Crew Go to Malta

At the end of the month, Jefferson was promoted to Squadron Leader and received news of a move to Malta. Sgt Scotney tells:

Several flights were made to test petrol consumption before setting off for Malta. The two

The Spitfire victim on Circus No.93 was an aircraft of 54 Squadron: Plt Offs Haws and Evans, acting as Target Support Escort were both shot down by Bf 109s. The next operation for Flt Lt Jefferson and crew came on 10 September when they took off at 13.00hr in Z7308, in the company of five other Blenheims of 18 Squadron for a shipping sweep off the Dutch Frisian islands in Beat 7:

The weather was overcast, with lots of low cloud. We suddenly came across a fishing smack – I recall the small superstructure which was obviously the wheelhouse. I can't bring to mind actually bombing it (the target seemed too small to warrant 500lb bombs), but I certainly machine-gunned it. The results were unobserved, as we lost it in the mist and low cloud. Although it looked diminutive and harmless, these so-called fishing smacks were packed with wireless equipment and were positioned to give the Germans early warning of enemy aircraft. I remember feeling guilty about the machine-gunning, and thinking, 'Suppose it was just a fishing boat.'

Although many 2 Group crews had second thoughts about attacking these innocent-looking fishing ships, Bomber Command HQ had ordered them on 3 April 1941 to attack any fishing vessels encountered, as they might very well be employed by the Germans as early-warning 'squealer' boats.

Four days later, on 14 September, the 18 Squadron crews were once again briefed for a low-level North Sea shipping sweep, this time off The Hague. Take-off for Flt Lt Jefferson and crew in Blenheim Z7308 was 16.30hr:

I clearly remember a small group of people waving us off as we taxied out. I also remember it being a Sunday and that we flew low, very low

18 Squadron groundcrew pose with Z7308 at Horsham St. Faith in September 1941. These unsung heroes worked all hours, often in the open and in atrocious weather to keep 'their' Blenheims in top condition. Z7308 served with 82, 18, 139 and finally 21 Squadron before it went missing on operations from Malta, 6 February 1942. Bryn Williams

legs, UK to Gibraltar, and Gibraltar/Malta would test the duration of the Blenheim to the limit. We flew to Portreath, well down on the north Cornish coast, spent six nights in a tent, then took off for the seven and a quarter hours' flight to Gibraltar. Uneventful really, except on two counts, a meeting with a fighter shortly before setting course across the Bay of Biscay at our optimum height of 10,000ft. Happily, it turned out to be a Spitfire on patrol, although a few nervous twitches occurred until a positive identification was made. It was a beautiful autumnal day, blue sky all around, blue sea below, a few scattered wispy clouds. The Spit floated in towards us, took a good look, and turned away.

Arrival at Gibraltar seven hours or so later was memorable. In 1941 the runway at Gibraltar was very, very short, ending with a drop into the sea. The wind direction around the Rock could change in an instant, and frequently did. Headwind one minute, tailwind the next. This made aircraft arrivals at Gibraltar very interesting for those on the ground, and a good knot of spectators was always guaranteed. We in Blenheim Z7895 'F' did not disappoint. As we approached, the wind turned and caught us up the back. Much too fast and unable to stop, we reached the end of the runway and, in desperation, Jeff did a violent swivel turn to starboard. The aircraft stood on its nose, bent the propellor tips and the port engine caught fire. I went up in the air rather like being in a fairground ride before the tail dropped down again. A Squadron Leader roared up on a motorcycle and shouted to Jeff, 'Press the fire extinguisher, you

bloody fool!' – which my skipper had already done. The motorcyclist was somewhat abashed when Jeff climbed out to reveal that he held the same rank. Gibraltar was then known as the aeroplanes' graveyard, and there really was a huge pile of wrecked aircraft, Wellingtons, I remember, being well represented.

We stayed in Gibraltar two days. My impressions? The huge sheer face of the Rock, eucalyptus trees, and horse-drawn carriages rather like those of nineteenth-century England. There were no spares available, especially propellors for Bristol Mercury engines, so the bent tips were hammered out straight and we took off for Malta, heading out to sea towards Algeciras. It was a blue, fine Mediterranean day, but this was not to last. The weather grew worse with strong winds and black cloud. We flew low, very close to the sea, and the whipped-up creamy wave tops were not far beneath us. At Cap Tenes, not too far from Algiers, and probably because we were experiencing persistent headwinds, we turned back for Gibraltar. A four-day wait, and then off again.

My memories of this near-seven-hours trip centre around worries about having to pass close to Pantellaria, a known Italian fighter base, a view of the conically-shaped Mount Etna, and a sighting of Ju 52 transports obviously winging their way to north Africa and Rommel. We were all flying as close to the sea as we could get. Arrival at Luqa soon followed; fortunately with no air-raid in progress as we touched down.

Accommodation was primitive, a former leper colony building known as the Poor House, food centred around tins of McConochie stew,

'tarted' up in various ways, and time was spent either being bombed or going out and doing the bombing. I have memories of persistent air-raids, low-flying Ju 88s immediately overhead, and the occasional Hurricane hurtling into the sea.

The first raid we did from Luqa, on 31 October (two days after our arrival), was an attack on a factory at Licata in Sicily. It was a bit like one of our circus operations over France, except that we had no fighter escort. A small formation, as I remember, probably nine, and this time, unusually, we weren't leading. In fact, we were in one of the less-favoured positions, somewhere at the rear. Not far to go, and this time I did watch the bombs all the way down to what seemed a pattern of ridiculously small, brown eruptions some eight thousand feet below. No flak whatsoever. A wheel round and a long shallow dive back to Malta.

We were attacked by three Macchi 200s, shortly after leaving the target. They appeared about a mile behind us and weaving to and fro at right angles to our flight path. This went on for some time, when suddenly one detached itself and came in very rapidly. It was firing lots of what I'm sure was .5-calibre red tracer. This streamed over our port wing without hitting us, or anyone else in the formation for that matter. The very strange feature of this attack was that not one Browning machine-gun (and there were eighteen of them) opened up on the Macchi. Why, I don't know. Perhaps there was a recognition doubt in our minds, although we certainly weren't taken by surprise: we had been watching them for a while before anything happened. But there it was – unharmed, they went back to their spaghetti and we all returned to our McConochie's.

My next four raids from Malta were all lengthy shipping sweeps. A Maryland would search for a target, find one, report its position, and the Blenheims would be sent out to locate it and attack. The day following our encounter with the Macchis we found and bombed a merchant ship escorted by a destroyer and a Caproni 310. I have a mind's eye picture of the Caproni – three engines, large and somewhat cumbersome, above us and outlined against the blue Mediterranean sky. What the function of the Italian bomber was I'm not sure – possibly to alert the destroyer. It obviously circled well above the ship it was protecting, while we approached as low as we could possibly get. An early sight of us could be obtained by the Caproni crew long before the destroyer could pick us up.

Again the next day (four sorties in four days) we attacked a Vichy French vessel, once more with the inevitable destroyer escort. Hits were confirmed on the merchant ship of 2 to 3,000 tons, which could have been unfortunate, since shortly after completing the attack I received a wireless message which gave us the specific order 'Do not attack, repeat, do not attack'. I suspect that when we were first briefed it was not known that our target was Vichy French. Once it was realized, the radio signal was sent – but too late. What the outcome of this mix-up was I don't know, we heard no more.

The next sortie I remember nothing of; the last one, on Guy Fawkes Day, 5 November 1941, appropriately, I vividly recall. The day started inauspiciously. Fine as usual, but after an early call, no breakfast was ready in the Sergeants' Mess. We resented this, feeling that if we could get up early, so could the cooks, especially as for some of us it was likely to be our last meal (as, indeed, for six crew members it was). While sitting at the roadside, waiting for transport to the aircraft, I saw an old Maltese farmer trundle slowly by in his horse and cart. I clearly remember wishing fervently that I could change places with him.

We had a formation of six. A Maryland had sighted a Rommel supply ship, with destroyer escort, somewhere between Tripoli and Benghazi. We carried two 500lb bombs, semi-armour piercing, 11sec delay fused. On reaching the designated area, low on the water, we commenced our square search. I don't know whether I was the first to see it, but away on our port beam, on the horizon, I saw the faintest smudge of smoke. I deliberately said nothing, hoping it would go unobserved by the others, but it was not to be. A voice broke in with something like 'Hello, formation leader [which was us], smoke on the port beam.' We wheeled towards it, and the attack was on.

Three pairs were to go in, two at a time, the others circling and waiting. Skimming the sea as close as we could, in we went. I saw the destroyer turn sharply and commence firing. The Italian crew used the sea as a kind of tracer aid, and it literally boiled. We were very, very low, released the five hundred pounders and pulled up to clear the superstructure. This was the critical moment – we were a sitting target. Jeff pushed the Blenheim's nose violently down, petrol drained from the carburettors, both engines cut. At this instant I thought we had been hit and were going in. But the engines picked up and we were away. Our partner was not so lucky. As I watched, he reared up vertically, light blue underbelly silhouetted against the sky, reached stalling point, flipped and plunged into the sea.

We circled, being fired upon by some of the destroyer's heavier armament – I saw eruptions in the sea, but falling well short. I also saw a large explosion, a great billow of white smoke or steam from the transport. It could have been the boiler going up. The next two Blenheims attacked and got away with it, but not the last pair. Again, obviously hit, the first of the two did a violent climb upwards, came straight down and disappeared. We had lost two out of six. The only consolation was a near certainty that the supplies for Rommel in that particular ship didn't reach him. I often wonder if the voice over the intercom which instigated our attack came from one of the lost crews.

The two Blenheims lost on 5 November were captained by Sgts H. Vickers and R.J. Morris; there were no survivors. The 3,000-ton merchant ship attacked was left sinking. Scotney concludes his story:

After my last sortie on 5 November I felt utterly drained, completely mentally and nervously exhausted. I really considered myself to be a liability to my fellow crew members. In retrospect, indicative of this was my failure to fire on the attacking Macchi, and my non-disclosure of seeing smoke on the horizon during my last trip.

I informed my CO, Wing Commander Smythe, who arranged for me to see the Medical Officer. He questioned me at some length, examined my record and recommended that I be rested. We were the most experienced crew on the squadron, having completed the most operations, and could reasonably be considered to have finished our tour. Twenty-five sorties was the number bandied about on Blenheim squadrons at that time; we had completed twenty-eight.

I went to an RAF Rest Centre at St. Paul's Bay, an almost rural, quiet part of Malta. There I stayed until February 1942, when I flew out (in a Wellington – on ops!) to Egypt, and subsequently returned to the UK in a French liner, the *Pasteur*, via South Africa and Freetown. Our losses in 18 Squadron during my whole tour were high. On three occasions aircraft in formation next to us were shot down. On two raids we lost two out of eight, and two out of six. Other losses occurred: my pilot, for example, went from Sergeant to Squadron Leader in just over seven weeks. In terms of promotion, he was stepping into dead men's shoes.

Back in the United Kingdom, Sgt Scotney attended an Air Gunner Instructors' Course at Manby, whereupon he was posted to the Central Gunnery School at Sutton Bridge. Here he remained as an instructor in the rank of Pilot Officer until May 1945, completing over 600hr flying in Wellingtons. In October 1945 he was posted to Bahrain, where he was awarded the Air Efficiency Award. He was finally demobbed in February 1947. Rejoining the Volunteer Reserve in 1950, he flew in Avro Ansons until the Reserve was disbanded in 1953. By that time he had risen to the rank of Flight Lieutenant. His pilot, Jefferson, ended the war as Wing Commander, DSO, AFC. Flt Lt Ralph Millns, the observer in Scotney's Blenheim crew, died on 26 February 1943 when his Mosquito IV DZ365 collided with another 105 Squadron aircraft while attacking a naval stores depot at Rennes in France.

18 Squadron officers, 5 October 1941. From the left: Sqn Ldr Banner; Fg Off Aldridge; Flt Lt Hervath (Adjutant); Wg Cdr Smythe (CO); Flt Lt Munro; Sqn Ldr Jefferson; Sqn Ldr Lerwill. Monty Scotney

CHAPTER TEN

Intruders, Commandos, Battleships and the 'Thousand Plan', December 1941–43

Night Intruding

The end of 1941 demonstrated the Blenheim's unsuitability for daylight operations over western Europe, but it was decided to keep the aircraft of 82, 110 and 114 Squadrons in service in a new role: night intruding. Intruding had been initiated at the end of the Battle of Britain when it was decided to strip eight short-nosed 23 Squadron fighter Blenheims of the still extremely secret AI and hold them in readiness for nuisance raids into France. Their aim was to try and harry Luftwaffe bombers at their French bases, venturing out for the first time on the night of 23 December 1940 when six Blenheims raided the Abbeville area. In addition to their five forward-firing Brownings and one Vickers gun in the turret, the aircraft carried eight 20lb or four 40lb bombs on these pioneering sorties.

Fg Off Ensor with Sgts Roberts and Langley in YP-B claimed the first night intruding 'probable' with an He 111 severely damaged east of Verneul on 2 January 1941. In fact, the Heinkel from III/KG55 was written off in the subsequent crash-landing at Villacoublai. The first confirmed victory was scored on 17 January, when Fg Off Willans caught He 111H5 3613 of III/KG26 in the circuit at Poix-Nord and sent it down in flames. On the night of 26 February, Plt Off Brown with Plt Off Langley-Ripon and Sgt Parsons in YP-X had an eventful night in the circuit over Lille airfield, where they mingled with about twelve enemy aircraft and claimed two shot down in a 50min running fight. One of their victims was probably Ju 88A5 0534 of 3(F)121, which was destroyed in a crash at Guerand. Over the next few months, 23 Squadron's tally mounted steadily, and crews were beginning to observe the unnerving effects of their audacious raids on their Luftwaffe opponents. For their leading role in night intruding Sqn Ldr Hoare and Fg Off's Ensor and Willans were awarded the DFC. Night intruding was still very much a case of learning the job at the sharp end, and 23 Squadron suffered six Blenheims and seventeen aircrew missing in four months of operations. Nevertheless, before the squadron fully converted to the Havoc for intruder work during April 1941, its fighter Blenheim crews had staked a claim to seven enemy aircraft destroyed, plus

114 Squadron observer bent over his bomb sight. For the Herdla raid a line was painted across the clear vision bomb panel which, if the observer kept his head in a certain fixed position, would result in accurate bomb release, the existing bomb sight being of no use at such a low level. Eric Ramsey

A 114 Squadron Blenheim is speeding away at zero feet while its rearward facing camera is recording the havoc being wrought on Herdla airfield, 27 December 1941. Bob Willis and Eric Bakker

three probables and six damaged.

Combined Operations

Before 1941 was out and the 2 Group night-intruder offensive was launched, the Blenheim became involved in a special event. 27 December 1941 witnessed the execution of the first combined Army–Navy–Air Force operations raid of the war: Operation *Archery*. The target on this raid was the destruction of the German iron-ore convoy assembly base at Vaagso on the Norwegian coast between Bergen and Trondheim. Five hundred and twenty-five Army Commandos were landed on the island by Royal Navy assault craft and successfully overpowered the German garrison in a sharp engagement, suffering only light casualties. In support of this raid, 404 (RCAF) Squadron dispatched two fighter Blenheims from Sumburgh on the Shetland Islands at 06.40hr to cover the landing, while Bomber Command contributed nineteen Blenheim and ten Hampden sorties. 404 Squadron's Plt Off Pierce in Z6341 'Z' and Sgt McCutcheon in V6181 'B' intercepted three Bf 109Fs over Vaagso, one of which

was claimed probably destroyed and another damaged. Two smokescreen laying Hampdens were shot down off Vaagso by shore flak, with only one pilot surviving. As a diversionary tactic, six crews of 110 Squadron from Lossiemouth carried out a shipping sweep off the coast near Stavanger with the aim of drawing off German fighters from the Commando raid. One Blenheim returned early with engine trouble, the remaining five found a convoy off Egero and went into the attack. On the run in one Blenheim hit the waves with one engine and bent the propellor back over the engine cowling. Its pilot immediately climbed and jettisoned his bombs in order to stay airborne and staggered back to base. The remaining four attacked the convoy but got a warm reception. Two Blenheims fell victim to a barrage of ships' flak, the other two were destroyed by Fw Kalweit and Fhnr Habermann, flying Bf 109s of I/JG77, and who had scrambled from Herdla airfield, just north of Bergen. No one in the four Blenheim crews survived.

Thirteen crews of 114 Squadron, in the meantime, had taken off from Lossiemouth at 09.20hr to attack the fighter airstrip at Herdla in an effort to pre-

vent German fighters intervening in the Commando landing. Twenty-one-years old Sgt Ian Webster, W.Op/AG in Sgt John Glen's crew with 114 Squadron has vivid memories of this occasion:

The airstrip, built on a rock headland north–south, consisted of a single runway with two rows of railway sleepers side by side, suitable only for fighter aircraft. It was necessary to bomb from 250ft for accuracy on such a small target but also in order that the 11sec delay bombs would dig into the hardwood sleepers – any lower and the bombs might have skidded off into the sea before exploding.

We were spread out in vics of three in order to target the whole length of the runway and the navigation by Fg Off Paul Brancker, navigator to the leader of this operation Wg Cdr Jenkins and CO of 114 Squadron, was excellent in the circumstances, having flown at 15 to 20ft above the sea for three hours and finding such a small target. John Glen, my pilot, was absolutely delighted when Wg Cdr Jenkins selected him to fly No.2 to himself on this operation. It is very hard work formating closely without colliding but John did an excellent job throughout the trip, including the bombing run. During the crossing of the North Sea from time to time the Wing Commander would look across to his No.2 and No.3 and give a wave of encouragement, and it gave a feeling of great confidence that we would survive this op.

We crossed the coast at the point selected just

23 Squadron Blenheim IFs practising formation flying, early 1940. During December 1940 eight of the squadron's aircraft were stripped of their AI and started specialist intruding over Luftwaffe bomber bases in France. Sybil Caban

south of the airstrip. By going inland further south than the target and flying low level still over land, turning and coming down a fjord to attack the target on the way out to the North Sea, complete surprise was achieved. Three 109s were in the circuit at about 1,000ft, probably waiting to land and refuel and one was starting to move down the airstrip, presumably to intercept us. At approximately two minutes past noon we bombed and watched the spurts of snow as the bombs dug into the snow-covered sleepers. As they exploded, the 109 taxiing-off flew into the bomb burst and crater – the aircraft in the circuit could have attacked us but it was thought that they had been waiting to land and refuel and, in view of the damage caused to the airstrip, they would have to head for the nearest airfield at Stavanger which was some distance to the south; their first priority would be to get there but it was considered that these may have run out of fuel on the way.

There was a great deal of light flak from ground defence and all AGs took great pleasure in machine-gunning large numbers of personnel running for shelter. We were greatly pleased with the result but, just as we congratulated ourselves on getting away with it, we had to do a tight turn to port to set course for Lossiemouth. The aircraft on the inside may have been hit by flak which caused it to slide into the aircraft alongside and together they dived vertically into the sea. There was no hope of survivors.

Indeed, there were no survivors when Flt Sgt R.W. Fisher's RAAF V6227 RT-Z and Sgt K.A. Davis's Z7500 RT-H collided and plunged into the water. Both aircraft came to rest at the bottom of the fiord more or less intact, but the Germans made no attempts to salvage the wrecks nor extract the crews. Only during the autumn of

'Abstürzendes Kampfflugzeug'. German war artist's impression of a Blenheim IV intruder crashing into the sea at night. Pieter Bergman

1945 were the remains of the six men recovered and buried at Bergen, where they still rest. Herdla airfield, home of the Bf 109s of 1/(Z)/JG77 and 3/JG77, was badly damaged in the 114 Squadron raid. Hits were scored on the operations room and hangars, a workshop truck was riddled with bullets and several groundcrew were killed and injured.

Having achieved their objective, the Commandos were subsequently taken off the island by the Royal Navy. The raid was regarded as a great success, but once more the Blenheim bomber crews had paid a heavy price. In recognition of his leadership on the Herdla raid, Wg Cdr Jenkins received the DSO, and for his superb navigation his observer Fg Off Brancker the DFC.

Further Intrusions

Only a few hours after the successful completion of Archery, 82 Squadron's Wg Cdr Roe led six crews on a late evening attack against Soesterberg airfield in the Netherlands. It signalled the restart of a determined RAF intruder campaign in support of Bomber Command, which would be waged until the end of the war with over 11,000 sorties flown, and a prelude to the decisively successful Mosquito intruder campaign of 1944–45. Typically, individual Blenheim crews were assigned an operational Luftwaffe aerodrome in Holland, western Germany or Belgium, which was subsequently visually identified. The intruders then flew around at a height of 2,000ft, dropping small bombs and strafing airfield installations and aircraft on the ground. When enemy aircraft were spotted landing or taking off these were engaged, in an effort to keep Luftwaffe night fighters away from the main RAF bomber force.

The extremely bad winter weather closing in, however, hampered the start of the night-intruder offensive. The three Blenheim squadrons combined could operate on only seven nights in January and early February, mounting sixty-four sorties, few of which were effective. Another factor complicating the intruder attacks was the efficient use of dummy airfields near the main Luftwaffe aerodromes, which were often attacked by the Blenheim crews. Four aircraft of 82 and 114 Squadrons were lost over Holland during the first five weeks of the offensive, at least two of which were shot down by light flak near their targets Schiphol and Soesterberg airfields. All twelve crew members perished. The operational height of only 2,000ft at which the intruder crews were operating clearly made them highly vulnerable to the airfield flak defences.

A sudden emergency arose on 12 February, when the German battleships Scharnhorst, Gneisenau and Prinz Eugen made an audacious dash from Brest through the Channel, under cover of atrocious weather conditions. Visibility was practically nil and the cloud was almost down to the storm-lashed seas on that day, which contributed decisively to the failure of both the RAF and the Royal Navy to hit any of the Kriegsmarine capital ships during their dash through the Channel and up the Dutch coast. In the some 300 RAF sorties dispatched in Operation Fuller, more than thirty aircraft fell to the withering fire from German warships and Luftwaffe fighters, with the majority of the Commonwealth crews finding a watery grave. 2 Group contributed thirty-seven Blenheim sorties in an attempt to find and bomb the ships, with only six crews catching a glimpse of the enemy off the Dutch coast. Two crews failed to return, with Sgt Reynold's Z7433 of 110 Squadron being destroyed off Texel by a Bf 109F of 5/JG1, probably flown by Oblt Max Buchholz. Plt Off Drysdale's T1922 RT-K of 114 Squadron was last seen

going down in a vertical dive off Kijkduin.

After the opening of Japanese hostilities in the Far East, it was decided to send both 82 and 110 Squadrons to this theatre in mid February, leaving only 114 Squadron at West Raynham to keep the intruder offensive going during the remainder of the month and March and April. Its crews harrassed the enemy airfields as best they could, but obviously just one squadron could accomplish little. The crews operated on eight nights between mid February and the end of March, dispatching a total of forty-one sorties. The cost was three Blenheims and crews, two on 26/27 and one on 27/28 March. On the latter night eight crews were briefed to intrude on Schiphol and Soesterberg. Two aborted their mission, but one of the crews which

did reach the target was engaged by the flak defences of Soesterberg at 22.26hr. Z7276 RT-N was seen to catch fire and, trailing orange flames, it slowly lost height to crash on the grounds of the Djimat estate at Zeist, scattering wreckage over 2,000sq m. It was journey's end for twenty-four-years old Wg Cdr Fraser Jenkins, DSO, DFC and his crew of Fg Off Paul Brancker DFC and Bar and W.Op/AG Flt Sgt Charles Gray, DFM. It was a tragic blow for 114

Squadron, the more so as this sortie to Soesterberg airfield was the final trip of the crew's second tour of Blenheim operations. The three men were buried at Amersfoort.

Eric Ramsey's Story

Plt Off Tony Compton and his crew of Sgt Eric Ramsey, observer and Sgt Ted Watkins, W.Op/AG, who joined 114 Squadron at this time, flew their first operation on the next night, 28/29 March 1942, an intruder to Schiphol in 'X' for Xray. Ramsey wrote in his diary:

We hit the Dutch coast about 5min before ETA, which shook me more than somewhat. The Dutch countryside looked quiet and mysterious in the moonlight, and no one seemed to bother

Sgt Eric Ramsey, observer (on right), in the entrance and exit hatch of a 114 Squadron Blenheim. West Raynham, spring 1942. Eric Ramsey

about our intrusion. Just as we turned on the last leg to the target, the searchlights came on and began to search the sky. Several times we were caught, but Tony coped very well and they did not hold us for long periods. Flak was coming up now, heavy bursts which seemed miles away, and coloured tracer which seemed to whip just by our tail. In spite of the fact that my mouth was as dry as a bird's cage, my PK felt like a piece of enemy cloth screwed up and the strange feeling in my stomach, I couldn't help smiling at

114 Squadron sergeant aircrew waiting for briefing at West Raynham in the spring of 1942. Left to right: Eric Ramsey (observer); Ian Webster (W.Op/AG); unknown W.Op/AG; Bruce White (observer); John Glen (pilot). Eric Ramsey

the aristocratic tone of Ted's voice as he gave Tony an unflustered running commentary from his turret. If Ted was as cool as he sounded, he was doing alright.

I located the target in the moonlight, and we ran on. I'd intended giving a very slow turn on the Mickey Mouse to drop the bombs in a long stick, but as soon as the target came in the sights, my hand had whipped over the handle, I'd yelled 'Bombs gone', and we were in a steep diving turn on the course for home, all in about half a second. I guess I was a little too excited and more than a little scared. The bombs fell in a salvo, but I'd had a good sight, and the results should have been OK. We came out over IJmuiden, where we had lots of coloured fireworks sent up at us, but we were feeling confident now; we were low over the sea, heading for England, and I looked back with mixed feelings of triumph and relief at the flaming onions, etc., which were still visible over the Dutch coast line.

I was able to alter course on DR [dead reckoning] from my Ijmuiden pin-point, and we hit our coast and West Raynham OK. Tony called, 'X for Xray off the flarepath', and then looked at me and grinned. We'd broken our duck!

With the gradual improvement of the weather, 114 Squadron flew fifty-two sorties (thirty-nine effective) against enemy airfields during April. The first loss of the month again was a severe one, when Jenkins's successor, Wg Cdr George L.B. 'Bok' Hull, DFC and his crew in Z7430

RT-Q failed to return from an intruder sortie to Schiphol on 17/18 April. After being badly shot up on their run in to the target by light flak and blinded by searchlights, Hull performed miracles bellylanding his Blenheim safely near Aalsmeer at 23.22hr. The three-man crew was soon taken prisoner, to spend the remainder of the war in Stalag Luft III Sagan. Two more

aircraft and one crew were lost during the remainder of the month. At the end of April 1942 the meagre intruder force received a welcome reinforcement when the reformed 18 Squadron at Wattisham began operations. This was of paramount importance, because of the recent Luftwaffe resumption of night bombing raids against British cities in the so-called 'Baedeker' offensive. The unit lost a crew almost immediately, when Plt Off R.M. Owen's Z7436 crashed between Goes and Wolphaartsdijk, Holland, during a night operation to Langenbrugge power station on 28/29 April with the loss of the whole crew.

The View from the Ground

Douglas Beagley, a rigger (airframes), was posted to 18 Squadron at this time and gives a fine impression of the Blenheim intruding effort from the groundcrew's point of view:

As soon as I went out on to the dispersal areas of the base at Wattisham I could see that these planes were old and very tired. For instance, the streamlined panels to the rear of the engines and above the wings (called by us 'the beetle backs') were retained by a series of 2BA screws entered into captive nuts. Unfortunately, these nuts were frequently stripped away and so many times the beetle backs were retained by a long

The frequent visits by the King and Queen to 2 Group stations were always a morale booster for the hardpressed Blenheim crews during 1941. In October of the year they visited West Raynham and 114 Squadron. Left to right: Wg Cdr Jenkins (OC, 114 Squadron, with his head concealed by one of the squadron aircraft, KIA, 27/28 March 1942); HM the Queen; Gp Cpt the Earl of Bandon (Station Commander); HM the King: AM Sir Richard Peirce (C-in-C, Bomber Command); AVM Stevenson (AOC, 2 Group). Bob Collis

two aircraft. Blenheim operations were winding down and so we were, no doubt, inheriting other people's 'left overs'. Of these twenty-two we were able to put two into the air.

The Big Ships Again

Coastal Command, meanwhile, continued its battle against Germany's capital ships in the hard-fought Battle of the Atlantic. After a sighting of the cruiser Prinz Eugen on 16 May heading south-west from Trondheim, AM Sir Philip B. Joubert de la Ferte, AOC-in-C Coastal Command, ordered the maximum effort strike. A mixed force of torpedo Beauforts, Hudson bombers and an escort of flak-suppression Beaufighters and six Blenheim IVFs of 404 (RCAF) Squadron were to be employed in an action similar to that a year earlier against the *Lützow* (see Chapter 6). In fact, the strike was to be the first co-ordinated 'Strike Wing' attack against a capital ship in history. Sqn Ldr Sam McHardy, DFC, a distinguished Blenheim fighter pilot who had risen to Flight Commander in 404 Squadron, recorded:

On 16 May there was a report that the German pocket battleship *Prinz Eugen* was breaking out of Norway and trying to return to Germany. We flew down to Leuchars close to St. Andrews in Fifeshire and went on stand-by with a force of torpedo Beauforts and some Beaufighters. My squadron was to provide fighter cover for a possible attack on the German ships. After a lengthy briefing, when it was indicated that we would first do a dummy torpedo attack on the Eugen followed by a quick climb up into the escorting Me 109s the adrenalin had really begun to flow. We hung around the Officers' Mess all that day waiting for the balloon to go up, but by nightfall the German force had not been sighted. After a restless night and a further briefing in Operations next morning we hung about again and half the chaps were becoming quite cuckoo in their behaviour owing to the pressure of delay and uncertainty.

Suddenly we were called to Operations and informed that the enemy force had been sighted heading for Lister Light down in the extreme south of Norway. After another briefing we were on our way at 18.00hr keeping low on the water to avoid radar detection. This is how we always flew, trying to keep below enemy radar. As we neared the enemy coast, there right ahead was the *Prinz Eugen* churning through the sea with a destroyer on every quarter in close attendance. The Beauforts went straight in with us

18 Squadron has just arrived at Ayr on 13 May 1942 for a spell of combined operations training. The squadron had started night intruding from Wattisham in late April 1942. Alan Ellender

strip of pinking tape which was doped on with red dope. Also the metal was so fatigued that if you put any weight on it it would pop inwards rather than outwards as it was intended.

The leading edges of the wings had to be kept coated with anti-freezing paste. This was a dark brown, thick paste which had to be smeared on all leading edges of the wings, tails, and radio masts. When this became dirty it was necessary to remove the old material and replace it with new, a very unpleasant but necessary job, we were told.

Our duty was to put aircraft over the German night-fighter fields in Germany, Belgium and the Netherlands at night. Planes were sent off at regular intervals and replaced one another. One could not help feeling sorry for the aircrews, with all that they faced. The flight out and back right across the North Sea, in these old and untrustworthy planes. Then to face the thick flak and the threat of night fighters; it was a daunting experience and many were lost. I was in charge of the aircraft with the most successful number of operations on the squadron. With its permanent Canadian crew and others it had managed to complete ten successful operations

before it too was shot down. Luckily for them, the Canadians were not in it that night.

It was quite a scene to see the Blenheims take off at night. They would taxi to the end of the runway and await clearance from the officer in charge of the flarepath and then, when he would flash his green lamp in their direction, they would run the engines up one more time and when at full rpm would pull down the lever to the right of the instrument panel and engage the nine pounds of boost and roll forward. The exhaust rings on the front of the engines would now start to glow red hot, like two angry eyes and sparks would emerge from the flame traps, which at times would also glow. The exhaust rings were painted with anti-glow paint. This was a rosy pink colour and was very obvious. The plane would slowly gather speed down the flarepath and lift slowly into the air and start its laboured climb to altitude.

For us it was not only the losses that bothered us, it was all the work. We would start early after breakfast and after a quick lunch and tea/dinner, we were back into the hangars to work on planes that were in a really bad state. At one time I recall we were all the way up to twenty-on their tails and, when the first aircraft were getting into range to drop, all hell was let loose as a huge barrage of AA fire burst in the sky all around. It seemed that huge shells were going off, fired from the main guns along with all the rest. At this stage Woody [Wg Cdr H.P. 'Pat' Woodruff, OC, 404 Squadron], who was leading, pulled up and the rest of us followed and in moments we were locked in combat with the Me 109s. In no time it seemed that Woody had one right on his tail. I was behind and able to call him up and warn him, then press in on the tail of the 109. I couldn't fire because of Woody just ahead, but the 109 wasn't having anyone on its tail and pulled out and disappeared. We were expecting a really hot reception, but after flying madly about for a while, trying to find a target and at the same time keeping out of trouble, the Me 109s disappeared. We thought we must have caught them at the end of their patrol and short of fuel. The Beauforts and Beaus were now turning away to withdraw and we followed suit.

As we drew away, a Beaufighter on my left appeared to be in trouble and was going down. I closed in and followed it down and it kept losing height until it finally struck the sea and dived under with a huge cloud of spray. Suddenly it popped up again and was on the surface for a few moments before going down. At this stage the pilot and the navigator emerged and were floundering around in the water but no dinghy seemed to be available as the one in the wing of the Beau had not burst out. I had a quick word with my crew and decided to drop our own aircraft dinghy. Fg Off Matthews, my air gunner, dropped our dinghy through the bottom hatch on a signal from me and it landed close to the men struggling in the water. When they were seen to climb aboard, I scuttled out of the area at high speed to try and catch up with all the others. It was getting dark when I reached Leuchars and I was one of the last to land.

The Free French Beaufighter pilot, W/O Sabbadini, and his navigator were later safely picked up by the Germans to become PoWs. For his gallant part in saving the crew, McHardy was awarded a bar to his DFC, and the *Croix de Guerre* with Palms after the war. Seven more aircraft were lost in the Wing Strike against the *Prinz Eugen* off Norway, but this time

no hits were scored on the capital ship. In September 1942, 404 (RCAF) Squadron began replacing its ageing Blenheim IVFs with the Merlin-engined Beaufighter IIF, while continuing to use a few Blenheims on offensive patrols until the following January.

18 Squadron aircrew at Wattisham, probably June 1942. Front row, on extreme right: Sqn Ldr Malcolm, 'A' Flight Commander. Fourth from right, front row: Plt Off Robb, Malcolm's observer. Alec McCurdy

The 'Thousand Plan'

May 1942 was a relatively quiet month in the Blenheim intruder offensive, with only fifteen sorties mounted on four nights for the loss of 18 Squadron's Plt Off Henry P. Palmer and crew in V6382. They were lost without trace while engaged on a sortie to Eindhoven on 6/7 May. Then, by the end of the month, it became clear that something big was in the offing. The Blenheims of 13 and 614 Squadrons from Army Co-operation Command were painted in night camouflage and moved to Wattisham and West Raynham, respectively, as a temporary reinforcement of the small 2 Group intruder force. A briefing on 30 May revealed that Bomber Command HQ had decided to launch a series of raids with

a thousand bombers on a few selected major German cities: the 'Thousand Plan'. The first city chosen to suffer in a devastating attack was Cologne. In support of the giant bomber stream of a record 1,047 aircraft, fifty-three Blenheim intruder sorties were despatched on the evening of 30 May, resulting in thirty-four attacks on St.

Trond, Juvincourt, Vechta, Venlo, Twente, and Bonn. Twenty-one-years old Sgt Ian Webster manned the twin Brownings in one of the 114 Squadron intruders heading for Bonn airfield:

We passed the outskirts of Cologne on the way to Bonn, which lies south-east of the main target. A large area of the city was already burning and the countryside around over which we were flying was illuminated by these fires and also by a clear sky and bright moonlight. We flew at approximately 300 to 400ft to discourage attack from below and, in the conditions prevailing, we could see and avoid any obstructions on the ground likely to be a hazard.

In these highly visible conditions we passed a searchlight battery about two fields to port of our track – there was one master, and one slave pointing upwards to the main attack. On hearing us and probably also seeing us, both turned their beams on us – the master light with the fierce blue light was blinding the pilot, which was rather dangerous at our height so I fired a long burst from the twin Brownings and the tracer bullets were most helpful in reaching the battery. The slave light went out and the master light returned to the main force. I cannot say whether I hit the light that went out or just discouraged the crew operating it but it achieved the object.

While passing Cologne we saw several aircraft coned by the lights and then boxed by a flak barrage and the sickening flash as an aircraft was hit in a vital spot and finally the bright flash of light and red as the aircraft and bomb load exploded with no chance of escape for the crew.

We arrived at Bonn and the navigator got a clear pinpoint from the river and the bridge and found the airfield. We climbed to 1,500ft and at 00.34hr bombs were dropped hitting the airfield and a building at the north-west of the field. One Blenheim of 114 Squadron failed to return from this target. We arrived back at base 04.45hr.

In fact, V5645 'R', flown by Plt Off John J. Fox, RNZAF was the only Blenheim intruder loss on the highly successful Cologne raid. The three-man crew perished and were buried in Sage War Cemetery. In all, forty Main Force aircraft were missing, with only nine lost to night fighters. Two nights later, a second thousand bomber raid was launched against Essen, but due to scattered bombing the outcome was a failure. Thirty-seven aircraft failed to return, at least five of which fell victim to night fighters. This time forty-eight Blenheims swarmed out to the Luftwaffe night-fighter aerodromes on the Main Force route, but only ten found and attacked their allotted targets. Three Blenheims, of 13 and 114 Squadrons, were lost, all without any survivors. On the third and final, thousand bomber raid against Bremen on 25/26 June the outcome was even worse. Of the 1,067 bomber sorties dispatched fifty-three failed to return and the bombing results were disappointing. Main Force effort included fifty-one Blenheims of 2 Group, which all returned safely. Despite the majority of fifty-six intruders (including thirty-one Blenheims) bombing and strafing their allocated airfields, Nachtjagd intercepted in force, claiming thirty aircraft destroyed. Among their victims were two 13 Squadron Blenheims bound for Venlo and St. Trond which were shot down by Bf 110 night fighters of NJG1 over Belgium, crashing at Houwaart and Aartselaar.

June 1942 witnessed the largest Blenheim intruder effort of the year, with 250 sorties flown by 13, 18, 114 and 614 Squadrons, some two-thirds of which resulted in successful attacks on enemy airfields. The price was surprisingly low: apart from three 13 Squadron aircraft and crews, 114 Squadron lost the same number, plus L8800 'C' crashing immediately after take-off from West Raynham on 4/5 June, killing the whole crew.

With the two ACC squadrons again taking up their Army Co-operation duties in early July, 18 and 114 Squadrons were left to bear the brunt of the intruder offensive. During July they carried out 108 sorties in support of Main Force raids, for the cost of ten aircraft and twenty-eight crew members killed, plus three more Blenheims written off in accidents in which four men died. The worst night occurred on 25/26 July, when twenty-one crews left West Raynham and Wattisham to attack Venlo, Vechta and Leeuwarden, to keep the enemy night fighters at bay while a Main Force raid took place on Essen. Sgt Eric Ramsey, observer in 114 Squadron, noted in his diary that night:

Our target Venlo was on the Dutch–German border just west of the Ruhr, right in the centre of the searchlight belt. Four of us on Venlo, the other three being Johnny Steele, Douggie Thorburn and Len Causley.

Slight flak on the way in, but the big moment was when we went into the searchlight belt. One light caught us, then another, another, and soon the ground seemed covered in lights, and all of them focused on us. Wilbur was working like a Trojan, throwing Zebra all over the place trying to get out of the lights, Ted was scanning the skies for fighters, I was doing the same, and also looking for a pinpoint, because we were approaching the target.

I saw a plane above us, then saw it dive as if to attack, and I realized it was our shadow on the clouds silhouetted by the searchlights. Ted saw a kite, but fortunately it didn't see us. We were lit up for 3 or 4min (it seemed like hours) but it must have been our lucky day, because we weren't bounced by night fighters. We finally got out of the lights, picked up a pinpoint on the river and turned towards the target.

On our port bow we saw tracer from an aircraft being fired at another kite, which burst into flames, spun down and exploded as it hit the deck. It crashed into a small German town, and it must have been one of our Blenheims, because there were no other bombers on our target. Very shaken, we flew on down the river and located the target. We bombed, and as we headed for home, we saw that the unfortunate Blenheim had caused a large fire in the town where it crashed.

We had a quiet trip out until we reached the coast, where the shore batteries sent us on our way with a concentrated and fairly accurate display of coloured fireworks. I was beginning to realize now that Wilbur's violent evasive action

Probably on the eve of the thousand bomber raids, 18 and 13 (ACC) Squadron aircrew are gathered in front of an intruder Blenheim at Wattisham. Alec McCurdy

had had considerable effect on my stomach, and I didn't eat my chocolate. As we flew low over the sea I was wondering which of the other three Blenheims that went to Venlo with us would not be returning.

When we landed, we found that two of the Venlo kites were overdue. With mixed feelings I waited for news. Len Causley's and Douggie Thorburn's were the two kites. Vic and I had a date tomorrow with Dorothy and Gwen. Vic was Douggie's navigator. I'd been boozing with Len and his crew last night. We'd been down about half an hour when we heard that Douggie had landed. He'd been chased all over Holland by a Ju 88, and Vic got a lot of laughs when he recounted the story. Besides Len and his crew we lost Tony Strasser and crew and Tubby Warnick and crew tonight. Tony was flying Queenie which was a squadron jinx, and Tubby was on his first op. I lost some good pals tonight.

25/26 July had turned out to be a black night for 114 Squadron. Sgt Leonard Causley and crew flying R3837 'T' had the misfortune of being intercepted by Oblt Reinhold Knacke, CO of 1/NJG1 and a leading night fighter ace with twenty-nine victories. They did not stand a chance and found their end at 01.20hr some four miles north of Venlo. Plt Off G.A. Strasser's V5635 'Q' left West Raynham at 23.15hr to intrude on Vechta, and was shot down at Delmenhorst, Germany. Finally, V6264 'X' of Canadian Flt Sgt Eugene E. Warnick and his RCAF crew crashed into the North Sea off the Dutch coast and disappeared without a trace, while on their way to Leeuwarden. All nine men died.

During September 1942 114 Squadron converted onto Blenheim Vs and flew out to North Africa later in the year. While operating the Blenheim IV the squadron had flown 731 sorties in 132 raids, losing thirty-nine aircraft or 5.3 per cent, thereby suffering the highest percentage losses in any Blenheim squadron during the war. Eight crews from 18 Squadron carried out the final Bomber Command Blenheim operations from the UK on 17/18 August, successfully intruding on Twente, Eelde, Borkum, Vechta and Rheine airfields.

Bill Gatling's Story

As W.Op/AG in the 18 Squadron crew of Flt Sgt L. Rule, RAAF (pilot) and Sgt M. Bradshaw (observer), Sgt Bill Gatling completed thirty-five Blenheim sorties during 1941–42. The majority of the crew's operations were carried out in, as he

End of the road for a veteran. L8800 'C' of 114 Squadron, which had survived operations with XV and 114 Squadrons throughout 1940, 1941 and early 1942, hit a tree on the edge of West Raynham on take-off for an intruder sortie to Schiphol airfield on 5 June 1942. It crashed and burned out, with Sgt Frank Cooke and his crew all perishing. Eric Ramsey

states, 'the rather dodgy hobby of night-intruder operations against enemy airfields in northern Europe'. Gatling ends the Blenheim intruder story on a humorous note:

One afternoon, while seated, not at the organ, but in the Sergeants' Mess and pondering the fact that my crew was on operations that night and also rather wistfully wishing that the offensive bomb load of a Blenheim was more in the category of heavier bombers such as Halifaxes and Wellingtons, I happened to glance at a neighbouring sergeant happily pouring a glass of beer from a bottle when a brilliant idea suddenly flashed through my normally vacant cerebellum. Why not collect all the empty beer bottles from the Mess bar and take them with us on our night operations? Why not indeed? After bombing the runways of the enemy airfields the air gunners could heave out their empties on to strictly military targets and, as we bombed from

only four or five thousand feet, the bottles would probably shatter with a great deal of noise, spraying broken glass all over the take-off area of the Luftwaffe, causing a certain amount of despondency and confusion.

Without further ado I immediately convened a general meeting of the local branch of the Air Gunners' Union... put forward my scheme and it was passed unanimously, as air gunners were always slightly miffed at the offensive power held in the hands of the navigator/bomb aimer. Off we went to see the Mess steward to gain his co-operation. He was thrilled at the idea of indirectly participating in the onslaught on Fortress Europe and readily agreed to supply us with all the empty bottles we needed on our little excursions.

That night the mess echoed to the merry rattle of empty bottles knocking together as the gunners collected their novel weapons from the bar and vanished into the night to their waiting aircraft. I should mention that the bottles were

carried in large bags which normally held our parachutes, these latter being carried separately – we wouldn't leave those behind, no blooming fear, not even for the sake of bottle throwing. Everyone returned from the night's operation more or less unscathed, all the gunners reporting that they had quite enjoyed throwing the bottles out of their turrets over the targets after their bombs had been dropped.

Two nights later my nefarious scheme received vindication when my own aircraft started its bombing run over a Luftwaffe airfield. We were suddenly held in a cone of searchlights, and once the bombing run had started it was inadvisable to take any evasive action. 'Throw your bottles out, mate', yelled my pilot, an Australian by birth, and I let fly with a hail of Watney's Pale Ale, Forest Brown and Guinness bottles. To the immediate relief of the occupants of our Blenheim the searchlights went out and we carried on bombing. Returning to base with no further unpleasantness, I told the Intelligence Officer at debriefing what had occurred and he, rather grudgingly, agreed to enter in his report 'Searchlight extinguished with bottle', which made the event singular instead of plural. I don't think I was too popular

with the Top Brass; probably this form of attack was considered to be not quite cricket, though bombs and machine-guns were.

Our campaign lasted a further week or two and then came the abrupt halt. Turning up for our usual cargo at the bar we were greeted by the bar steward who was wearing a very long face. 'Sorry lads, I can't give you any more bottles', he said. 'Why ever not?' we all chorused, or words to that effect. 'Because my supply of beer depends upon the number of empty bottles that I send back, and as you blighters are using them all up we are soon going to run out of beer.' There was a pregnant silence. His argument, considering the impending disaster to the mess was irrefutable. So that was the end of the Great Empty Bottle Campaign against the Third Reich in 1942.

A few months later Dr Goebbels's department issued the following statement: 'All British flyers are drunk when they are operating over Europe.' After collecting all the broken glass and labels together they must have decided that our bottles were not empty when we carried them on board our aircraft. They were wrong.'

Dieppe

Following the final Blenheim intruder sorties, the home-based aircraft were employed in offensive action once more one day later. In support of the ill-fated Canadian assault landing at Dieppe on 19 August, fourteen Boston crews and six Blenheim crews of 13 ACC Squadron, opened the RAF's contribution at the break of dawn. They were to drop 100lb phosphorus bombs on the landward side of enemy flak guns, to shield the landing craft as they approached the beaches. At briefing, the crews had been told that there were only a couple of machine-gun posts defending the area, but Intelligence was seriously in error. Having all successfully finished their smoke-laying, Plt Off Cecil L. 'Jackie' Woodland and his 13 Squadron crew in V5380 were shot down and killed in a hail of fire over the port, with Flt Lt Eric L. Beverley in Z6089 and Plt Off A. Jickling in N3545 nursing their badly damaged aircraft back to Thruxton. Also belonging to the first wave of smoke-screen layers, Wg Cdr H.C. Sutton in V5534 led in four Blenheim IVs of 614 ACC Squadron just before dawn. However, on the run in to the landing beaches, Flt Lt J.E. Scott's V5626 was subjected to a burst of 'friendly' fire from one of the allied

escorting vessels, which all but severed his jaw and instantly killed Flt Sgt G.R. Gifkins, his W.Op/AG. Undaunted, Scott pressed on in the company of Flt Lt P.G. Roberts in V6002, but, due to damage to his bomb release gear, he was unable to release his load. Aided by his observer, Sgt W. Johnson, Scott brought his crippled aircraft back across the Channel to crash-land near Friston. As he bellied-in, the smoke bombs exploded, badly burning Scott, but he still managed to pull his unconscious observer clear of the burning wreck. Sadly, Sgt Johnson died in hospital 36 hours later, but Flt Lt Scott recovered and received the DFC in September.

At 10.50hr eight further Blenheims of 614 Squadron left Thruxton as part of the second wave of smoke-screen layers. German infantry, shooting at them from the cliffs, scored many hits on the low-flying aircraft, but all successfully completed their task this time and returned to base safely.

After this final major operational task many of the remaining Blenheims in Great Britain were seconded to other roles, apart from training duties in a number of OTUs. 516 Squadron, for example, was formed at Dundonald on 28 April 1943 by renumbering No. 1441 (Combined Operations) Flight. Equipped with Blenheim IVs and other types, the squadron was tasked to co-operate with combined operations training units in western Scotland, carrying out practice attacks on shipping and landing craft, laying smoke screens, gas spraying, low-level reconnaissance training and demonstration flights to Army units. This vital work was done in preparation for the invasion of the continent. After D-Day the requirement for such a unit declined and on 2 December 1944, 516 Squadron was disbanded.

Another role in which the Blenheim soldiered on in Britain was radar calibration. For this purpose, Nos. 526 and 527 Squadrons were formed on 15 June 1943, with 528 Squadron following fourteen days later, and with Blenheim IVs as their main equipment. The units became engaged in calibrating radar stations in southern England, Lincolnshire and East Anglia. On 1 September 1944, 527 Squadron absorbed No. 526 at Digby, while 528 Squadron was disbanded on that date, 527 taking over its aircraft. Until after the surrender of Germany in May 1945, Blenheims remained on 527 Squadron's strength.

From Defeat in Greece to Victory in *Torch*, 1940–43

In the shade of a building at Khormaksar airfield, Aden, onlookers watch L1479 of 8 (B) Squadron taxiing by, 1939–40. This aircraft fell to Italian fighters near Nasiyeh, Eritrea on 18 August 1940. S. Lunn, via Blenheim Society

Fifty Blenheim Is were dismantled, packed into crates and shipped from Avonmouth to Basrah in early 1939. On arrival, they were wheeled up to the civil airport where a small detachment of airmen reconstructed them, whereupon they were test-flown and re-equipped the three Vincent light bomber squadrons based in Iraq (at Habbaniya and Shabah): Nos. 30, 'Shiny' Fives (55) and 84. Over the next year seven more Middle East Command squadrons received the Blenheim. The majority, Nos. 8, 11, 39, 45 and 211, received the Mk I, with 113 Squadron converting to the Mk IV and 203 to the Mk IVF. Thus, when Italy entered the war at midnight on 10 June 1940, the Blenheim formed the backbone of the RAF's bomber force in the Middle East.

Before dawn on the first day of the war, six 211 Squadron crews flew reconnaissance sorties over Libya, which furnished targets for the rest of the command. El Adem airfield was bombed

and strafed by twenty-six aircraft of 45, 55 and 113 Squadrons at the break of day, meeting with fierce opposition and three Blenheims were shot down. Later the same day a second attack was mounted, resulting in eighteen Italian aircraft being destroyed or damaged on the airfield. Until October 1940 the normal practice was that one raid per day was carried out on Libya, so that each of the four Western Desert Blenheim bomber units (Nos. 45, 55, 113 and 211), operated every fourth day. 39 Squadron came into action for the first time on 12 June, when seven Blenheims attacked the Italian airfield at Diredaewa in Abyssinia. 30 Squadron, the bomber Blenheims of which had been fitted with four-Browning belly-packs, acted in the long-range fighter defence role against Italian bombers raiding Alexandria during the second half of 1940, its crews claiming several S.79s damaged or destroyed in combat.

Back to Africa

Mussolini's dream of rebuilding a Roman Empire encompassing the whole of the Mediterranean took shape with a first successful thrust, mounted from Libya towards Egypt during September 1940. His aim was clear: control over the Suez Canal would give him control over the eastern Mediterranean. Within a matter of weeks, his 250,000 strong troops had advanced 50 miles into Egypt, but the reinforced British and Free French forces soon wrested the initiative. In a counteroffensive against vastly superior numbers starting on 9 December, they swept the Italians out of Egypt and by early 1941 the allied forces had moved deep into Libya. Nos. 11, 39, 45, 55 and 211 Squadrons supported the offensive, often operating with fighter escorts to keep losses down. 39 Squadron handed over its last remaining four Blenheim Is to 11 Squadron on 17 January 1941, which subsequently took them to Greece, where they were lost to enemy action.

With a view to protecting their interests in northern Africa, the Free French Air Force in Britain created its first Blenheim unit on 1 August 1940 with Escadrille Topic, which was equipped with eight (later eleven) Blenheim IVs and IVFs. The crews of Topic were trained at RAF Odiham and Andover during the height of the Battle of Britain, to be shipped to eastern north Africa in late October. By the end of the year Topic was incorporated into a new unit, Groupe réserve de bombardement No.1 (GRB1), which was formed on 24 December. Equipped with Lysanders and fourteen Blenheim IVs and IVFs, its crews saw action against Vichy French and Italian forces in southern Libya during the following two months. Twenty operational sorties were flown, during which 10 tons of bombs were dropped and 18,000 rounds of ammunition fired. Losses, however, amounted to two

30 Squadron's L1097 at Amman. This aircraft, the first of a batch of 450 Mk Is delivered to the RAF between February 1938 and March 1939, was the first Blenheim to reach India. It served with 30, 60, 11 and again 30 Squadrons, before being relegated to 72 OTU, where it was written off on 28 January 1943. Don R. Neate

The fully intact Blenheim T1867 of GRB1 as it was found in the Sahara near the Libyan-Chad frontier in March 1959, after being lost on 5 February 1941. SHAA

Blenheims missing and four more severely damaged in crashes, with five aircrew posted killed or missing, three wounded and another three taken prisoner. Most of these aircraft had force-landed in the desert after their crews became lost over the wide expanse of the Sahara. Blenheim T1867, for example, set off from its base at Ounianga in Chad on 5 February 1941 to bomb the strategic Italian-held oasis Al-Kufrah in Libya, a return flight of some 1,300km over monotonous desert terrain. The crew of Lt Claron (observer) found and bombed the target, but on the way back they got lost and Sgt Le Calvez belly-landed the aircraft at position 19 degrees 45min N, 23 degrees 20min E, some 350km east of their base. No trace was ever found of the aircraft nor of its crew until 29 March 1959, when two soldiers patrolling the Libyan frontier discovered the fully intact aircraft and the remains of the crew.

In mid February 1941 GRB1 moved to Sudan to take part in combined allied operations against strong Italian forces (350,000) in Ethiopia and Abyssinia. Plagued by the harsh desert living conditions, frequent mechanical failure and lack of spares, the unit had an average of only two or three serviceable Blenheims available for operations throughout the Ethiopian campaign. Reinforced in late April by six rather worn out aircraft from 14 Squadron in Egypt (which had converted from Welleseys in September 1940), the hard-working Free French crews kept up pressure on the Italians.

Free French Air Force Blenheim Units

The following data are listed:
unit: command: period during which the unit had type on strength: mark(s) of aircraft used

Escadrille Topic: RAF Middle East: 5 months (Aug 1940–Dec 1940): Blenheim IV and IVF

Groupe réservé de bombardement (GRB) No.1: RAF Middle East: 10 months (Dec 1940– Sep 1941): Blenheim IV and IVF

Groupe de Bombardement (GB) Lorraine: RAF Middle East: 11 months (Sep 1941–Oct 1942): Blenheim IV and V

Groupe de Bombardement (GB) Bretagne: RAF Middle East: 1 year 9 months (Jan 1942– Sep 1943): Blenheim IV and V

Groupe I/17 Picardie: RAF Middle East: 2 years 3 months (June 1943–Aug 1945): Blenheim IV and V

Greek Air Force Blenheim Unit

32 Mira: 1 year 7 months (Oct 1939–Apr 1941): Blenheim I and IV

Yugoslav Air Force Blenheim Units

21 Eskadrila: Blenheim I
22 Eskadrila: Blenheim I
201 Eskadrila: Blenheim I
202 Eskadrila: Blenheim I
203 Eskadrila: Blenheim I
204 Eskadrila: Blenheim I
215 Eskadrila: Blenheim I
216 Eskadrila: Blenheim I
217 Eskadrila: Blenheim I
218 Eskadrila: Blenheim I
The Yugoslav Air Force operated sixty-two Blenheim Is between November 1937 and 17 April 1941, the day of the country's surrender; a few surviving aircraft were subsequently incorporated in the Croat Air Force

Their morale received a boost on 13 May, when Sgt Chef Jean, W.Op/AG in GRB1's CO Commandant Astier de Villatte's crew, shot down a CR 42 fighter over the Blenheim's target, a field aerodrome at Az-Zozo. By mid August, the successful allied thrust into Ethiopia had ejected the Italian forces from this theatre, thus ending Mussolini's short-lived East African empire. During the campaign, GRB1 had completed eighty-five sorties against the odds, with just one aircraft and crew lost in an accident on 2 June. Through war attrition, however, the unit only had two serviceable Blenheims left on strength by early autumn 1941.

Failure in Greece

Meanwhile the Italians had opened another front, by invading northern Greece on 28 October 1940. About half of the small Greek bomber force at the time consisted of twelve Blenheim IVs in 32 Mira (Squadron), which had recently been purchased from Britain. Middle East

Fg Off B. Wade's L1391 VA-J 'Doughnut Doris' of 84 Squadron, at Menidi, Greece. All B and C Flight 84 Squadron Blenheims had a name or emblem painted on their noses, a habit taken over from 107 Squadron in the UK. Other names sported were 'The Musso Menace' and 'The Queen of Shaibah'. Don R. Neate

View forward from the observer's seat in a 211 Squadron Blenheim I, probably taken in early 1941. Eric Bevington-Smith

Command immediately replied by dispatching several RAF units from Egypt to aid the Greeks. 30 Squadron's Blenheim Is and IFs were the first to arrive at Eleusis near Athens on 29 October, followed by 84 and 211 Squadrons in the second half of November. Over the next two months 11 and 113 Squadrons reinforced the Blenheim strike force in Greece. 30 Squadron carried out the first bombing raid of the campaign on 8 November against shipping in the port of Sarande, near the Albanian border. Over the following months the Greek and the British crews mounted hundreds of bombing and strafing sorties against the Italians in support of the Greek Army in Albania, operating both from the Athens area and from forward airstrips in the mountainous north of Greece. Soon, however, they began suffering heavily from Fiat CR 42 and G.50 and Macchi 200 fighter attacks. It was a black day on 7 December when a complete vic of 84 Squadron (L8455, L8457 and L1381) was shot down over the port of Valona by 150th Gruppo CR 42s, while L1535 and L4926 from 211 Squadron crashed in the hills around Lamia due to icing. Eleven aircrew were killed. Apart from the fighter opposition, an acute shortage of spares and the unpredictable and extremely severe weather conditions hampered the operational effort of the Blenheim strike force in Greece during the winter months of 1940–41. Nevertheless,

the crews valiantly kept up pressure against the Italian forces throughout this period. On 28 March 1941, the anniversary of the creation of the Regia Aeronautica was properly celebrated by six fighter Blenheims of 30 Squadron 'A' Flight, which strafed Lecce airfield on the heel of

Italy at dawn. Row after row of aircraft drawn up in review order were machine-gunned, resulting in the destruction of one S.81, with twenty-five other aircraft damaged. Only one of the attacking Blenheims received serious damage with a hit in the starboard engine, Sgt Tony Ovens making a perfect emergency landing at Paramythia where the damage was repaired.

Seeing the Italian invasion of Greece failing and wishing to secure his southern flank before invading Russia, Hitler came to Mussolini's aid and declared war on Greece and Yugoslavia on 6 April 1941. Supported by an armada of about a thousand Luftwaffe aircraft, one million German soldiers launched a blitzkrieg in the Balkans. At this time ten bomber and reconnaissance Eskadrilas (Flights) of the Yugoslavian air force (JKRV) operated a total of fifty-six Blenheim Is, sixteen of which had been licence-built by Ikarus AD at Zemun during 1938–40. Their crews put up a brave but unequal fight, and the large majority of the aircraft were destroyed in air combat, by flak and on the ground during the first few days of the campaign. By 12 April the JKRV was down to only five or six Blenheims still airworthy. Five days later Yugoslavia capitulated, and the Greek and British forces were pushed back south into the

Death of a pilot. 84 Squadron's Flt Lt R.A. Towgood suffered a failure of his port engine on landing at Menidi in L4833 VA-U, 5 February 1941, with fatal consequences. Don R. Neate

211 Squadron aircrew gathered at Paramythia, northern Greece in early 1941. Left to right: 'Embros' (Greek for 'Hello', Greek liaison officer); unknown W.Op/AG; Sgt Bill Baird (W.Op/AG); unknowkn Ops. Sgt; Sgt James Dunnet (observer); Sgt Tam Hughes (W.Op/AG); Sgt 'Nobby' Clark (observer); Sgt Strudwick (pilot); Sgt Len Page (observer). James Dunnet

heart of Greece. Most of the British Blenheim units were forced to abandon their forward airstrips on the Larissa plain and withdrew to the Athens area. Their crews were kept busy, flying standing patrols and ground support operations over the constantly changing front line, reconnaissance sorties and convoy and fleet escort missions. In a concentrated spell of operations, 30 Squadron's fighter Blenheim crews destroyed or damaged thirteen Ju.88s and S.79s in air combat between 10 and 25 April, for the loss of only one aircraft. Although the Blenheims aquitted themselves well in the several roles into which they were pressed, just as in the French campaign they suffered heavily from intense mobile flak fire and roaming Messerschmitt fighters while attacking Axis armoured columns. In a virtually vain effort to reduce losses, 84 Squadron's Blenheim Is were fitted with an armoured headshield for the pilot and a belt-fed Browning 'scare gun', fitted beneath the nose of the aircraft. In a similar effort, two sheets of armour plate were fastened behind the pilot and the observer in 211 Squadron's aircraft. If nothing else, these field modifications at least proved a morale booster for the aircrews.

The end for 211 Squadron came on Easter Sunday, 13 April. In mid afternoon, six crews at Paramythia were ordered to man the six remaining Blenheims for an attack against advancing German troops on the Florina–Monastir road near the Greek–Yugoslav border. It was the third unescorted operation the hard-working squadron mounted that day, in a desperate attempt to check the Axis advance into the country. Wg Cdr 'Paddy' Coote, Wing Commander in charge of operations in northern Greece, took Sgt James Dunnet's (observer) place in L4819, as he wanted to assess the German progress. After having dropped their bombs on target from 7,000ft, three Bf 109E-4s of 6/JG27, led by Hptm Hans-Joachim Gerlach, bounced the formation. 211 Squadron's new CO, Sqn Ldr A.T. Irvine smartly turned the short-nosed Blenheims to the west, diving down a valley into the sinking sun, but not one of the six bombers pulled out. Four aircraft were shot down between 16.05 and 16.07hr. At only 300ft, Fg Off Alan Godfrey hurriedly baled out of L8449, his cockpit a mass of flames, as did Sgt James, piloting L1539. The two remaining machines flew away to the east, each with a 109 on its tail, but there was no escape.

Fg Off Herbert's L4819 and L8478 in the hands of Sqn Ldr Irvine were destroyed at 16.08 and 16.09hr, with the loss of all six crew members. Sgt Dunnet recalls:

Following the debacle of Greece and Crete, my squadron had passed into the historical records... 'On one mission, all the Blenheims of No.211 Squadron were shot down with the loss of the Squadron Commander and the Commander of the Western Wing.' 'Fate had decreed that Wg Cdr Coote would take my place as the observer on that Easter Sunday. As the six Blenheims climbed into the afternoon sun, glinting over the mountains surrounding the 'Shangri-La' valley of Paramythia, high in a remote area of northern Greece, I thought of my crew in L4819... 'Herby', flying over the same Macedonian territory as in the first World War had his distinghuished father, holder of the Order of St. Saviour of Greece ... 'Jock', the W.Op/AG and fellow Scot... Together we had shared ops in England with the Blenheims of 57 Squadron, then across France and the Mediterranean, to Malta and the western Desert with 'Two Eleven' before flying to Greece in November 1940 after Italy had invaded on 28 October.

Blenheim L1434 flown by Flt Lt L.B. Buchanan, DFC, which was shot down into Lake Prespa at 16.07hr, was lifted from it in June 1993 by a combined team of Greek Air Force and Army personnel, and is now in the Tatoi Athens museum.

Throughout the morning of 15 April large numbers of Bf 109s roaming the Larissa Plain strafed Niamata, home of 113 Squadron. All ten of its unprotected Blenheims, fuelled and bombed up for a

211 Squadron Blenheim Boys at the Acropolis, Athens, in early 1941. Flt Sgt Bill Young, W.Op/AG (in middle) perished when L4819 crashed near Pisodherion on the fateful 13 April 1941 raid. Bea Cashford

Towards the end of the Greek campaign, Bf 109s and 110s made a habit of ground-strafing British airfields. Only a tattered tail unit remains of four Blenheims from 11 and 211 Squadrons thus destroyed at Menidi on 20 April 1941 by III/JG77 and II/ZG26. Don R. Neate

further raid against the advancing tanks, were wrecked. By this time, only twenty-two work-weary and worn Blenheims were serviceable between 11, 84 and 211 Squadrons in Greece, plus fourteen Blenheim IFs of 30 Squadron. When the country finally surrendered on 23 April, 30 Squadron hurriedly airlifted most of its personnel to Crete, with up to thirteen men crammed into each Blenheim for the 180 miles or 45min haul to Maleme airfield.

N3560 of 11 Squadron has come to grief at Heraklion, Crete, after flying out of Greece on 21 April 1941. Eric Bevington-Smith

The Cretan Catastrophe

Crete was the next target for the victorious German forces. During the short but fierce battle of Crete, the remainder of 30 Squadron operated from Maleme for twenty-seven days in appalling circumstances, aided by nine Blenheim IVFs of 203 Squadron which were flown in from Egypt. Nos. 14, 45 and 55 Squadrons, with Blenheim IVs, tried to stem the tide from Egypt (a long 800-miles return haul), but

their numbers were depleted in one grim week ending on 27 May. On 21 May, Ob Lt Homuth, Fw Kowalski and Lt Schmidt, flying Bf 109Es of I/JG27 destroyed five out of seven 14 Squadron Blenheims over the Capuzzo–Tobruk road. An estimated twenty-four Luftwaffe aircraft were wrecked in a successful 14 Squadron raid early on 25 May against Maleme airfield, (where the Germans were cramming Ju.52s on to the landing grounds), but later that day a complete vic from the same unit (T2065, V5510 and T2003) was shot down into the sea off Crete by two Bf 109s of II/JG77. All nine men aboard perished. At dusk next day the same tragedy unfolded, when two out of three 45 Squadron aircraft fell to ObLt Höckner of 6/JG77 in the target area. Sgt N.H. Thomas and crew in T2339 were all lost, while two men from T2350 were taken prisoner. The third Blenheim, V5592, escaped only to get lost over the desert on its return, and finally crashed. Plt Off J. Robinson and his W.Op/AG, Sgt A.F. Crosby, were picked up after walking for four days, the crew's observer Sgt W.B. Longstaff was never seen again. On 27 May six out of nine Blenheims (from 14, 45, and 55 Squadrons) were lost in crashes and collisions in Egypt while taking off or returning from strikes on Maleme, resulting in the death of nine aircrew. There was no stopping the Germans at this time and Crete fell on 31 May. One adverse consequence of shifting major fighting elements of the slender Middle East resources to Greece and Crete was that Rommel's newly arrived Afrika Korps had few problems in driving the depleted allied forces back to the Egyptian border during March 1941.

After the evacuation of Greece and Crete the remnants of the Blenheim squadrons reassembled in Palestine, most of them converting to the Mk IV, and with 30 Squadron reforming on Hurricanes. The crews now found action against the Vichy French in Syria. Early in May hostilities also broke out in Iraq, where the pro-Axis ruler Raschid Ali, supported by his German masters, attacked the RAF base at Habbaniya. A relief force was dispatched at once to ward off the threat that the British might be excluded from the Iraqi oilfields. Known as 'Habforce', it was supported by a small detachment of Blenheim IVs from 84 and 203 Squadrons, and the threat was ended by 12 July.

Desert Victory

Greece and Crete had been lost but with Egypt, Iraq and Syria now in British hands, the Middle East remained firmly under their control. All available forces could now be directed on a single front in the western desert, and the struggle for control in the Mediterranean could begin in earnest. The lull in the fighting during the following summer months was eagerly seized upon to strengthen the RAF Middle East Command substantially in Egypt. The end of this retrenchment period saw the bulk of its light bomber force consisting of six Blenheim IV squadrons: Nos. 8, 11, 14, 45, 55 and 84. 113 Squadron was re-equipped with Blenheim IVF 'strafers' for the ground-support role. The Free French contributed two further units. On 2 September 1941 GRB1 was incorporated into a new Wing, 'Groupe de Bombardement (GB) Lorraine'. Lorraine, which came under British operational control, comprised two squadrons, 'Metz' and 'Nancy', and was equipped with twenty-one Blenheim IVs taken over from RAF stock.

The autumn of 1941 was spent with the 8th Army preparing for a new offensive into Libya, Operation *Crusader*, which was planned to start in mid November. On the 15th a mighty air offensive was launched before its start, concentrating on Axis supply columns and on airfields in an effort

Above **Sleek tools of war. Free French Blenheim IVs of Groupe Lorraine casting long shadows in the Egyptian desert in the autumn of 1941. Note the famous Croix de Lorraine unit marking painted over the former RAF roundel.** SHAA

Below **Bull's-eye! 84 Squadron strikes at German supply columns and tanks in the western desert, 4 December 1941.** Arthur Gill

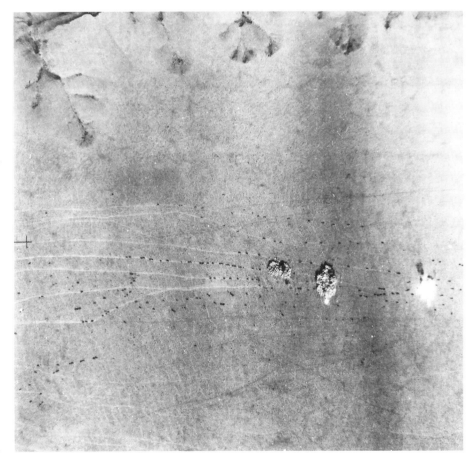

to win air superiority. Over the next three months the Blenheim crews were on a constant diet of formation raids, both by day and by night, with occasional single aircraft sorties thrown in. After losing his crew in the Greek campaign, Sgt James Dunnet was posted to 11 Squadron, crewing up with Plt Off 'Robbie' Robinson, a Belgian escapee pilot who flew under a pseudonym:

My Log Book for November 1941 details entries for raids on Derna, Tobruk, El Adem, attacking tanks, MT, AFVs and assorted Army co-op. targets in support of Operation *Crusader*. On 21 November, the day the besieged Tobruk garrison finally broke out, we took off to bomb a fort called El Erg. We were to land at an advanced fighter base some hundred and fifty miles into Libya. Aerodromes on the European model were non-existent in the desert. Where a strip of flat scrubland could be found, it was quickly turned into a landing ground and given an identifying number. But on being ordered to fly from one LG to another, sometimes resulted in settling the Blenheim down on one piece of desert to be greeted with a dismissal and a waving arm pointing towards another patch a few miles away, where a lookalike collection of petrol bowsers, dug-outs, tents and aircraft would be dispersed. Living conditions at these LGs were basic. Water was rationed to two pints daily, one pint going to the cookhouse and the other at the individual's discretion for him to wash, drink, or shave. We usually slept in our clothes, in shallow dug-outs covered by a tarpaulin, or tent. Desert sores, caused by the sand penetrating all protective layers and sand-papering skin into festering blisters, were a constant source of irritation. Food consisted of bully beef and biscuits or a vegetable stew cooked during the day, as no fires were allowed at night. Fresh crews arriving from the UK were usually greeted with the ribald comment, 'If we had some bacon, we could have some bacon and eggs, if we had some eggs!'

Such was existence at a desert landing ground in 1941. As we approached LG 125 on 21 November and prepared to land, there came an alarming shout from the W.Op/AG and the Blenheim rattled from a burst of fire from a Hurricane on our tail. Hydraulics shot away and the Bristol Mercury making terminal noises, Robbie managed to belly flop our stricken Blenheim in the desert. Although the air around our spreadeagled Blenheim resounded with frustrated outcries against trigger-happy fighter types, we watched with horror 'our' Hurricane (of 33 Squadron) approach to land. A stream of red Very lights flashed up at the

Wg Cdr C.D.C. Boyce, CO of 84 Squadron, during the second half of 1941, and his gunner Sgt Chinnery returning to their base in Egypt from a raid in the western desert, December 1941. Don R. Neate

pilot, but to no avail. Appalled by his action, he completely forgot to lower his undercarriage and a much crumpled Hurricane crunched belly-down into the desert. Later that day, I was told that, on being helped out of the cockpit, he was heard to mutter, 'My God, I've just shot down a Blenheim.' Then he fainted.

A greater disaster however was to follow, as our gaze abruptly lifted from the wrecked fighter to the clear blue skies. Heading in our direction were ten Ju.88s. 'Eighty eights', I shouted, looking wildly around at the flat scrubland, bare of any cover from the menacing roar of the approaching bombers.

'They are our Blenheims', Robbie called, unperturbed. 'Run, for God's sake', I yelled, appalled that we were trapped in open desert, beside the obvious target of a sitting Blenheim. A memory flashback of the last days in Greece and Crete triggered my legs into a sprint towards a distant Bofors gun pit. The scream of diving Ju.88s finally convinced Robbie and, as I glanced back, he had started to follow me. Then I tripped as the ground tilted with the first stick of bombs. My mind raced with chaotic thoughts... to be caught in the open, hopeless predicament that was here, now, was not the

way I had ever envisaged ending... the rattle of the 88s' gunners as they hosepiped the ground made me lift my face out of the gritty dust. There was a dense cloud of black dust from the explosions to my left... if I got in there, I would be concealed from the ground strafing. Out of the corner of my eye, I saw a second stick of bombs falling as I raced into the acrid smelling black haze and flung myself prone. An explosion behind me made the earth heave into my chest as I hugged the ground. Blindly, with a mental sight on the Bofors gun pit, I ran on, and dived into the sandbagged enclosure.

My Log Book entries for that fateful day record 08.20hr take-off time in N6146 from LG 76, a flying time of 2.40hr. At 14.10hr, I returned to our base near Sidi Barrani. For Robbie, it was journey's end at LG 125. He had been instantly killed by that second stick of bombs. As the Blenheim carrying me as passenger headed towards the east, some lines of a poem by Stephen Spender drifted into my memory:

The names of those who in their lives fought for life
Who wore at their hearts the fire's centre.
Born of the sun they travelled a short while towards the sun
And left the vivid air signed with their honour.'

Sunset in the desert, 1941. A last Blenheim IV is coming in to land. Arthur Gill

The customary formation raids in the western desert created a heavy concentration of bombs in a relatively small area, which gave maximum bombing results. A full squadron raid by 84 Squadron, for example, destroyed an estimated fifty-three Axis vehicles at El Adem on 6 December. Although Hurricanes and Tomahawks usually provided escort for the Blenheim formations, frequent losses were incurred by the Bf.110s of III/ZG26 and by the superior Bf 109F fighters now equipping JG27. The German fighters delivered a first blow on 22 November, when pilots of 1/JG27 destroyed four out of six Blenheims of 45 Squadron, plus three escorting Tomahawks of 3 (RAAF) Squadron over the Acroma–El Adem road. On 20 December another memorable operation took place, when four Lorraine aircraft plus eight Blenheims of 45 and 84 Squadrons, in the company of nineteen escorting Tomahawks, set out to attack retreating German tanks on the Tokra–Benghazi road. On approaching the target area at 09.30hr, twelve Bf 109Fs of I and III/JG27 bounced the formation and immediately a 45 Squadron Blenheim and

a Tomahawk plunged down in flames. With the formation badly split up, it was every man for himself and the allied aircraft sped back home. Although his aircraft was badly shot up, one of the Lorraine gunners claimed a Bf 109F destroyed in the ensuing combat, with another 45 Squadron aircraft and three more Tomahawks falling to the Messerschmitts' gun fire during the next few minutes. Two Free French crews did not make it back either, including the one of Lt Colonel Pijeaud, AOC of Groupe Lorraine. Terribly burnt, he baled out of his doomed aircraft, only to be taken prisoner by an Italian desert patrol a few days later. Undaunted, Pijeaud managed to escape from the hospital at Derna in the company of two British aircrew and, after four days in the desert, they were picked up by friendly forces. Sadly, in Alexandria hospital, Pijeaud succumbed to his wounds and to the hardships of his march through the desert. His observer was altogether more fortunate: after a seven-day trek through the desert, Lt Guigonis was discovered by an allied patrol and brought back to his unit.

84 Squadron Blenheims are forming up after take-off for a raid on Rommel's tanks in the desert, December 1941. The Hurricane escort is milling overhead. Arthur Gill

This armourer needed a strong back to load 250lb bombs into the bomb bay of a Blenheim IV of 84 Squadron in the desert! Arthur Gill

Takoradi, across the continent to Cairo, delivering a total of thirty-one Blenheims, fifty Hurricanes, sixteen Beaufighters, twelve Toma-hawks, seven Warhawks, six Baltimores, four Bostons and one Maryland. The five- or six-day journey gave us wireless operators valuable experience in H/F, M/F and D/F communica-tions. No radio silence in this part of the world! The general plan for the air convoys was to fly in open formation at about 3,000ft, subject to the weather conditions at the time. As we progressed along the route the weather pattern changed from rain and thunderstorms to dust storms and poor visibility. Accommodation throughout was fairly basic, sleeping in native-type mud and straw huts at several staging points. I recall having a month's stay at Maid-uguri (northern Nigeria) and had the back of my briefcase eaten by termites while it was hanging on the mud wall of my hut.

July 1942 saw us leading one of the first convoys of American Warhawks. These were flown by West Point boys from Accra and we led them with a Beaufighter. While the Blenheim IV and later the Mk V Bisley were the mainstays as convoy leader aircraft, we did quick conversions on to other types (Beaufighters, Baltimores, Marylands and Bostons). We oper-ators really appreciated the relative comfort of the American aircraft – the airborne radios in these aircraft were a delight to operate. Hardly any convoy completed the route without some mishap or other. Our first Tomahawk convoy lost one aircraft at El Fasher (Sudan) when it was flipped over by a sand devil when on its final approach to land. Another trip saw a Hurricane drop out of the formation and forced land in the bush. We dropped him some rations

Intensive supporting operations contin-ued throughout the first five weeks of 1942, notably in the strategic area of the pass of Halfaya (or 'Hellfire'), which bordered Axis-held Libya and Egypt. After having successfully completed 381 opera-tional sorties during which 175 tons of bombs had been dropped, Lorraine was withdrawn to Syria for a well-earned rest and regrouping in February. Crusader had cost the Groupe five Blenheims, with six aircrew perishing, another six missing and one severely injured.

With the successful allied advance in Crusader slowly grinding to a halt during January 1942, the Free French unit Nancy was relegated to guiding allied aircraft safely across the Sahara on the Takoradi route. Onwards from the first reinforce-ment flight on 20 September 1940 (consisting of four Blenheims guiding six Hurricanes), this 3,697-miles trans-African ferry route to Cairo became one of the main reinforcement lines of aircraft to the Middle East. The Blenheim served with distinction in this role, as Sgt W.Op/AG Fred Burton explains. He had completed a tour of operations in 21 Squadron during 1940 before he and his pilot (Flt Lt Gauthier) found themselves

posted overseas to Takoradi in the former Gold Coast in early 1941:

This was to be our home for the next twelve months. We stayed in Cairo in between convoys instead of in Takoradi, which was healthier, and continued to fly the route until 1943. Altogether my crew led some twenty-five convoys, which had all been assembled at

Blenheim IV of groupe Lorraine, taken during a bombing raid against Halfaya in January 1942. Note the full-length rudder tri-colour banding and individual aircraft number (5) painted on the tail unit, and the Croix de Lorraine unit markings on both the wings and fuselage SHAA

In the scorching desert heat of a Libyan landing ground, two Blenheim IVs of Group Lorraine are revving up their Mercury XV engines prior to setting out on a mission in early 1942. SHAA

and radioed his position to the nearest staging post. He was eventually picked up.

The return trip back to Takoradi was made in a variety of aircraft. We never quite took to flying in the back of a Bristol Bombay which used the same route. However, sometimes we were lucky to get aboard a BOAC Class 'C' flying boat at Cairo which followed the Nile down to Lake Victoria in East Africa, then down the River Congo via Stanleyville, Leopoldville, to Lagos lagoon. From there, a land plane back to Takoradi for a few days' rest before taking another convoy up the route.

By the end of October 1943 more than 5,000 aircraft had been ferried to Egypt via the Takoradi route, which contributed decisively towards victory in the desert.

With Nancy serving on the Takoradi route during 1942, Metz was seconded to RAF Coastal Command and reinforced by four Blenheim Vs in August 1942. Its crews carried out anti-submarine patrols along the Lebanese and Palestine coastline during August and September, with one Axis submarine attacked and claimed heavily damaged by the crew of Capt

Mendousse. The end of GB Lorraine's Blenheim period came in October 1942, when the whole Groupe was transported to the United Kingdom to form 342 Squadron (or GB I/20 'Lorraine') with Douglas Bostons. Meanwhile, a second Free French Groupe de Bombardement in North Africa, GB 'Bretagne', had been created in Chad on 1 January 1942. Its first squadron, Nantes, received six Bristol Blenheim IVs and a few Glenn-Martin 167s for reconnaissance and bombing missions in support of the advance of the Free French ground forces into Tunisia, reinforced by five Blenheim Vs in April.

Meanwhile, fortunes had once more shifted in the desert, and Rommel was driving back the allied forces during February and March 1942. By April his Afrika Korps had penetrated Egypt and seemed to be making a decisive push for the Suez Canal. Only 60 miles west of Alexandria, at El Alamein, the allied troops managed to make a stand and check the German advance. Most of the remaining Blenheim squadrons now shifted from day to night-time operations, as Wg Cdr Dick 'Boffin'

Maydwell recalls. He was appointed CO of 14 Squadron in May 1942:

When I took over command of No.14 Squadron at Ismailia in the Canal Zone, the morale of both aircrew and groundcrew was at a very low ebb. The previous month, while operating in the western desert, the squadron had lost twenty-one Blenheims along with twenty-eight aircrew, and only two of those Blenheims destroyed were through enemy action. The cause of this disaster was a changeover from daylight formation bombing to night bombing, because there was insufficient fighter cover available for day operations. Therefore the first priority was to get the pilots' confidence back into night flying and particularly night take-offs with full bomb load. The crews recently posted from the Operation Training Unit in Kenya had flown only an unloaded Blenheim on circuits and bumps in moonlight, and therefore the sudden change to having to take off in pitch dark conditions on a poorly lit flarepath in the desert with a full bomb load was simply above their ability, and so there had been crashes.

Before we started any flying at Ismailia, I grounded all the aircraft in the squadron for four days for thorough maintenance and a good clean out of sand. Group HQ then gave us permission to night fly at Kabrit, which had a

A GB Lorraine Blenheim IV being serviced at Rayak, Syria, in March 1942. Lorraine was withdrawn into Syria after "Crusader" in early 1942 for a well-earned rest and regroup, having lost five aircraft and twelve aircrew during the campaign. SHAA

long and excellent runway. I organized ten inexperienced crews to carry out night take-offs and landings under fairly easy conditions in good visibility for five nights and only one crew failed the test and had to be posted away.

In June the squadron moved to LG116. We were nomads and therefore used to moving from one landing ground to another at short notice. The movement order was a simple statement on one sheet of paper. I always endeavoured to keep paperwork down to a minimum. Every section of the squadron (equipment, maintenance, cooks and so on) all knew the lorries allocated to them and their airmen and also the loads they had to carry.

Situated about 30 miles south east of Mersa Matruh, LG116 was typical of the many forward airfields in the desert. It was just a rectangular, cleared area, with a number of white-painted, 44gall drums positioned around the perimeter to aid sighting from the air. A windsock was placed at one side and the field was then declared operational. Maydwell continues:

On arrival at LG116, where a tented camp was set up, the importance of hygiene was vital to the health of every member of the squadron. There were thousands of flies in the western desert at the best of times, but if cleanliness were poor then there would be millions of flies, and that would bring real trouble. Also, all tents had to be be fully anchored, because gale-force sandstorms blew up without warning.

I warned all aircrew that avoidable accidents were a serious offence, such as landing with the undercarriage up or colliding with empty fuel drums. I put a Flight Commander under close arrest for two days for beating up the camp on

an unauthorized flight, and that certainly cooled him down. I was keen to keep every Blenheim serviceable because I had flown a Maryland from Takoradi via Khartoum to Cairo and realized the difficulties of delivering aircraft to the Canal Zone, and therefore did not want them broken in stupid accidents.

At this time the pilots had confidence in their night-flying ability, and flew intruder operations to Crete for a period of three weeks with very few casualties. Although it was a long haul both ways, the flights were successful and kept the enemy airfields at Heraklion and Maleme shut down. Enemy aircraft returning to Crete had no diversions, because the Wellingtons were covering the airfields around Athens. As Commanding Officer I did my fair share of operations, but, of course, it is no help to the war effort if a large number of COs with experience get shot down. However, there is a happy medium, and at least I avoided the hopeless attitude of one Blenheim CO I served under whom all the aircrew referred to as 'A one trip a month, Charlie, and make it safe'!

Some aircrew had been discussing the fact that the Blenheim had a rather poor bomb load and later on an Australian pilot suggested carrying a crate of empty beer bottles, as additional armament. These could be dropped through the back hatch by the W.Op/AG, as

Sqn Ldr Hugh Malcolm, 'A' Flight Commander of 18 Squadron, showing off his motorcycle at Wattisham, summer 1942. Promoted to Wing Commander and OC 18 Squadron, Malcolm was killed in action on 4 December 1942 during a raid on Chouigui aerodrome in Tunisia. For his exceptional devotion to duty and intense determination to fight to the very end, he was posthumously awarded the Victoria Cross, one of three VCs awarded to Blenheim aircrew during the war. His squadron bore the brunt of daylight operations in the Bisley Wing during November–December 1942, suffering the highest casualties of all four squadrons, with eleven aircraft and crews lost in action. Alec McCurdy

screaming 'no hopers' to divert the Germans into thinking they were unexploded bombs.

The second trip that I ran to Crete was probably the most enjoyable I have ever experienced. I was the pilot of the first aircraft that took off that night. It was almost a full moon. We set course for Heraklion and later the mountains of Crete came into view. It was a wonderful sight to see Mount Ida clear and sparkling in the moonlight. We crossed the main ridge at 8,000ft and saw the airfield at Heraklion in operation with a full flarepath lit up. I glided down to 4,000ft to confuse the sound locators and dropped two 250lb bombs on the main hangars. The flarepath was extinguished in a flash. After that attack, I flew close to the slopes of Mount Ida and circled round the summit, which was as clear as crystal in the moonlight. Then I turned down a wide valley before gliding towards the airfield, where I dropped two more 250lb bombs. There was not much light AA. Finally, after keeping out of range for a further fifteen minutes, I flew towards the airfield at full speed in a dive and at 4,000ft my airgunner pushed out twelve empty beer bottles from the hatch, which screamed down to the runway. No point in being shot down when dropping beer bottles! The return trip to LG116 was completed without incident, and I was glad to see the red flashing beacon near the coast. I made a wide sweep before landing at LG116 with a smooth touch down after 4hr 45min. It was a very pleasant trip. No. 14 Squadron completed fourteen nights of intruder operations on Crete. Aircraft serviceability was good and no Blenheims force landed in the sea.

In the desert, the cooks of No. 14 Squadron achieved miracles of improvisation and provided everyone with appetising meals, however impossible the conditions. The Officers' Mess was not specially favoured. Everyone had the same rations. The health of the squadron was good. There were as many heroes on the ground as there were in the air and they suffered their casualties too. There were always problems with spares for the Blenheims, but there were no forced landings away from base. I remember one aircraft landing with one propeller, the other engine had seized up and the propeller flew off. The aircraft flew better, because there was no feathering device!

Our aircrew were outstanding. They came from the UK, Australia, Canada, Denmark, New Zealand, Palestine, South Africa and South America. Personally, I had an Australian navigator and a W.Op/AG from Argentine. There was splendid comradeship and a wonderful team spirit throughout the squadron. For most of the time we lived a nomadic existence, erecting our tents and moving from place to place. Conditions were often harsh and uncomfortable, luxuries were non-existent and rations limited. The exhilaration of operations and feeling of fighting in a great crusade certainly created a determination to carry out every operational flight with increased vigour. However, there was always a chance of being burnt alive, drowned, badly injured or taken prisoner of war. It calmed the nerves to put your fate in the hands of Almighty God, and have faith that you would return safely.

Because the German forces advanced across the desert at great speed, 14 Squadron carried out a well organized withdrawal from LG116 to LG97 on the Alexandria–Cairo road on 29 June. Six weeks later, the squadron moved to Cairo, where they said farewell to the Blenheims and started conversion to the Marauder B26A. They had been preceded by Nos. 8 and 55 Squadrons, which respectively re-equipped on Wellingtons and Marauders during the spring of the year.

Enter the Bisley

The final development of the Blenheim was the Mk V, which was designed in the summer of 1940 as a ground-attack aircraft with a solid nose mounting four .303 Browning machine-guns for the Army support role. Specifications for such an aircraft had been issued after the Luftwaffe had shown how to fill in the army co-operation role to devastating effect with the Ju 87 Stuka during the Battle of France and the RAF had deemed the Blenheim IV to be suitable for further development in this direction. Only AD657 and AD661, the two prototypes of the MkV with a solid nose, were officially named the 'Bisley', after the famous shooting ranges in Surrey. Still the name stuck with the air and groundcrews later operating the aircraft.

After the two prototypes had been completed in early 1941, the Army's and the RAF's thinking on the subject of army support had changed considerably. The Battle of Britain had clearly marked the end of the much too vulnerable Ju 87 as the Army's ideal concept for ground attack. It was also clear that any army-support aircraft would have to be able to take care of its own defence, because complete air superiority would be unobtainable for many years to come in any theatre of war. It was therefore decided to fit the Hurricane with bomb racks and 20mm cannon to fill in the support role for the time being, and to abandon the Blenheim Mk V as a ground-attack aircraft. Instead, the Bisley design was modified to become a high-level bomber. It was very similar to the Blenheim IV, with a glass nose fitted with a chin turret for rearward defence. However, an increase in all-up weight of some 20 per cent was hardly compensated for by an increase of only 30hp in the Bisley's Mercury 25 or 30 engines. It was therefore underpowered, slower and had a shorter range than the Mk IV.

The Blenheim V was prone to engine cuts on take-off, which usually occurred as the extra 9lb boost was cut out at a height of a few hundred feet, and usually with fatal consequences for the crew. The three men aboard BA808 K-King of 13 Squadron had a lucky escape when their starboard engine caught fire at 300ft after taking off from Canrobert for a night raid against the docks at Tunis on 15 December 1942, causing the aircraft to crash with a full fuel and bomb load on the muddy salt lake depression of Garaet Guellif. Fg Off Rodney Broughton, here sitting on the wing of BA808, and his crew of Sgts Frank Westbrook (observer) and Andy Smith (W.Op/AG) took off next evening in another Bisley, and again suffered an engine cutting on take-off. Only by applying full rudder and ground-looping the aircraft, did Broughton avoid hitting the bomb dump. Frank Westbrook

Specification of the Blenheim Mk V	
ENGINES	two 950hp Bristol Mercury XV or 25 nine-cylinder, air-cooled, super charged radials
WINGSPAN	56ft 1in (17.10m)
WING AREA	469sq ft (43.57sq m)
LENGTH	43ft 11in (13.34m)
HEIGHT	12ft 10in (3.86m)
WEIGHT EMPTY	11,000lb (5,000kg)
FULL LOAD	6,500lb (2,955kg)
MAX. BOMB LOAD	1,000lb (454kg)
MAX. ALL-UP WEIGHT	17,500lb (7,955kg)
PERFORMANCE (with full load):	
economical cruising speed	140mph (225kmh)
max. speed	260mph (419kmh)
stalling speed	70mph (113kmh)
range with full load	1,600miles (2,580km)
service ceiling	31,000ft (9,455m)

In March 1941 the Air Ministry placed an order for 1,195 Blenheim Vs (later cut back to 942) to be built at the Rootes Group's shadow factory at Blythe Bridge in Staffordshire, the first aircraft rolling off the production lines in September. But it took almost a year before operational squadrons and OTUs began to receive Mk Vs. Nos. 13, 18, 114 and 614 Squadrons, having trained for the army support role, traded their Blenheim IVs for Bisleys during August and September 1942. Douglas Beagley, a rigger (airframes) with 18 Squadron at West Raynham comments:

We could see that the new aircraft only had one advantage over what we had had and that was that they were new. The trouble was, to our eyes, that the aircraft was the same basically but

its weight had gone up. It had a new nose, more roomy which was good, and had a new rear turret which it could well use. Then there were two more guns fitted under the nose, firing rear-wards under the direction of the navigator. It used a sight which incorporated a mirror and we were wondering how efficient it would be.

As soon as the aircraft arrived we were set about modifying them. We removed some armour plate, which was even under the engines as I recall, but although this reduced the weight this was countered when we fitted bomb racks under the wings between the engines and the fuselage. We all wondered what it was going to be like getting all this into the air.

Someone who can tell more about this is Flt Sgt Jack Brown, who served as W.Op/AG with 18 Squadron in the crew of Flt Sgts Bill Williams (pilot) and McCombie (observer). During the spring and summer of 1942, the crew completed twelve intruder sorties on to Luftwaffe air-fields from Wattisham, before converting to the Bisley in August:

I have a copy of Air Ministry Air Publication 1530.C, Pilot's Notes Blenheim V Aeroplane, Section 2, Note 23: 'Engine Failure. The air-craft will not maintain height on one engine except when quite light.' This was pretty depressing news and proved totally correct when we lost an engine on trials, lost height at about 300ft per minute, giving Bill about 4min to find a field in which, expertly as ever, to put her down, wheels up, near Ely, without injury to any of us but farewell to Bisley 805. A fortnight later we flew down to Filton to collect 870, and within a few days we had another engine failure but managed to land undamaged but unhappy.

No operations were flown with the Bisley from the United Kingdom, and it was decided to employ the aircraft in Egypt.

Nos. 15, 16 and 17 Squadrons of the South African Air Force received Bisleys during the second half of 1942, the first unit becoming operational during July in the anti-shipping and ground-attack roles. Its crews scored an occasional success against Axis supply shipping, notably on 25 October 1942. 16 and 17 (SAAF) Squadrons operated Bisleys for a short while during early 1943 from Kenya, Egypt, and the Aden Protectorate for anti-submarine patrol duties.

Operation *Torch*

By the autumn of 1942 the planning of Operation *Torch* was in full swing, which would involve large-scale amphibious landings by British and American troops in Vichy French north Africa (Algeria and Morocco) with the purpose of taking the enemy forces in Libya and Tunisia from the rear as they were steadily retreating after their defeat at El Alamein. *Torch* was launched on 8 November with allied land-ings in Algeria. Vichy French resistance crumbled within days and the allied troops advanced into Tunisia, engaging the rem-nants of the Afrika Korps and the Italian Army there. British forces under General Montgomery, the victor of El Alamein, meanwhile pushed the Afrika Korps back into Libya and beyond. During November Nos. 13, 18, 114 and 614 Squadrons flew out from the United Kingdom to north Africa, where they arrived at Blida airfield near Algiers and formed 326 (Bisley) Wing. Under the command of Gp Capt Laurence Sinclair, GC, DSO, DFC, it was attached to the First Army and started flying supporting missions on the 14th, together with the Free French Blenheim crews of Nantes. Douglas Beagley continues his story when the 18 Squadron groundcrew arrived at Blida:

The French had all taken off and were in the hills. We found everything neat and tidy with planes in the hangars but no people to care for them or fly them. We went right out on to the field and found our planes now sixteen in number (one had lost his way to Blida and had crashed) and two spares. I went out and found one of my favourite pilots, Flt Lt Eller. When we walked up he and his crew were refuelling their plane from four-gallon cans! A long and very boring job. His first words were, 'Am I glad to see you', and with that he climbed down off the wing to greet us.

Blenheim V BA727 of 114 Squadron being serviced at Canrobert, early 1943. By this time, the North African Bisley Wing had been withdrawn from daylight operations due to exceedingly high losses on daylight raids. Bill Burberry

Ground crew bombing up a 114 Squadron Bisley at Canrobert, Algeria, 1943. Bill Burberry

Life was very basic at this time. We existed on emergency rations and had what we could carry in our small side bags. We were still fully armed as we were not sure whether the French would return and fight. There were some units that fought for two weeks. We also slept out and we lived on the far side of the field. We were supplied by a couple of British trucks which shuttled back and forth from Algiers. Of course, there was some confusion as this was our first attempt at a large-scale invasion, we would be short of fuel and for a long time we had no tools. Also other squadrons flew in, 114, 13 and 614. It was some time before their crews arrived, some were torpedoed and when they arrived it was without equipment and so one squadron of personnel was supporting four squadrons of

planes. It meant that everyone was out servicing planes, the cooks and clerks were set to refuelling and doing whatever they could manage, sometimes under the supervision of technical people. They all worked hard and very long as you may imagine.

There was great confusion as we had four squadrons of Bisleys and no way of knowing which was which. We soon fell into the habit of doing four aircraft when only one might be needed. For instance, if you were assigned to do a daily inspection on 'V' Victor, you did all four on the base. Each squadron had its letter in a different colour painted upon the side, but we were not sure which squadron was which. Also, soon after the base was invaded by a couple of hundred American C-47s which had flown in.

We started flying operations immediately, of course. We first had to remove the long-range tanks but these were retained in, I think, two aircraft in each squadron, to accomplish long-range reconnaissance.

Targets for the Bisley Wing mainly consisted of transports and Axis airfields in the Tunis area, with the aim of reducing the enemy bombing of allied lines. These operations were flown both by night and in daylight with Spitfire escorts. However, fighter escorts did not

Left to right: Sgt Frank Westbrook (obs.); Fg Off Rodney Broughton (pilot), and Sgt Andy Smith (W.Op/AG). Operating over Bizerta harbour on the night of 19 April 1943, their Bisley was riddled with fifty-seven cannon shells from a Ju 88, but Fg Off Broughton brought 'F' for Freddie safely back to base. Frank Westbrook

always materialize as the bad winter weather rendered the forward airstrips, from which the fighters operated, unusable. As a result the Bisley crews often had to press home their attacks unescorted, which proved costly on many occasions. Flt Sgt Jack Brown, W.Op/AG in Flt Sgt Bill Williams's crew with 18 Squadron, experienced this on his squadron's second raid in north Africa, a low-level, cloud-cover formation attack on Bizerta airfield on 17 November:

Wg Cdr Malcolm was always keen to have Bill flying as No.2, tucked in tight on his port side since close formation by the leading 'vic' of three is the secret of keeping the whole of the twelve near enough together to present a rearward, effective firepower from twenty-four turret-mounted guns combined (being the main aim of formation daylight work). We were told that there would be no German fighter opposition and, of course, we had no fighter escort.

We flew in 828 for about three hours, low over the Med. and then out in over the coast. There was a lot of air turbulence and tragically two of the rear box of six collided and crashed straight in, blowing up in one big flash of flame. To sit looking astern, as we gunners did, and to watch six lads with whom you had recently had breakfast blown to glory was a grisly prelude to what lay about 20 miles ahead.

We were to fan out on the bombing run so that all bombs should be dropped within a few seconds of each other. Bombs in the main had 11sec delay fuses for low-level work to avoid blowing yourself up. It follows that if No.12 is eleven seconds behind No.1, he's in big trouble. We turned in to bomb and all Hell broke loose. There was a lot of ground defence fire, but worst of all there were some Messerschmitt Bf 109s either on the ground, in the air or just landing. As we flew over about 25ft up, one came straight up behind us and opened up with his cannon. We had dropped our bombs but were only just clear of the target when I saw the starboard engine well on fire. I also had a fair bit of turret damage. We could not speak to each other as the intercom had failed. It was clear that she would either blow up or the engine would stop and she would drop. Bill did the only thing possible and put her down flat on the only bit of level ground ahead.

Bill and I got out safely with only superficial damage, but our navigator was trapped. Fortunately some French troops managed to get the fire out before the tanks blew up and he was rescued, and recovered in a few weeks. So ended our 18 Squadron service and so began two and a half years as PoWs.

13 Squadron kept operating its Bisleys in North Africa until December 1943. Here, aircraft 'A' is serviced in the field. Rev. Leonard S. Rivett

On the 17 November raid, cloud cover prevailed until the aircraft were about 20 miles from the target. Undeterred, Wg Cdr Malcolm pressed on and Bizerta was successfully bombed and many dispersed aircraft were raked by machine-gun fire. The price for the crews' daring was high: apart from the two aircraft lost in a collision over Cap Ferrat, two further Bisleys of 18 Squadron fell victim to Bf 109s. Thanks to Malcolm's skillful and resolute leadership the remaining aircraft kept a tight formation and returned safely to base, although several aircraft were marked with severe battle scars. Beagley continues: 'Immediately, we started sustaining losses. I lost quite enough friends, I recall one chap, an ex-London policeman, with whom I became friendly, a W/O Beers. Just before we went overseas, when we knew nothing of what we were to face but feared the worst, he told me that not one of the aircrew would wear out a pair of shoes. He was so right.'

W/O Beers was killed instantly in one of the Bisleys that collided on the 17 November raid. At the end of the month, the Bisley Wing moved 150 miles closer to the frontline, to Canrobert airfield. From this new base the Wing kept up its close-support offensive for the 1st Army. After a successful attack on tanks in an olive grove south-east of Chouigui on 3 December, Wg Cdr Malcolm led off a mixed group of ten Bisleys from 13, 18, 114, and 614 Squadrons from their forward base at Souk el Arba in the late afternoon on the next

day, to attack Chouigui aerodrome. Immediately after take-off, BA804 of 114 Squadron developed engine trouble and crash landed without injuring the crew. There was no fighter cover available for the raid, and when the formation was bounced by a horde of fifty to sixty Bf 109s and Fw 190s of I and II/JG2 before reaching the target area, the cannon-armed fighters reaped havoc amongst the Bisleys. One after the other, five bombers plunged down during the next five minutes with only one crew surviving. Three other badly shot-up aircraft struggled back to nearby allied territory to crash-land in the desert. Determined to press on and undaunted by the overwhelming odds, Malcolm in BA875 flew on towards the target. Only 15 miles west of Chouigui his Bisley was shot down in flames too, he and his crew all perishing. For his exceptional bravery beyond the call of duty, Wg Cdr Malcolm was awarded a posthumous Victoria Cross. Flt Lt Wray Eller, Flight Commander in 18 Squadron recorded of the raid:

Personally, the sadness of losing nearly all my friends is my overriding memory. However, incidents do stand out. It was a beautiful winter's day with nothing helpful like cloud cover. The target was a satellite aerodrome (racecourse) but it was never located; it was believed we had been given the wrong map reference.

In the Chouigui area we were jumped by a large force of Me 109s, variously estimated at fifty or sixty plus; in all the excitement this

could be an exaggerated guess but there is no doubt that we were greatly outnumbered and quite inevitably had no chance. Formation became impossible to keep, as one by one we were shot down and it was every man for himself. My navigator was quite badly wounded; he has always joked that the bullets meant for me hit him by rebounding off my armour-plated seat. My air gunner, Norman Eckersley, was slightly wounded but claimed one Me 109 certainly and one probable. He was awarded an immediate DFC.

In the excitement, I forgot to open the hatch as we approached the deck and we were trapped inside the blazing plane until we finally forced it open. What caused me enormous concern was the fact that I lost my expensive Jermyn Street forage cap in the fire! My air gunner was also trapped, wounded in his turret, but we managed to kick in the Perspex and haul him out. To cap it all, we were instantly fired upon by ground troops, all happily bad shots, and equally happily our own men.

Flt Lt Eller was awarded the DFC and resumed operational flying in Bisleys with 18 Squadron on 29 December. Following the 4 December disaster, 326 Wing was hurriedly withdrawn from daylight operations and now became engaged in night-intruder work, attacking Axis transport, airfields and ports under cover of darkness. In daylight coastal reconnaissance patrols were also flown. Beagley concludes:

The squadron received some replacement Bisleys, not many. We still operated a little at night but we just did not have the planes or crews to be of much use. We also made some modifications to the planes. The rear-firing under guns had been removed to save weight, and we had tried to smooth the open positions over. But we had no materials and few tools. I tried with others to make a streamlined fitting from the metal cut from the petrol cans. But we had only 1/8in drills and 3/32in rivets. The result was that the fitting blew off quite regularly, but there was little else we could do about it. Also it was very hard to do accurate work with no hangar to use and, combining that with the short supply of tools and materials, it was very discouraging.

We were also operating from a plateau in the Atlas Mountains; this was putting an additional strain upon the overburdened engines and the results were obvious. We were suffering more cases of engines cutting on take-off. On 7 March 1943 we moved a short distance to a place we called Oul Mene and again we were poorly supported and trying to make something work which was obsolete before we even started with it. It was here that we first saw some Douglas Bostons and started re-equipping. I well remember what happened at this place one afternoon: three Bisleys took off for an air test. They accelerated down the dirt track which was our runway and all three left the ground and started to climb slowly. One after the other, all three had engines cut and all three crashed one right after the other. Luckily no one was killed or even hurt as I recall, but I wonder whether you can imagine the state of our morale? If you can, then ask yourself what was the state of the morale of those poor chaps who had to fly the things? It was a pity the Bisley was ever built, it seems to me.

In March 1943 18 and 114 Squadrons were stood down for conversion on to the Boston. Although there were strong rumours in 13 and 614 Squadrons that they too were to receive new aircraft, these, in fact, were yet more Bisleys. During the following weeks 13 Squadron personnel removed some of the heavier items of equipment to make the aircraft more airworthy. These included the observer's radio and the back-firing guns with their periscopic sight, a large water container (in case of a crash in the desert) and some armour-plating. As a result it was found that most aircraft could just about maintain height on one engine. The crews soldiered on in night raids against Axis airfields and ports in the Tunis and Bizerta area, as Sgt Frank Westbrook vividly recounts. He was an observer with 13 Squadron, in the crew of Fg Off Rodney

Broughton (pilot) and Sgt Andy Smith (W.Op/AG):

Our brief on 19 April 1943 was to search the coastline and harbours for shipping bringing in supplies and barge concentrations ready for the evacuation of Axis troops. We took off at 02.30hr in 'F' Freddie and spent some time searching the harbours at Bizerta and Tunis without finding any really worthwhile targets, so I decided to return along the coast and have another look at Bizerta from a lower level – we usually bombed from around four or five thousand feet.

We were approaching the harbour again, when Andy called on the intercom that he had just seen another Blenheim. His last words were almost drowned by the noise of bursting cannon shells, together with a smell of cordite and a sharp pain in my right leg – we had been caught cold by a Ju.88. Since we were over the harbour, I released the bombs immediately and Rod took evasive action. I assume that the German pilot thought the explosions from our bombs was the aircraft crashing and we didn't see him again. My assumption proved to be correct, because the German communique next day (our Intelligence bods received these regularly) claimed one Boston shot down at exactly that time and place; it was interesting that the German pilot's aircraft recognition was even worse than Andy's! I moved back to my seat next to the pilot to examine my leg as best I could. It was dark and it would have been very risky to show a light when there was a possibility of enemy fighters about. I pulled up my trouser leg and felt a warm sticky patch above my right ankle.

I opened up the emergency field dressing, bound up my leg and moved back to the front seat to try to find out where we were after all that evasive action.

I picked up the coastline and followed it east as far as Bone, then set course inland for Oul Mene. Rod had announced that, apart from the port engine being a bit rough, all the controls seemed to be working normally, but as we approached Oul Mene, he found that he could not lower the undercart, so called for the ambulance and firetender to stand by. Flying Control acknowledged the message and told him to land on the grass at the side of the runway. Belly landings can always go wrong for, after all, you are going to make contact with the ground at around 100mph. However, it was a successful landing and the thing I remember most was the horrible grinding sound as the plane scored a path along the ground. The aircraft was a write-off.

While recovering in hospital, Westbook was informed that BA727 'F' for Freddie had been hit by fifty-seven cannon shells without destroying it, although one had come very close, because it was found lodged in the port petrol tank. Some four weeks after this event, the north African campaign ended with the surrender of all Axis forces on 12 May. After three years of hard and bitter fighting, the Mediterranean was open and the threat to the Suez Canal was finally ended. The allies could start to prepare for the invasion of southern Europe.

By this time there were only few Blenheims left in operational service in the Middle East. The remaining two RAF Bisley squadrons flew daytime coastal patrols and U-boat hunts until 13 Squadron re-equipped with Baltimores in December 1943, and 614 was finally disbanded in February 1944. During February and March 1943 eighteen Bisleys were transferred from Middle East stock to the Turkish Air Force to supplement earlier deliveries of Mk IVs. The USAAF in north Africa received Bisleys BB179, EH347, EH443 and EH458 on 1 October 1943, but the reason why remains obscure. At the end of September the Free French Groupe Bretagne ended its Blenheim operations to convert on to Martin B-26 Marauders. The French kept a handful of Blenheim IVs and Vs in operational service in Groupe I/17 Picardie, a small unit which was employed in coastal surveillance patrols off Syria from July 1943 onwards, probably until after VJ Day in August 1945.

The under-nose, rear-firing blister gun pack of Bisley No. 443 was crushed in during a crash-landing near Damas on 9 November 1944. Pilot of this Groupe de Bombardement I/17 'Picardie' aircraft was Commandant Allot. SHAA

CHAPTER TWELVE

Fighting the Japanese Assault, December 1941–43

A major part of the RAF's strength in the Far East was built up with Blenheims in the three years preceding the outbreak of war in the Pacific in December 1941. 62 Squadron was equipped with twelve Blenheim Is in 1938 and flown out from Cranfield to Singapore in August of the following year and stationed at Alor Star, the most northerly airfield in Malaya, during 1941. 34 Squadron was also transferred there in the autumn of 1939, losing four out of eighteen aircraft en route between RAF Watton and Tengah, Singapore. At the end of 1941 it had seventeen Mk IV bombers on strength at Tengah. After converting from Wapitis to the Blenheim I bomber, No. 60 Squadron was involved in patrols along the Indian coast during 1939–40, before moving to Mingaladon in Burma in mid February 1941. Due to the rapidly deteriorating political situation, a 60 Squadron detachment was deployed to its war station at Kuantan for the defence of Malaya in November. Finally, 27 Squadron flew out twelve short-nosed

fighter and bomber Blenheims to reinforce Singapore in February 1941, moving to Sungei Patani in August. On the eve of the outbreak of war, the Far East Blenheim strike force totalled forty-seven aircraft, plus fifteen in reserve. In all, only 362 mostly outdated Commonwealth aircraft (233 serviceable) were available. At the same time, it was estimated that at least 500 aircraft would be required to defend British interests successfully in the Far East. To make matters worse, aircraft spares and replacement engines were practically non-existent in Malaya, because these had been absorbed in supplying units in the African desert.

Malaya

The increasing apprehension regarding Japan's intentions towards British territories in the Far East finally came true in the early hours of 8 December 1941, when enemy invasion troops beached at Kota

Bharu on the eastern coast of Malaya, eighty minutes before the air attack on Pearl Harbor. In fact, the Kota Bharu invasion was a 'feint', intended to draw attention from the main landing area further to the north around Singora and Patani in Siam. The ruse worked: crews of the four Blenheim squadrons and their colleagues of 8 (RAAF) Hudson Squadron were briefed shortly after midnight on 7/8 December to take off at first light for an attack on the Japanese invasion fleet, expected off the coast of Kota Bharu. However, by the time they became airborne, the enemy forces had already landed at Kota Bharu, with the last wave of barges disembarking at 06.00hr. The Japanese fleet then slowly withdrew to the north-east in anticipation of the expected dawn air attacks. Thus the strike force was dispatched too late to try and contain the invasion. 8 (RAAF) Squadron took off first, together with eight Blenheims of 60 Squadron, for the 150-miles flight to Kota Bharu, arriving over the target area by

Blenheim Is L8382 MU-J and L8609 MU-X of 60 Squadron, Mingaladon, June 1941. Both these aircraft were in action against the Japanese invading Malaya during December 1941. M.C. Bunting, via Joe Warne

Left to right: Plt Off A.M. Johnstone (pilot) and his W.Op/AG Flt Sgt G.W. Gregory of 60 Squadron, who were shot down on 9 December 1941, while flying V5931, a 34 Squadron Blenheim IV. This shot was taken at Calcutta in August 1945, while these men were on their way home after release from Japanese captivity. M.C. Bunting, via Joe Warne

ditching in the sea. His crew perished, but Bowden kept hanging on to the tailwheel floating in the sea and was picked up a day later by a Japanese destroyer, thus becoming the first allied airman prisoner of war. The returning Blenheim gunners claimed two Zero fighters shot down. Wg Cdr Vivian comments:

> We had plenty of trouble with the Zeros who used to stay just out of range of our rear VGOs until the gunner took off his empty ammo pan to change it, and then came in. (We counter-acted this by fitting twin Brownings.) The best way of getting away from a Zero was to dive within a few feet of the ground if we could and just go flat out. This proved quite successful with the Mk I on the few raids we did with them.

The first wave of raiders was followed by eight Blenheim Is and IFs of 27 Squadron, which lifted off from Sungei Patani at 06.45hr for a dawn strafing and bombing attack on the invasion forces at Kota Bharu. Due to blinding rainstorms, no attack could be carried out, but on their return the crews found that their base had been thoroughly bombed and machine-gunned, with L6669 destroyed plus two other Blenheims damaged. The squadron was thereupon diverted to Butterworth.

34 Squadron from Tengah was thrown in next against the invading hordes, bombing and strafing targets in the same area. However, Oscar fighters (possibly of the 64th Sentai) intervened and V5827 was so severely shot up that it force-landed at

08.00hr. Plt Off Kingwill, observer to 60 Squadron's CO, Wg Cdr Vivian, recalls:

> We flew in loose formation, myself and Dick Vivian in the lead. We were to carry out independent, low-level attacks on any enemy ships we could find. Off Kota Bharu there was a 10–15,000-tons transport already on fire. There were numerous landing craft moving to and from the beach. Vivian flew around out to sea to size up the situation. Two or three Blenheims decided to drop their bombs on the transport. We followed in behind and could see that she was red-hot inside with bodies sprawled all over the decks, so we decided not to waste our bombs on it. It was apparent that the main invasion force had withdrawn. Vivian picked out a group of landing craft as a target. We dropped our bombs in a stick across them, but by the time the 20sec fuses had burned, the craft had moved some yards away. We could see the crews firing at us with automatic weapons. One of the boats overturned in the explosion which followed, and the others must have been badly shaken. It was a neat bit of bombing but not particularly effective.

The burning 10–15,000 ton transport in fact was the 9,794-tons *Awagisan Maru*, which had been successfully bombed by Hudson crews of 1 (RAAF) Squadron a few hours before the Blenheim crews came

into the fray. 60 Squadron's L4829, piloted by Flt Lt G.P. Westropp-Bennett, was hit during the attack and caught fire, 'Paddy' Bennett then diving his blazing Blenheim into a Japanese landing craft, killing himself, his crew and all sixty enemy soldiers aboard. This sacrificial attack was later praised by the Japanese over Saigon Radio. The Canadian Flt Lt Bill Bowden's L4913 was shot up by AA and disintegrated upon

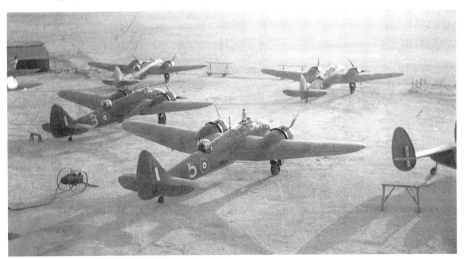

Reinforcement of the depleted Blenheim force in the Far East came in January 1942, when 84 and 211 Squadrons were transferred from the western desert to Sumatra. Depicted here is the first Flight of 84 Squadron's Mk IVFs at Heliopolis, Egypt en route to the Far East. Arthur Gill

Machang fighter strip. The other Blenheim IVs flew back to Butterworth only to be surprised over the airfield by more Oscars, this time probably of the 59th Sentai. V5633 was damaged and crashed, and V5636 was damaged with its Australian gunner Sgt K.R. Burrill wounded, but he retaliated by shooting down his assailant. Shortly after Oscars of the 64th Sentai roared in over the airfield boundary and strafed the Blenheims while they were being refuelled, damaging four more aircraft. Sqn Ldr Harley Boxall, in the meantime, was leading eleven Blenheims of 62 Squadron from Alor Star in an attack on shipping and landing craft at Patani. Although they were jumped by Nate and Oscar fighters on turning for home, all aircraft escaped from the ensuing 10min combat. After landing back at base around noon, the Blenheims were serviced and bombed up again, but were caught on the ground in an air raid by twenty-seven Sally bombers of the 60th Sentai. Four Blenheims were completely destroyed and another five damaged, leaving only two squadron aircraft serviceable.

History had repeated itself when, just as in May 1940 in the German blitzkrieg in the West, about half of the RAF aircraft were destroyed on the ground by the overwhelming might of the Japanese Air Force on the first day of war. The remaining Blenheims and Hudsons stood by at Kuantan and Butterworth for the rest of the day. Despite the fact that Flt Lt Dobson and his 60 Squadron crew had spotted the main invasion fleet further to the north during the early morning raids, the depleted allied strike force was not ordered off to hunt after it. By midday on 8 December, Siam's army surrendered to the Japanese, who quickly put the airfields at Patani and Singora to good use as forward bases for fighter and bomber units to support the landing forces.

Due to the severe attrition in only one day of war, RAF Far East HQ decided to establish a Bomber Pool at Tengah, Singapore, where the eighteen surviving Blenheims of 34 and 60, and also those of 27 and 62 Squadrons were concentrated during the next few days. At 12.45hr the next day 34 Squadron dispatched six aircraft, half of them flown by 60 Squadron crews, to attack Singora on the Kra Peninsula, where the main Japanese landings were taking place. Plt Off P.N. Kingwill, observer in Plt Off A.McC Johnstone's crew of 60 Squadron, who flew

Flt Lt Gill's V6375 of 84 Squadron, guarded by a local Arab at Sharjah on 15 January 1942. Arthur Gill

in 34 Squadron's V5931, has vivid memories of the occasion:

We approached Singora at 6,000ft, with no cloud in sight, and at 16.00hr I picked out Singora airfield and saw quite a number of aircraft on the ground. We did a steady run-up and I watched for the leader's bombs, but at the point that I judged the bombs should go, nothing happened. The leader's observer must have decided to do a dummy run. The formation started to turn quite sharply to port and, on the outside of the turn, we could not keep up. We then spotted five lots of enemy aircraft in formations of nine about 2,000ft above us and two miles away. Out at sea were the invasion ships and I counted twenty transports at anchor. Isolated from the rest of the formation,

it was obvious that the enemy fighters would be on us unless we did something quickly. We decided to have a go at the transports and did a run-up on the one nearest our heading. Having set the bombsight, I pressed the release when the target came into line, but the bombs failed to release... I selected another ship, did a run-up and selected the other bomb for release. Again nothing happened, so Johnnie tried to dive-bomb them off. He selected a ship and dived down to about 4,000ft, pressed his release button and pulled out.

By this time we were right in the middle of the fleet with about eighty AA and goodness knows how many small arms firing at us. We were wearing our tin hats over our flying helmets and at that time this seemed to be a singularly inappropriate piece of headgear. I

The Ragged Irregulars: 84 Squadron aircrew celebrate Christmas 1941 at Gambut in the desert. Most of these Blenheim Boys were killed or taken prisoner while operating against the Japanese during the following months. Eric Oliver

therefore transferred it to my seat where it might serve a more useful purpose. Johnnie selected a ship for the other bomb, dived down to 2,000ft, released and pulled out. Because of the violent evasive action we were taking, I did not see the bombs strike, nor was I sure that they had come off. Johnnie gave the engines +9 lb boost which was permissible for five minutes. We kept in a shallow dive, heading for the shore at 220kts, the object being to get low over the jungle to take advantage of the excellent camouflage of the Blenheim. I gave Johnnie a course to steer for the Malayan border, and asked 'Ace' Gregory if he could see anything of the enemy fighters. He said that he thought we'd got away unseen, but no sooner had he finished speaking than there was a burst of fire and he shouted that he'd been hit. In fact, his turret had been hit and put out of action. I looked back and saw him crouched down by the rear armour plate with both guns almost straight up. Almost immediately, Johnnie pointed to his port rev counter which was showing that the engine was idling. I heard a second burst and felt the bullets hit the aircraft. We were almost at tree-top height so I thought it unlikely that fighters would attack from below. Eventually I saw a fighter through the blister from the seat alongside the pilot – it was a low-wing, fixed undercarriage job with a radial engine, almost dead astern and closing in rapidly. At about 50yd it opened fire and I could actually see the bullets coming from the guns in the wing roots and the jagged tears in the metal wing covering where they struck. As the fighter broke away, I could see four more coming in line-astern.

The defenceless Blenheim was further riddled by Nakajima Ki.27 (Nate) fighters of the 1st Sentai and, when its starboard engine also began to falter, Plt Off Johnstone had no option but to crash in the jungle at a speed of about 120kts. Luckily the aircraft missed all the heavy trunks, but both wings were torn off, the fuselage falling to the floor of the jungle. Flt Sgt 'Ace' Gregory scrambled out quickly as the fuselage had broken at his turret and, though badly bruised, he managed to release a side panel in the cockpit section and helped his wounded pilot and observer out. Being under continuous fire from the Japanese fighters, they found shelter behind thick tree trunks. Having dressed their wounds, they set fire to their aircraft

and soon there were two tremendous explosions – the bombs had definitely not released. Although the crew attempted to escape through the swampy jungle, shortly after they were picked up by Thai soldiers and handed over to the Japanese, Johnstone being sentenced to death on 12 December for taking up arms against the Imperial Japanese Army. This was later commuted to three months imprisonment. The three men received very harsh treatment over the next three and a half years, including slave labour on the infamous Thailand–Burma 'Railway of Death', but happily all survived the war.

V5829 was crash-landed some 15 miles south of Mersing by Sqn Ldr Finan O'Driscoll of 34 Squadron after being shot up in the fight with the Nates of the 1st Sentai, the whole crew returning safely to Tengah. Another crew from 60 Squadron was less lucky. Flt Lt Joseph A.B. Dobson crashed his severely battle-damaged V5598 near Haadyai. Dobson, Flt Sgt George R. Smith and Sgt Ernest F.W. Fowler were captured, the pilot being beheaded and his crew being shot in the following week. The crew have no known grave and are commemorated on the Kranji Memorial.

In the meantime, the remaining 62 Squadron Blenheims were prepared at Butterworth for a similar raid on Singora airfield, but only Sqn Ldr Arthur 'John' Scarf in L1134 PT-F was airborne, awaiting his comrades to follow him when a Japanese air raid caught the others on the ground, wreaking havoc and destruction. Undaunted, Scarf decided to carry out the raid singly. Before reaching the target a swarm of Ki.27 fighters bounced the lone short-nosed Blenheim. Stubbornly, Sqn

L8364 of 84 Squadron crashed at Sembawang, Singapore during a night landing on 26 January 1941. Arthur Gill

Flt Lt John Wyllie at the controls of his 84 Squadron Blenheim IV over the western desert, 1941. Arthur Gill

Ldr Scarf pressed on, managing to bomb Singora, while his gunner Cpl Cyril Rich emptied his single Lewis machine-gun into rows of parked aircraft, and making good their escape at low level. However, the fighters now persisted in their attacks, and soon Scarf's left arm was shattered and bullets smashed into his unprotected back. Finally, the fighters left the seemingly doomed bomber alone. Aided by his observer, Flt Sgt Freddie 'Paddy' Calder, and Cyril Rich, Scarf flew the riddled Blenheim back to Alor Star, where he belly-landed without injury to his crew. Sadly, hours later, Scarf succumbed to massive secondary shock and his weakened condition. Not until after the war did the true story of Scarf's exploit become known; his widow receiving the third Blenheim Air Victoria Cross on 30 July 1946.

Butterworth aerodrome had been heavily damaged, with Blenheims L1133 and V5379 being wrecked and most of the other aircraft rendered unserviceable. After this raid only ten out of the original fifty Blenheims were still flyable, an attrition rate of 80 per cent in forty-eight hours of war. During the remainder of December the rapidly dwindling number of Blenheim crews valiantly kept up pressure on the advancing enemy in single aircraft raids or by small formations, but it was all in vain. The Japanese swept down the Malayan peninsula at such a pace that by Christmas the remnants of the Blenheim squadrons were withdrawn to

Tengah, Singapore to regroup. Only nineteen Blenheim IVs, plus five Mk Is and IFs were still serviceable and these undertook night raids over Malaya and strikes on the landings under way on the Borneo coast.

Sumatra

By the end of January 1942 the situation at Tengah too became hopeless, being on the receiving end of constant air attacks, and all RAF bomber units were withdrawn to Palembang airfield in Sumatra. Singapore finally fell on 15 February, with 138,708 prisoners of war being taken. 60 Squadron gave up what were left of its Blenheims to 34 and 62 Squadrons, with which the unequal and bitter fight was carried on until all Blenheims were lost and the majority of the aircrew were posted killed or missing in action. Replacing these war losses was a painstaking business, as Sgt Fred Burton, W.Op/AG, experienced:

It was early January 1942, following a delivery to the Middle East, that my crew and I were told that we would be part of a formation of three Blenheim IVs which we were to take out to Singapore to reinforce the squadron there. A Lt Pocock of the South African Air Force was the formation leader. My pilot was Flt Sgt Les Millen, DFM and Flt Sgt Dickie Carr, DFM was the navigator – both these fine chaps were ex-18 Squadron in the UK. Our aircraft was Z7897. To ensure that we would get top priority to return to our Middle East unit following the safe

delivery of the aircraft, we were all issued with a yellow authorization card, signed by the C-in-C M.E.

We set course from Fayoum Road airfield on 4 January 1942 but returned after 30min as the leader's W/T was unserviceable. We took off again the following day and landed at Lydda [Palestine] some two hours later. Various snags on the aircraft delayed us for two days but on 8 January we were off again (with a large sack of Jaffa oranges in the back) to Habbaniya [Iraq]. From there the route was Bahrein Island, Sharjah, Karachi, Jodhpur, Alahabad, Calcutta, Akyab [Burma], Toungoo, Zayatkin [Rangoon]. We arrived at Zayatkin on 15 January. Here we were in trouble – most aircraft had massive mag-drops and required considerable attention.

We were grounded for a week during which we watched RAF Brewster Buffaloes operating from our airfield. Other things were happening, however. Singapore was almost at the point of being run-over by the Japanese. What were we to do with our aircraft? Finally, we were briefed to take the three Blenheims to a squadron based at Palembang in Sumatra. On 24 January we left Rangoon at 01.30hr and headed south towards the Amdaman Islands and after 5-hr flying made a landfall with north-west Sumatra. We were looking for a small airfield called Lho-nga and finding it proved quite difficult After flying around the coastline for a while (fuel now getting very low indeed), we spotted an inlet leading to what looked like a grass field. Our leader decided to go in and, to our great relief, the field turned out to be the place we were seeking. We all got down OK but had to use almost full throttle to taxi (the grass was so long). Surprisingly, we had been expected and a large stack of five-gallon fuel cans were made ready for refuelling. We left the working party to do just that and were then taken to some building or other to be fed and bedded for the night.

We left the next day, stopping off at Pakan-Baru to refuel, then on to Palembang. This was the end of the road. It had taken us twenty-two days and over forty-one flying hours. We thought the aircraft were really clapped out and would certainly require extensive servicing before they could be used operationally. After such a long trip all sorts of snags appeared. We were just thankful that we had arrived in one piece and were handing the aircraft over. Having reported to the appropriate authorities and handed over the aircraft, we sat around the flying control tower for several hours waiting for the next move. During this time we watched a single Blenheim IV come into the circuit for landing. The aircraft touched down too far up the runway and overshot the end, which happened to be a drop of six feet on to a road.

18 Squadron detachment to Portreath in May 1941. From the left: Sgt Bill Proctor (W.Op/AG); Plt Off George Milson (pilot); Sgt Jim 'Dinty' Moore (W.Op/AG); Sgt Ron Millar, RNZAF (observer.). Apart from Sgt Moore, these men were posted to 84 Squadron and the Far East in January 1942 to be taken prisoner by the Japanese three months later. Plt Off Milson completed fifty-four daylight and nine night operations in Blenheims during 1940–42, Sgt Millar three fewer. The crew's W.Op/AG, Sgt Moore completed three tours of daylight operations, ending the war as Flight Lieutenant, DFC. Jim Moore

Palembang and force-landed in swamps at the mouth of the Loempo River on 23 January, the crew travelling in native boats and by car to Palembang. V5782 crashed at Rangoon on 25 January, Sgt R.A. Headlam, RAAF and his observer, plus one ground crew passenger perishing. Z9577 and a 211 Squadron aircraft force-landed in rice-fields near Lho-nga in northern Sumatra, wrecking both aircraft, on 4 February. The crews had been wrongly briefed on the location of the airfield, causing the unnecessary loss of two valuable aircraft. Three more 84 Squadron aircraft did reach Sumatra but never got to Palembang, and three other Blenheims were held up by defects and never got beyond Burma. Flt Lt John Wyllie, who led the first flight of 84 Squadron to the Far East, recorded:

When I took my flight in for a landing in northern Sumatra we found that the map reference located the aerodrome on the side of a rocky mountain! It had been a long flight from Rangoon and we were very short of petrol. I searched towards the coast over flat country and was just about to order the other pilots to follow me and make belly-landings in the paddy fields when I saw the 'drome. I tanked up at once and took off again to watch for the flight the Wing Commander was leading. The intercoms never worked. But I spotted them, flew in beside him and waved for him to follow me. He did, and I got my first Brownie point!

Palembang aerodrome at this time was subjected to increasing bombing and strafing attacks, and therefore it was decided to divert the majority of the aircraft and personnel from it on 23 January and move to Palembang 2 (P2), some 25 miles further to the south-west. By the end of the month just twenty Blenheim IVs of 34, 84 and 211 Squadrons plus eight Mk Is and IFs of 62 and 27 Squadrons were available at P1 and P2 for night bombing raids and shipping strikes. However, only a handful of these aircraft were serviceable at any time, the greatest number available from 84 Squadron, for example, was only ten. There were no spares, refuelling facilities and armament stock were insufficient and the units suffered from an almost complete lack of transport. Living conditions were appalling, crews sleeping on mattresses on the ground while being plagued by mosquitoes, and food was very poor. But no one complained and the brave Blenheim crews carried the war to the enemy almost

The aircraft was a write-off. We saw the crew later (unharmed) – they had flown that aircraft all the way out from the UK! What a waste.

Luck was with Burton and his crew, as they were flown out in a Dutch Lockheed Lodestar after a week's stay at Palembang, during which time they had been subjected to several Japanese air raids.

As reinforcement of the depleted Far East strike force became a pressing necessity, 84 Squadron was hurriedly withdrawn from Libya to Egypt in January 1942. It received a new CO, Wg Cdr John Jeudwine, and was re-equipped with twenty-four reconditioned Blenheim Mk IVs. Loaded with a three-man crew, two passengers, an extra 55gall overload tank, personal kits, spares

and tool kits, the all-up weight of each aircraft was 14,800lb. Soon followed by twenty-four aircraft of 211 Squadron (which had reformed after the Greek campaign with the Mk IV), the Blenheims flew out in eight sections to Singapore, via Iraq, India and Burma, during the second half of January. One newspaper headline in Cairo reported 'Air Armada Leaves Egypt for Singapore!' While en route, Singapore had become untenable and the squadrons were ordered to Palembang (P1) in Sumatra instead. Only thirty-four Blenheim IVs of the two reinforcement squadrons actually reached Sumatra, 84 Squadron losing three aircraft and one crew on the last legs of the journey. Z9570, in the hands of Plt Off Macdonald missed

every night, mainly against Ipoh, Singora, the Anambas Islands and Japanese troop transports off Sumatra.

With the enemy advancing, the Sumatran aerodromes came under regular air attacks in the course of February. Six Blenheims were destroyed in a bombing and strafing attack on P1 airfield on the 7th (V6133, Z6282 and Z7799 from 84, plus two from 211 and one from 34 Squadron). During the same attack Flt Lt Linton's 211 Squadron Blenheim, which was returning from a reconnaissance sortie, fell victim to 59th Sentai pilots. After a sighting of a major Japanese invasion fleet north of Banka Island on 11 February, an all-out attack by all twenty-three available Blenheims was ordered. However, a few minutes after midnight, disaster struck: three heavily loaded Blenheims of 84 and 211 Squadrons all struck the tops of tall trees due to the flarepath being wrongly laid out and crashed. Plt Off B.L. West, RAAF and his 211 Squadron crew escaped alive with cuts and broken bones; four of the other two crews perishing unnecessarily.

On 14 February 1942, the Japanese finally invaded Sumatra Island. In warm pouring rain, during this and the following day, the last raids from Palembang 2 were mounted by 84, 211 and 62 Squadrons, bombing and strafing Japanese troop-carrying barges which were coming up the Moesi River. Flt Lt John Wyllie continues:

After several missions against supposedly Japanese-held positions in Malaya (one was a completely deserted aerodrome) they sent a big airdrop of paras into Palembang 1 (on the 14th) and landing-barges full of troops up the Moesi River. We had a fighter Blenheim (of 27 Squadron) on our 'hidden' aerodrome. It came from Malaya. Our ground crews checked it out and said that it was OK, but the pilot refused to take any more action against the Japs whose Navy Zeros flew circles round the Blenheim fighters and had shot down all his companions.

I volunteered to take it up on 14 and 15 February to attack the landing barges coming up the Moesi River. I fired short bursts from five forward-firing machine-guns, over a hundred rounds a second, into the barges until we came to the cruiser which was unloading the men into the barges. I made three attacks on her from very close to sea-level then (much to the relief of my airgunner in the back, who had been using his twin guns as well, on what he kept shouting was 'bloody suicide') we went back to the boats on the river. We had taken a few hits ourselves but nothing hit me or my gunner, though things buzzed around our ears a couple of times and one bullet passed through my trouser leg just above my instep. So Brownie point number 2.

Hundreds of Japanese soldiers were killed in the air attacks on 14 and 15 February,

for the loss of 27 Squadron's L1258 and K7173. On the 16th the few remaining Blenheims retreated to Kalidjati airfield in Java, while most of the ground personnel were being evacuated to India. 27, 34 and 211 Squadrons handed over all their remaining, battered Blenheims (twelve Mk IVs and seven Mk Is and IFs) to 84 Squadron on order from RAF HQ at Bandoeng two days later. Twenty crews from all four units, under the command of Wg Cdrs Jeudwine and Bob Bateson (211 Squadron CO, later in the war to gain fame as a Mosquito fighter-bomber leader in the 2nd TAF), were now to take a last desperate stand against the crushing might of the Japanese advance. From their new base, situated about 80 miles east of Batavia, cloud-cover bombing raids were mounted against shipping in the Banka Straits and on Palembang 1, which was crowded with about 150 Japanese aircraft. Flt Lt Wyllie recalls:

From Kalidjati I did seven operations, five of them with considerable success: 1. (21 February) A 'must get through' venture to destroy an oil refinery the Dutch had forgotten to blow up near Palembang. To do it I had to take three aircraft through a storm at close to typhoon winds. One of the other two went down in the storm. However, between us, the other plane and my crew and I, left a pretty furious blaze; 2. (23 February.) The Japanese moved into Sumatra and used P1 but, as far as we knew, had not yet started operating from P2. The Japs had a 'standing cover' over it of a couple of Navy Zeros. It was a nice cloudy day and I played a game of hide and seek with them, now you see me, now you don't. Coming out of one cloud my bomb-aimer-navigator shouted, 'We're right on, we're right on!' Luck. I had come out of a cloud immediately over the runway with Japanese aircraft parked wing tip to wing tip on each side of it. (They had not learnt about dispersal at that time.) So we put down a string of bombs, but had to get back into cloud-cover without waiting to see the results. Then, still using the cloud cover, I went to P 2 to see if the Japs had found it yet; they had, but had very little defence set up. We went up and down the field twice, at low level, using the four machine-guns with which our machine was equipped. Then back to Kalidjati. When Jeudwine told AVM Maltby the news of our discovery, the old man, he was an ex-1914–18 war pilot, said I should report to him personally.

This involved a flight over 6,000ft mountains and a distance of over 100 miles. The only available machine was the fighter Blenheim I had used before. Our Flight Sergeant shook his

113 Squadron en route to Moulmein to bomb port facilities, 11 February 1942. This was one of many low- and medium-level direct support operations flown in the period 30 January to 23 February 1942, with a total of 160,128lb of bombs delivered by 113 Squadron. Chappy Chapman, via Tony Day

Sgt Folliet-Foster of 113 Squadron, an American in the RAF, taking the cross off the ex-convent used as HQ and quarters by the squadron in the centre of Asansol in mid or late 1942. The offending pilot was severely burned when, on taking off from Agartala on 12 September 1942, in Z7985 a bomb dropped off which caused the aircraft to burst into flames Chappy Chapman, via Tony Day

head and said that he didn't know if we'd make it. He gave me a fitter to take with me. At Bandung, where we had to land, one wheel came down, the other stayed up. Dutch fighter pilots added to my problems by flying up from under our machine, pointing back at our one-up, one-down condition and making life even more difficult by giving me their slipstreams. I made a successful crash landing out on one side of the flying field. Minutes later an immaculate formation of Japanese bombers came over and dropped forty-eight bombs in the field all around us. I went on and reported to the AVM then returned by road to Kalidjati. More Brownie points.

On 24 February six crews of 84 Squadron were detailed to carry out a cloud-cover raid on Palembang 1, in an effort to create maximum disruption to the Japanese Air Force which was using it as its main base for operations against the allied airfields in western Java. While the crews were walking up to their dispersed aircraft at Kalidjati, sixteen Ki-21 bombers of the 75th Sentai screamed into view at low level and wrought havoc among the Blenheims and airfield installations. However, three

Blenheims were still airworthy and these became airborne, setting course across the Sunda Straits. The vic of three was led by Sqn Ldr Passmore, No. 2 being Sgt Cosgrove and No. 3 was Plt Off Fihelly. Over the sea, Sgt Cosgrove waggled his wings to indicate that something was amiss and headed back to base. Then there were two heading into the hornet's nest.

Eric Oliver's Story
Sgt Eric 'Ollie' Oliver, W.Op/AG in Plt Off Brian Fihelly's crew and a veteran of the Greek and Desert campaigns, recounts:

We droned on over the thick jungle for about two hours. The cloud cover we had hoped for was very sparse and we felt naked and vulnerable as we flew through the bright sunshine over south Sumatra. Our navigator Tommy, in his usual professional manner, gave time checks as we came up to our ETA at the target. As we neared Palembang I was beginning to feel the eyestrain of constantly scanning every portion of sky in turn in order not to be caught out by a surprise attack, particularly from up-sun. This was learnt

from the pattern of attack used by the Luftwaffe in north Africa. When Tommy called out 'Palembang ahead', I dared only give a swift glance ahead but observed that a column of smoke was still rising from the oil refinery that the Dutch had blown up ten days previously when they evacuated the town. Not daring to have my vigilance distracted further, I quickly resumed my search pattern. The sharp crackle of machine-gun fire forced me to look sharply across to Passmore's aircraft, now on our port side and slightly below some 400yd away. Three Japanese fighters were hanging on to the tail of his aircraft like terriers at the heels of a bull. 'Fighters', I yelled into my intercom and away we swung to starboard. Only then did I see another three fighters (Ki 27s of the 11th Sentai) that had sneaked up below us and were snapping at our heels, just like their comrades attacking the other Blenheim. I had been caught out, despite all my training to 'beware of the Hun in the sun'. They must have been aware that our weak spot was underneath and they were exploiting it methodically.

I was now too busy defending the aircraft to think much about our mission, but I knew we weren't going to be deterred until we had made a determined effort to do the job we had set out to do. I heard Tommy's controlled voice on the intercom giving Brian, our pilot, the usual approach instructions, 'Left, left – steady – hold it', and then, 'Bombs gone'. Under the circumstances, we had to abandon our attempt to

About 25 per cent of all RAF and Commonwealth bombing sorties mounted from India during the second half of 1942 were directed at the important and fiercely defended Japanese-held harbour of Akyab, on the western coast of Burma. The demise of 113 Squadron's V5589 over Akyab was captured by the rear-facing camera mounted on the CO's (Wg Cdr Walter) aircraft, at 10.50hr on 9 September 1942. Sgt John Reid, RAAF successfully ditched his aircraft in the sea, to be taken PoW together with his crew. On this raid three Blenheims of 113 and 60 Squadrons (V6507, V5589 and V5425) were shot down, a third of the attacking force. On the credit side, both ships attacked were sunk, including the supply ship Niyo Maru. Imperial War Museum

bomb the airfield runway and had been forced to settle for the oil refinery. This was hit, as Tommy told me later, and huge columns of black smoke erupted as we cleared the target area.

Meanwhile, I had my hands full as the three attackers hung on our tail and took turns at trying to close in to administer the coup de grâce. They tried to hide out of sight, under the tail, in order to seize any opportunity to rake us with gunfire whenever Brian attempted to make any turn away from a straight course. At the same time, it seemed to me that this was the only time I could get in a good shot at them as I couldn't fire directly astern.

Aided by the 9lb boost that Brian had thrown in to give the engines maximum power, we ran for home. Brian was desperately seeking the protection of that elusive cloud in which to hide. Tommy was down on his belly trying to get a bead on our attackers with the rear-firing Brownings fitted in a blister under the nose of the aircraft. I was getting off bursts from my own guns in the turret. This really was a different kind of fighter attack from those experienced against the Germans in north Africa. There, with far superior speed, they had run rings round us with constant diving attacks and quick bursts of cannon-fire. On this occasion the Japs seemed not to have the speed to outrun us and the aircraft were obsolescent and with fixed undercarriages. The three of them seemed to take turns popping up from beneath our tail while I desperately tried to manoeuvre the arc of the incendiaries from my twin Brownings into what I hoped was a vulnerable part of the enemy.

Suddenly, I realized that the twin arcs of incendiary were now one. A gun had jammed! Not daring to take my eyes away from the action to look for the cocking handle to clear the stoppage, I reached down and accidentally nudged it out of its storage position and it fell to the floor of the turret. There was nothing left but to lower the seat to allow me to reach for it on the floor. This I did and desperately hooked the handle on to the breech-block and quickly cleared the stoppage. While this was taking place, I was low down into the aircraft and completely unsighted as to what was going on outside. As I raised myself quickly back up into position, I was horrified to see, in the space of 30sec, that a new situation had developed.

Brian had spotted a cloud to starboard that would no doubt afford us refuge and was banking away to get under cover. This, of course, gave our enemy a lot more fuselage surface at which to fire. When I thought about the situation later, I realized that the attacker, having seen me disappear from the turret and the twin guns suddenly point helplessly upwards, without a doubt assumed that I had been killed or wounded and was closing in for the kill. Our sudden turn toward the cloud afforded him every opportunity. When I reappeared, he was on our tail and less than 100yd away so I lined the guns straight at him, firing a continuous burst for about 10sec while shouting through the intercom to Brian to 'Turn left, turn port'. Suddenly, the Japanese just stood up, like a begging dog, on his tail and seemed to hover there while I still blasted at him, finally sliding away out of sight.

The suddenness of this incident caused me to shout out aloud something like 'Wow!'. I made no attempt to avert my eyes to see where he had gone but held my position, waiting for the next attack. I knew there were two more Japs somewhere beneath the tail, though I couldn't see them. I was sweating under my flying helmet as I gazed around, desperate not to be caught unawares again. Then Tommy's voice came over the intercom, 'Are you OK, Ollie?' 'I'm OK so far', I replied. Then suddenly we were engulfed as we flew into the cloud. A wave of relief swept over me and I prayed that the cloud would stay with us until we got back to the coast. It didn't, but it did provide cover long enough for us to lose our attackers.

The tension then eased and we held an excited discussion on the recent events. Tommy said that he feared his rear-firing guns had not been much good and that he'd seen little of the action. Brian was concerned that we were not flying on full power and were losing height. While all this discussion was taking place, I still kept a watchful eye all around the sky about us as we were now out of cloud cover and back in brilliant sunshine. I took time, however, to take stock of the damage we had sustained. There were numerous bullet holes in the tailplane and fuselage but the ones that made me sweat were the four holes in the Perspex of the gun-turret. Two appeared at one side, where they had entered

the cupola, and two exactly opposite, where they had exited. I puzzled for a moment as to how they had not blown my head off. It then dawned on me that the incident with the jammed breech-block had caused me to lower myself into the turret to clear the stoppage. Clearly, that action had saved my life.

When Brian commented that the starboard engine was losing power and running badly, I turned to look at it. Suddenly, a stream of smoke billowed in the slipstream, past my position. The feeling of relief I was savouring at having come out of the incident in one piece suddenly turned to dismay as I felt sure that the smoke would soon turn to flames. It was then that I

spotted the shiny surface of the tailplane and realized that it was covered in oil. It seemed obvious that an oil feed had been severed by a bullet and we were losing oil badly. I reported my findings on the intercom and there followed a discussion on our chances of survival. By now, we were almost down to the minimum height for baling out. Below us lay the solid jungle of Sumatra. It was certain that, if we did bale out, we would be hung up in the tree-canopy and very likely miles apart. It was a prospect that none of us fancied. Our discussion was interrupted by a loud bang and a sudden lurch as the propeller dropped off and fell to the jungle below as the engine seized up. As Brian brought the Blenheim under control, decisions had to be made – and quickly! Baling out was now out of the question; we were far too low. The likelihood was that we would have to ditch in the middle of the Sunda Straits.

Reporting our situation by radio was a non-starter. Far East Command, in their infinite wisdom, had not made provision for radio communication since we arrived in this war zone and I had no frequencies to work to. We

were now flying on the port engine only and, while a Blenheim could fly on one engine in normal circumstances, this engine was losing power, causing us to lose height rapidly. Unless the coast appeared pretty soon crashing in the jungle would be inevitable. The situation was tense and all conversation ceased. Only a short while before I had been thinking of the yarn I would be spinning over a beer to my brother aircrews, back at base. Now my thoughts were concentrated on home, back in England, and what the hell was I doing here, anyway?

Only minutes later, Plt Off Fihelly successfully ditched his Blenheim near the coast

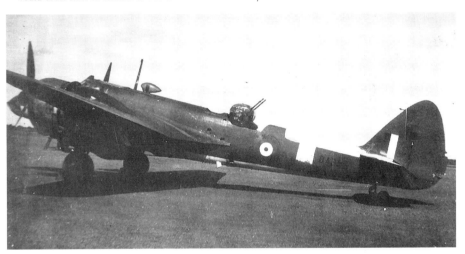

Bisley BA928 of 113 Squadron with an unusual paint job, early 1943. Joe Ward, via Tony Day

in four feet of water and the three men scrambled into their dinghy. The following night the crew were rescued by native fishermen, who supplied them with a skiff, food and water, and they set out to row to Java and to freedom by crossing the Sunda Strait. After a few days the crew were stranded on a small island in the Strait, exhausted and with no rations left. By pure coincidence, a yacht with Royal Navy survivors from HMAS *Perth* had anchored off the island, and the overjoyed Plt Off Fihelly and crew were taken on board. Next night, the yacht set sail to cross the Strait, but, only a few miles from the freedom of the Indian Ocean, it was intercepted by two Japanese destroyers and the game was up. The crew spent the next three and a half years in miserable captivity.

The last day of February witnessed a repeat Japanese precision bombing raid against Kalidjati airfield. But in a concerted effort the air and groundcrews of 84 Squadron managed to lay out a landing and take-off path between the bomb craters and that evening instructions were received to carry out an all-out attack on a large Japanese convoy approaching the coast. That night a total of twenty-six sorties were flown in the remaining six combat-worthy Blenheims. Flt Lt Wyllie and his crew did three in Z9723:

1. On this trip we found the Japanese fleet which were covering the landings further along the coast. We got caught and held in a pyramid of searchlights, an action which guided all the other aircraft out on the hunt to bomb the Japs. We discovered that the Japs used their aircraft at night from an aircraft carrier, and a fighter came and sat on our tail waiting for us to get out of the massive display of anti-aircraft fire. I did a steep falling turndown to sea level under a typically huge 'bomber's moon'... and returned to Kalidjati to bomb up and refuel.
2. On our second sortie I flew at sea-level from the start and remarkably quickly found a vulnerable target. A six to eleven thousand ton cargo ship with a centre castle which suggested passengers or troops. We flew over her at mast-head height, bow to stern and dropped four 250lb, tail-fused bombs. I had 11sec to get clear and turn to see what effect the bombs had had. There was a tremendous explosion below her bridge in her centre castle, followed by another explosion in the same area, perhaps caused by explosives in a hold there. (Brownie point.)
3. This sortie started in a similar way to the previous one except that I believed there were likely to be more ships close inshore. I was right. We came on a fleet of them, mostly at anchor, in a line along the coast near Tjeribon. We attacked two from low level and broadside to us but were greeted with enough flak to make it unhealthy to wait around to check results. (Brownie points.)

Surprisingly, only one aircraft was lost on the gallant 28 February/1 March effort. His Blenheim Z9723 damaged in a fighter attack, Sgt Sayers had been forced to land in a paddy-field near Rangkasbitung, without serious injury to the crew. Early next morning enemy forces landed on Java near Kalidjati airfield. The attack came so swiftly that 84 Squadron was overrun on the aerodrome before the few remaining Blenheims could get into the air. Flt Lt Wyllie wraps up his story:

Within an hour of our landing at Kalidjati there were Japanese tanks on the aerodrome. I tried to get one aircraft off but came under too much fire from the tanks. I then joined the CO in his car.

He had got the squadron personnel away southwards, in trucks up back roads, and decided to set up a decoy with three of us with Tommy-guns in the back of his car driving on the main road away to the east. It was quite exciting, Chicago-gangster stuff. Squadron casualties were few but the men of a newly arrived anti-aircraft battery, in barracks beside the aerodrome, were completely wiped out. So was our much loved and respected Flt Sgt Bill Slee (i/c servicing aircraft). He tried to get out to another plane and was shot down and killed right in front of me.

Sixty-five survivors of 84 Squadron that made good their escape from Kalidjati reached Tjilatjap, the only port on the south coast of Java, on 5 March. They found two 30ft-long lifeboats and a motor launch, and set sail to Australia on the night of the 6th. Within an hour disaster struck, one lifeboat and the motor boat being holed on some rocks although everyone managed to wade ashore. The following day twelve men, under the command of Wg Cdr John Jeudwine, set sail in the remaining lifeboat. Miraculously, they reached Australia, after a journey of about a thousand miles which had taken them forty-four days. They made arrangements with the US Navy for the submarine *Sturgeon* to try and pick up the remaining survivors off the coast of Java. Sadly, some seven weeks after the departure of Jeudwine and his crew, the party of survivors that had stayed behind were captured by the Japanese and taken prisoner. Many of them did not survive their ordeal in captivity while others were very sick men when they were released in the autumn of 1945. When John Wyllie finally got home he was pleasantly surprised to learn that he had been awarded the DFC on 28 February 1942.

Burma

Meanwhile, with a view to establishing an offensive bomber capacity in Burma, 113 Squadron had arrived at Mingaladon airfield on 7 January 1942 from the Middle East with twelve Blenheim IVs. At its new base the unit incorporated those 60 Squadron aircraft that had not flown out to Malaya. Reinforced by 45 Squadron during the second half of February, the two units were thrown into the breach to try and stem the advancing enemy in Burma. They suffered heavily in the retreating

battle, especially from bombing and strafing attacks on their airfields. On 25 February, for example, five 45 Squadron aircraft were wrecked in an 8th Sentai raid on Mingaladon. The last serviceable Blenheim of 113 Squadron flew out to Dum Dum in India on 10 March, taking, in addition to its crew, a load of two evacuee women, three children, three trunks, seventeen suitcases, a sewing machine and a wire-haired terrier with it. By this date 45 Squadron had nine serviceable Blenheim IVs, which represented the entire bomber strength in Burma. Yet against the odds, 45 Squadron unloaded 31,500lb of bombs on enemy airfields, troop concentrations and other targets during the last weeks of March. A most successful, last-ditch effort was undertaken on the morning of the 21th, when nine Blenheims of 45 Squadron and their Hurricane escort wrote off sixteen Japanese aircraft in an attack on Mingaladon aerodrome, plus eleven in the air, two of which fell to the concentrated Blenheim turret gunners' fire. Amazingly, all of the bombers returned safely, although most had battle scars. Next day, the Japanese retaliated, destroying nine Blenheims in a hail of bombs on Magwe airfield. By the end of March, when most Royal Air Force units finally withdrew into India, eight Blenheims had failed to return from operations, with a further twenty-three aircraft lost on the ground.

Another gallant episode followed on 9 April, when nine Blenheim IVs of 11 Squadron, based in Ceylon, attacked a marauding Japanese fleet 180 miles off the island. Only near-misses were scored, and, immediately after the bombing, a swarm of Japanese carrier-based A6M Zeros broke up the formation. In a running battle, four of the bombers were shot down (Z7896, Z9574, R3911 and Z7803). Finally, V5592, flown by the formation leader Sqn Ldr Ken Ault, fell foul to three Zeros just before reaching the coast. There were no survivors among the sixteen aircrew. Of the four aircraft that returned to base, three were holed like colanders, one (Z7759) being wrecked on landing. Further attacks on the Nagumo Force were ordered, as Sgt Wal McLellan, RAAF, a pilot with 45 Squadron recorded:

In mid April about ten Blenheim crews from various squadrons gathered in Calcutta for 'Special Duties' and I and my crew were among them. On arrival we were briefed in a locked

Z7691 and Z7643 of 60 Squadron went up with a bang in a bomb-carrying Oscar attack at Dohazari, with two other aircraft damaged, early in the morning of 2 May 1943. Depicted are the remains probably of Z7691. A few weeks earlier, on 25 March, six aircraft of the unit were bombed-up and ready to take off when six Sally bombers dropped their bombs on the southern end of the strip; Z9828 was written off by a direct hit and three other Blenheims received severe damage. Bill Ward, via Tony Day

room in the Grand Hotel that we were on stand-by to attack the elusive Japanese Fleet supposed to be on its way to Calcutta. The crews did not receive this briefing with a great deal of enthusiasm, as we all knew that No. 11 Squadron had been badly mauled attacking the main Japanese Fleet off Ceylon. It was finally agreed that four of us would attack from low level and the rest from high level, thus splitting the attack from the Zeros. We were bluntly told that it was not expected that any of us would survive, but other Blenheim squadrons would attack from the Calcutta area, if we could not stop the Japs. The Japs would have died laughing if they had known how small, obsolete and unreliable our total strike force was in India Command.

We stood by for a week, restricted to the grounds of the Grand Hotel, waiting for the order to take off from Dum Dum, but on the seventh day we were told that Intelligence had established that both Japanese Fleets had returned to Singapore. Our high tension relieved, we all got very drunk before returning to our squadrons.

Following their mauling during the first three months of war in the Pacific, 60 Squadron reformed at Lahore in India in the spring of 1942 with Blenheim IVs. In May 1942 the squadron resumed operations, often in the company of 45 and 113 Squadrons, against Japanese targets in Burma. Meanwhile, during late April six crews of 113 Squadron had been temporarily based at Loiwing in southern Yunnan, China, to attack Japanese troops advancing in the area. 34 Squadron's Blenheim IVs joined in the concerted air offensive against the spearheads of the Japanese thrust in Burma during June. Despite an acute shortage of spares, tools and equipment, both the air and the groundcrews worked extremely hard trying

to assist the retreating British Army. Operating from Asansol and Dohazari, Akyab (a major port for the Japanese) was frequently bombed and machine-gunned and several aerodromes, coastal shipping and communications were attacked. At the end of May, and at the instigation of the Army, 113 Squadron experimented in the low-level dropping of 250lb 'oil bombs' against the village of Minbya, where Japanese troops were reported to be billeted. This method of bombing with the forerunner of the napalm bomb was not pursued further, however, because it was considered too dangerous for the aircrews dropping them.

On 22 May 1942, just before the end of this phase of the war in the Far East, W/O

Farewell to the Blenheim. 113 Squadron leaving Feni for central India to re-equip after being withdrawn from operations in mid 1943. Joe Ward, via Tony Day

Martin Huggard of 60 Squadron, with observer Sgt John Howitt and Flt Sgt Jock Mcluckie, W.Op/AG, lifted Z9808 into the air from Dum Dum for an attack on Akyab airfield, while a simultaneous raid was to be carried out by 113 Squadron on barges in the Mayu River. Having successfully bombed their target and while diving out to sea, Jock was watching five Ki 43 Oscars of the 64th Sentai taking off from a satellite airstrip near Akyab, which were led by the famous ace Lt Col Takeo Kato (eighteen victories) and soon the lone Blenheim came under attack. However, with magnificent flying the crew managed to escape destruction and Mcluckie damaged the Oscars piloted by Sgt Maj Yoshito Yasuda and Capt Masuzo Otani during an encounter which lasted for some

35min. Having survived an estimated twenty-five attacks, Mcluckie finally scored hits on Lt Col Kato's Oscar, which dived into the sea in flames, killing the pilot. After their leader had been shot down, the remaining fighters circled the spot where Kato had gone in and were soon out of sight. During the very-low-level evasive action, Z9808's starboard wheel had struck the sea and was banged back up into the wheel housing, breaking the hydraulic lines. On returning to base, 'Paddy' Huggard did a beautiful one-wheel landing, but the aircraft was a write-off due to strain on its airframe. This certainly was one operation which deserved decorations for the gallant crew, but they were not forthcoming.

Patrolling the State of Bihar in India

became an added task for the crews of 34, 60 and 113 Squadrons during August, where nationalist saboteurs were trying to wreck the vital railway system in order to disrupt British control over the region. Both 34 and 113 Squadron each lost an aircraft and crew during these Internal Security Reconnaissance Flights. Of the former, Flt Sgt Goss, RCAF and crew, flying T2245, were murdered by the natives after making a successful ditching in the Ganges near Kohitar (due to engine failure) on 15 August.

Meanwhile, raids against the Japanese in Burma, where the fighting had stabilized, continued unabated in the midst of the monsoon season. On operations the crews often had to contend with considerable turbulence, hail, heavy rain and electric thunderstorms, and plough through black, almost purple storm clouds which went up to 30,000ft. Regularly, aircraft fell to the

weather, ground fire and Japanese fighters, but on occasions the Blenheim hit back. For example, during a raid on Shwebo airfield on 29 October by eight aircraft of 60 and 113 Squadrons, 60 Squadron's W.Op/AGs Sgts Houlgrave and Carruthers each shot down an intercepting Oscar fighter and combined fire probably destroyed the remaining Japanese. On the debit side, Sgt Minchin, RAAF's Z9745 was badly shot up and crash landed at Agartala.

During this month, No. 167 Wing was formed to control all Blenheim squadrons in Burma. By this time the British forces had been replenished to such a degree that they could go on a limited offensive again down the Arakan, with the aim of retaking Akyab. In October 1942, the Mk V or Bisley began to arrive on the scene, 60 and 113 Squadron receiving the first aircraft. However, 60's crews did not like the Bisley

and were quite content to keep their old Mk IVs. As a typical effort in this period, the wharf at Akyab was once more the target for seven Blenheim IVs and one Mk V of 60 and 113 Squadrons on the morning of 10 November, escorted by eight Mohawks from 155 Squadron. Racing in in pairs at zero feet, the formation hurled their 250lb bombs into a 500-ton coaster, which was sunk, and damaged a 1,500-ton supply ship unloading at the jetty. V6491, with Sgt Conan Allen, RCAF and crew, was seen to roll over on to its back and plunge into the water of the harbour, apparently the victim of light flak. As the bombers came out of the target area, they were bounced by between twelve and twenty fighters, but the Mohawks came to the bombers' rescue and no further Blenheims were lost. A repeat raid was mounted on the early afternoon of the same day, nine crews of 34 and 60 Squadrons bombing the same target from low and medium level, with an escort of eight Mohawks from No. 5 Squadron. Flt Sgt Graham Clayton, W.Op/AG in 60 Squadron, recalls:

The shipping attacks on Akyab were pretty dicey. The attack on 10 November was particularly harrowing. Of the two ships at the wharf, one was a flak ship, armed to the teeth. We went out into the bay and attacked from virtually sea-level. As we got close, I could see tracer slipping by and looked over the front – only once – the amount of flak being hurled at us was simply scary. I was glad I wasn't the pilot having to fly straight into the stuff. We dropped our stick of 250lb bombs, one of which we saw went into the side of the larger ship, then we pulled away to head for home. Then came the fighters. There seemed to be Oscars everywhere. We got down on the deck, to be joined by another Blenheim, but three fighters attacked us at once. I could see pieces falling off one that I had a go at and it swung away to head back to Akyab. However, one of the other ones got the Blenheim with us and he started to burn. He could not go on and ditched it. I did see a couple of the crew get out on the wing and took time to radio their position to base. However, they were too close to Akyab and finished up as PoWs. Two more passes were made at us but no hits by either side and we eventually eluded them and returned to base.

On the afternoon Akyab raid on 10 November, one ship was sunk and gunners in the bomber formation claimed four out of an estimated twelve to fifteen Oscars of

the 64th Sentai shot down. 5 Squadron Mohawks shot down two further Oscars. On the debit side, two low-level attacking Blenheims of 34 Squadron were destroyed in the fighter attacks, with Fg Off Howe, RAAF in 'N' and Sgt H. Elliott RCAF in 'H' and their crews lost. As a result of these frequent Blenheim strikes on shipping at sea and in port, the Japanese were forced to abandon the seagoing Burmese supply routes after 10 November.

In January 1943, 34 Squadron left the battle zone, its place taken by the rebuilt 11 Squadron. 11, 60 and 113 Squadrons kept harassing enemy positions and supply lines along the front in direct support of the first British ground offensive down the Arakan. 42 Squadron, after converting from the Beaufort to the Bisley, joined the Blenheim Wing during March. However, by this time the advance had ground to a halt and the reinforced Japanese troops and Air Force took the initiative again, forcing the Commonwealth units back to the Indian border. No clear-cut tours of operations were in vogue in the Far Eastern theatre at this stage; Graham Clayton, for example, did sixty-two operations between May 1942 and May 1943 before he was screened. His pilot Sqn Ldr J.E. Morphett, RAAF, DFC completed 421 hours on Blenheim operations in 60 Squadron before he was taken off operations.

The covering of the withdrawing troops continued from April to July 1943. On 13 May, twenty-two Blenheims of 11 and 60 Squadrons, with an escort of thirty-five Hurricanes carried out a most successful low-level attack on supply dumps at Kappagaung without loss. This raid ended 60 Squadron's Blenheim era, and in July the unit, together with 34 and 113 Squadrons, began conversion training on to the Hurricane IIC, or 'Hurri-bomber'. Before August 1943 was out, the last remaining Blenheim units in the region (11 and 42 Squadrons) also withdrew, to re-equip with the Hurri-bomber. The battle-weary Blenheims, their airframes stress-fatigued and their engines worn out, were given an honourable retirement after two and a half years of sterling war service in the Far Eastern theatre.

CHAPTER THIRTEEN

The Spirit of the Blenheim

PILOT:

Pilot Officer E.R. Mullins
RAF S/N 41865

OBSERVER:

Sergeant R. Lowe
RAF S/N 581231

GUNNER:

Aircraftsman Patrick Ahern
RAF S/N 625621

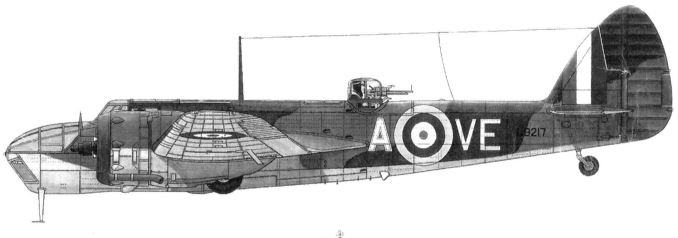

BATTLE RECORD

Target	Date
Waalhaven	5/10/40
Maastricht	5/11/40
Sedan	5/14/40

SQUADRON

No. 110 (Hyderabad) Sqn.
No. 2 Group, Bomber Command
Royal Air Force
Wattisham, England

Of the total of 6,260 Blenheims and Bolingbrokes built between 1935 and 1944, only a few dozen survive today. It is sad to record that not a single intact Blenheim I is still in existence and the only complete Blenheim IV remaining is BL-200 of the Finnish Air Force, which is presently awaiting full restoration for static display at Tikkakoski.

Salvage operations which were undertaken during the 1990s have provided the remains of several Blenheim Is and IVs, the first being recovered was L1434 of 211 Squadron, which was brought to shore from Lake Prespa, Albania in June 1993.

During 1996 the Albanian crash sites of several other Blenheims were being investigated by British Embassy personnel, which led to the positive identification of L8374 of 84 Squadron at Permet in the south-east of the country. This Blenheim I (one of a batch built by Rootes Securities between November 1938 and August 1939) went missing on operations on 20 December 1940. Further searches will, it is hoped, result in the salvaging of L8536 from 211 Squadron in Topove (which crashed on 6 January 1941), and of a second 211 Squadron aircraft that is reported to have ditched off the Albanian

Side-view drawing of Blenheim IV L9217 of 110 Squadron. This aircraft completed two operations: to Waalhaven airfield on 10 May and to the Maastricht bridges on 12 May before it was shot down on 14 May 1940 to crash at Torcey on the outskirts of Sedan. In all, 110 Squadron lost five aircraft in the Sedan area on that day. John Geary

coast. During the summer of 1996 the skeleton of an unidentified Blenheim, minus its nose section, was pulled from the sea off Crete. Finally, a group of Norwegian researchers have been involved in salvaging two 114 Squadron Blenheims, V6227 and Z7500, which both crashed into the sea near Herdla aerodrome on 27 December 1941. In the summer of 1997 a plaque was erected near the site of the crash to commemorate the six gallant men from these two crews who died on the famous Herdla raid.

Restoration

Fortunately, a few dozen Canadian-built Bolingbrokes have survived the ravages of time, the majority of which were purchased in flying condition, for around Canadian $100 each by farmers as war surplus in 1947. The Bolys were cannibalized and many components were put to good use in farming machinery, the airframes left standing on the farmers' yards out in all weathers for decades. As a result of the booming interest in old aircraft during the 1970s and 1980s, some forty often derelict and dilapidated hulks of Bolingbroke airframes and various battered components have been recovered. Many of these have

Members of a Norwegian salvage team posing in 1996 with the remains of the twin Brownings of Blenheim V6227 or Z7500 of 114 Squadron, which crashed near their target, Herdla aerodrome, on 27 December 1941.
Torstein Saksvik

The skeleton of a Blenheim on the jetty after being pulled from the sea off Crete, July 1996. This aircraft was probably lost in 1941, the crew of three all escaping safely.
Ron Hicks

Having rested in Lake Prespa for over fifty-two years after falling victim to a Bf 109E of 6/JG27 on 13 April 1941, 211 Squadron Blenheim I L1434, flown by Flt Lt L.B. Buchanan, DFC saw daylight again in June 1993. The aircraft's wing section, plus its two Mercury engines and propellors (in the background) have been retrieved from the lake by a Greek Army and Air Force recovery team. These items are now on display in the Tatoi, Athens Museum. James Dunnet

After a three-year restoration, the newly finished Belgian Blenheim is shown to the public for the first time at the Brustem/St. Trond airshow in September 1996. Bart Beckers

Wes Agnew. After lingering in airfield hangars for over two decades, it was decided to restore the aircraft to static condition in 1994 and transported to Brustem airbase. Despite being plagued by a constant lack of finance, the project was finally concluded in September 1996 by a dedicated team of volunteers and the aircraft is now a static exhibit in the Royal Museum of the Army and Military History in Brussels. In commemoration of the gallant AASF and 2 Group attacks on the Meuse bridges on 11 and 12 May 1940, the aircraft is sporting the colours of 139 Squadron's L9416 XD-A. This aircraft, piloted by Fg Off Pepper, DFC, crashed on 12 May near Hoepertingen, in eastern Belgium, on its return from an ill-fated raid on the Maastricht bridges, when seven out of nine Blenheims were destroyed.

One Bolingbroke IVT is presently on display at the Royal Air Force Museum, Hendon, restored as Blenheim IV L8756. The original aircraft was one of a batch of 130 aircraft built by Rootes Securities between September and November 1939, and had a long-serving career with 139 Squadron, 9 AOS and 12 PAFU, before it was finally struck off charge on 4 May 1944.

Flying Again

In 1979 Graham Warner privately, but with the assistance of the Imperial War Museum at Duxford, Cambridgeshire, took the brave and far-reaching decision to restore, to flying condition, the derelict remains of Bolingbroke IVT 10038. The aircraft had originally been purchased from Wes Agnew by the former RAF pilot Ormond Haydon-Baillie, who was tragically killed in a flying accident in July 1977. Before being shipped over to the United Kingdom in 1974, 10038 had been sitting out in the open in Manitoba for almost thirty years. During the next eight years well over 40,000 man-hours and £300,000 were spent on the project by a dedicated and mainly volunteer team. Several components of another Boling-broke, 9893, were also used in bringing 10038 back to life again. After completing the meticulous rebuilding, it was correctly finished in the markings of 105 Squadron's V6028 GB-D. This was the aircraft that Wg Cdr Edwards, DFC had flown on the daylight Bremen raid on 4 July 1941, which earned him the Victoria Cross.

formed, or still form, the basis of restoration projects in Canada, the USA, Belgium and the United Kingdom. Largely thanks to the efforts of Wes Agnew, a well known Canadian collector, seven Bolingbrokes today are on static display in aviation museums around Canada or are being restored. Another three aircraft went to the USA where they are reported as undergoing restoration.

In 1969 the Belgian Air Force purchased the wreck of a Bolingbroke Mk I, formerly serving with No. 3 Bombing and Gunnery School at MacDonald, Manitoba, from

V6028 sported the contemporary colours of 2 Group, Bomber Command (sky, or duck-egg blue, on all its lower surfaces and with the upper surfaces painted in dark earth and dark green to the official Camouflage Pattern A), to represent the gallant but costly daylight attacks flown by 2 Group during 1940–41. The Blenheim Team's dream came true on 22 May 1987, when, for the first time in over forty years, their impeccably restored Blenheim IV took to the air again.

Disaster struck less than a month later when, due to a grave pilot error, D for Dog crashed on Denham's golf course, a sad end of the world's only airworthy Blenheim. Yet, undaunted by this blow, Warner and his team decided to put a second Blenheim back in the air. Greatly supported by the Blenheim Appeal Fund and the newly formed Blenheim Society, restoration started in January 1988 on a replacement derelict airframe and the engines of Bolingbroke 10201 and on the outer wings of Boly 9703, which had been purchased from Strathallan in Scotland. Five years of

Many Bolingbrokes have formed, or still form, the basis for Blenheim restoration projects around the world. Here depicted are:

Above: **Bolingbroke IV 9040 YO-O of 8 RCAF (BR) Squadron at Seward, Alaska, 1942. Note the spinners on the propellors of this aircraft which completed 682hr 10min of flying in the RCAF before being struck off strength on 6 September 1946.** Lloyd W. Manuel

Below: **Bolingbroke IV 9009 YO-M of 8 RCAF (Bomber Reconnaissance) Squadron being serviced in the outdoors during the severe weather conditions in Alaska during 1942. Clearly visible is the squadron crest, the musk ox, and the motto 'Determined to Defend' on the nose of this aircraft. It was on the RCAF strength between 8 April 1941 and 1 October 1946, completing 582hr 10min of flying.** Lloyd W. Manuel

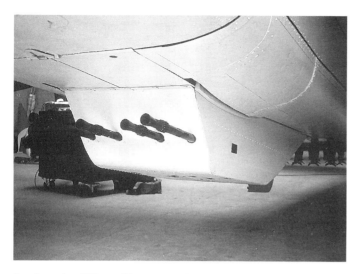

Four Browning .303in machine-gun pack fitted under the bomb bay of L8841 QY-C of 254 Squadron, Duxford, May 1997, in the Blenheim IVF configuration. NBS Aviation

Sliding hatch over the cockpit on L8841. Clearly visible are the bulging observation blisters, and the Venturi tube on the extreme left. Also note the familiar scalloped, asymmetrical shape on the pilot's port side of the nose, to improve his view on take-off and landing. NBS Aviation

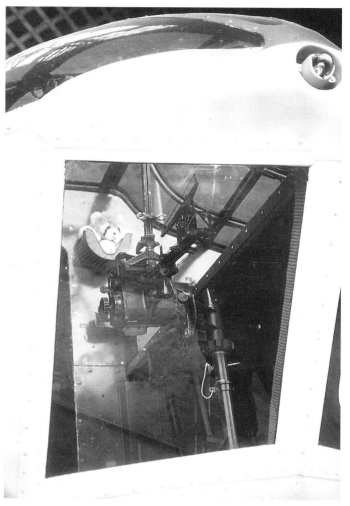

Front close-up with bomb-aiming windows and bomb sight on L8841. Note the cabin fresh-air intake in the right upper corner. NBS Aviation

QY-C's completely rebuilt and functional Bristol B Mk 4 hydraulically-operated retractable dorsal turret with twin Browning .303in machine-guns. NBS Aviation

The pilot's office in L8841, viewed from the entrance hatch. NBS Aviation

Rear view of undercarriage leg detail on L8841. NBS Aviation

painstaking hard work followed, including the building a four-Browning gun-pack and light bomb carriers, which were later fitted to the belly of the aircraft, as in the Mk IVF fighter Blenheim intruder configuration. With the restoration brought to a perfect end in early 1993, it was decided to paint it in the markings of Z5722 WM-Z, flown by Wg Cdr the Hon. Max Aitken, DFC, when he was CO of 68 Squadron. Finished in matt black, it represented the pioneering night-fighting role in which many fighter Blenheims IF and IVF served during 1939–41. The efforts of the Blenheim Team were finally rewarded on 28 May 1993 when Z5722 made its maiden flight. The original aircraft was the second in the final batch of 420 Blenheim

IVs built by A.V. Roe & Co. at Chadderton, being delivered to the Fighter Interception Unit in May 1941. It went on to serve with 600 and 68 Squadrons and was finally written off in a crash on take-off from Coltishall on 6 June 1942.

Starring at numerous official ceremonies and in main air shows all over Europe, where millions of spectators have already been able to witness the wonderful sight and hear the deep roar of a Blenheim, the aircraft will continue to attend these feasts of aviation history. Every few years it will be refinished in a different colour scheme to represent the wide variety of roles in which the Blenheim, Bisley and Bolingbroke served in World War II. After starting out as an all-black night fighter, in

1996 the sky, grey and green colour scheme of Coastal Command was applied and the aircraft was marked L8841 QY-C of 254 Squadron. This unit operated Blenheims IF and IVF in both Fighter and Coastal Commands between November 1939 and September 1942. The original L8841 was built by Rootes Securities in late 1939, and served with 233, 254 and 404 (RCAF) Squadrons, finally being struck off charge on 15 October 1944. In the future other schemes will follow, such as the light and dark brown desert colours of the Western Desert units. With her sleek and yet warlike lines gracing the sky, the Spirit of the Blenheim and the memory of its gallant crews will thus be kept alive into the next century.

Above: **Pilot's instrument panel and flying controls in L8841. Note the open forward hatch.** NBS Aviation

Left: **Close-up of the engine and propellor controls, and trim wheels on the centre console to the pilot's right-hand side.** NBS Aviation

Right: **Centre-section with wing spar, facing forward, in L8841. On the left-hand side are the bomb winch, hydraulics and electrical lines.** NBS Aviation

Rear fuselage interior of L8841 with the Bolingbroke radio operator's seat forward of the gun turret, and lowered turret gunner's seat. NBS Aviation

Interior shot of QY-C looking aft, showing the mid fuselage section with wing spar, and rear fuselage with the gun turret. Note the meter on the left, installed for display flying, and the bomb winch, hydraulic and electrical lines on the right. NBS Aviation

Experiences

Several particularly interesting accounts from Blenheim aircrew could not be included in the relevant chapters because their length would have unbalanced those chapters. Three such accounts are presented here.

'PER ARDUA AD ASTRA AD TERRA FIRMA'

...by Plt Off Paddy Quirke, an 18 year old pilot with 107 Squadron. Paddy and his crew of Sgts D.C. Hawkins (observer) and K.E. Murray (W.Op/AG), had been posted from the Aircrew Pool at West Raynham to 107 Squadron at Wattisham on 23 June 1940. Quirke describes their first – and last – Blenheim operation, on 30 June 1940:

Fortunately for me, a chum from FTS (Flying Training School) days, Plt Off Tony Vinson, was already in my squadron and I was introduced without delay to all the best 'Locals', notably the 'Pig' in Ipswich, where we were able to forget for a while that the average 'life expectancy' at the time was just two weeks.

This was the era of daylight raids, but luckily for me, I thought, the powers that be had just decided that such raids were far too costly and that in future raids would only be carried out if there was adequate cloud cover; failing this, with a fighter escort.

As fate decreed, the whole week I spent at Wattisham was memorable in that the sun shone all day and every day from a cloudless sky. This period of waiting was no good for morale and at the end of the week it was decided that, cloud or no cloud, into action we must go. So it came to pass that on the Sunday morning, instead of being bound for church, I was on my first op, experiencing feelings of excitement tinged with apprehension and wondering what my gallant crew must be thinking in the hands of this totally inexperienced boy skipper. Concentrating on taking off in formation with all the complexity of cockpit drill, gills closed, flaps down, fine pitch, hot air, full boost, watch speed, undercarriage up, etc., soon put these thoughts out of my mind.

This was the real thing at last, our target was, for me, some unknown airfield in France called Merville, where we were to drop our four 250lb bombs on some enemy aircraft our Intelligence had reported as being present in large numbers. Since we were flying in formation, I only had to keep station on the left of my section leader. My memories are of circling over some airfield in the south of England at about 10,000ft, waiting to pick up our fighter escort before heading off across the Channel.

Shortly after reaching the coast of France, my section leader started veering off at a tangent to the direction of the rest of the squadron. Yours not to reason why, at the time, but subsequently I have sometimes wondered whether we had been detailed to act as a decoy to draw fighters from the main body of the raid. If this was the intention it worked, but at a cost. It was not long before I heard a shout from my air gunner on the intercom 'Fighters above left!' and quickly glancing in that direction, I saw four 109s looking as though they were about to pounce on us. Horror of horrors, the worst had happened, heart in mouth, cold sweat etc., there we were, just the three of us, no cloud cover, no fighter escort. I knew from conversations in the Mess that 109s were what everyone feared most.

It was then that I saw our section leader calmly putting on his tin hat. This looked ominous indeed. Sure enough the tracer soon started to overtake us, passing lazily by, and at the same time I was aware of the sinister sound and smell of machine-gun fire of my air gunner who was having a go at the attackers. In this situation the tactic was to close ranks in order, in theory, to concentrate our fire power. In actuality we were virtually sitting ducks, all bunched together, waiting to be picked off in turn. Even with full boost, the German fighters were able to make rings around us, approaching from behind, firing a burst and then circling round time and again one after the other.

As the pilot I was unable to see what was going on in the rear but every so often I would catch sight of a 109 passing by on one side or the other after having fired a burst at us. It was about this time that the awful realisation suddenly hit me that these chaps were trying to kill me. There was no way in which I could use the forward mounted gun by way of defence or retaliation. There was nothing for it but to press on regardless. Minutes later I saw smoke and flames starting to pour from the port engine of my opposite number's plane which then started to drop back, losing height and finally disappearing from sight. [Blenheim R3823, Plt Off R.H.M. Bennett (pilot), Sgt A.B. Langford (observer) and Sgt D.S. Harrison (W.Op/AG), all killed when their aircraft crashed at Wittes, 14 kms SE of St Omer, France, and buried in Wittes Churchyard].

All the time tracer was whistling by, little silvery specks, looking quite harmless. I was very glad of the armour plate at my back which seemed to provide protection from the bullets I could hear cracking through the fuselage and tailplane, jerking the control column in my hands. Who goes next I wondered? Must keep in tight formation, why are we on our own? Where is the fighter escort and the rest of the squadron? All these thoughts crowded through my mind.

We still seemed to be heading towards our target, and at full boost, how much longer the engines would stand it was anyone's guess, bearing in mind one's instructions not to exceed five minutes through the gate at a stretch. However I did not have long to worry about this aspect of the situation because almost immediately I saw my section leader in trouble with his port engine on fire. This as far as I was concerned was a signal to go it alone. [Blenheim R3870, Sqn Ldr H. Pilling AFC (Pilot), KIA; Sgt F.A.S. Roche (observer), POW, and Sgt H.T. Denison (W.Op/AG), KIA. R3870 crashed at Ecques, 9 kms SSE of St Omer, France].

At that moment the starboard engine spluttered and coughed just as I half rolled the plane and with the stick back made for the deck in a vertical dive, hotly pursued by a 109. It was not until I tried to pull out and nothing seemed to be happening that I realised that the tail must have been shot up. We were heading straight for a wooded area. I was aware of my observer instinctively raising his arm to shield his face from the impending impact. Miraculously we came out of the dive, just clearing some trees but severing some telephone wires, before flopping down in a convenient field where we slithered to a halt with turf spewing through the floor of the nose and splattering the cockpit and crew.

Other than a bruised hip, sustained by my air gunner who had fallen out of his turret into the well of the plane during all the excitement, and a slight cut on my nose, as a crew we were virtually unhurt. We needed no encouragement to abandon ship – the crash had actuated the

Above: **A brand new Blenheim IV has just arrived with 82 Squadron, probably as a replacement aircraft after the Gembloux debacle on 17 May 1940.** Coll. Paul Lincoln

Right:. **N6192 of 107 Squadron, here depicted at Wattisham shortly before the outbreak of war, was shot down at Marck (Pas de Calais) during a raid on troop concentrations near St Omer on 27 May 1940, with Sgt H. Warman and his crew all being lost without a trace. On the same raid, Wg Cdr Basil Embry, DSO, AFC, 107's CO, was shot down in L9391.** Coll. Blenheim Society

fuel jettison valves and high octane was pouring out from both wing tanks, soaking the ground all around the plane.

No sooner were we out of the plane than back the victor came, spraying bullets all around us and making us dive for cover in a most unseemingly fashion. We decided he must have run out of ammunition for he soon made off and left us to carry out a most vital task, namely, to destroy our aircraft since we had landed in enemy territory.

As luck would have it we had been spared a conflagration but now there was nothing for it but to follow the procedure laid down. This entailed extracting the Verey pistol from its mounting in a tube used for signalling purposes and using it as an incendiary device. For some reason I had great difficulty in releasing the pistol and eventually had to chop it out with the small axe provided for an emergency of, I felt sure, a different nature.

Having thus obtained the pistol and armed with the five rounds provided, I told my crew to keep well away while, from what I hoped was a

safe distance, I took a pot shot at the fuel-soaked ground surrounding the aircraft. Four times I fired, setting fire to an adjacent cornfield and the surrounding foliage. With my last cartridge there was nothing for it but to shoot at point blank range. Expecting to be incinerated or blown to kingdom come, I fired the last shot from a position where I could not possibly miss and immediately took to my heels as though my life depended on it, which I thought it did. In fact nothing dramatic happened, the fuel started to burn quite gently and the fire spread surprisingly slowly until all was alight and the ammunition was crackling and popping like some giant firework.

It was then that I suddenly remembered that the bombs were still on board and might therefore explode at any minute. There was no reason to hang about, the plane was well alight and of no possible use to the enemy, besides, the thought of those bombs, although only 250s, was enough to make even my air gunner with his gammy hip, take off at a rate of knots to what we hoped was a safe distance.

My last memories of No. L9467 were of a large explosion followed by an enormous perfect smoke ring ascending slowly into a cloudless sky, above what to all appearances was a tranquil and serene countryside basking in the heat of a midsummer day. The reality was that from

Above: **Blenheim R3594 'D' was one of the few Blenheims that survived the Battles of France and Britain. It served with 57, XV, and 114 Squadrons, finally to be destroyed in a crash after flying into a tree on final approach to Oulton on 27 November 1940. Wg Crd J. Cox, CO of XV Squadron and his crew of Plt Off Philip Camp (on right) and Sgt V.F.E. Treherne, DFM, (on left) are about to board 'D' for Dog in the second half of September 1940 for a raid on shipping in Ostend.** Coll. Philip Camp

our position on the edge of a large cornfield we could see the German search parties spread out across the flat countryside, obviously intent on our capture. My air gunner with his handicap very nobly suggested that we leave him by running for it ahead of the patrols. Quite wrongly we opted to stay together and, as a result we were picked up shortly afterwards. For us the war was over – but that is another story.

The average age of my crew was 19. Pilot, 18; observer, 19; W.Op/AG, 20. The Germans thought we must be scraping the barrel. I suppose in a way we were, they were desperate days, but we were rolling out the barrel. Two lessons to be learnt: 1. Practice shooting with a Verey pistol. 2. Escape before being captured.

'NIGHT FLIGHT TO MALTA'

...by Sgt James Dunnet, observer with 57 Squadron. In mid-September 1940, three 57 Squadron Blenheims were selected for ferrying to Malta. Navigation in 1940 consisted of drawing on a map a line between base and destination, and using a hand held mechanical computer to work out the triangle of velocities from the vectors of air speed and course, track and ground speed and direction. There were no facilities in the Blenheim for such refinements as astro navigation. Very accurate navigation though was required on the long ferry flight to find the small island of Malta – especially for the Blenheim IV with its limited range of 1,460 miles. James Dunnet crewed up with Plt Off Richard 'Herby' Herbert and Sgt Bill 'Jock' Young, and after long range petrol endurance tests, set out in the late hours of 24 September for the long flight over France to Malta:

In the art of flying, there is a calculated position on the flight path, known as 'the point of no return'. It is the time on the flight when a decision has to be made to continue or to return to base, flight times being exactly equal. The factors involved in the problem are considerable: weather conditions, aircraft performance, petrol consumption, and in wartime, the chance of fighter interception. Once the decision has been taken to go on from that critical point, there can be no turning back.... There is however, another 'point of no return' – the moment of self realisation in the individual psyche. A famous composer once explained how there was one point – the *crise* as he termed it – in classical music, where all the individual notes must express their meaning into a revelation of Truth behind the creation. Unless this climax was reached, the artistic conception was lost, dissolved into unfulfilled nothingness. In later years, I was to discover in the esoteric doctrines of the East, that this *crise* is also known and understood. Many are the Paths leading ultimately to the same destination, and one such Path I was to discover during a wartime flight from England to Malta.

Of the subsequent personal 'crise' of that night, there was no hint as I drew track lines on the maps and charts, and calculated our point of no return. We were one of three Blenheim Mark IV bombers of No. 57 Squadron, due to be ferried as much-needed replacements to the Middle East. We left our base at Thorney Island around midnight, on a dismal night in September 1940, and as we bumped and jolted in the blackness of the truck taking us out over the drome to the dispersed aircraft, a kaleidoscope of recent scenes came whirling through my mind ... the last toast of success to our trip. 'Herby', Frankie, Jock, Johnny, all seated beside me now. The raised glasses, smiling confident faces, what were their thoughts now. No one spoke in the swaying night ... the Wing Commander wishing all success, the Met man rushing in with a last weather chart ... what would everyone at home be doing now – sleeping of course, they had no idea that we were taking off tonight. The little fireside group of the family, a drowsy peke with just the tip of its pink tongue sticking out, how long would it be before I saw home again. I'd had forty-eight hours leave, a hasty farewell, then I was in the air again, test flight after test flight, up and down the Welsh coast to check the ultimate endurance of our aircraft. Could the Blenheim make the long haul to Malta?

Finally everything was ready, inspection certificates signed up. With brimming tanks, there would be just enough fuel to take us to Malta at the most economical cruising speed. Only three Blenheims were to go from the squadron, the three that had proved the best petrol consumption. Each aeroplane carried urgently required spares and stores for Malta. No extra fuel tanks were fitted. If they could not take off tonight, then none of the crews would go. It was September, the weather was getting worse, the moon was on the wane, hardly visible. It had to be tonight, or a long wait for the next opportunity.

'OK, Frankie, your kite'; the truck halted alongside a dark outline. Overcoated ground crews moving covers away, cursing as a knot stuck.... 'Good luck chaps, see you at Malta....' The truck rumbled a short distance. Johnny and his crew clambered down, lugged their kit out. 'Bet we get there first,' my air gunner yelled. 'OK, a quid on it; good luck,' a dim receding figure called back, and then it was our turn. The small suitcase I had with me held the regulation twenty pounds, no more. We were careful with the thought of our fuel endurance assuming top priority. I looked around and shivered. A black night, a thin watery moon hung dismally overhead. 'OK?' asked Herby, my pilot, a small slight-looking youngster. He was twenty, the same age as myself. Jock (Bill) Young was the baby at nineteen, but we had already lived through a year of wartime flying, and we thought we were the best! 'Fine, let's go!', I grinned back at him, and climbed up the wing into the cockpit. The spluttering of starting engines broke through the night, then a bellowing roar as the other two aircraft revved up. Concentration was now focussed on the preparatory details before take off. I had a rolled pile of maps to organise in the cramped

Sgt James Dunnet, observer, poses with a 57 Squadron Blenheim at either Wyton or Lossiemouth in 1940.
Coll. James Dunnet

cockpit together with navigation computer, pencils, rulers, and all the other impedimenta of a wartime navigator.

The engines deafened me as they were opened out, I drew the helmet tight about my ears, the bluish flame of the exhausts held my gaze as we moved out ... couldn't see anything in the pitch blackness of a wartime aerodrome ... the other planes? Probably taken off ... the tail swung round, a faint row of blue dots stretching in front of us. Ahead, a green light winked out, the Bristol Mercury engines suddenly screamed into full power ... tail up ... the blue dots of subdued runway lights streaming past merged into a thin line. Were we never going to get off the deck? The blue line came to an abrupt end, the wheels bounced ... up, steady, a slight sinking feeling as the undercarriage was retracted, some-

The port undercarriage failed to lock down on this 57 Squadron Blenheim, in the summer of 1940, which resulted in a bent propellor. Coll. James Dunnet

thing flashed beneath the wing tip ... good show, just cleared the hangers!

Out over the Channel, we climbed steadily on course. It seemed to be a bit lighter up here, cloud in front. Above them everything seemed so remote, a feeling of being utterly alone, the other two members of the crew might have been disembodied hosts. The purring engines lulled a sleepy satisfaction. It was beginning to get cold. I wriggled deeper into my Irvin jacket. Ah! The French coast, Le Havre down there through a gap in the thick cumulus, someone was bombing hell out of the place, the searchlights were furious, groping and wavering like giant antennae ... a beam of bluish light swung past our tail, little angry red splashes dotted the night .... we continued steadily on our course for Malta.

Now, there was an unbroken mass of fleecy cloud ahead. Cumulus, stretching away to the horizon. Didn't look too good. The air was getting a bit bumpy. Herby eased the stick back, but the cold greyness climbed with us, to enfold us for a second, then to break away in nebulous wisps ... soon there was only the enveloping cloud, no gaps to be seen. We flew on and hoped.

This was nothing like the forecast that the Met. briefing had so confidently given us. 'Nothing in your way except a run out Cold Front which is over the Marseilles area, and will be no trouble to you.' The Met. man's voice echoed in my ears; I recalled with a grin, an old line shoot piece of aircrew humour ... 'there we were, upside down, in a cloud, and nothing on the clock!'... I glanced back at my pilot. His face was tense, set. He said nothing, concentrating on throttle settings, mixture control and trim.

Then we were enveloped in wet clammy murk smothering us in its clinging folds. Instruments! A dozen of them to focus the attention. Herby's face looked strained. I knew that he was determined to press on and not turn back.... We tried to climb up out of the turbulent mass. Still the everlasting greyness.

Then the storm came, as we knew it would, and with the lashing rain, soft slushy ice which quickly formed and slid away. The Blenheim shuddered and jolted, my navigation instruments were picked up by invisible hands and hurled into awkward corners, dribbles of water oozed through the roof and fell on my frustrated face. My roll of carefully prepared maps were soon a soggy mess on the lurching floor. I looked out at inky blackness. We were alone, the three of us against the sound and fury of the elements. Worse was to come. We were to encounter all the brilliant fireworks of an electrical thunderstorm, the most dangerous phenomenon an aviator can meet.

A sizzling sheet of concentrated fury suddenly lit up the scene with face-blanching power. The Blenheim whirled and bucked upwards, a wing sliced earthwards and we fell through space to end with a spine-snapping jerk like a puppet pulled up abruptly on its strings. The safety straps tightened on my knees as my head shot towards the roof, the whirling rain whipped savagely at the perspex. A flickering bluish flame licked around the outlines of the plane. Fascinated, I stared out of the perspex nose. The rain streaming from the front of the cockpit came darting at me like points of multicoloured fire. It looked for all the world as if we were heading into a concentrated burst of tracer. I could only stare in a sort of hypnotised horror at this dazzling exhibition of the raw power of Nature. All the loose paraphernalia in the cockpit danced madly for a moment in mid air, then clattered and bounced from my navigation table to the sodden floor. I made a frantic grab at my computer as the negative 'G' forces floated it into space, and abandoned it for a muscle-wrenching grab at a bulkhead as my stomach tore downwards against the next violent upthrusting rush to the sky. Herby was wrestling with the stick and throttle controls, his face dead white. With a sickening jolt and lurch, we went into a half spin, then levelled out again for a brief moment. Vivid sheets of lightning illuminated the jet blackness, hissing sleet lashed protesting metal, the crack of thunder exploded above the struggling engines, then ice started to form and build on the wings.

A hoarse voice came through the headphones, 'My aerial has gone,' Jock cried incredulously, 'We've been hit by bloody lightning!' Could three youths and some fragile metal survive against the naked fury of enraged Nature? A great hand suddenly seemed to whisk the plane heavenwards as if it were a small boy's toy ... up ... up ... then with a contemptuous flick threw us back into the raging maelstrom. My teeth bit into my tongue as another vast shaking jerk wrenched the wheel from the pilot's white knuckled hands; a frantic grab, a twist, and everything was under control again, the madly gyrating aircraft shuddered and steadied.

Then the port engine spluttered, coughed harshly, and died. 'Jump,' shouted Herby, fighting the Blenheim from dropping into a spin, 'I can't hold her much longer. Jump ... Jump!' This is it, I thought, and yelled through the mike to Jock, enclosed in his rear gunner's cockpit. There was only the ear splitting crackle of sparking electrics ... had he gone? Grabbing my 'chute, I jumped to my feet, swaying drunkenly on the heaving floor, and yanked the slide roof open. A torrent of water swept into the cockpit, a hasty glance at the speed and height indicators, the altimeter needle spinning rapidly anticlockwise, Herby jerked his head impatiently at me. Jump? Into that? Better make your mind up quick, she was going to spin at any second. I had a flash of intense admiration for the way in which Herby was fighting desperately at the controls, stick hard over to port, then violently over to the other side. My God! To jump into that blackness of elemental rage, the 'chute would be soaked and useless under the weight of water, but it was suicide to remain, falling every second, being whirled and tossed through the skies. The brief moments I stood there, my face lashed with the driving sleet, my eyes hurt with blinding flashes, my ears appalled with the triumphant roar as the heavens tore apart, those split seconds expanded into a form of mystical consciousness. I was witness to a dawn of Creation, the beginning and end of the Universe ... then with a choked, half-drowned roar of protest, the port engine opened up and bellowed defiance to the Gods!

We were in that storm for four hours.

Somewhere south of Marseilles, as the first light steadily tinged the eastern sky a pale pink, I made a facetious entry in my Log: 'Came the Dawn!'. I turned to my pilot, and grinned. He smiled back wanly. Jock's voice came hoarsely through the intercom: 'do you want a bearing?'. Even though it was now bright morning, we had nothing to check our position. We had probably been flown far off our original course. Our compass had likely been affected by the electrical storm, and petrol was running short. We set an approximate course for Malta, radio silence was abandoned, the risk of fighter interception was less than the very real fear of having to ditch in the sea through lack of fuel. Jock, wireless oper-

ator and air gunner, hammered an SOS through the ether, and for QDM's (magnetic bearings) to lead us in.

Soon we were panting with sweat, the hot Mediterranean sun blazed down on us. Our eyes were dry and gritted, and hurt as they looked down on the molten shimmering metal of the sea, intense glowing blue beneath, intense burning blue above. We flew in a sphere of merging sky and sea. The Blenheim was flying magnificently, twin engines purring like a kitten

beside a warm hearth. A glance at the fuel indicator showed enough petrol for an hour and a half, and Malta was at least an hour and a half away.... Bearings were now coming through almost continuously, Malta responded magnificently to our call for help, and had obviously got a good fix on our position. We were heading straight for the island. If only we could keep in the air. What a temptation it was to open the throttles wide and go hell for leather for Malta, but that most certainly would have

In the Mark IV, the Blenheim observer was sitting sideways to the direction of flight, and working at his chart-table in the nose of the aircraft. Depicted is Sgt Philip Camp of XV Squadron in his 'office', sometime in the spring of 1940. Coll. Philip Camp

resulted in a watery grave, the extra power eating up their precious fuel over a few short miles at speed. We would literally have to sit and sweat it out through the unclouded sky, peering ahead, eyes smarting, head throbbing, wood and metal inside the cockpit blistering hot to the touch. 'How far is Malta?' Herby asked in a weary monotone – for the umpteenth time I thought....

Nearly an hour had passed, a quick glance at the fuel dials showed the reason for his query. 'Not far now, not far, only a few miles, we should see it soon, keep her going.' We'll never make it, I thought. Seven and a quarter hours was the maximum endurance laid down for the trip. We had been flying for well over eight now, and the needles of the tanks were flickering at the zero line. Where is that bloody cloud which they told us we would see over Malta, I could see dozens of clouds on the horizon. Thank God, the makers of the Blenheim, Bristol's, had put a safety margin on these tanks, there can only be a trickle of petrol left in them now. A suspicious cough, a faltering beat in the steady engine note ...God! Don't let us down now after coming this far; ah! they picked up again... 'How much farther?' Herby inquired in an angry vexed mood, 'How much farther?'. His clenched hands gripped the control column a bit tighter, juggled some more with the mixture controls, strained eyes lifting from needles now resting limply at the empty mark, to peer ahead as if willing the island to materialise out of the empty blue sea.

Then suddenly, it was there, a high conical hill appeared, a slightly smaller one, brown and scorched, bare looking, a small island off the main one ... yes! it was Malta! I grabbed the mike and howled delightedly to the other two 'Malta, down there, look, look'. Again the engines gave an ominous warning splutter, but we were at ten thousand feet, and Malta was ahead and below. Herby shoved the stick forward with a tired grin, and closed the throttles. We glided down over the white and grey patchwork of Valetta, raced over the sandy parched earth, and with a last dying burst from the valiant Mercurys, lifted over the aerodrome boundary, and rumbled on to the dusty landing field.

We sat very still and quiet in the plane after the props had ceased turning. How had we done it? I looked at my Log. We had been in the air for eight hours and fifty-five minutes, an hour and forty minutes over our estimated maximum endurance! 'I never thought a Blenheim would fly for that long,' said Herby in a nonchalant tone, as he heaved himself stiffly out of the cockpit. 'I wonder where the others are? They don't seem to be here'. Later that day, we waited as the shadows lengthened into the dusk, and knew that Frankie, Dave and all the carefree youths

who had so cheerfully flown away with us into the night, would never see the dawn. Our journey had taken us to the edge of the stars. Their destination had lain somewhere far beyond....

After being posted to 211 Squadron and Greece, 'Herby' Herbert and 'Jock' Young were both killed on 13 April 1941, during the squadron's final operation of the Greek campaign. James Dunnet, on the other hand, completed about 70 operational Blenheim sorties with 57, 211 and 11 Squadrons, plus another nineteen in 8 Squadron as Flight Lieutenant Bombing Leader, and survived the war unscathed. He remained in the RAF with a Permanent Commission, specialising in Armament and Fighter Control until he retired in 1966.

'SHIPPING STRIKE'

...by Flt Sgt Peter Saunders, observer, who had crewed up with Sgt Bill O'Connell RCAF (pilot) and Flg Off Les Harrell (W.Op/AG) at 13 OTU before being posted to 226 Squadron at Wattisham in July 1941. Saunders vividly recounts his crew's first shipping strike, against a convoy off IJmuiden, on 26 August 1941:

It was 8.15hr on an August morning, and the crew room was a hubbub of noise. Not that that, of course, was in itself unusual, only today there seemed more of it. In a corner a portable gramophone, under the jealous guardianship of a boyish-looking Sergeant, gave forth agedly and protestingly the wailing, plaintive voice of Bing Crosby, to the obvious delight of his sponsor, for he was perched alongside, industriously and with the aid of a scrap of emery paper preparing a needle for his next ten inches of rapture. At one end of the long crew-room table a Flight-Lieutenant and a Warrant Officer were playing shove-ha'penny, while a burly, cheerful looking Sergeant looked on and tendered his advice from time to time. On the other end of the table there was a game of *vingt-et-un* in progress, while on a bench in a corner of the room two Flying Officers were quietly playing chess. A few sat reading and some lay just lazing and relaxed in their chairs or on the table, yawning and smoking alternately and watching their smoke rings curl gracefully upwards towards the roof. But for the most part they were talking, noisily in groups or in pairs, talking of anything under the sun – discussing, arguing, reminiscing or merely gossiping. There was a good deal of laughter and joking, fooling and horseplay, and there were high-spirited faces and voices.

There was an air of expectancy, of tension, about it all, for it was 'stand-by'. In the Mess the previous evening, the 'Battle Order' had gone up on the notice-board, and there had been the usual flurry of excitement to see who of us were on it, and to see if we could guess what sort of target it would be, and where. There had been the usual disappointment of new crews, if they found that their names were not on the list, and the customary, good-natured grumbling of the old hands who discovered that they were. Now we were congregated in the crew-room, impatiently hoping for further news, and as we waited we debated all the possibilities and probabilities. It was a short Battle Order, with only six crews named on it, but that of course was no indication to us whether or not it was to be a 'big show', because we were so short of crews and aircraft that we could never muster a large number at any time. What we did know, however, was that we were carrying delay-fused bombs, and that meant only one thing – a low-level attack.

'Shipping it is, I'll bet', said one. 'Might be the docks again at Rotterdam. Just another friendly visit.' 'I've got the target', says a wag. 'We're going to bomb Hitler in his bath at Berchtesgaden!' 'It'll be ships all right', protested Johnny ('Johnny' Onions), this being the first time he had opened his mouth. 'Ships and plenty of them, especially the kind with lots of guns. Wouldn't be my luck to get put on a nice, quiet, peaceful 'do''.

We were accustomed by this time to Johnny's 'grievances'. He bemoaned his lot constantly, and a casual observer might have been shocked into believing that he meant it. In a way I suppose he did, but everyone who knew him knew also that Johnny did his job well and shirked nothing. He was an old hand, a 'regular'; he had good work to his credit on the squadron, and when we talked shop this always ensured him a ready audience, for knowledge drawn from the experience and skill of others is of too great value to be neglected or ignored. It also ensured him an interested, if not always sympathetic, ear to his laments, although they were frequently amusing enough by themselves to merit attention. He grumbled when he was on an 'Op', and he grumbled if he wasn't. In the crew-room, waiting for briefing, we used to remark that Johnny's face was like a barometer of prospects – its expression in inverse ratio to the chances of the 'Op' taking place, or being cancelled. If the weather was fair and the sky clear, Johnny would be sitting like the personification of all glumness. From time to time he would get up from his chair and look out and up at the sky. A small, dark cloud would give him hope; a bank of overcast moving across would

Flt Sgt Peter Saunders, observer with 226 Squadron, 1941-42. Coll. Peter Saunders

start a smile at the corners of his mouth; ten-tenths cloud and rain descending would find Johnny at last looking as happy as a sandboy, a permanent broad grin across his features. He would rise, close one eye, and placing an imaginary telescope to it would state: 'I see no ships!'

For Bill and Les and me the prospect of a shipping attack was exciting. We had been briefed already for three similar sorties; the first had been cancelled before take-off and on the other two occasions we had swept our patrol line but, finding nothing, had returned disappointed. We knew, of course, something of what to expect; we had read all the available Intelligence reports, we had listened to the stories of the crews who had been on previous attacks, and Johnny in particular had rubbed it in with a wealth of alarming detail which made us realise that these raids were by no means picnics. We had trained too, as hard as we had been able, and as often as we could get a machine we had flown down to our dummy-ship range and

there applied all we had learned, practising low-level attacks until we could get hits or near misses with all our bombs. This was Bill's job, for it had been found by experience that the pilot could in this form of attack bomb more accurately and easily than the observer. No bomb-sight was used; we would approach at nearly ground level, and the pilot would judge the time of release of the bombs a split second before the target shot beneath us. We tried to make these practices as realistic as we could imagine them to be, taking evasive action and flying as low as we could all the time. Bill's bombing became more and more accurate, and we felt that we had prepared ourselves reasonably well for the real thing. But the real thing, we knew, would be very different.

It was just on ten when the door opened and the Wing Commander (Wg Cdr V.S. 'Buttles' Butler, KIA 8 March 1942 whilst leading a low level daylight raid against the Ford Motor Works at Matford, near Paris, in Boston Z2209) came in. He was a big man, tall and heavily

Bill O'Connell, Saunders' Canadian pilot with 226 Squadron during 1941-42. He is here depicted posing in front of Mosquito 'P' of 21 Squadron in late 1943, as Sqn Ldr, and decorated with the DFC. Coll. Bill O'Connell

built, with an amiable looseness about him and an air of boyish diffidence which was misleading because it hid a directness which could be at times startlingly blunt. As he walked in there was a sudden and expectant quiet: the murmur of voices died away, the laughter was hushed, and Bing Crosby, with cruel abruptness, forgot his dream about the lady with the light brown hair. 'Briefing will be at quarter past ten', said the C.O. 'All crews not on the Battle Order outside please'. Then with a grinning: 'Don't forget your tin hats, chaps', he turned and went into the Navigation Room.

At 10.14hr and a half Johnny climbed on to

his chair and gave one last despairing look at the sky. 'Not one single little cloud', he announced. 'We've had it this time, all right.' The Wing Commander returned, followed by the other briefing officers – Navigation, 'Met', Armament, Intelligence and Signals. We took our places around the table and the briefing commenced. 'Settle down, lads', began the Wingco. 'As you've probably guessed, today's effort is going to be a shipping sweep off the Dutch coast. You will set course, Base to Sheringham, Sheringham to Position A here on the map – that is 330 degrees IJmuiden eight miles – and then beat down the patrol line to Position B.

With a bit of luck you should find a medium-sized convoy just about the start of your beat. It should be steaming south, speed about eight knots. Number of ships uncertain, but it'll probably be well escorted. If you find it each man will pick his own ship and go right in. You know the rest. Keep as low as you can; come round behind after you have attacked and pick up formation again as soon as you get out of range. Then come straight back. You won't have any fighter escort. OK. George.' And he handed over to the Navigation Officer.

Step by step the briefing proceeded; all the necessary aspects were thoroughly covered. The

1941 Coastal Raider. This 53 Squadron Blenheim IV at St Eval has the perspex cupola removed from its gun turret. Note the small bomb racks beneath the fuselage. Coll. Peter Cundy

Wing Commander looked at his watch. 'It is now ten fifty three and a half', he said. 'Into aircraft eleven twenty, start up engines eleven twenty-five, take-off eleven-thirty. You will set course at eleven thirty-seven. Give 'em a bang, boys! All the best.'

As we filed out of the crew-room and into the bus which was waiting to take us to the dispersal points, we felt the usual curious mixture of emotions. Everyone was talking and laughing and seemingly gay. New hands, like Bill, Les and myself, were either gayer or quieter than the rest, for all this was still so much a novelty to us and we were keyed up to the highest

pitch of tension and excitement. We felt at the same time elation and apprehension; we were aware of our 'greenness' and we desperately wanted to acquit ourselves well. The ground crew was waiting for us as we reached our aircraft, A for Apple. 'Think you could hit a ship, Bill?', I asked. 'You find it – I'll hit it!' he rejoined, and climbed aboard.

At 11.24hr the stillness of the air was shattered by the roar of the engines of F for Freddy bursting into life, and one by one the others followed suit. With engines spurting and brakes squealing intermittently the six Blenheims moved slowly round the field and

turned, ready to take off. At 11.30hr to the minute, F for Freddy, with a thunderous surge of its engines, started to move across the grass, slowly at first but gathering speed until it rose gently and gracefully into the air. The rest of us followed in quick succession, and soon we were getting into formation for the flight. Ken, our Northern Irish Flight Commander (S/Ldr. J. Shaw Kennedy) was leading in F for Freddy; Johnny was Number One in the second 'Vic' of three, we were his Number Two and Smithy (who had joined the squadron only a week or two before ourselves) was pilot of Number Three. At 11.37hr Ken turned us over the flying-field and we set course for Sheringham. The countryside beneath us looked so quiet and peaceful that it was difficult to believe that we were setting forth upon a mission of destruction, and I remember feeling lonely and a little disappointed because while we were going out, keyed-up and grimly eager, the people below were going heedlessly and blissfully about their jobs, unaware of whither we were going, or why. They looked small and unimportant – yet this was England, these hamlets and homesteads – this was home, and it was lonely to watch it nestling there, happy and warm and green, as we sped over it and away. But at the same time I felt that we were privileged.

Soon we saw Sheringham ahead of us and, beyond, the unbroken greyness of the North Sea stretching out to the distant skyline. I caught a glimpse of the Market Square, of quiet streets and of trim houses as we roared overhead, then the next moment we were over the cliffs and the sea was beneath us. 'Have a good look, Les', I called out over the intercom. 'We might like to see that place coming back.' 'Don't worry', he gave back. 'I won't miss it. We'll drop in for a pint on the way home!'

We crossed the North Sea at about thirty feet. Ken held the course and the rest of us kept with him in formation, a distance of one and a half to two spans between each aircraft. We could see Johnny, alongside on the left and slightly in front of us, looking mournful but grim, while behind in his gun-turret Butch, his air gunner, kept grinning at us and making rude but unintelligible grimaces and gestures. I decided I wanted a smoke, and consoled myself with a fresh tablet of chewing gum. It was always thrilling flying so low over the sea and in such tight formation, but the sea itself became monotonous, unbroken anywhere except for the white horses and misty spray. It almost lulled one into believing that this was the end of the world, or like the land of the Lotus Eaters, remote from everyone and everything, where quiet dulled the senses to danger. It seemed

'We could see the ships now. There were about eight of them, heavily laden and low in the water, in the middle of the convoy. In front and behind and on the seaward flank were dotted the protecting escort vessels.' Coll. Art Edwards

impossible that this desolate peacefulness might be suddenly shattered, that we might shatter it ourselves at sight or sign of quarry. I gave myself a pinch and scanned the horizon for tell-tale smudge or smoke. 'See anything, Pete?' enquired Bill. 'Not a sausage.' He motioned upwards at the sky with his thumb. 'No 'Huns-in-the-sun' either. Jerry must be having a half holiday.'

We were within a few minutes of Position A, the start of our patrol line, and so far we had seen no sign of either ships (which we were looking for) or scouting enemy fighters (who might be looking for us). The flatness and disappointment of our two previous shipping sorties – when we had returned without having seen a thing – was beginning to descend upon

us. I looked at my watch. 'We're due to turn in two minutes' time', I told Bill. 'Looks like being another blank'. 'Yeah. All this goddamned way for nothing'. Raising an imaginary telescope to one eye, he mimicked Johnny: 'I see no ships. I see no ship...'. He broke off suddenly. 'Look, Pete, look! To starboard! No, there, there! They are ships, by God!'

I looked where he was pointing, excitedly. A cluster of faint but unmistakable wisps of smoke were rising above the horizon. It was a convoy all right, although we were too far away as yet to be able to see the ships themselves. Ken had seen it as well, for he had shot ahead, turned slightly to starboard and was now streaking low across the water in the direction of the rising smoke. We followed suit. There was a new note

of urgency, of exhilaration in the roar of the engines as the throttles were thrust forward. The blood pounded through my veins and I drew a deep breath to take hold of my excitement. The sea rushed past beneath us like a grey, weaving film. The hunt was on.

We could see the ships now. There were about eight of them, heavily laden and low in the water, in the middle of the convoy. In front and behind and on the seaward flank were dotted the protecting escort vessels. They were steaming along slowly and apparently unaware of our approach, feeling secure no doubt in their closeness to the shore and to the defences of the port of IJmuiden, which we could see two miles or so the other side of the convoy. I marked the convoy's position on my chart and noted the time in my log. Then I loosened the stowage ring on my Vickers, clamped a pan of ammunition on top of the breech, and swung the gun down ready for use. We buckled on our steel helmets. I called to Les: 'Don't forget the Leica. Try and take an exposure just after we've bombed'. 'Don't worry', he replied. 'I'll get you a Candid Camera snapshot. I hope I can get in a squirt with my guns as well.' 'Go for the flak ships, Les,' warned Bill. 'They're the bastards to watch.'

Ken waggled his wings sharply and we opened out to nearly line abreast. There was little more than a mile to go. Ahead the water spouted up jaggedly; minute stabs of orange showed on the deck of the nearest vessel. 'They've spotted us!' yelled Bill, and the next moment tracer was flying past us and spouting into the sea all round. We jinked madly through it. They were getting our range; the tracer was coning us and above the sound of the engines we could hear bullets dully punching their way into the aircraft. I pulled my tin hat forward and snapped the catch of my gun to 'fire'. Less than half a mile to go. The ships were looming large now – big black hulks which rocked and towered drunkenly as Bill wrenched and kicked at the controls to fling A for Apple through the searing, twisting coils of flak.

'We'll take that big bastard', he yelled and threw the aircraft in its direction. We beat Johnny by a second. We saw him twist and head alongside us, then he side-slipped and aimed himself for the vessel on its left. 'Give 'em hell, Bill!' I shouted, and grabbed the Vickers. As I pulled it into my cheek to take aim I saw a flash to my right. Smithy's port engine was on fire and black smoke was belching from it. I fired into the flashes from a flak ship ahead, then next moment the whole horizon tilted and it was out of my sights. I saw Smithy's port engine a mass of fire; it was a huge orange glow and flames were leaping along the wing. He was holding her straight and going right in.

We lurched sickeningly. Bill pulled her straight, and there was nothing in front of us now but the black, solid mass of our ship. They were firing right into us; stabs of flame were spitting from the deck and we felt bullets slapping and splintering all over the aircraft. I could see men clustered round the guns – tensed, labour-ing figures in blue trousers and singlets. I swung the Vickers round and fired. The tracers leapt forward; I clamped my second hand on the butt and held it on the nearest turret. I saw some of the figures falling and one leap jerkily into the sea, then next moment the rails and masts and funnel were rushing at us. They hovered menacingly, and then we were up and over and diving for the water on the other side.

We were still jinking violently. I heard Les' twin Brownings take up the rattle. He was getting in his 'squirt'. Then they fell silent. We were turning. I craned round but the port wing still blocked my view. Then: 'Bloody fine!', roared Les. 'You've got her! She's going up. Oh, lovely! You've got her, Bill!' He was jubilant. 'Try and get a photograph', Bill called back. Hardly had he spoken when there was a violent, grating crump right underneath us. The whole airframe trembled and shook violently, and the nose gave a sickening downward lurch. The sea

This photo symbolises the dreaded 1941 shipping strikes. In mid-afternoon on 16 June 1941, Blenheim V6034 'D' of 21 Squadron clipped the mast of its target ship, a 'squealer' off Borkum, losing half of the outer wing section and crashing into the North Sea seconds later. Flt Sgt Reg Leavers DFM and his crew, who were on the last op of their first tour, all perished. Coll. Jim Langston

They Went In Low. A hand-held Leica shot taken by a Blenheim W.Op/AG during a strike on a six-ship convoy in the Heligoland Bight on 30 July 1941. Coll. Don Bruce

was terrifyingly near. Bill righted her and his face looked tense and grim. 'Christ! That one was close.' I drew my fingers across my forehead and found beads of sweat.

'Look', he said, and pointed. The coastal guns were firing now. We were caught between them and the convoy, and we still had a mile or more to fly before we were through the gauntlet and safe to turn for home. I could see our ship now and I yelled to Bill to look. She was broken in the middle. Her stern was low and her bows jutted crazily out of the water. A pall of smoke and steam was rising from her. 'You certainly hit her, Bill', I said.

'She'll be under soon.' I felt very happy.

Bill was calling Les. 'I want to know if he got a photograph', he explained, 'but he doesn't answer'. 'Hullo, Les. Hullo, Les', I tried. There was no reply. 'He might be hurt', called Bill. 'Go through and see, Pete'. I removed my parachute harness and steel helmet and loosened the pin on the bulkhead plating behind the pilot's seat. The plating hinged down and I tried to squeeze through the space. It was too small, so I took off my Mae West and this time succeeded in wriggling through head first into the well of the aircraft. Crawling over the dinghy I came out into the space forward of the turret, and there I

found Les. His helmet was off and he was lying against the step. His face was drawn and deadly white, but when he saw me the glimmer of a smile came on his face and he raised his thumb in the old way. 'We pranged it.' I gave him back the 'thumbs-up' and nodded. 'Where did it get you, Les?', but I knew already. There was a jagged hole behind the turret where the cannon shell had entered; the turret pillar was twisted and the metal showed gashed and bent. There was a sickening smell of cordite and oil and blood. I looked at Les. His right flying boot was a wet, red pulp. A hole showed where the metal had gone in behind his ankle; it had come out through his calf on the other side, and the lamb-skin lining of his boot gaped crimson and matted. He was bleeding badly. I took out my sheath

'Crawling over the dinghy I came out into the space forward of the turret, and there I found Les. His helmet was off and he was lying against the step. His face was drawn and deadly white, but when he saw me the glimmer of a smile came on his face and he raised his thumb in the old way.' The gun turret interior in a Blenheim IV, taken from the catwalk. Coll. Ken Whittle

knife and started to cut away his boot, but the blade was too long and he winced involuntarily. He was saying something and I took off my flying helmet to hear. 'The hydraulic pipes are gone. Tell Bill to shut off the turret supply – he might be able to save the juice.'

I crawled through to Bill and told him. 'O.K.', he nodded. 'How is Les?' 'Through the leg.' 'Bad?' 'Pretty bad, but I think he'll be all-right.' 'Fix him up, Pete.' 'I will. Have you got a sharp pocket knife?' He found one and passed it to me. I collected the first-aid kit and my Mae West and crawled back to Les. Then I put the Mae West under his leg, in order to cushion it from the vibration of the aircraft, and carefully cut off his flying boot. His leg looked ghastly; I could do nothing to dress it properly, so I padded it loosely with gauze and cotton wool. There was a great pool of blood on the bottom of the well, and I knew that he would not be able to stand the loss of much more, so

I gave him a shot of morphia and put a tourniquet on his leg just behind the knee. It was quiet now, except for the steady beat of the engines. I had no idea where we were, for I could see nothing from the well, but we must have got safely away and headed for home. It was comforting to see Bill's back through the space in front. He looked solid and confident. I went forward to check our course.

'It's O.K.' Bill said. 'I can see the others in front – I'll follow them.' 'Will we make it?' 'I hope so', he grinned, 'provided the 109s don't catch us up. I saw some milling around just before we turned. The engines seem OK. How's Les?' 'Must be having plenty of pain, 'though you'd never know. He hasn't said a word. I've given him some morphia – that should help.' 'Good.' 'I'll go back and stay with him.' 'OK. I can cope here.'

Les was still conscious when I got back and his face was hard with pain. 'How do you feel,

Les?' I asked. 'It's OK. I didn't … get the photograph.' 'That's all right, Les. Don't worry about that.' 'I caught this, when I was trying to get it.' 'Yes. Now take it easy. Rest as much as you can.' The morphia didn't seem to be dulling his pain, so I broke another ampoule in my fingers and gave him it. I kept the tourniquet on for about fifteen or twenty minutes at a time and loosened it in between. The bleeding was much slower. The second shot of morphia, too, was taking effect: Les was looking more comfortable and his eyes were closed.

We were beginning to climb. I felt it and momentarily wondered what was happening. Then it came to me and I knew gratefully what it was – the coast of England must be in sight! I clambered up into the turret and looked forward. About two miles in front of us stretched an unbroken line of white. It was the sea washing on the coastline, and behind and beyond rose the gentle cliffs in green and gold. And there to starboard, warm and friendly, was Cromer! I looked along the coast to the south-east and saw Sheringham. There were the same sleepy, trim houses and quiet streets. There was no clamour, nothing was changed, but it was welcoming us back.

I went below. Les was lying quietly, his eyes open. This time I gave 'thumbs-up' to him. He grinned wearily but gamely; I think he knew what I was telling him. In twenty-five more minutes we should be home. The engines were singing now. The air felt different and the sky above looked warm and friendly. I went forward to Bill. 'How's the pressure?' 'I couldn't say. I'll test it shortly. We'll make it.'

I made my way back to Les and loosened his tourniquet. The bleeding was almost stopped now but his leg lay weak and limp. I lifted the dinghy and laid it against the step of the well; then I placed our parachutes on top and gently moved Les across against the pile, so that it would soften the landing for him. He was very weak. Bill was trying to attract my attention. I looked forward and saw him make a motion with the flat of his hand. I knew what he was indicating: the pressure was too low and he

could not get the undercarriage down. We should have to make a belly landing.

We must be over base now; we were turning and losing height. Bill fired a warning Verey signal, the 'Colours of the Day', and I thought of the figures who would be down there below on the flying field, watching us anxiously and waiting. I put my arms beneath Les' shoulders and braced my back against the dinghy. I could not see a thing, but I knew from the sound of the engines that we were on our final approach. The tension was agonising. We were gliding in now; the motors were almost silent, and I waited for the ground to hit. We touched – more gently than I had feared: there was a sudden, jarring shock and then Bill throttled quickly forward – in order to cushion the impact – and we were sliding smoothly along the ground. It was beautifully done.

I threw open the hatch, and as I climbed out the Station Commander was alongside in his car. He was out in a flash and running towards us. 'Are you

all right?' 'Air gunner's wounded, sir.' An ambulance was there as I spoke and the Doc. was out before it had stopped. 'The air gunner', said the Group Captain briefly, and the Doc. was climbing up before he had finished speaking. I went up after him. Les' face was drawn again and white with pain. He opened his eyes and smiled wearily. 'Doc', he said, 'I hope you've got my size in wooden ones.'

After many months in hospital, Flg Off Harrell took his honourable discharge from the RAF, and went back to civilian life. On the run in during the 26 August strike, T7305 of 226 Squadron fell victim to ship's flak and crashed into the North Sea near the convoy with its port engine blazing. 19 year old Sgt Gilbert V. 'Smithy' Smith of Townsville, Queensland, Australia and his crew all perished. With a new W.Op/AG, Bill O'Connell and Peter Saunders went on to complete their tour of ops with 226 Squadron in June 1942.

Battle damage. V6525 of 18 Squadron has been severely shot up by Bf109s during a Circus raid on the Hazebrouck railway yards, 22 June 1941. Coll. Dennis Denton

RAF and Commonwealth Squadrons Operating the Blenheim and the Bolingbroke

The following data are listed: Squadron; RAF Command(s); unit code; period during which the unit had types on strength; Mark(s) of aircraft employed. Note: RCAF squadrons operating in Canada routinely underlined the unit number and individual aircraft codes to avoid confusion with similarly coded overseas units.

Abbreviations: AASF (Advanced Air Striking Force); ACC (Army Co-operation Command); BC (Bomber Command); CC (Coastal Command); FC (Fighter Command).

6 Squadron; RAF Middle East; JV; 3 months (Nov 1941–Jan 1942); Blenheim IV

8 Squadron; RAF Middle East; HV; 4 years 10 months (May 1939–Mar 1944); Blenheim I, IV and V

8 (RCAF) Squadron; 1939–42 YO, from 1942 GA; 2 years 8 months (Dec 1940–Aug 1943); Bolingbroke I and IV

11 Squadron; RAF Middle East, RAF India; OY and YH prewar, EX wartime; 4 years 3 months (July 1939–Oct 1943); Blenheim I and IV

13 Squadron; ACC, RAF Middle East, 326 Wing North Africa; OO; 2 years 5 months (Jul 1941–Dec 1943); Blenheim IV and V

13 (RCAF) Squadron; 1939–42 AN, from 1942 MK; 8 months (Oct 1941–Jun 1942); Bolingbroke IV

13 (Hellenic) Squadron; RAF Middle East; no known sqn code; 1 year (Oct 1942–Sep 1943); Blenheim IV and V

14 Squadron; RAF Middle East; CX; 2 years (Sep 1940–Sep 1942); Blenheim I and IV

XV Squadron; BC; LS; 11 months (Dec 1939–Nov 1940); Blenheim IV

15 (SAAF) Squadron; RAF Middle East; no sqn code; one year (Jul 1942–Jul 1943); Blenheim V

16 (SAAF) Squadron; RAF Middle East; no sqn code; 8 months (Nov 1942–Jun 1943); Blenheim V

17 (SAAF) Squadron; RAF Middle East; no sqn code; 5 months (Jan 1943–May 1943); Blenheim V

18 Squadron; ACC, BC, RAF Middle East, 326 Wing North Africa; GU prewar and WV wartime; 4 years 2 months (May 1939–Jul 1943); Blenheim I, IV and V

21 Squadron; BC; JP prewar and YH wartime; 4 years 4 months (Aug 1938–Dec 1942); Blenheim IV

23 Squadron; FC; MS prewar and YP wartime; 2 years 6 months (Dec 1938–May 1941); Blenheim IF and IVF

25 Squadron; FC; RX prewar and ZK wartime; 2 years 2 months (Dec 1938–Jan 1941); Blenheim IF

27 Squadron; RAF India, RAF Far East; PT; 2 years 11 months (Jun 1939–May 1942); Blenheim I and IF

29 Squadron; FC; YB prewar and RO wartime; 2 years 3 months (Dec 1938–Mar 1941); Blenheim IF

30 Squadron; RAF Middle East; DP prewar and VT wartime; 3 years 5 months (Jan 1938–May 1941); Blenheim I and IF

34 Squadron; BC, RAF·Middle East, RAF Far East, RAF India; 34 and LB, EG from Sep 1939; 5 years (Aug 1938–Aug 1943); Blenheim I, IV and V

35 Squadron; BC; TL; 6 months (Nov 1939–Apr 1940); Blenheim IV

39 Squadron; RAF India, RAF Far East, RAF India, RAF Middle East; XZ; 1 year 8 months (Jun 1939–Jan 1941); Blenheim I

40 Squadron; BC; BL and LE; 11 months (Dec 1939–Nov 1940); Blenheim IV

42 Squadron; RAF India; AW; 9 months (Feb 1943–Oct 1943); Blenheim V

44 Squadron; BC; 44; JW and KM; 1 year 3 months (Dec 1937–Feb 1939); Blenheim I

45 Squadron; RAF Middle East, RAF India; OB; 3 years 3 months (Jun 1939–Aug 1942); Blenheim I, IV and IVF 'strafer'

52 Squadron; RAF Middle East; no known sqn code; 5 months (Oct 1942–Feb 1943); Blenheim IV

53 Squadron; ACC, BEF Air Component, CC; TE prewar and PZ wartime; 2 years 8 months (Jan 1939–Jul 1941); Blenheim IV

55 Squadron; RAF Middle East; no known sqn code; 3 years 2 months (Apr 1939–Jun 1942); Blenheim I and IV

57 Squadron; BC, CC; EQ prewar, DX and QT wartime; 2 years 9 months (Mar 1938–Nov 1940); Blenheim I and IV

59 Squadron; BEF Air Component, ACC, CC; PJ prewar, BY, TR and WE wartime; 2 years 6 months (May 1939–Oct 1941); Blenheim IV

60 Squadron; RAF India, RAF Far East; AD prewar and MU wartime; 4 years 3 months (Jun 1939–Aug 1943); Blenheim I, IV and V

61 Squadron; BC; 61 and LS; 1 year 3 months (Jan 1938–Mar 1939); Blenheim I

62 Squadron; BC, RAF Far East; 62 and JO, FX from Sep 1939; 4 years (Feb 1938–Feb 1942); Blenheim I

64 Squadron; FC; XQ prewar and SH wartime; 1 year 5 months (Dec 1938–Apr 1940); Blenheim IF and IVF

68 Squadron; FC; WM; 5 months (Jan 1941–May 1941); Blenheim IF and IVF

69 Squadron; Malta; no known sqn code; second half of 1941; one Blenheim IV

82 Squadron; BC; OZ prewar and UX wartime; 4 years 1 month (Mar 1938–Mar 1942); Blenheim I and IV

83 Squadron; BC; 2 months (Sep–Oct 1938); Blenheim I

84 Squadron; RAF Middle East, RAF Far East; UR prewar, PY and VA wartime; 3 years 2 months (Feb 1939–Apr 1942); Blenheim I, IF, IV and IVF

86 Squadron; CC; BX; 7 months (Dec 1940–Jun 1941); Blenheim IV

88 Squadron; BC; RH; 1 year 1 month (Feb 1941–Mar 1942); Blenheim I and IV

90 Squadron; BC; 90 and TW prewar, WP and XY wartime; 3 years (May 1937–Apr 1940); Blenheim I and IV

92 Squadron; FC; GR; 6 months (Oct 1939–Mar 1940); Blenheim IF

101 Squadron; BC; LU prewar and SR wartime; 2 years 10 months (Aug 1938–Jun 1941); Blenheim I and IV

104 Squadron; BC; PO prewar and EP wartime; 2 years (May 1938–Apr 1940); Blenheim I and IV

105 Squadron; BC; GB; 1 year 7 months (Jun 1940–Nov 1941); Blenheim IV

107 Squadron; BC, CC; BZ prewar and OM wartime; 3 years 7 months (Aug 1938–Feb 1942); Blenheim I and IV

108 Squadron; BC; 108 and MF prewar, LD wartime; 1 year 11 months (Jun 1938–Apr 1940); Blenheim I and IV

110 Squadron; BC; AY prewar and VE wartime; 4 years 6 months (Dec 1937–May 1942); Blenheim I and IV

113 Squadron; RAF Middle East, RAF Burma, RAF India; BT prewar, VA wartime; 4 years 3 months (Jun 1939–Sep 1943); Blenheim I, IV, IVF 'strafer' and V

114 Squadron; BC, AASF, BC, CC, RAF Middle East, 326 Wing North Africa; FD prewar and RT wartime; 6 years 2 months (Mar 1937–May 1943); Blenheim I, IV and V

115 (RCAF) Squadron; 1939–42 BK, from 1942 UV; 2 years (Aug 1941–Aug 1943); Bolingbroke I and IV

119 (RCAF) Squadron; 1939–42 DM, from 1942 GR; 1 year 10 months (Jul 1940–Jun 1942); Bolingbroke I and IV

121 (RCAF) Squadron; Jan 1942; May 1942 JY, May 1942; Oct 1942 EN; 1 year 9 months (Aug 1942; May 1944); Bolingbroke IV

122 (RCAF) Squadron; AG; 3 years 1 month (Aug 1942–Sep 1945); Bolingbroke IV

139 Squadron; BC, AASF, BC; SY prewar and XD wartime; 5 years 3 months (Jul 1937–Sep 1942); Blenheim I, IV and V

140 Squadron; CC (?); ZW; 2 years (Sep 1941–Aug 1943); Blenheim IV

141 Squadron; FC; TW; 7 months (Dec 1939–Jun 1940); Blenheim IF

143 Squadron; CC; HO; 10 months (Dec 1941–Sep 1942); Blenheim IV

144 Squadron; BC; 144 and PL; 1 year 9 months (Sep 1937–May 1939); Blenheim I and IV

145 Squadron; FC; SO; 7 months (Oct 1939–Apr 1940); Blenheim IF

147 (RCAF) Squadron; SZ; 1 year 7 months (Jul 1942–Mar

1944); Bolingbroke I and IV

162 Squadron; RAF Middle East; GK; 1 year 4 months (Jul 1942–Oct 1943); Blenheim V

163 (RCAF) Squadron; no sqn code; 1 year (Mar 1943–Mar 1944); Bolingbroke IV

173 Squadron; RAF Middle East; no known sqn code; 1 year 7 months (Jul 1942–Feb 1944); Blenheim IV

203 Squadron; RAF Middle East; CJ and NT; 2 years 7 months (May 1940–Nov 1942); Blenheim IV, IVF and V

211 Squadron; RAF Middle East, RAF Far East; LJ prewar and UQ wartime; 2 years 10 months (May 1939– Feb 1942); Blenheim I and IV

218 Squadron; BC; HA; 5 months (Jun 1940–Sep 1940); Blenheim IV

219 Squadron; FC; FK; 1 year 5 months (Oct 1939–Jan 1941); Blenheim IF

222 Squadron; FC; ZD; 6 months (Oct 1939–Mar 1940); Blenheim IF

223 Squadron; RAF Middle East; AO; 8 months (May 1941–Jan 1942); Blenheim I

226 Squadron; BC; MQ; 10 months (Feb 1941–Dec 1941); Blenheim IV

229 Squadron; FC; RE; 6 months (Oct 1939–Mar 1940); Blenheim IF

233 Squadron; CC; ZS; 4 months (Oct 1939–Jan 1940); Blenheim IV

234 Squadron; FC; AZ; 5 months (Oct 1939–May 1940); Blenheim IF

235 Squadron; FC, CC; LA; 1 year and 11 months (Feb 1940–Dec 1941); Blenheim IF and IVF

236 Squadron; FC, CC; FA; 2 years 5 months (Oct 1939–Feb 1942); Blenheim I and IVF

242 (RCAF) Squadron; FC; LE; 1 month (Dec 1939); Blenheim IF

244 Squadron; RAF Middle East; no known sqn code; 2 years 1 month (Apr 1942–Apr 1944); Blenheim IV and V

245 Squadron; FC; DX; 5 months (Nov 1939–Mar 1940); Blenheim IF

248 Squadron; FC, CC; WR; 1 year 8 months (Feb 1940–Jul 1941); Blenheim IF and IVF

252 Squadron; CC; PN; 5 months (Dec 1940–Apr 1941); Blenheim IF and IVF

254 Squadron; FC, CC; QY; 2 years 10 months (Nov 1939–Sep 1942); Blenheim IF and IVF

272 Squadron; CC; XK; 6 months, (Nov 1940–Apr 1941); Blenheim IVF

285 Squadron; FC; VG; 3 months (Dec 1941–Mar 1942); Blenheim I

287 Squadron; FC; KZ; 3 months (Nov 1941–Feb 1942); Blenheim IV

288 Squadron; FC; RP; 2 months (Nov 1941–Dec 1941); Blenheim IV

289 Squadron; FC; YE; 3 months (Nov 1941–Jan 1942); Blenheim I and IV

404 (RCAF) Squadron; CC; EE; 1 year 10 months (April 1941–Jan 1943); Blenheim I, IF and IVF

406 (RCAF) Squadron; FC; HU; 2 months (May 1941–Jun 1941); Blenheim IF and IVF

407 (RCAF) Squadron; CC; RR; 3 months (May 1941–Jul 1941); Blenheim I and IV

415 (RCAF) Squadron; CC; GX; 3 months (Dec 1941–Feb 1942); Blenheim IV

454 (RAAF) Squadron; RAF Middle East; no known sqn code; 3 months (Nov 1942–Jan 1943); Blenheim V

459 (RAAF) Squadron; RAF Middle East; BP; 2 months (Feb 1942– Mar 1942); Blenheim IV

489 (RNZAF) Squadron; CC; XA; 3 months (Jan 1942–Mar 1942); Blenheim IV

500 Squadron; CC; MK; 8 months (Apr 1941–Nov 1941); Blenheim IV

516 Squadron; Command?; no sqn code; 1 year 8 months (May 1943–Dec 1944); Blenheim IV

521 Squadron; CC; 50; 9 months (Jul 1942–Mar 1943); Blenheim IV

526 Squadron; Command?; MD; 1 year 11 months (Jun 1943–May 1945); Blenheim IV

527 Squadron; Command?; WN; 1 year 11 months (Jun 1943–May 1945); Blenheim IV

528 Squadron; Command?; no sqn code; 1 year 4 months (Jun 1943–Sep 1944); Blenheim IV

600 Squadron; FC; MV prewar and BQ wartime; 2 years 10 months (Sep 1938–Oct 1941); Blenheim IF and IVF

601 Squadron; FC; YN prewar and UF wartime; 1 year 2 months (Jan 1939–Feb 1940); Blenheim IF and IVF

604 Squadron; FC; WQ prewar and NG wartime; 2 years 5 months (Dec 1938–May 1941); Blenheim IF

608 Squadron; CC; UL; 7 months (Feb 1941–Sep 1941); Blenheim I and IV

614 Squadron; ACC, RAF Middle East, 326 Wing North Africa; LJ; 2 years 7 months (Aug 1942–Feb 1944); Blenheim IV and V

APPENDIX III

Royal Air Force Units, Other than Squadrons, Operating the Blenheim

Note: Some of these units had large numbers of Blenheims on strength for a period of many years (like the Operational Training Units, see Chapter 2); others only had a few and used them only for a short time.

AAC Flight - Anti-Aircraft Co-operation Flights of 9, 10, 11, 12 and 13 Groups.

AACU - Anti-Aircraft Co-operation Unit 1, 6, 7, 8, 22.

A&AEE - Aeroplane and Armament Experimental Establishment.

1 AAS - No.1 Air Armament School.

ACSEA CS - Air Command South East Asia Communications Squadron.

Admiralty (An estimated 30 Blenheims went to the Admiralty in early 1944, purpose not clear).

ADU - Aircraft Delivery Unit.

AFDU - Air Fighting Development Unit.

AFEE - Airborne Forces Experimental Establishment.

AFTU (I) - Advanced Flying Training Unit (India).

AGME - Aircraft Gun Mounting Establishment.

1 AGS - No.1 Air Gunners School

1 (I) AGS - No.1 (Indian) Air Gunners School.

AI-ASV School - Airborne Interception-Air to Surface Vessel (radar) School.

Air Service Training.

AOS - Air Observers School 1, 3, 5, 9.

ASR Flight - Air Sea Rescue Flight.

ASR Flight ME - Air Sea Rescue Flight Middle East.

2 ASU - No.2.

ATA - Air Transport Auxiliary.

BARU - British Airways Repair Unit.

BATF - Beam Approach Training Flight 6, 7, 8, 1508.

BDU - Bombing Development Unit..

BGS - Bombing and Gunnery School 5, 7, 9, 10.

Blenheim Collection Flight.

Blenheim Delivery Flights 3, 17 and 18.

Blenheim Flight.

1 CACF - No.1.

Calibration Flight Blida.

1 Cam (Camouflage?) Flight.

3 CDF IAFVR - No.3.

CF - Communications Flight 1653, East Africa, 13 Group, 81 Group, 201 Group, Hal Far, Hendon, India, Iraq, Khartoum.

CFS - Central Flying School.

CGS - Central Gunnery School.

CU - Communications (or Conversion) Unit 1672.

ECFS - Empire Central Flying School.

ESW - Electrical & Wireless School (Cranwell).

2 FF - No.2 Fighter Flight.

FF Flight - Free French Flight.
FIU - Fighter Interception Unit.
Flights: Nos 404, 405, 1300, 1301, 1302, 1303, 1401, 1402, 1403, 1404, 1405, 1416, 1434, 1438, 1442, 1483, 1508, 1572, 1573, 1578, 1579, 1580, 1581, 1582, 1653.
3 Flight Indian Air Force.
35 Flight SAAF.
1482 (Target Towing) Flight.
Flight Sudan.
Y Flight.
Z Flight.
FP or FU - Ferry Pool or Unit 2, 4.
FPP or FPU - Ferry Pilots Pool or Unit 1, 2, 3, 4, 6, 7.
FFAF - ?
Free French Desert Patrol Flight.
FTU - Ferry Training Unit 301, 305, 307, 311.
FU - Ferry Unit 9.
FTS - Flying Training School 6, 9.
12 Group Pool.
2 Group TF - 2 Group Training Flight.
2 Group TT Flight - 2 Group Target Towing Flight.
ICS - India Communications Squadron.
MECCU - Middle East Check and Conversion Unit 1, 2.
1 METS - No.1 Middle East Training School (became RAF (Middle East) Central Gunnery School).
METS - Middle East Training School 3, 4, 5.

Middle East Communications Flight.
1655 Mosquito Training Unit.
MU - Maintenance Unit Nos 5, 6, 9, 10, 15, 19, 20, 23, 24, 27, 32, 33, 36, 39, 103, 108, 114, 133, 136, 162, 166, 226, 308, 315, 319, 326.
North African Practice Flight.
1 OADU - No.1 Overseas Aircraft Delivery Unit.
OAFU - Observers Advanced Flying Unit 1, 9.
1, 9 OAO - No.1, 9
PAFU - Pilots Advanced Flying Unit 9, 12. (12 PAFU used over 200 Blenheims).
PDU - Photographic Development Unit.
PRRP - ?
PRU -Photographic Reconnaissance Unit.
1 PRU - No.1 Photographic Reconnaissance Unit.
RAE - Royal Aircraft Establishment.
RAFC - Royal Air Force College.
431 Reconnaissance Flight (Malta).
3 RFU - No.3.
RMU - Radio Maintenance Unit 2, 3, 4, 5, 6, 8.
Royal Air Force Film Unit.
2, 3 RS - No. 2, 3 Radio School.
RSU or RSS - Radio Servicing Unit or Section 1, 3, 7, 51, 54.
2 SAC - No.2 School of Army Co-operation.
SDF or SD Flt - Special Duties Flight.
Sea Rescue Flight.

SFPP - Service Ferry Pilots Pool.
17 SFTS - No.17 Service Flying Training School.
SF - Station Flight Abbotsinch, Andover, Denham, Dyce, Heston, Odiham, Wyton.
3 SGR - No.3 School of General Reconnaissance.
STT - School of Technical Training 6, 10.
TFPP - Temporary Ferry Pilots Pool.
TFU - Telecommunications Flying Unit.
TURP - ?
WG - Wing No.'s 70, 71, 72, 73, 74, 75, 76, 77, 78, 79, 249, 298.
74 Wing Calibration Flight.
OTU - Operational Training Unit Nos 1 (used 24 Blenheims), 2 (used 114 Blenheims), 3 (used 19 Blenheims), 5 (used 47 Blenheims), 6 (used 54 Blenheims), 12 (used 3 Blenheims), 13 (used 265 Blenheims), 15 (used 4 Blenheims), 17 (used 184 Blenheims), 20 (used 1 Blenheim, T2438), 42 (used 121 Blenheims), 51 (used 101 Blenheims), 52 (used 1 Blenheim, K7170), 54 (used 176 Blenheims), 55 (used 7 Blenheims), 56 (used 2 Blenheims, L9294 and P6896), 60 (used 109 Blenheims), 63 (used 2 Blenheims, AZ897 and BA156), 70 (used 141 Blenheims), 71 (used 1 Blenheim, Z7769) 72 (used 85 Blenheims), 75 (used 28 Blenheims), 79 (used 31 Blenheims), 132 (used 72 Blenheims), 142 (used 1 Blenheim, Z6173), 152 (used 7 Blenheims).

Glossary

AA	anti-aircraft
AFV	armoured fighting vehicle
AG	air gunner
AOC	Air Officer Commanding
ASR	air–sea rescue
Baedeker raids	bombing offensive against British cities of historical and cultural significance during 1942
Beat	stretch of German-held coastline and sea
BEF	British Expeditionary Force
CH	Chain Home (radar stations)
Channel Stop	RAF operation intended to close the Straits of Dover to enemy shipping during daylight
Circus	RAF bombing operation, strongly escorted by fighters to lure German fighters into combat
DFC	Distinguished Flying Cross
DFM	Distinguished Flying Medal
DSO	Distinguished Service Order
ETA	estimated time of arrival
FAA	Fleet Air Arm
FIU	Fighter Interception Unit
Flak	German anti-aircraft gun or gunfire
Fringe target	target on enemy coastline
Fuller	RAF operation to prevent the passage of German capital ships through the Straits of Dover
GC	George Cross
GP	general purpose (bomb)
IAS	indicated air speed
JG	Jagdgeschwader, Luftwaffe day fighting wing
KIA	killed in action
MIA	missing in action
Mickey Mouse	a sequential hand-operated electrical switch which enabled the observer to 'straddle' the target, as opposed to the original idea of dropping the bombs singly or in a cluster
MT	motor transport
Nachtjagd	Luftwaffe night fighting arm
NJG	Nacht Jagdgeschwader, Luftwaffe night fighting wing
OC/CO	Officer in Command/Commanding Officer
OTU	Operational Training Unit
PAFU	Pilots Advanced Flying Unit
PRU	Photographic Reconnaissance Unit
Ramrod	fighter-escorted bombing operation, designed to destroy a specific target
Ritterkreuzträger	holder of the Knight's Cross
SASO	Senior Air Staff Officer
SDF	Special Duty Flight
Sentai	Japanese Army Air Force's main operating unit, about thirty aircraft strong
SOC	struck off charge
Squealer	small German ship, often disguised as fishing vessel, equipped with radio to report movement of RAF aircraft
Torch	allied invasion of north Africa, November 1942
Vorpostenboot (Vp)	German Navy Flak ship and auxiliary minesweeper
W.Op	wireless operator
WIA	wounded in action

Bibliography

Aders, Gebhard and Held, Werner, *Jagdgeschwader 51 'Mölders'* (Stuttgart, 1985)

Air Ministry, Pilot's Notes: Blenheim I Aircraft (1943)

Air Ministry, Pilot's Notes: Blenheim V Aeroplane (1942)

Air Ministry Historical Branch, The Second World War 1939–1945, Royal Air Force. The RAF in Maritime War (unpublished)

Anon, Table des matieres de l'histoirique du Groupe de Bombardement 'Bretagne' des origines (Decembre 1940) a 1945 (unpublished, archives SHAA)

Anon, 84 Squadron History. January 14th– March 17th 1942 (unpublished)

Ashworth, Chris, *RAF Coastal Command 1936–1969* (Sparkford, 1992)

Baczkowski, Wieslaw, *Samolot bombowy Bristol Blenheim Mk I–IV* (Warszawa, 1995)

Bingham, Victor F., *'Blitzed' The Battle of France May–June 1940* (Walton-on-Thames, 1994)

Boiten, Theo, *Blenheim Strike* (Walton-on-Thames, 1995)

Boiten, Theo, *Nachtjagd. The night fighter versus bomber war over the Third Reich, 1939–1945* (Ramsbury, 1997)

Bowman, Martin W., *The Reich Intruders* (Sparkford, 1997)

Bowyer, Chaz, *Bristol Blenheim* (London, 1984)

Bowyer, Chaz, *For Valour. The Air VCs* (London, 1992)

Bowyer, Michael J.F., *2 Group RAF. A complete history, 1936–1945* (London, 1974)

Braham, Wg Cdr J.R.D. 'Bob', DSO, DFC, AFC, CD, *'Scramble!'* (London, 1985)

'Bristol' Blenheim, Journal of the Blenheim Society, 1988–96

Brookes, Andrew, *Bomber Squadron at War* (London, 1983)

Bruin e.a., Robbie de, *Illusies en Incidenten. De Militaire Luchtvaart en de Neutraliteitshandhaving tot 10 mei 1940*

Butterworth, Albert, *With Courage and Faith. The story of No. 18 Squadron Royal Air Force* (Tonbridge, 1989)

Camelio, Paul and Shores, Christopher, *Armee de l'Air* (Warren, Michigan, 1976)

Charles, Lt-Col, Historique du Groupe de Bombardement I/20 Lorraine (unpublished, archives SHAA)

Chorley, William R., *Royal Air Force Bomber Command Losses of the Second World War. Vols I (1939–1940), II (1941) and III (1942)* (Earl Shilton, 1992–94)

Commonwealth War Graves Commission, The War Dead of the Commonwealth, Germany 3–5 and 6; Netherlands 191–247 and 451–539 (Berkshire, 1985, 1988–89)

Cull, Brian and Lander, Bruce with Weiss, Heinrich, *Twelve Days in May* (London, 1995)

Dargasse, Philippe, Temoinage sur la chronologie du Groupe 1/17 'Picardie' FAFL (unpublished, archives SHAA)

Day, Tony, The Airwar over the Arakan 1942–1945. An Arakan Aerial Anthology by 'Those who served there' (unpublished MS, Penticton, BC, 1989)

Dean, Jack, *'The Phoenix Bombers'*, Airpower, Vol. 27, No.1 (January 1997)

Decker, Cynrik De and Roba, Jean-Louis, *België in Oorlog 5. Luchtgevechten boven België 1941–1942* (Erpe, 1994)

Fearnley, Len, *Blenheim Odyssey* (Farnham, 1990)

Fellowes, Air Cdr P.F.M., (ed.), *Britain's Wonderful Air Force* (London, 1942)

John Foreman, *Air War 1941: The Turning Point, Part 1 and 2* (Walton-on-Thames, 1993–94)

Girbig, Werner, *Jagdgeschwader 5 'Eismeerjäger'* (Stuttgart, 1976)

Goulding, James and Moyes, Philip, *RAF Bomber Command and Its Aircraft 1936–1940* (London, 1975)

Gunn, Peter B., *RAF Great Massingham. A Norfolk Airfield at War 1940–1945* (King's Lynn, 1990)

Halley, James J. and Corbell, Peter M. (eds.), *Aeromilitaria*, No.1/77 (Shepperton, 1977)

Henry, Mike, *Air Gunner* (London, 1964)

Holliday, J.E. (ed.), *The RAAF PoWs of Lamsdorf* (Holland Park, Queensland, 1992)

Jeudwine, Wg Cdr John R., History of 84 Squadron from 3.1.42 to 7.3.42 (unpublished, 1942)

Jones, Flt Lt T.W., *Aim Sure. 75 Years of Number 15/XV (Bomber) Squadron* (1990)

Keller, Otto, *Das Leben eines Seemannes* (Offenburg, 1996)

King, Peter, *Knights of the Air* (London, 1989)

Altes, A. Korthals, *Luchtgevaar. Luchtaanvallen op Nederland 1940–1945* (Amsterdam, 1984)

Kostenuk, Samuel and Griffin, John, *RCAF Squadron Histories and Aircraft* (Toronto, 1977)

MacDonald, Callum, *The Lost Battle. Crete 1941* (London, 1995)

Mason, Francis K., *Battle over Britain* (London, 1969)

McHardy, Wg Cdr E.H. (Sam), Someone on My Shoulder (unpublished MS, n.d.)

Middlebrook, Martin and Everitt, Chris, *The Bomber Command War Diaries. An Operational Reference Book, 1939–1945* (Harmondsworth, 1985)

Millar, Flt Lt R.D., Narrative of Personal Experiences of War in the Far East (unpublished, n.d.)

Ministry of Information, *The Campaign in Greece and Crete* (London, 1942)

Moyes, Philip J.R., Bristol Blenheim I (Profile No. 93)

Oughton, James D., Bristol Blenheim Mk IV (Profile No. 218)

Persch, Helmut, Meine Zeit bei der Kriegsmarine (unpublished, Koblenz, 1993)

Prosser, Sgt P. Rollo, Wartime Diary on WOp/AG service with 235 Squadron, 1940 (unpublished, 1940)

Public Record Office Files:
AIR 14/801. March–October 1941. Daylight attacks on enemy shipping at sea
AIR 16/514. Interpretation Report No. 2491, 2 Group Bomber Command, on Ramrod XII, 15 October 1941
AIR 20/4057. Daily reports on enemy shipping and land objectives attacked by Blenheims of No. 2 Group in: East Frisian Islands; Dutch Islands; Holland and Belgium; 'B' raids against industrial targets, 12 March–25 May 1941
AIR 20/4057. 2·Group War Room 14 days reports on (1) Coastal sweeps and fringe operations; (2) Operations against industrial targets or shipping in port; (3) Operations with fighter escort; (4) Summary of all operations in (A) Norway and Skagerrak; (B) Denmark and Schleswig Holstein (N.Frisian Islands); (C) Heligoland Bight and East Frisian Islands; (D) Holland, 12 March–3 June 1941
AIR 27 Various: 18, 23, 25, 29, 53, 57, 59, 82, 110, 139, 219, 226, 235, 242, 254, 404, 600, 601, 604 Squadron Record Books
AIR 37/47. Daylight bombing attacks on Germany and Occupied Territory: photographs 1941

RAF Museum (Hendon)
B3260. Retrospective Diary of Special Duty Flight

Ransom, Derek, *Battle Axe. A History of 105 Squadron Royal Air Force* (1967)

Rawlings, John D.R., *Fighter Squadrons of the RAF and Their Aircraft* (London, 1976)

Rawnsley, C.F. and Wright, Robert, *Night Fighter* (London, 1968)

Ring, Hans and Shores, Christopher, *Luftkampf zwischen Sand und Sonne* (Stuttgart, 1969)

Ring, Hans and Girbig, Werner, *Jagdgeschwader 27* (Stuttgart, 1994)

Robinson, Anthony, *Night Fighter. A Concise History of Night Fighting since 1914* (London, 1988)

Ronnest, Ole, Aalborg. 13th August 1940 (unpublished manuscript, 1996)

Schenk, Peter, *Invasion of England 1940. The Planning of Operation Sealion* (London, 1990)

Scott, Stuart R., *Battle-Axe Blenheims. No 105 Squadron RAF at War 1940–1* (Stroud, 1996)

Shipley, Eric, *139 (Jamaica) Squadron* (Pontefract, 1990)

Shores, Christopher F., *Pictorial History of the Mediterranean Air War, Vol. I and II* (London, 1972–73)

Shores, Christopher and Cull, Brian with Malizia, Nicola, *Malta: The Hurricane Years 1940–41* (London, 1987)

Shores, Christopher and Cull, Brian with Malizia, Nicola, *Air War for Yugoslavia, Greece and Crete 1940–41* (London 1987)

Shores, Christopher and Cull, Brian with Izawa, Yasuho, *Bloody Shambles. Vol. 1 and 2* (London, 1995, 1996)

Sniderhan, Capt Mike, *404 Squadron History* (Winnipeg, 1991)

Terraine, John, *The Right of the Line: The Royal Air Force in the European War 1939–1945* (London, 1985)

Warner, Graham, *Spirit of Britain First* (Sparkford, 1996)

Wheeler, Hugh F.C., Bristol Blenheim – Operational Training Units (unpublished, Peterborough, 1996)

Whittle, Ken, *An Electrician Goes to War* (Swindon, 1994)

Wisdom, T.H., *Wings over Olympus* (London, 1942)

Wood, Derek and Dempster, Derek, *The Narrow Margin* (London, 1969)

Wyllie, John, *Johnnie Purple. The Story of a Bomber Squadron in Sumatra, 1942* (London, 1972).

Acknowledgements

I am deeply grateful for the splendid support I have received in the preparation of this book from many air and ground crews who operated the Blenheim, from their next of kin, from former Luftwaffe and Kriegsmarine veterans who fought the aircraft, and from fellow researchers and aviation organizations: Len 'Abbie' Abbs (photographer, 211 Sqn); Wes Agnew; the Aircrew Association; A.L. Allen (wireless electrical mechanic, 25 Sqn); Rodney Armstrong (pilot, 21 Sqn); Arthur Asker (observer, 226 Sqn); Guy Avery (pilot, 139 Sqn); Jock Bain (pilot, 21 Sqn); Rosemary Bareham; Bill Barnes; Derek L. Barnes; Jack Bartley (W.Op/AG, 21 Sqn); Donald A. Bassil (radar mechanic 25 Sqn); The Battle of Britain Fighter Association; Douglas Beagley (fitter IIA, 18 Sqn); Bart Beckers; Pieter Bergman; Eric Bevington-Smith (observer, 211 Sqn); Iris Bonnor; Martin Bowman; Bill Bradshaw (W.Op/AG, 21 and 18 Sqns); Chuck Brady (W.Op/AG, 236 Sqn); David Brandwood-Spencer; H. Layton Bray (pilot-navigator, 8 RCAF Sqn); Geoff Brazier (observer, 235 Sqn); A.C.L. Brown (W.Op/AG, 114 and 55 Sqns); Jack Brown (W.Op/AG, 18 Sqn); Joseph Buerschgens (pilot, 7/JG26); Bill Burberry (W.Op/AG, 114 and 13 Sqns); Fred Burton (W.Op/AG, 21 Sqn); Richard Butt; Albert Butterworth; Sybil Caban; Philip J. Camp (observer, XV Sqn); Canadian Airforce Association; Bea Cashford; Jack Caslaw (pilot, 25 Sqn); James Cathcart; Graham Clayton (W.Op/AG, 60 Sqn); Les Clayton (groundcrew, 18 Sqn); Bob Coles (observer, 139 Sqn); Ken Collins (observer, 82 Sqn); Bob Collis; Combined Aircrew Association, Australia; Peter G. Cooksley; Doug Cooper (pilot, 110 and 21 Sqns); Bill Corfield; Noel 'Paddy' Corry (pilot, 25 Sqn); Croydon Aviation Research Group; Keith Cudlipp (W.Op/AG, 105 Sqn); Peter Cundy (pilot, 53 Sqn); Antony F. Day; Les Deadfield (groundcrew, 18 Sqn); Cynrik de Decker; Ken Dee (pilot, 14 Sqn); Freddy Deeks (observer, 110 and 107 Sqns); Irene Deeks; Hans de Haan; Jack M. Derbyshire (pilot, 236 Sqn); Nelson Derkson (A.I. operator); Rob de Visser; John Douch (pilot, 18 Sqn); Timothy Dubé (Canadian Aviation Historical Society, Ottawa Chapter); George Dunbar (fitter, 'A' 211 Sqn); James Dunnet (observer, 57, 211 and 11 Sqns); The Dutch Embassy, Pretoria, South Africa; Alan Ellender (groundcrew fitter I, 18 Sqn); Wray Eller (pilot, 18 Sqn); Paddy Embry; Henry Emden; Wolfgang Falck (St Kpt, 2/ZG76); Ralph Fastnedge (observer, 139 Sqn); Philip Felton (observer, 21 and 82 Sqns); A. Sid Fenerty (observer, 8 RCAF Sqn); Eric Forbes (observer, 82 Sqn); Bill Gatling (W.Op/AG, 18, 110 and 614 Sqns); John Geary; Betty and Hugh George (Blenheim Society); Brian Gibbs; Jeanne Gibbs; Arthur M. Gill (pilot, 84 Sqn); Al Glazer; Sally Goldsworthy; Alex H. Gould (pilot, 144 Sqn); Bob Gould; Bill Graham (groundcrew, 211 Sqn); Beryl Griffiths; Wyb-Jan Groendijk; Peter B. Gunn; Vic Hand; Gilbert Haworth (observer, 44 Sqn); Mike Henry (W.Op/AG, 110, 101, 21, 105 and 107 Sqns); Wilf Hepworth (observer, 139 Sqn); Wim Hermans; Wilf Hewlett (W.Op/AG, XV, 139, 107 and 21 Sqns); Ron Hicks; John A. Hill (armourer, 8 RCAF Sqn); Jim Holdaway (observer, 45 Sqn); Julian Horn (Watton Museum); Len Hunt (observer, 59 Sqn); John A. Hurst; Ab A. Jansen; Charles A. Joy; Jörn Junker; Irene Kohl; Aubrey Lancaster (observer, 235 Sqn); Stanley W. Lee (101, 18 and 113 Sqns); Dickie Leven (pilot, 107 Sqn); Ted Long (pilot, 34 Sqn); Bill Magrath (observer, 64 and 82 Sqns); Tommy Mann (ground crew, RAF Watton); Lloyd W. Manuel (pilot, 8 RCAF Sqn); Jim Martin (observer, 110 and 18 Sqns); Peter Martin; Michael J. Martinson; Dick Maydwell (pilot, 53 Sqn and CO, 14 Sqn); Alec McCurdy (pilot, 59 and 18 Sqns); Don McFarlane (observer, 82 Sqn); Douglas McKenzie (pilot, 82 Sqn); Tony Mee (W.Op/AG, 82 and 105 Sqns); H.W. 'Tubby' Mermagen (CO, 222 Sqn); George Milson (pilot, 18 and 84 Sqns); Jim Moore (W.Op/AG, 18 Sqn); Stan Moss (pilot, 13 OTU); Bert Mowat (W.Op/AG, 248 Sqn); Simon Muggleton; E. Roy Mullins (pilot, 110 Sqn); Dick Muspratt (pilot, 53 Sqn); John Muter (pilot, 147 Sqn RCAF); National Archives of Canada; Don R. Neate; Henk Nootenboom; Terence O'Brien (pilot, 53 Sqn); Bill O'Connell (pilot, 226 Sqn); Mollie O'Connell; Eric 'Ollie' Oliver (W.Op/AG, 84 Sqn); Hans Onderwater; George Parr (observer, 18 Sqn); Vic Parsons (observer, 235 Sqn); Colin Pateman; Charles Patterson (pilot, 114 Sqn); Roger Peacock (W.Op/AG, 90 and 40 Sqns); Eileen Peckover; Helmut Persch (13th Vp. Flo.); Maria E. Petroulakis; R.D. 'Fiery' Phillips (observer, 34 Sqn); H. Pleasance (pilot, 107 Sqn); Doug Pole (observer, 235 Sqn); Ernst Pörschmann (flak gunner, battleship Lützow); Ray Price (observer, 254 Sqn); Mrs J.M. Prosser; Paddy Quirke (pilot, 107 Sqn); RAAF Historical Branch; Eric Ramsey (observer, 114 Sqn); Hal 'Tubby' Randall (pilot, 254 Sqn); RCAF Airforce Magazine; John Reid (pilot, 113 Sqn); Allan P. Richardson (W.Op/AG, 211 Sqn); Audrey Richardson; G.A. 'Jimmy' Riddle (observer, 211 Sqn); Eino Ritaranta; Ian 'Robbie' Robinson (observer, 59 Sqn); Walter S. Robinson (pilot, 82 Sqn); Ole Ronnest; Dickie Rook (observer, 114 and 105 Sqns); Jim Rowand (pilot, 404 RCAF Sqn); Peter Russell (fitter 2E, 53 Sqn and 70 OTU); 'Rusty' Russell; Lt Mark A. Said AFM; Torstein Saksvik; Peter Sarll (pilot, 21 Sqn); Peter Saunders (observer, 226 Sqn); Ron Scholefield (observer, 139 and 105 Sqns); Jeff Scholefield; Gerhard Schöpfel (St Kpt and Kommandeur III/JG26); Gerhard Schubert (13th Vp. Flo.); Monty Scotney (W.Op/AG, 18 Sqn); Sectie Luchtmachthistorie Koninklijke Luchtmacht; Denis Shanahan (observer, 114 Sqn); Vera Sherring; George Shinnie (W.Op/AG, 139 Sqn); Edwin Shipley (pilot, 8 Sqn and 71 OTU); Bill Sise (pilot, 254 Sqn); Peter Smith (pilot, 59 Sqn); Les Spong (pilot, 139 Sqn and several OTUs); 25, 30, 101, 145 and 604 Squadron Associations; William Stapledon; Terry Staples (pilot, 114 Sqn); Pat Stapleton (W.Op/AG, 614 Sqn); Norman Steele; Helen Stephens; Harry Stewart (AG 236 Sqn); Peter Stubbs (groundcrew, 211 Sqn); Flt Lt David S. Sully (25 (F) Sqn); Ralph Tallis; D.V. (Vic) Thomas (pilot, 6 B and G School); Tommy Thompson (pilot, 18 Sqn); Paul Todd (pilot, 101 Sqn); Pat Townley (W.Op/AG, 13 Sqn); Len Trevallion (pilot, 13 Sqn); Ron Tucker; Turkish Air Force Historical Branch; Dick van der Heul; James Waddington; Hugh Wakefield (observer, 235 and 272 Sqns); Joe Warne; Eric Watson; Eric Webster; Ian Webster (W.Op/AG, 114 Sqn); Frank Westbrook (observer, 13 Sqn); Hugh Wheeler; Ken Whittle (W.Op/AG, 139 Sqn); Bryn Williams (fitter 18 Sqn); Mike Williams; Ray L. Williams (groundcrew, 211 Sqn); Charles Willis (CO, 8 RCAF Sqn); C. Wind (archief gemeente Westvoorne); John Wray (pilot, 53 Sqn); Pip Wray; Ronny Wright (pilot, 248 Sqn); John Wyllie (pilot, 84 Sqn).

Index

COMMONWEALTH AIR FORCE PERSONNEL

Adams, D.G., Sgt RAAF *98, 116*
Adams, Peter A., Sgt *74*
Adkin, Fred, AC1 *19*
Ahern, Patrick, AC2 *44, 160*
Aitken, Max, Sqn Ldr-Wg Cdr the Hon. DFC *82, 165*
Aldridge, Fg Off *119*
Alexander, J.O., Flt Lt *97*
Allen, Conan Sgt RCAF *159*
Anderson, Don, Plt Off *69*
Anderson, Michael H., Plt Off MiD *66*
Appleby, Michael B., Flt Sgt *75*
Ashfield, G. Fg Off *65*
Asker, Arthur, Flt Sgt *85*
Atkinson, 'Attie', Sqn Ldr-Wg Cdr DSO DFC *75, 78, 101-102, 104*
Attenborough, Douglas, Sgt *96*
Ault, Ken, Sqn Ldr *156*
Austin, Ron, Sgt *102*
Avery, Guy, Plt Off *16, 70*
Bader, Douglas, Wg Cdr *114*
Baird, Bill, Sgt *133*
Baker, Tommy, Flt Lt DFM *93*
Balzer, Christian, Sgt RAAF *98*
Bandon, the Earl of, 'Paddy', Wg Cdr-Gp Cpt DSO *49, 59, 93, 124*
Banister, Sgt DFM *67*
Banner, Sqn Ldr *119*
Bareham, Jack 'Bish', Sgt DFM *19, 55*
Barker, Jack, Sgt *80*
Barlow, E.C. 'Kekki', Wg Cdr *50*
Barnes, Tom, Cpl-Sgt *11*
Barnwell, John, Ptl Off *8, 67*
Baron, Norman, Sgt DFM *90*
Bartlett, Plt Off *96*
Bartlett, George A., Wg Cdr DFC *57*
Bartley, Jack, AC1 *45-46, 48*
Bateson, Bob, Wg Cdr *152*
Beagley, Douglas, *124, 142, 144*
Beatson, Walter G.C., Plt Off *99*
Beers, W/O *144*
Bell, J. Plt Off *88*
Bendall, J., Sgt *106*
Bennett, L.C., Wg Cdr *58*
Berg, N.W., Sgt *116*
Bevan, James E.S., Sgt *86, 88*
Beverley, Eric L., Flt Lt *129*
Biden, Plt Off *48*
Birch, Arthur M.A., Wg Cdr *75*
Blackmore, John, Sgt *80*
Blair, Donald, Sgt *58-60*
Bone, Dave, Flt Sgt DFM *108*
Bonnett, Sgt *71*
Booth, Anthony, Plt Off *43, 51*
Booth, Arthur, Wg Cdr *112*
Booth, G.F., Sgt *17-18*
Bowden, Bill, Flt Lt *147*
Box, Leslie, Sgt *79*
Boxall, C. Harley, Sqn Ldr *148*
Boyce, C.D.C., Wg Cdr *136*
Bradley, James W., Sgt *99*
Bradshaw, Bill, LAC-Sgt *56, 97, 107-109*
Bradshaw, M., Sgt *128*

Braham, John 'Bob', Plt Off *67*
Brancker, Paul, Fg Off DFC and Bar *121-123*
Brandwood, Bill, Sgt-Fg Off *87-88, 106-107*
Brett, John, Flt Sgt *85*
Broadland, Sgt *47-48*
Broadley, A.B. 'Ben', Flt Lt DFC *105*
Brooker, M.D., Sgt *85*
Broom, Ivor, Sgt *89*
Broughton, Rodney, Fg Off *141, 143, 145*
Brown, Plt Off *120*
Brown, Sgt *43*
Brown, C.D., Plt Off *78*
Brown, Jack, Flt Sgt *142-143*
Brown, John, Sgt DFM *75*
Brown, P., Sgt *85*
Buck, D.W., Sgt *107*
Buchanan, L.B., Flt Lt DFC *133, 162*
Bullivant, Ian A., Flt Sgt *79*
Burrill, K.R., Sgt RAAF *148*
Burt, C.J., Sgt *58*
Burt, Kenyon O., Wg Cdr DFC *88*
Burton, Fred, Sgt *138, 150-151*
Butler, Wg Cdr *99*
Byatt, J., Sgt *55*
Caban, Edmund, Flt Sgt DFM *88*
Calder, Freddie 'Paddy', Flt Sgt *150*
Carr, Dickie, Flt Sgt DFM *150*
Carruthers, Sgt *159*
Cathles, N.A.C., Sgt *105*
Causley, Leonard, Sgt *127-128*
Chandler, E.F., Sgt *104*
Charney, F.R.H., Sqn Ldr DFC *106*
Chinnery, Sgt *136*
Chippendale, Sgt *92*
Chown, C.M., Sgt *85*
Christensen, S., Plt Off *47*
Clark, 'Nobby', Sgt *133*
Clayton, Graham, Sgt *159*
Clements, Sqn Ldr *18*
Close, Sgt *67*
Coakley, Ken, Sgt *109*
Cole, Reg, Sgt *63*
Collins, Ken, Sgt *102, 105*
Compton, Tony, Plt Off *123*
Cooke, Frank, Sgt *128*
Cooper, Joseph H., Sgt *52-55*
Cooper, T.E., Plt Off RNZAF *92*
Coote, Paddy B., Wg Cdr *133*
Coote, Ted, LAC *43*
Corfield, Jimmy, Plt Off *24*
Cormack, J.A., Sgt RAAF *111*
Corry, Noel 'Paddy', Plt Off *65, 68-69*
Cosgrove, W.N.P., Sgt RAAF *153*
Crawford, T. Alvin, Sgt *28*
Cronan, John, Plt Off *50-51*
Crosby, A.F., Sgt *134*
Cross, Dick, Flt Lt *51*
Crozier, Sgt *52-54*
Cue, H.D., Sgt *88*
Cunningham, John 'Cat's Eyes', Fg Off *67*
Davidson, William, Plt Off RCAF *98*
Davies, LAC *43*
Davies, Sgt *112*

Davies, T.C., Flt Sgt DFM *86*
Davis, Frank, Sgt *75*
Davis, K.A., Sgt *122*
Deadfield, Les, LAC *114*
Deane, C.H., Sgt *78*
Dejace, Leonard 'Paul', Plt Off *63*
Delap, Miles, Sqn Ldr-Wg Cdr DFC *19, 58*
Dew, Ron, Sgt *70*
Dickens, Louis W., Wg Cdr AFC *45*
Dobson, Joseph A.B., Flt Lt *148-149*
Downes, H.T.H., Sgt *81*
Drysdale, Robert E., Plt Off RCAF *123*
Dukes-Smith, H.F., Flt Lt *109*
Duke-Woolley, Plt Off *67*
Dunford-Wood, H.D.S., Fg Off *55*
Dunnet, James, Sgt *56-57, 133, 136*
Dunning, J., Sgt *75*
Dupee, Sgt DFM *67*
Eames, Peter K., Sgt DFM *57*
Eckersley, Norman, Plt Off DFC *144*
Edmunds, E.G., Flt Lt DFC *107-108*
Edwards, Hughie I., Flt Lt-Wg Cdr VC DFC *70, 86, 105-106, 162*
Edwards, 'Nobby', Sgt *24-26*
Ellen, Flt Lt *49*
Eller, Wray, Flt Lt DFC *142, 144*
Elliott, H., Sgt RCAF *159*
Elsmie, George R.A., Wg Cdr DFC *74-75*
Emden, H.L., Fg Off *17*
Embry, Basil, Wg Cdr-ACM Sir *19, 45, 50*
Ensor, Fg Off DFC *120*
Evans, Plt Off *117*
Fairbairn, G.M., Flt Lt *102*
Fairbank, E.T., Fg Off *85*
Farmer, Sgt *70, 100*
Felton, Philip, Sgt *104*
Fihelly, Brian, Plt Off RAAF *153, 155*
Fisher, R.W., Sgt RAAF *122*
Flury, W., Sgt *78*
Folliet-Foster, Sgt *153*
Foster, 'Foss', Plt Off *78, 81-82*
Fowler, Ernest F.W., Sgt *149*
Fox, Sgt *102*
Fox, John J., Plt Off RNZAF *127*
Frankish, Claude, Plt Off *44*
Free, C.W., Sgt *27*
Fry, Tony, Flt Lt DFC *72*
Galt, R.B., Plt Off *112*
Garland, Fg Off *45*
Gatling, Bill, Sgt *128*
Gauthier, Flt Lt *138*
Gifford, Plt Off *25*
Gifkins, G.R., Flt Sgt *129*
Gill, Arthur, Flt Lt *14, 148*
Gilroy, Fg Off *31*
Girling, Ken, Flt Sgt *108*
Glen, John, Sgt-Fg Off *29, 31, 121, 124*
Goddard, H.G., Flt Lt *67*
Godfrey, Alan, Fg Off *133*
Goode, George, Sqn Ldr DFC *105*
Goss, Flt Sgt RCAF *158*
Graham, R.O.M., Sqn Ldr *78*
Graham-Hogg, D., Sqn Ldr *89*
Grant, 'Scottie', Sgt *80*
Gray, Charles H 'Dolly', Flt Sgt DFM *123*

Green, R.W.J., Flt Sgt DFM *86*
Greenwood, Bill, Sgt *58-59*
Gregory, G.W. 'Ace', Flt Sgt *147, 149*
Gregory, W.J. 'Sticks', Sgt *67*
Griffith, John, Plt Off *73, 82*
Guesford, Arthur E., Flt Sgt *78*
Guest, Jack, AC1 *52, 97*
Gunning, Dickie, Sgt. DFM *19*
Halahan, 'Bull', Wg Cdr *65*
Hale, E.R., Plt Off *57*
Halling-Pott, J.R., Sqn Ldr *64*
Hanson, H.L., Sgt *107*
Harrell, Les, Plt Off *90*
Harriman, Plt Off *46*
Harris, Sqn Ldr *92*
Harrison-Broadley, Fg Off *104*
Harte, F.A., Wg Cdr SAAF *106*
Haworth, Gilbert, Cpl *12-13*
Haws, Plt Off *117*
Hayes, Norman, Plt Off *42*
Headlam, R.A., Sgt RAAF *151*
Heath-Brown, J.A., Plt Off *58*
Heavyside, LAC *49*
Henry, Mike, Sgt *61-65*
Hepworth, Wilf, Sgt *102-104*
Herbert, Richard 'Herby', Plt Off-Fg Off *100, 133*
Herrick, Mike, Plt Off DFC *68-69*
Hervath, Flt Lt *119*
Hickinbotham, Jack, Flt Sgt *75*
Hickman, G.W., Sgt *81*
Hicks, Plt Off RAAF *114*
Hindle, Sgt *89, 106*
Hislop, Bruce E., Plt Off RAAF *92*
Hoare, Sqn Ldr DFC *120*
Hogg, D.W., Plt Off *67*
Holland, Cpl *58*
Holmes, M.P.C., Plt Off *43*
Hooker, E.A., Sgt *25, 27-28*
Hopkinson, K.W., Sgt *90*
Hopkinson, R.A., Plt Off *57*
Houlgrave, Sgt *159*
Houston, Matthew C., Sgt *109*
Howe, Fg Off RAAF *159*
Howitt, John, Sgt *158*
Huckins, Harry, Sgt *56, 58, 108-109*
Hudson, R.M., Plt Off RAAF *99*
Huggard, Martin H. 'Paddy', W/O *158*
Hughes, Tam, Sgt *133*
Hughes, W., Flt Lt *90-91*
Hull, George L.B. 'Bok', Wg Cdr DFC *124*
Humphries, Dave, Plt Off *67*
Hunt, Len, Sgt *72-73*
Hunt, Theo 'Joe', Sqn Ldr-Wg Cdr DFC *55, 104, 106*
Hunter, Alistair, Fg Off *67*
Hurst, R.G., Wg Cdr *86*
Ibbotson, Jack, Flt Sgt RNZAF *109*
Ingham, Jerry, Sgt *80*
Inman, Ted, Sgt *102*
Irvin, Jack, Sgt *80*
Irvine, A.T., Sqn Ldr *133*
James, A.G., Sgt *133*
James, B.B., Plt Off *52*
James, F.L., Sgt *27*

Jefferson, T.G. 'Jeff', Sgt-Wg Cdr DSO
    AFC *110-115, 117-119*
Jenkins, Fraser, Flt Lt-Wg Cdr DSO DFC
    76-77, 99, 121-124
Jennings, Clifford, Flt Sgt DFM *75*
Jeudwine, John, Wg Cdr *151-152, 156*
Jickling, A., Plt Off *129*
Johnson, Sgt *99*
Johnson, W., Sgt *129*
Johnstone, Sgt *89*
Johnstone, A.McC. 'Johnnie', Plt Off
    147-148
Johnstone, F.M.W., Plt Off *95, 97*
Jones, Sgt *58*
Jordan, C.B., Plt Off *45*
Joubert de la Ferte, Philip B., AM Sir *125*
Judson, Alan, Sqn Ldr *89*
Keighley, Flt Lt *48*
Kemp, J.R.M., Sgt *89-90*
Kennedy, Plt Off *82*
Kennedy, J. Shaw, Flt Lt-Sqn Ldr *85, 98-99*
Kercher, John, Wg Cdr DSO *93, 96*
King, Flt Sgt *59*
King-Clark, Plt Off *67*
Kingwill, P.N., Plt Off *147-148*
Kirk, Sgt *99*
Koranski, M., Sgt *116-117*
Labouchere, Fg Off *92*
Lancaster, Aubrey, Sgt *50-51*
Langley, Sgt *120*
Langley-Ripon, Plt Off *120*
Lart, de V, E.C., Wg Cdr DSO *59-60*
Lascelles, F.A.G., Wg Cdr DFC *96-97*
Laughland, Plt Off *82*
Leavers, Rex, Flt Sgt DFM *82*
Lerwill, George, Sqn Ldr DFC *97, 107-109,
    119*
Leyland, R.H., Sgt *65*
Linton, Flt Lt *152*
Little, Cpl *67*
Llewellyn, Wg Cdr *50*
Lloyd, Phil *50-51*
Locke, Sgt *89*
Longstaff, W.B., Sgt *134*
Loveitt, Ray, Flt Sgt *81*
Lowe, Sgt *116*
Lowe, R. Sgt *44, 160*
Lyon, Flt Lt *63*
Macdonald, Plt Off *151*
MacIlwraith, John, Sgt *75*
Magrath, Bill, Sgt *58-59*
Maguire, Sgt *90*
Maher, 'Paddy', Sqn Ldr *28-29*
Malcolm, Hugh, Sqn Ldr-Wg Cdr VC *126,
    140, 143-144*
Maltby, P.C., AVM *152*
Mann, Jackie, Wrt Off *73*
Mann, Ronald, Sgt *75*
Manwaring, Flt Lt *43, 51*
Maple, Johnnie, Sgt *80*
Marshall, H.K., Plt Off *75*
Martin, Jim, Flt Sgt *108*
Matthews, Fg Off *126*
Maxwell, Sqn Ldr-AVM *62*
Maydwell, Dick 'Boffin', Flt Lt-Wg Cdr
    61, 139-140
McCombie, Flt Sgt *142*
McCutcheon, Sgt *121*
McFarlane, Don, Sgt *57*
McHardy, E.H. Sam, Plt Off-Wg Cdr DFC &
    Bar, C de G *49, 125-126*
McKenzie, Douglas, Plt Off-Fg Off *17, 19,
    48, 52-53, 55*
McKenzie, Donald J. Sgt *28*
McLellan, Wal, Sgt RAAF *156*
Mcluckie, Jock, Flt Sgt *158*
McPherson, Andrew, Fg Off *17*
Mee, Tony, Sgt *87-88, 106-107*

Mermagen, H.W. 'Tubby', Wg Cdr *14*
Merritt, A.E., Sgt *53*
Millar, Ron, Sgt RNZAF *72, 85, 151*
Millen, Les, Flt Sgt DFM *150*
Miller, Jock, Sgt-Fg Off *87-88, 106-107*
Millns, Ralph, Sgt-Flt Lt *110, 112-114, 119*
Mills, F.G., Sgt *57*
Milson, George, Sgt-Plt Off *72, 85, 151*
Minchin, Sgt RAAF *159*
Moore, Eric, Plt Off *72*
Moore, Jim 'Dinty' Sgt-Flt Lt DFC *72, 84,
    151*
Moore, 'Pony', Fg Off *13-14*
Morphett, J.E., Sqn Ldr DFC RAAF *159*
Morris, Plt Off *49*
Morris, G.E., Plt Off *65*
Morris, R.J., Sgt *119*
Morrison, Sgt *49*
Mortimer, Q.E., Sgt *106*
Morton, Plt Off *95*
Mossman, Fg Off *28*
Mounser, W.H., Sgt *85*
Mullins, E. Roy, Plt Off *44, 160*
Munro, Flt Lt *119*
Munt, Jack, Sgt *73*
Murray, Sgt *70*
Muspratt, Dick, Plt Off *63*
Muter, John, Fg Off, RCAF *21*
Myers, Thomas H., Flt Lt *74-75*
Mynott, Leonard, Sgt *88*
Newell, 'Tich', Sgt *80*
Newland, Plt Off *48*
Nice, Frank, Sgt *24-26*
Nichol, James 'Nick', Wg Cdr DSO *92-96*
Nickleson, John M., Flt Sgt RCAF *114, 117*
Nightingale, F.G., Sgt *67*
Norton, H.D., Plt Off *72, 78*
Oates, John, Sgt *60-61*
O'Brien, Sqn Ldr *67*
O'Connell, Bill, Sgt-Plt Off RCAF *90, 97-98*
O'Driscoll, Finan, Sqn Ldr *149*
Oliver, Eric 'Ollie', Sgt *153*
Orme, Frank, Plt Off RCAF *97*
Osborne, 'Ozzie', Sgt *78, 82*
Osborne, 'Ozzie', Sgt RCAF *90-92*
Outhwaite, Johnny, Sgt *47-48*
Owen, R.M., Plt Off *124*
Ovens, Tony, Sgt *132*
Page, Len, Sgt *132*
Paine, S.L.T., Sgt *99*
Palmer, Henry P., Plt Off *126*
Pardoe-Williams, Hugh, Plt Off *43*
Parsons, Sgt *120*
Partridge, Thomas N. 'Tim', Fg Off-Wg Cdr
    DFC *23, 86, 111-113*
Passmore, A.K., Sqn Ldr *153*
Patterson, Charles, Flt Lt-Wg Cdr DSO DFC
    92-93
Peacock, Roger, AC2-Sgt *10, 14-15, 20, 24*
Peacock, R.J. 'Pissey', Fg Off DFC *45*
Pearson, John E., Sgt *114*
Peirce, Richard, AM Sir *124*
Pennington Legh, Alan, Flt Lt *49-50*
Pepper, N.E.W., Flg Off-Wg Cdr DFC *42,
    102-103, 162*
Percival, Plt Off *55*
Petley, Lawrence V.E., Wg Cdr *86*
Pike, Kenneth, Plt Off *96*
Pleasance, Fg Off *53*
Plessis, Du, Stephen A., Sgt *75*
Pocock, Lt SAAF *150*
Portal, Charles, ACM Sir *101*
Powell, 'Sandy', Flg Off *61, 63*
Prince, Sgt *17*
Proctor, Bill, Sgt *151*
Proudlock, Michael S., Plt Off *75*

Pugh, Sgt *68-69*
Pughe Lloyd, Hugh, Air Cdr *101-102, 107*
Quillian, Plt Off *114*
Ramsey, Eric, Sgt *123-124, 127*
Redfern, Sgt *114*
Reid, John, Sgt RAAF *154*
Reynolds, Peter L., Sgt *123*
Rhodes, Plt Off *67*
Rich, Cyril G., Cpl *150*
Richmond, 'Rich', Sgt *61*
Ridgman-Parsons, R., Sgt *81*
Robb, Plt Off *126*
Roberts, Sgt *120*
Roberts, P.G., Flt Lt *129*
Robertson, G.P. Plt Off *55*
Robins, Augustine S.Q., Sqn Ldr *74-75*
Robinson, Ian 'Robbie', Sgt *78, 81-82*
Robinson, J., Plt Off *134*
Robinson, 'Robbie', Plt Off *136*
Robinson, Walter S., Plt Off *96*
Robson, H., Sgt *17*
Roe, H.J., Fg Off-Wg Cdr *105, 112, 122*
Rogers, Dennis A, Plt Off *74*
Rogers, Dick, Plt Off *56, 58*
Rolfe, Bernard, Plt Off *68*
Rolland, Graham C., Plt Off *93*
Rook, Richard 'Dickie', Sgt *70, 78, 88*
Rost, Ronald J.B., Sgt RAAF *86*
Rotherham, R.C., Fg Off DFC *43*
Rule, L., Flt Sgt RAAF *128*
Russell, Peter, LAC *30-31*
Sargent, J.S., Sgt DFM *104*
Sarll, Peter, Fg Off-Sqn Ldr *46-47*
Saunders, Peter, Sgt *90, 99*
Sayers, Sgt *156*
Scarf, Arthur S.K. 'John', Sqn Ldr VC
    149-150
Scivier, Don, Wg Cdr AFC *106*
Scotney, Montague 'Monty', Sgt-Flt Lt
    110-114, 116-117, 119
Scott, J.E., Flt Lt DFC *129*
Searles, Flt Lt *31*
Selkirk, Bill, Wg Cdr *109*
Shayler, Doug, Sgt *75*
Shepherd, Sgt *102*
Sherring, Charles, Plt Off *76*
Shuttleworth, Dick, Sqn Ldr *97*
Sidney-Smith, Eric, Flt Lt-Sqn Ldr DFC *86,
    88, 102-103*
Sinclair, Laurence, Gp Capt GC DSO DFC
    142
Slade, Plt Off *92*
Slade, Ralph, Plt Off *88*
Slater, Plt Off *58*
Slattery, L.J. AC1 *17-18*
Slee, Bill, Flt Sgt *156*
Smart, Doug, Sgt *63*
Smith, A., Sgt *86*
Smith, Andy, Sgt *141, 143, 145*
Smith, Christopher D.S., Flt Lt DFC *65*
Smith, George R., Flt Sgt *149*
Smith, J.O.N., Fg Off DFM *112*
Smith, Norman, Plt Off *43*
Smythe, Wg Cdr *114, 119*
Spong, Les, Plt Off *27*
Standfast, P.H., Plt Off *105*
Stanford, Sgt *46*
Staples, Terry, Sgt-Wg Cdr OBE DFM *74,
    80*
Stapleton, Wg Cdr *116*
Stevens, V.A., Sgt *114, 116*
Stevenson, Donald F., AVM *78, 86, 96, 98,
    124*
Stewart, Harry, Sgt *68*
Stewart, Russell, Sqn Ldr RNZAF *109*
Stocks, P., Sgt *88*
Stone, Fg Off *31*
Strasser, G.A. 'Tony', Plt Off *128*

Strudwick, Sgt *133*
Stubbs, Richard T., Sqn Ldr DFC *98*
Sutton, H.C., Wg Cdr *129*
Symes, Flt Lt *48*
Syms, T.E., Flt Lt *59*
Tallis, Ralph, Flt Lt DFC *75*
Thomas, Edward W., Plt Off *76*
Thomas, N.H., Sgt *134*
Thomas, 'Tommy', Sgt *67*
Thompson, Flt Lt-Sqn Ldr *102-104*
Thompson, Tommy, Sgt *101*
Thorburn, Douggie *127-128*
Thripp, Freddie, Flt Sgt *106*
Tilsey, John, Sgt *80*
Toft, K.S., Flt Lt *48*
Towgood, R.A., Flt Lt *132*
Tracey, Charles, Sgt *112, 117*
Trent, Len 'Mad', Plt Off VC, DFC *53*
Tudge, H.J.C., Fg Off-Sqn Ldr *84, 111*
Tuppen, Alan, Sgt *106*
Turner, Sgt *104*
Turner, E.V., Sgt *59*
Twist, W.H., Sgt *104*
Ullmer, Robert W., Sgt *90, 101, 103*
Vickers, H., Sgt *116, 119*
Villa, Plt Off *82*
Vivian, R.L. 'Dick', Wg Cdr *147*
Waddington, Martin, Sqn Ldr *91-92*
Wade, B., Fg Off *131*
Waigh, Sgt *70*
Wales, Alan, Plt Off *43*
Walker, Sqn Ldr *65*
Walsh, Kevin H., Sqn Ldr *92*
Walter, Wg Cdr *154*
Ward, Wesley Newell 'Leslie', Flt Sgt *28*
Wardell, 'Rusty', Sqn Ldr *48*
Warnick, Eugene E. 'Tubby', Flt Sgt RCAF
    128
Watkins, T.J., Flt Lt DSO *104*
Watkins, Ted, Sgt *123*
Watson, Flt Lt *45*
Watson, M.L., Sqn Ldr *104*
Webster, Ian, Sgt *121, 124, 126*
Wellburn, F., Flt Lt *86*
Wellings, Donald, Plt Off *57*
Wells, Jimmy, Sqn Ldr *42*
Werner, Plt Off *80*
West, B.L., Plt Off RAAF *152*
Westbrook, Frank, Sgt *141, 143, 145*
Westropp-Bennett, G.P. 'Paddy', Flt Lt *147*
White, Adrian, Plt Off *88*
White, Bruce, Sgt *124*
Whitford-Walders, N., Fg Off *107*
Willans, Fg Off DFC *120*
Williams, Bill, Flt Sgt *142-143*
Williams, Maurice, Plt Off *24*
Williams, Reginald E., Sgt *75*
Williams, Tommy, Sgt *106*
Williams, W.A., Sgt *105*
Wilson, L.R., Sgt *85*
Wilson, R.S., Plt Off *112*
Wilson, W. Sgt *45*
Windram, P., Flt Lt *81*
Wood, Plt Off *116*
Woodburn, J.D., Sgt DFM *107*
Woodcock, F., Sgt *116*
Woodger, D.N., Plt Off *67*
Woodland, Cecil L. 'Jackie', Plt Off *129*
Woodruff, H.P. 'Woody', Wg Cdr *126*
Woolbridge, Flt Sgt *92*
Woolman, J.H., Sgt *107*
Workman, Plt Off RAAF *109*
Worthington-Wilmer, Ivor C.B., Flt Lt *56*
Wray, John, Fg Off *18*
Wright, D.L., Sgt *67*
Wright, H.W., Sgt *76*
Wright, K.H., Sgt *59*

Wright, Ronny, Plt Off *74*
Wrightson, L.H., Sgt *102*
Wyllie, John, Flt Lt DFC *150-152, 156*
Young, Bill, Flt Sgt *133*

FINNISH AIR FORCE PERSONNEL
Eskola, Armas, Capt-Maj *32-37*
Laakso, Harri, Ens *38-40*
Lumiala, O., Maj *37*
Nynäs, Anders, Cpl *38-40*
Oinonen, O., Sgt-Sr Sgt *33-34, 36*
Pättiniemi, Reino, Cpl-Sr Sgt *37-40*
Raty, J. Ens-Lt *33-34, 36*
Telajoki, E., Lt *38*
Veijola, K., Lt *39*

FREE FRENCH AIR FORCE PERSONNEL
Allot, Commandant *145*
Astier de Villatte, Commandant *131*
Claron, Lt *131*
Guigonis, Lt *137*
Jean, Sgt Chef *131*
Le Calvez, Sgt *131*
Mendousse, Capt *139*
Pijeaud, Lt Colonel *137*
Sabbadini, W/O *126*

GERMAN AIR FORCE PERSONNEL
Adolph, Walter, Oblt-Hptm *44, 92*
Ahnert, Heinrich W., Fw *79*
Brunsmann, Heinrich, Gefr *61*
Bucholz, Max, Ofw-Oblt *49, 123*
Dinger, Fritz, Lt *99*
Eissler, Uffz *61*
Esser, Gefr *61*
Ewerts, Fw *68*
Friedrich, Oblt *61*
Fröse, Uffz *61*
Galland, Adolf, Obstlt *85, 110*
Gerlach, Hans-Joachim, Hptm *133*
Goebel, Siegfried, Ofw *98*
Habermann, Fhnr *121*
Höckner, Walter, Oblt *134*
Homuth, Gerhard, Oblt *134*
Imhof, Georg, Oblt *58*
Kalweit, Fw *121*
Kind, Uffz *76*
Knacke, Reinhold, Oblt *128*
Koenig, Hans-Heinrich, Lt *92, 98*
Kowalski, Fw *134*
Maier, Maj *68*
Menge, Fw *61*
Müller, Hans, Lt *97*
Muschter, Fritz, Uffz *99*
Oemler, Uffz *81*
Petermann, Fw *61*
Pingel, Rolf, Hptm *82*
Priller, Josef, Oblt *82*
Roth, Ofw *92*
Schmidt, Uffz *61*
Schmidt, Lt *134*
Stark, Alfred, Fw *46*
Stolte, Paul, Oblt *72*
Tamm, Maj *67*
Viedebannt, Helmut, Lt *75*

JAPANESE AIR FORCE AND NAVY PERSONNEL
Kato, Takeo, Lt Col *158*
Otani, Masuzo, Capt *158*
Yasuda, Yoshito, Sgt Maj *158*

TURKISH AIR FORCE PERSONNEL
Alniz, Lt *29*
Gonluyuce, Lt *29, 31*
Iyigun, Lt *29*
Konnulu, Lt *29*
Yumlu, Lt *29*

PLACES
Aalborg *57-61*
Aalsmeer *124*
Aartselaar *127*
Abbeville *52, 54-55, 120*
Aberdeen *57*
Accra *138*
Accroma *137*
Agartala *153, 159*
Akyab *150, 154, 157-159*
Alahabad *150*
Aldergrove *11, 68*
Alexandria *130, 137, 139, 141*
Algeciras *118*
Algiers *118, 142-143*
Al Kufrah *131*
Alor Star *146, 148, 150*
Ameland *28, 74, 89, 98*
Amersfoort *123*
Amiens *18*
Amman *131*
Amsterdam *35, 53*
Andover *20, 27, 130*
Antrea *36*
Antwerp *61*
Argostoli *108*
Arras *50*
Artukainen, Turku *35*
Asansol *153, 157*
Ashbourne *20*
Aston Down *65*
Athens *132-133, 162*
Aveiro *101*
Avonmouth *130*
Aylsham *28*
Ayr *125*
Ayrapaa *38*
Az Zozo *131*
Bahrein *119*
Baltrum *78*
Bandoeng *152-153*
Basrah *130*
Bawdsey *65*
Benghazi *119, 137*
Benson *72*
Bergen (Norway) *74, 121-122*
Berlin *76*
Betheniville *53*
Bethune *84, 116*
Bicester *14, 20, 25-28, 35*
Bircham Newton *45, 50-51, 72*
Bizerta *143-145*
Blankenberge *90, 92*
Blida *142*
Blythe Bridge *142*
Bodney *46, 57, 75, 87-89, 96-97*
Bone *145*
Bonn *126-127*
Bordeaux *48, 76*
Borkum *64, 66, 82, 89, 111-112, 117, 128*
Boscombe Down *63*
Boulogne *61-64, 70, 72, 78, 81, 90*
Bourne *113*
Breendonk *43*
Bremen *18, 86, 127, 162*
Bremerhaven *96*
Brest *76, 123*
Brighton *65*
Bristol *8*
Brussels *162*
Brustem *162*
Buerat *109*
Bury St. Edmonds *67*
Butterworth *147-150*
Cairo *109, 138-141, 151*
Calais *50, 61-64, 67, 70, 72-73, 81*
Calcutta *147, 150, 156-157*

Candlesby *113*
Canrobert *141-144*
Cap Ferrat *144*
Cap Griz-Nez *82, 85*
Cap Tenes *118*
Capuzzo *134*
Carnaby *25*
Castel Vetrano *108-109*
Castleton *74*
Catania *107*
Catfoss *20, 25*
Chadderton *10, 165*
Chalons *43*
Chatham *82*
Chellaston *16*
Cherbourg *67, 72, 89, 111*
Chipping, Norton *28*
Chivenor *72*
Choques *82, 84, 86*
Chouigui *140, 144*
Church Fenton *11, 20, 23*
Cintra *101*
Cley *67*
Cologne *24, 70, 92-94, 96, 114, 126-127*
Coltishall *165*
Condé-Vraux *43*
Cordova, Alaska *22*
Cranfield *14, 20, 146*
Cromer *78*
Crotone *105*
Croydon *33*
Cuxhaven *96*
Damas *145*
Damville *109*
Deauville *61*
Debden *65*
De Kooy *88*
Delft *86*
Delmenhorst *128*
Denham *163*
Den Helder *90, 98*
Derby *16*
Derna *136-137*
Detling *50-51, 56, 61, 63, 72, 76, 82*
Dieppe *98, 129*
Digby *129*
Dinant *46, 50*
Diredaiwa *130*
Dixemunde *52*
Dohazari *157*
Dover *73, 78, 81, 91*
Driffield *67*
Dum Dum *156-158*
Dungeness *70*
Dunkirk *49-52, 56, 61-66, 70, 85-86*
Duxford *14, 162, 164*
Dyce *35, 57*
Edinburgh *27*
Eelde *128*
Egero *121*
Eggersund *81*
Eindhoven *27, 126*
El Adem *130, 136-137*
El Alamein *139, 142*
El Fasher *138*
Eleusis *132*
Elgin *56*
Elisenvaara *35-36*
Ely *94, 142*
Emden *61*
Epernay *48*
Eplessier *55*
Esbjerg *59*
Essen *127*
Estoril *101*
Feltwell *19, 27*
Feni *158*
Filfla *109*

Filton *8-10, 32-33, 142*
Finmere *28*
Flamborough Head *27*
Florina *133*
Flushing *11*
Folkestone *73*
Fort Philipe *91*
Freetown *119*
Friston *129*
Gambut *149*
Garaet Guellif *141*
Gelsenkirchen *107*
Gembloux *47-50, 58*
Genk *44*
Geragh, Londonderry *80*
Gianaclis *29*
Gibraltar *100-102, 118*
Givonne *48*
Glasgow *8*
Goes *124*
Gorskaja *37-38*
Gosnay *117*
Gothenburg *35*
Grantham *29*
Gravelines *89-90, 110, 114*
Great Massingham *86*
Greenock *106*
Grendon Underwood *27*
Groningen *89*
Guerand *120*
Haadyai *149*
Haamstede *57*
Habbaniya *16, 130, 135, 150*
Halfaya *138*
Halli *40-41*
Hamburg *33*
Hamm *18*
Hankoniemi *36*
Hanover *18, 71*
Harlaxton *29*
Harwich *61*
Hawkinge *73, 82*
Hazebrouck *84, 110*
Heligoland *76, 85, 88, 91, 96, 98, 111*
Heliopolis *15, 147*
Helsinki *33*
Hendon *162*
Heraklion *134, 140-141*
Herdla *120-122, 161*
Hinckley *11*
Hinton-in-the-Hedges *28*
Hoepertingen *42, 162*
Homs *106-107*
Hook of Holland *45, 65, 72, 78, 97, 117*
Horncastle *113*
Hornchurch *116*
Horsham St. Faith *70, 84-85, 111-112, 116, 118*
Hotsola *38*
Houwaart *127*
Huumola *38*
Ihantala *38*
IJmuiden *97, 112, 117, 124*
Immola *33, 37*
Inverness *56*
Ipoh *152*
Ipswich *61, 64*
Ismalia *139*
Jodhpur *150*
Joensuu *36, 38*
Juist *96*
Jurby, Isle of Man *28*
Juva *35*
Juvincourt *126*
Kabrit *139*
Kalidjati *152-153, 155-156*
Kappagaung *159*
Karachi *150*

Karhusuo *38*
Kasimovo *37-38*
Kassel *48*
Katitsanlampi *40*
Katwijk *72, 97*
Kemi *40*
Kethel *97*
Khartoum *30, 140*
Khormaksar *130*
Kiel *81, 87-88, 112*
Kijkduin *123*
King's Lynn *50, 72*
Kinloss *58*
Kivennapa *38*
Knapsack *93-94*
Kohitar *158*
Koivisto *38*
Kopernikus *43*
Kota Bharu *146-147*
Kristiansand *35, 79*
Kronstad *33*
Kuantan *146, 148*
Kuolismaa *40*
Lahore *157*
Lamia *132*
Lampedusa *102-106*
Langenbrugge *124*
Langerooge *78*
Lannion *99*
Lavajarvi *39*
Lecce *132*
Leeuwarden *88, 127-128*
Leningrad *33, 37-38*
Lens *110*
Leopoldville *139*
Les Andeleys *56*
Le Havre *91, 98-99, 111-112*
Le Touquet *90-91*
Leuchars *75, 79-80, 125-126*
Levashovo *37-38*
Lho-nga *150-151*
Licata *118*
Liikala *38*
Lille *99, 116, 120*
Lisbon *105*
Lister *81*
Liverpool *28*
Llandudno *28*
Loiwing *157*
London *35, 62, 65, 68, 88, 114, 144*
Longueil, Quebec *21*
Lonstrup *58*
Lossiemouth *19, 56-58, 121-122*
Luonetjärvi *33, 35-36, 41*
Luqa *101-109, 118*
Lydda *150*
Maassluis *97*
Maastricht *42-46, 56-57, 160, 162*
MacDonald *162*
Machang *148*
Magwe *156*
Maidstone *50, 72*
Maiduguri *138*
Mainila *38*
Malmπ *33*
Manby *119*
Manston *10, 22, 42, 66, 78, 81, 89-92,*
    114, 116
Margate *90*
Martlesham Heath *9-10, 65*
Méharicourt *42*
Menidi *131-132, 134*
Mensuvaara *38*
Mersa Matruh *140*
Metz *18*
Minbya *157*
Minden *18*

Mingaladon *146, 156*
Mombasa *30*
Monastir *133*
Moulmein *152*
Mountain View, Ontario *21*
Münster *18*
Muonio *40*
Nairobi *30*
Nakuru *29-31*
Nanton, Alberta *21*
Nanyuki *29*
Nasiyeh *130*
Netheravon *17*
Neuwerk *96*
Newcastle *59*
Newmarket *67*
Niamata *133*
Nicosia *30*
Nietjarvi *39*
Nordeney *78, 86*
North Coates *43*
North Walsham *28*
North Weald *53, 65, 67*
Northolt *67*
Norwich *70, 96, 116*
Odiham *130*
Oostvoorne *56*
Orfordness *92-93*
Oslo *35*
Osnabrück *18*
Ostend *61-62, 78, 90, 98*
Onttola *34, 38-40*
Oul Mene *144-145*
Oulton *72, 110-111*
Ounianga *131*
Pakan-Baru *150*
Palembang *150-153*
Palermo *109*
Pantellaria *101, 104, 118*
Paramythia *132-133*
Paris *52, 92*
Patani *146, 148*
Pearl Harbour *146*
Permet *160*
Perth *35*
Petroskoi *37*
Pisodherion *133*
Pitkaranta *38*
Plivot *18, 44-45*
Poix *19, 53*
Poix Nord *120*
Poling *65*
Pont a Vendin *110*
Portraith *101, 118, 151*
Portsmouth *67, 72, 100*
Prestwick *88*
Quadrath *93*
Ramsgate *51, 90*
Rangkasbitung *156*
Rangoon *150-151*
Rayak *140*
Rennes *119*
Rheims *48*
Rheine *128*
Rotterdam *42, 48, 71, 76, 79, 86-89, 95-97,*
    111-112
Runnymede *75, 88*
Rye *116*
Sage *127*
Salmijarvi *40*
Sarande *132*
Scheveningen *42, 66, 111*
Schiedam *97*
Schiermonnikoog *57, 98*
Schillig Roads *19*
Schiphol *33, 123-124, 128*
Sea Island (B.C.) *21*
Sedan *44-46, 48, 97, 160*

Sembawang (Singapore) *149*
Seward *163*
Sfax *104*
Shabah *130*
Shandhur *29-30*
Sharjah *148, 150*
Shwebo *159*
Sidi Barrani *136*
Siikakangas *36*
Silloth *35*
Singapore *16, 146, 151, 157*
Singora *146, 148-149, 152*
Sirkka *40*
Soesterberg *122-123*
Sola *75*
Souk el Arba *144*
Speke *10*
Spitalgate *28-29, 31*
St. Andrews *125*
St. Eval *63*
St. Kruis *46*
St. Omer *50, 61, 70, 81, 85, 97, 114*
St. Trond *126-127, 162*
St. Valérie *52, 54-55*
Stanleyville *139*
Stavanger *19, 35, 57-58, 74, 76, 121*
Stert Flats *27*
Stockholm *33, 35*
Strathallan *163*
Strijen *93*
Strijensas *93*
Sumburgh *121*
Sungei Patani *146-147*
Sutton Bridge *119*
Swanton Morley *86*
Takoradi *30, 138-140*
Tali *38*
Tallinn *37*
Tampere *32-33, 38, 41*
Tengah (Singapore) *146-150*
Terschelling *74, 79*
Texel *25, 74, 76, 79, 88-89, 99, 117, 123*
The Hague *42, 115, 117*
Thornaby *19, 74-75*
Thorney Island *15, 56, 64, 67, 72-73, 100*
Thruxton *129*
Tikkakoski *41, 160*
Tjilatjap *156*
Tobruk *134, 136*
Tokra *137*
Tongeren/Tongres *42, 45*
Topove *160*
Toungoo *150*
Trapani *104*
Tripoli *102-107, 119*
Trondheim *121, 125*
Tunis *141, 145*
Turweston *28*
Twente *126, 128*
Upper Heyford *12*
Upwood *20-21, 94*
Vaagso *121*
Vaala *40*
Valona *132*
Värtsilä *33, 37*
Västeras *35*
Vechta *126-128*
Veltwezelt *45*
Venlo *126-128*
Verneul *120*
Vesivehmaa *40*
Viipuri *38*
Villacoublai *120*
Vitry *52*
Vitska *38*
Vlieland *94*
Vust *60*
Vytegra *37*

Waalhaven *42, 66, 88-89, 160*
Waddington *12*
Warmwell *13*
Wattisham *17, 45, 50, 61, 65, 76, 90, 97,*
    99, 104, 108, 124-127, 140, 142, 160
Watton *17, 24, 46-48, 51, 53, 55, 58, 71,*
    90, 97, 104, 146
West Raynham *62, 74, 78, 99, 123-124,*
    126-128, 142
Weston Zoyland *27, 54*
Wilhelmshaven *17*
Wittering *69*
Woensdrecht *94*
Wolphaartsdijk *124*
Wyton *10, 18, 42, 45, 50, 54*
Ypenburg *42*
Zandvoort *117*
Zayatkin *150*
Zeebrugge *92*
Zeist *123*
Zemun *132*

ROYAL AIR FORCE
AND COMMONWEALTH UNITS
No. 9 Air Obervers School *162*
No. 18 Blenheim Delivery Flight *15*
No. 3 Bombing and Gunnery School *162*
No. 6 Bombing and Gunnery School *21*
Central Flying School No. *12*
Fighter Interception Unit *65, 165*
1441 (Combined Operations) Flight *129*
No. 3 Ferry Pilots Pool *12*
3484M *23*
1 OTU *25*
2 OTU *20, 25*
5 OTU *23, 65*
13 OTU *20, 24-30, 92*
17 OTU *19-21, 26, 92, 110*
42 OTU *20, 27*
51 OTU *20*
54 OTU *20, 22-23*
60 OTU *23*
70 OTU *29-31*
72 OTU *29, 131*
75 OTU *29*
79 OTU *30*
No. 12 (Pilots) Advanced Flying Unit *12,*
    28, 31, 162
No. 1 Photographic Reconnaissance Unit
    72
1 (RAAF) Squadron *147*
3 (RAAF) Squadron *137*
8 Squadron *130, 135, 141*
8 (RAAF) Squadron *146*
8 (RCAF) Squadron *21-22, 163*
RCAF Central Training Establishment *21*
Special Duties Flight *65*
No. 3 School of General Reconnaissance
    29
1 Squadron *65, 67*
5 Squadron *159*
11 Squadron *56, 130-132, 134-136, 156-*
    157, 159
12 Squadron *45*
13 Squadron *126-127, 129, 141-145*
14 Squadron *131, 134-135, 139, 141*
XV Squadron *18, 42, 44-46, 50, 53-54, 128*
15 (SAAF) Squadron *142*
16 (SAAF) Squadron *142*
17 (SAAF) Squadron *142*
18 Squadron *12, 16, 18, 24, 42-45, 56, 62,*
    71-72, 76, 79, 82-88, 90-91, 93, 96-98,
    100-101, 107-112, 114, 116-120, 124-
    128, 140, 142-145, 150-151
19 Squadron *65*
21 Squadron *19, 24, 45-46, 51-52, 55-58,*
    71, 74-75, 78, 82, 85-86, 88-90, 93, 96-
    97, 101, 104, 109, 111, 118

23 Squadron *64, 67, 69, 120, 122*
25 Squadron *64-67, 69*
27 Squadron *146-148, 151-152*
29 Squadron *8, 64, 67, 69*
30 Squadron *16, 130-135*
33 Squadron *136*
34 Squadron *146-152, 157-159*
35 Squadron *20-21*
39 Squadron *130*
40 Squadron *18, 42, 50-52, 54, 62*
42 Squadron *81, 159*
44 Squadron *12*
45 Squadron *130, 134-135, 137, 156-157*
46 Squadron *67*
53 Squadron *18-19, 43, 56, 61, 63, 71, 76*
54 Squadron *82, 117*
55 Squadron *109, 130, 134-135, 141*
57 Squadron *16, 18, 42, 45, 56-57, 100, 133*
59 Squadron *18, 45, 56, 64, 71-73, 76, 78, 81-82*
60 Squadron *131, 146-150, 154, 156-159*
62 Squadron *146, 148-151*
64 Squadron *23*
68 Squadron *165*
74 Squadron *81*
82 Squadron *14, 16-17, 19, 25-26, 46-49, 52-53, 55, 57-61, 71, 75, 87, 93, 96-97, 102, 104-106, 118, 122-123*
84 Squadron *14, 130-138, 147-153, 155-156, 160*
86 Squadron *29*
88 Squadron *71, 97, 117*
90 Squadron *14, 20-21, 23*
91 Squadron *73, 92*
101 Squadron *62, 65, 78, 81*
104 Squadron *20*
105 Squadron *82, 86, 93, 105-107, 111, 119, 162*
107 Squadron *17-19, 43, 45-46, 50-51, 53, 62, 71, 75, 79, 85-86, 93, 101, 105-107, 109, 112, 131*
108 Squadron *20*
110 Squadron *17, 19, 24, 42, 44, 46, 51, 61, 71, 76, 78, 81-82, 97, 104-106, 108, 116, 120-121, 123, 160*
113 Squadron *130, 132, 135, 152-159*
114 Squadron *10-11, 18, 45, 70-71, 74-75, 78-80, 87, 89, 92-94, 96, 98-99, 120-123-124, 126-128, 142-145, 160-161*
139 Squadron *16-18, 27, 42, 44-45, 70-71, 82, 86-88, 90-93, 96, 98, 100-104, 111-112, 116, 118, 162*
145 Squadron *64-65*
147 (RCAF) Squadron *20-21*
149 Squadron *62*
152 Squadron *99*
155 Squadron *159*
203 Squadron *130, 134-135*
211 Squadron *29, 56, 130, 132-134, 147,*

151-152, 160, 162
219 Squadron *64, 67, 69*
222 Squadron *14*
226 Squadron *24, 71, 85-87, 90-92, 95-99, 117*
233 Squadron *165*
235 Squadron *22, 43, 45, 50-52, 56, 67, 71, 76, 78, 83*
236 Squadron *56, 63, 68, 71*
242 Squadron *114*
248 Squadron *49-50, 56, 71, 74*
254 Squadron *56, 71, 74, 98, 164-165*
258 Squadron *82*
402 Squadron *92*
403 Squadron *116*
404 (RCAF) Squadron *49, 71, 121, 125-126, 165*
464 Squadron *27*
487 (RNZAF) Squadron *53*
500 Squadron *76*
516 Squadron *129*
526 Squadron *129*
527 Squadron *129*
528 Squadron *129*
600 Squadron *42, 64, 66, 69, 165*
601 Squadron *64-66*
604 Squadron *42, 64-67, 69*
607 Squadron *92*
614 Squadron *126-127, 129, 142-145*
167 Wing *159*
326 (Bisley) Wing *142-144*

FINNISH AIR FORCE UNITS
Finnish Air Force Signal School *37*
Finnish Air Force Technical School *41*
Finnish Air Force Test Flight *41*
1st Lennosto (Haemeen Lennosto) *41*
Lentolaivue 16 *37*
Lentorykmentti 3 *41*
Lentorykmentti 4 *35*
(Pommitus)Lentolaivue 41 (P)LeLv 41) *35, 41*
(Pommitus)Lentolaivue 42 (P)LeLv 42) *35-37*
(Pommitus)Lentolaivue 43 (P)LeLv 43) *41*
(Pommitus)Lentolaivue 44 (P)LeLv 44) *35-36*
(Pommitus)Lentolaivue 45 (P)LeLv 45) *35*
(Pommitus)Lentolaivue 46 (P)LeLv 46) *35, 38*
(Pommutus)Lentolaivue 48 (P)LeLv 48) *35-36, 38, 40*
T-LeR4 *35*

FREE FRENCH AIR FORCE UNITS
Escadrille Topic *130*
GB Bretagne *139, 145*
GB Lorraine *135, 137-140*
GB I/20 Lorraine (342 Squadron) *139*
GRB1 *130-131, 135*

Groupe I/17 Picardie *145*
Metz *135, 139*
Nancy *135, 138-139*
Nantes *139, 142*

JAPANESE AIR FORCE AND NAVY UNITS
1st Sentai *149*
8th Sentai *156*
11th Sentai *153*
59th Sentai *148, 152*
60th Sentai *148*
64th Sentai *147-148, 158-159*
75th Sentai *153*

LUFTWAFFE UNITS
3(F)121 *120*
Stab I/JG1 *44*
I/JG1 *45*
2/JG1 *42, 44*
3/JG1 *72*
5/JG1 *123*
I/JG2 *144*
3/JG2 *50*
II/JG2 *144*
III/JG2 *46, 82*
1/JG3 *49*
3/JG21 *51*
JG26 *82*
Stab JG26 *82, 85*
I/JG26 *82, 92*
II/JG26 *82, 92*
4/JG26 *92*
III/JG26 *81-82*
JG27 *137*
I/JG27 *134, 137*
1/JG27 *137*
2/JG27 *45*
3/JG27 *44*
II/JG27 *45*
6/JG27 *42, 133, 162*
III/JG27 *137*
2/JG52 *111*
3/JG52 *79, 98*
JG53 *109*
I/JG53 *45-46, 96*
4/JG53 *99*
6/JG53 *97*
III/JG53 *45*
4/JG54 *57*
I/JG76 *51*
I/JG77 *76, 121*
3/JG77 *122*
II/JG77 *134*
5/JG77 *61*
6/JG77 *134*
1(Z)/JG77 *122*
III/JG77 *134*
Stab I/KG1 *68*
4/KG2 *43*

2/KG3 *65*
I/KG26 *58*
4/KG 26 *68*
III/KG26 *120*
II/KG53 *67*
KG54 *48*
III/KG55 *67, 120*
KüFlGr 106 *66*
KüFlGr 906 *66*
NJG1 *127*
1/NJG1 *128*
3/ZG1 *42*
II/ZG26 *46, 134*
III/ZG26 *137*
II/ZG76 *88, 94*
5/ZG76 *90, 92*
III/ZG76 *75*
8/ZG76 *75*

REGIA AERONAUTICA UNITS
23rd Gruppo *105-106, 108*
150th Gruppo *132*

AXIS (MERCHANT) NAVY UNITS AND VESSELS
Admiral Scheer *17*
Alvisa da Mosto *107*
·Aspen *112*
Awagisan Maru *147*
Beatrice Costa *104*
Brarena *104*
Canadolite *99*
Capo Faro *107*
Cigno *102*
Foscarini *102*
Gneisenau *19, 123*
Gunlog *99*
Hipper *19*
Iridio Mantovani *107*
Iseo *107*
Karabishes-Meer *91*
Lützow *81*
Montello *103*
Nagumo Force *156*
Nita *105*
Niyo Maru *154*
Oranjefontein *89, 97*
Preussen *104*
Prinz Eugen *123, 125-126*
Scharnhorst *19, 123*
Tembien *104*
U-31 *19*
Volturno *107*
Vp1 *107* 86, 88
13th Vorpostenboot Flotilla *86, 88*
Vp1304 *79*
Wachtfels *104*
Westerdam *97*
Zuiderdam *97*